D1519207

RACE AND EDUCATION
IN NEW ORLEANS

MAKING THE MODERN SOUTH

David Goldfield, Series Editor

RACE & EDUCATION IN NEW ORLEANS

CREATING THE SEGREGATED CITY, 1764–1960

Walter C. Stern

Louisiana State University Press
Baton Rouge

Published with the assistance of the University of Wisconsin's Office
of the Vice Chancellor for Research and Graduate Education

Published by Louisiana State University Press
Copyright © 2018 by Louisiana State University Press
All rights reserved
Manufactured in the United States of America
First printing

Designer: Michelle A. Neustrom
Typeface: MillerText
Printer and binder: Sheridan Books, Inc.

Maps by Mary Lee Eggart

Library of Congress Cataloging-in-Publication Data

Names: Stern, Walter C., 1979– author.
Title: Race and education in New Orleans : creating the segregated city, 1764–1960 /
    Walter C. Stern.
Other titles: Making the modern South.
Description: Baton Rouge : Louisiana State University Press, [2018] | Series: Making
    the modern South | Includes bibliographical references and index.
Identifiers: LCCN 2017043569| ISBN 978-0-8071-6918-6 (cloth : alk. paper) | ISBN
    978-0-8071-6919-3 (pdf) | ISBN 978-0-8071-6920-9 (epub)
Subjects: LCSH: Segregation in education—Louisiana—New Orleans—History. |
    Education—Louisiana—New Orleans—History. | New Orleans (La.)—Race
    relations—History. | New Orleans (La.)—Social conditions—18th century. | New
    Orleans (La.)—Social conditions—19th century. | New Orleans (La.)—Social
    conditions—20th century.
Classification: LCC LC212.523.N49 S84 2018 | DDC 379.2/630976335—dc23
LC record available at https://lccn.loc.gov/2017043569

The paper in this book meets the guidelines for permanence and durability of the Committee
on Production Guidelines for Book Longevity of the Council on Library Resources. ∞

for Nelsie,

- - - - - - - - - - - - - - - - -

and for my mother, Lynne Rothschild Stern

CONTENTS

Illustrations follow page 84

TABLES

MAPS

ACKNOWLEDGMENTS

Race and Education in New Orleans began at Tulane University in New Orleans and matured at the University of Wisconsin in Madison. While my name is on the cover and any errors of fact or interpretation are entirely my own, this book owes its existence to the people and places that nurtured it.

At Tulane, Larry Powell helped me find my voice as a historian. The standards he sets for scholarship, community engagement, and the writer's craft remain an inspiration, and I am grateful for his continued friendship and support. Rosanne Adderley, Randy Sparks, Rachel Delvin, and Emily Clark also contributed mightily to my growth as a scholar, as did Jana Lipman, Justin Wolfe, and Thomas Adams. Liz Skilton and Rien Fertel were a source of friendship throughout my time at Tulane.

Clarence Mohr and Donald DeVore of the University of South Alabama also aided this project's development. Clarence's tough questions pushed me to refine my arguments, while Donald's decades of work on African American history and the history of education in New Orleans provided a road map for my research. As even casual readers of the endnotes will recognize, this book would not have been possible without the breadcrumbs that Donald left for me and future researchers to follow. Arnold Hirsch also deserves recognition for his willingness to discuss this project during its gestational phase and the model he offered through his own work.

A slew of librarians, archivists, and administrators supported my research and helped me secure the images that are included in the book. These include Lee Hampton, Chris Harter, and Andrew Salinas at the Amistad Research Center; Irene Wainwright and Gregory Osborn at the New Orleans Public Library; Daniel Hammer, Bobby Ticknor, Erin Greenwald, and Matt Farah at the Historic New Orleans Collection; Lee Miller, Sean Benjamin, Ann Smith Case, and Lori Schexnayder at the Louisiana Research Center at Tulane; Eric

Wedig at Tulane's Howard-Tilton Memorial Library; Catherine T. Wood at the Boston Public Library's Norman B. Leventhal Map Center; the librarians at Lusher Charter School and McDonogh 35 High School; and the staffs at the Conveyance Division at Orleans Parish Civil District Court, the Louisiana State Museum, the National Archives and Records Administration in College Park, Maryland, the New Orleans Notarial Archives, the New Orleans Notarial Archives Research Center, the Southeastern Architectural Archive at Tulane, the Archives of the Archdiocese of New Orleans, the Wisconsin Historical Society, and the University of Wisconsin–Madison Libraries' Interlibrary Loan Department. While all of these individuals aided my work, none contributed more than Sybil Boudreaux, Florence Jumonville, and James Lien, formerly with the Louisiana and Special Collections Department at the University of New Orleans's Earl K. Long Library. They fielded numerous requests while confronting damaging cuts to their budget.

I am also grateful for multiple sources of financial assistance I received throughout this project. Support for this research was provided by the University of Wisconsin–Madison Office of the Vice Chancellor for Research and Graduate Education with funding from the Wisconsin Alumni Research Foundation. Additional funding from the Wisconsin Center for Education Research (WCER) covered the production costs for many of the maps that anchor the text. At Tulane, I received financial support from the School of Liberal Arts, the Center for Ethics and Public Affairs at the Murphy Institute, the Cowen Institute for Public Education Initiatives, and the History Department. The US federal government and State of Louisiana also provided essential support through Medicaid and multiple tax credits and deductions.

My understanding of and approach to my topic developed thanks to the conversations and correspondence I had with others in the field. Al Kennedy helped me better understand the Orleans Parish School Board Collection. Richard Campanella prepared two of the maps and responded to my numerous questions relating to New Orleans geography, census statistics, and outdated addresses. Michael Schwam-Baird, formerly of the Cowen Institute, helped me with enrollment data. Jamin Wells carefully read and helped me make sense of a sprawling early draft. Leslie Gale Parr and Pamela Tyler shared their experiences researching New Orleans history. Alecia Long, Kent Germany, and Mary Niall Mitchell thankfully discussed the project with me in person or via email.

Ansley Erickson, Karen Benjamin, John Rury, Tracy Steffes, Jack Dougherty, Lawrence Vale, Alexander Von Hoffman, Jeanne Theoharis, and Tess Bundy either commented on portions of this project or were kind enough to field questions about it at conferences. Sylvie Mathé and Gérard Hugues of Aix-Marseille Université organized a conference and special issue on New Orleans which helped me refine many of the ideas that went into this book. For permission to draw upon material from my article, "Public Schools and Ghetto Formation in Interwar New Orleans," which originally appeared in *E-rea* 14, no. 1 (2016), I am grateful to Sylve and Nathalie Vanfasse.

Libby Neidenbach graciously shared her unpublished dissertation, which enabled me to bring Marie Couvent's story to life. Joe Trotter granted me permission to cite an unpublished essay that he presented at the 2016 Future of the African American Past conference, and Larry Vale shared an unpublished work in progress on public housing in New Orleans. I also benefited from Ken Ducote's encyclopedic knowledge of New Orleans school buildings and the primary sources he shared with me. Mary Lee Eggart made most of the maps, turning my crude first drafts into works of art. Liz Hauck provided research assistance.

In addition to easing my transition to Madison, my colleagues in the Department of Educational Policy Studies at the University of Wisconsin–Madison have provided me with a remarkably supportive intellectual community. Bill Reese deserves special mention for reading and commenting on the entire manuscript, as does Adam Nelson for the feedback he provided on portions of the manuscript and for his stellar leadership of the department and willingness to serve as a sounding board for my ideas. This book's prose is sharper, its organization tighter, and its arguments clearer thanks to Bill's and Adam's editorial suggestions. Additionally, Jake Leonard and Mary Jo Gessler ensured that the funding that supported this research flowed to the right places, while also helping me feel at home in EPS.

I also want to thank the students from my spring 2014 and 2015 seminars on Race and Education at Bard Early College–New Orleans and the students from my 2016–2017 seminars on Cities, Schools, and the Urban Crisis and Education and the Civil Rights Movement at the University of Wisconsin–Madison. Their comments and questions pushed me to think more deeply about my own work and the limitations and biases I may bring to the study of race and power.

At LSU Press, Rand Dotson moved this project form one phase to the next, Gary Von Euer and Neal Novak provided editorial assistance, David denBoer prepared the index, and M'Bilia Meekers coordinated marketing. This book is also better thanks to David Goldfield's and Kent Germany's incisive comments. I am very thankful for their interest in and commitment to the project.

Before Tulane and the University of Wisconsin–Madison, my professors at Yale and my editors at KPLU Public Radio in Seattle and the *Savannah Morning News* helped me become a better thinker and writer. My friends in New Orleans also provided invaluable support for my work and welcome distraction from it. A list of friends and neighbors too long to mention formed the community that sustained me throughout this process.

Additionally, I thank my father- and mother-in-law John and Carol Munson for never questioning my decision to quit my job and return to school when their daughter was newly pregnant with our second child. In fact, they always made me feel as though I had made an excellent choice. Their willingness to provide childcare and carpool during their visits to New Orleans and Madison helped me stay on top of this project, and they generously assisted during lean times. Yet even more than their unqualified support, I am grateful for their love and friendship. The same goes for the rest of the Munson clan and all of its hyphenated and nonhyphenated offshoots.

My brother Maury, sister-in-law Emily, and nieces Gracie and Cate Stern were also regular sources of support. On a practical level, they hosted me during research and conference visits to Washington, DC, spoiling me almost as thoroughly as they spoil my sons. I cannot wait to repay the favor by teaching Gracie and Cate about the benefits of an advanced degree in the humanities. More importantly, they help me maintain a sense of perspective in relation to my work. I cannot imagine my life without them.

Succinctly capturing the ways my mother Lynne Stern has supported me throughout my life is not easy. She taught me to love the written word from a young age, encouraged me to excel in intellectual and other pursuits, and continues to believe in me far more than she should. While she still occasionally suggests I should consider legal history, she never gave me a hard time about not going to law school. She also regularly looked after my sons to give me more time to work, made excellent choices at the Farmer's Market for our Tuesday night meals, and was overly generous when finances were tight. Additionally, she is quite fun to be around. The relationship I developed with her was one of the real joys of returning to New Orleans—and one of the hardest parts about leaving the city.

While my father Maurice Stern died during the very early phases of this project, I could not avoid thinking about him as I worked on it. Since he was a contemporary of some of the individuals I wrote about and lived in a neighborhood whose origins I studied, I developed a better sense of the world he grew up in through this project. I also thought about him as I searched for the right words to use, remembering in particular a news article that I had written late in his life and which he mailed back to me after underlining the words and phrases he found particularly effective. He loved language and life, and I would have loved sharing this book with him.

Last but not least are my sons Arthur and Ben and my wife Nelsie. I am incredibly grateful that several phases of writing this book gave me the flexibility to take Arthur and Ben to and from school most days, to sit in on their judo practices, and to spend my late afternoons watching their latest Lego creations, drawings, and imaginary worlds take shape. While I paid for this flexibility by working later into the night than was wise or healthy, I will take the joy of their company over sleep any day. As this project reached its end, they provided encouragement and feedback and made the task of editing much more enjoyable during our Wednesday afternoon coffee dates.

Without Nelsie, this journey would have been as unimaginable as it would have been lonely. I am grateful for her willingness to let me talk through my ideas, for her ability to ask questions that forced me to develop a deeper understanding of my subject, and most of all for her love. I am also thankful for her insistence that I return to school and for her support of our move to Madison.

Her work with New Orleans schoolchildren grounded my more abstract perorations and pressed me to think about my historical study's contemporary relevance. More importantly, she makes even the most mundane aspects of life enjoyable and worthwhile. I am grateful for her love and that she lets me love her as deeply as I do. Nearly twenty years ago, we sat on a porch on Tybee Island and talked about where we wanted to be in five and ten years. I do not remember the details of what we said, but I cannot imagine anything better than the opportunity to share my life and future with her.

RACE AND EDUCATION
IN NEW ORLEANS

SCHOOLS, RACE, AND POWER

Ruby Bridges awoke early on the morning of Monday, November 14, 1960. In the bedroom she shared with her three younger siblings, Ruby's mother Lucille carefully readied her for school. The six-year-old pulled on a starched white dress, slipped into a pair of shiny black shoes, and fixed a large white bow in her hair.[1]

Lucille, her husband Abon, and their children had moved from the southwestern hill country of Mississippi to New Orleans two years earlier, settling in a rooming house apartment near the Industrial Canal in the city's Ninth Ward. The Bridges were among the thousands of African Americans who moved to New Orleans during the 1950s in search of greater opportunity. Like postwar black migrants throughout the country, the family left a rural county with a long history of racial oppression and of black community organizing for a city with a mix of the same.[2]

All of the residents on Ruby's block were African American, and she embraced the comfort and safety of her new neighborhood. She spent most afternoons looking after her sisters and brother while playing jacks, jumping rope, and climbing the large China ball tree near her house. Abon, a Korean War vet, had learned auto repair in the service and worked as a gas station attendant, while Lucille worked evenings, at one point cleaning hotel guest rooms and at another building caskets in a factory.[3]

As the time approached for Ruby to head to school, four white US marshals stepped onto the Bridges' screen porch and knocked on the front door. The marshals were there to protect Ruby as she desegregated the all-white William Frantz Elementary School, located five blocks from her home. On the far side of the Industrial Canal, three other African American first graders— Gail Etienne, Leona Tate, and Tessie Prevost—were preparing to desegregate a second white elementary school. The admission of these four girls to two formerly white schools followed decades of legal activism on the part of black New Orleanians and the National Association for the Advancement of Colored People (NAACP).[4]

Lucille and Ruby climbed into the backseat of one of the marshals' waiting cars, then drove along France Street before heading west on North Galvez. As they crossed Alvar Street, Ruby spotted barricades, policemen, and a large, shouting crowd. "I actually thought it was Mardi Gras," Bridges recalled. "They were throwing things and shouting. And so—that sort of goes on in New Orleans at Mardi Gras. I really didn't realize until I got into the school that something else was going on."[5]

The car parked in front of the school, and she and her mother exited it, followed by a trio of marshals from a second car. The crowd erupted, shouting racist epithets and hurling items at the Bridges. Once Ruby was inside the school, white parents rushed into the building to remove their children. As one mother explained to a news reporter, "We don't want the niggers going in that school. It's a white school."[6]

In the days following Ruby's start at Frantz, the crowds grew larger and more raucous, and rioting soon engulfed the city. Bands of white teenagers roamed the Central Business District, attacking any black person who crossed their path. With the exception of two white children who remained at Frantz, whites orchestrated a total boycott of the two technically desegregated elementary schools. Mobs enforced the boycott by attacking white parents who dared to bring their children to school.[7]

This grassroots violence capped years of official resistance to desegregation following the Supreme Court's 1954 decision in *Brown v. Board of Education*. In Louisiana, as in other southern states, the legislature attempted to outlaw the NAACP, encouraged the governor to abolish public education in the event of desegregation, and authorized him to defy federal court orders so as to preserve segregation. African Americans turned to the federal judiciary to overcome these tactics, and a district court judge ultimately issued restraining orders to more than seven hundred state and local officials to permit the desegregation of New Orleans public schools to proceed. But this violent, carnivalesque start did not bode well for the process. Seven years passed before desegregation reached the high schools, where violence and discrimination continued to undermine African American hopes for expanded educational opportunity and equity.[8]

Alongside Little Rock, George Wallace's stand in the schoolhouse door, and "busing" in Boston, what became known as the 1960 New Orleans School Crisis persists as a prime example of white "backlash" against desegregation and the broader civil rights movement. In perhaps the most controversial variant of the backlash thesis, *Brown* mattered only to the extent that it "radicalized southern politics" and encouraged the white violence that pushed northerners to support civil rights legislation.[9] That claim is woven into popular explanations of postwar American history, most notably in high school and college textbooks and curricula. In these venues, "backlash" against school desegregation, the civil rights movement, and the Great Society frequently explains "white flight" to the suburbs, white working-class abandonment of the Democratic Party, and the emergence of a radicalized Right. For many people, the term serves as a heuristic for understanding the collapse of inner cities and a once robust American welfare state.[10]

In New Orleans, the School Crisis undoubtedly sparked a backlash that sharpened the politics of white supremacy. But this was nothing new. Rather, it was the latest episode in a long-running battle over schools, race, and the future of the city. This book examines the political economy of race and education in New Orleans during the two centuries *preceding* Ruby Bridges's brave walk, and it highlights the limited effectiveness of "backlash" as a framework for understanding postwar American history.[11] When making sense of *Brown*, the transformation of cities and suburbs, the black freedom struggle, and the persistence of white supremacy in shaping modern politics, "backlash" conceals more than it reveals.[12]

Race and Education in New Orleans argues that schools profoundly shaped the development of New Orleans's racial order and urban landscape. By taking a long view of the interplay between race, education, and urban change, it underscores the fluidity of race as a social construct and the extent to which segregation often evolved through a dynamic, improvisational process.[13] Schools were central to that process as policymakers and residents repeatedly turned to educational institutions to strengthen or disrupt the prevailing racial order. Time and again, schools became the focal point of social, economic, and racial crises. They offered residents the means to envision competing futures and the state the mechanism to grant certain futures while denying others.

The centrality of schools to New Orleans's development and social structure began with the arrival in 1727 of twelve Ursuline nuns from France, whose focus on educating European, Native American, and African-descended free and enslaved girls muddled racial and gender hierarchies. During the antebellum era, the parallel founding of a white public school system and a privately operated but partially publicly funded black school known as the Catholic Institution revealed starkly divergent visions of community advancement and social order. Drawing upon the revolutionary traditions of Haiti, France, and the wider Atlantic world, students, educators, and board members from the Catholic Institution placed education at the forefront of their effort to build a new democracy during the Civil War and Reconstruction. Bolstered by federal and state support for African American civil and political rights, they also pushed New Orleans to become the only southern community—and one of the few cities in the nation—to desegregate its public schools during the 1870s.

While New Orleans segregated its racially mixed public schools immediately following Reconstruction, during the late nineteenth and twentieth centuries the structure and nature of black education never became firmly fixed.[14] The more white residents and officials sought to restrict black schooling, the harder blacks fought back, pushing whites to develop more novel strategies for maintaining and strengthening the racial order even as they bent to black demands for expanded educational opportunity.

Chronologically, this book begins with the circa 1764 kidnapping and enslavement of a seven-year-old girl named Marie Justine Sirnir in western Africa, and it ends with six-year-old Ruby Bridges's entrance into Frantz Elementary two hundred years later. In between, it traces Sirnir's rise to educational prominence in nineteenth-century New Orleans and the centrality of schools to antebellum understandings of race, citizenship, and community development. As the story moves into the twentieth century, two themes related to urban geography become paramount. The first involves the conflict over land and resources that stemmed from New Orleans's inhospitable physical environment and historically inadequate investment in public education and other civic improvements. The second concerns the tension between black residents' demands for greater educational opportunity and white residents' opposition to black schools near their homes.

New Orleans's limited amount of habitable land meant that blacks and whites, rich and poor, and immigrants and natives traditionally lived near one another on the highest, driest land available between the Mississippi River and what New Orleanians called the woods, the undeveloped former cypress swamps that stretched north toward Lake Pontchartrain. While this had been the case since the city's founding as a French colonial outpost in 1718, by the early twentieth century the city's severe shortage of school facilities threatened the stability of its residentially integrated neighborhoods. As a tight job market and compulsory education (introduced in New Orleans in 1910) pushed school enrollments skyward, schools became particularly valued—and value-laden—commodities, both for families seeking to climb the economic and social ladder and for neighborhoods seeking such amenities as paved streets and modern sewerage, drainage, and water facilities.[15] The suspension of school construction during World War I exacerbated the city's educational bottleneck, intensifying the competition for buildings once construction resumed after the war.

Since wealthy New Orleanians generally did not send their children to public schools, the struggle for school facilities often pitted middle- and working-class whites against blacks. Black residents had disproportionately fewer schools than whites and continually pressed for more and better accommodations. But white residents insisted that they receive additional facilities first. Whites also feared that black schools near their homes would mark their neighborhoods as black, thereby decreasing their property values and their chances of securing future public and private investment. For ordinary black and white residents, who largely maneuvered within institutional structures that affluent whites controlled, public schools represented the future. In this environment, the struggle for new schools both revealed and institutionalized anxieties about race, status, and opportunity.

To explore the relationship between racial politics, economic development, and school placements, *Race and Education in New Orleans* offers street-level views of individual neighborhoods and their schools. In the Tremé neighborhood, for instance, the Bayou Road School's racial designation changed four times between the Civil War and 1950 as black aspirations for educational opportunity collided with white anxieties over status and territorial control. Responding to both white residents' opposition to black institutions near their homes and black residents' demands for more and better school facilities, officials pushed black schools into the city's least desirable sections, which was the case in Louis Armstrong's childhood neighborhood. These black schools created racial boundaries around otherwise racially nondescript areas, providing justification for later slum clearance and redevelopment. Conversely, an ambitious post–World War I school construction program spurred the

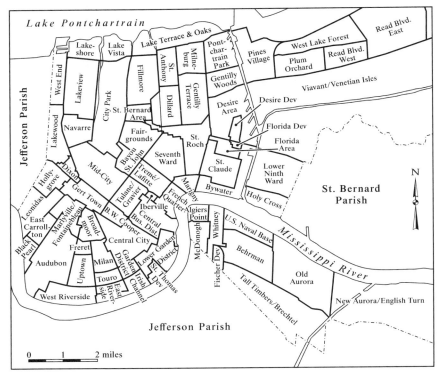

Map I.1   New Orleans neighborhoods, 2004.
Map based upon Greater New Orleans Community Data Center, "Neighborhoods in Orleans Parish," 2004.

growth of well-appointed white subdivisions in areas such as Broadmoor and Fontainebleau on the city's former fringe (see map I.1 for neighborhood locations). Since the US Supreme Court repeatedly rejected attempts to segregate neighborhoods by law during the interwar period, schools became the most powerful tools available for officially designating areas as either white or black.[16]

After World War II, schools played a still greater role as federal policies encouraged the concentration of additional white schools in nascent suburbs and black schools in inhospitable sections of the city. These moves had a profound effect. By 1973 a Great Society antipoverty agency lamented that "New Orleans has had a city within a city for some time." The city's poor population, the group noted, was concentrated in an "inner city sprawl[ed] amidst

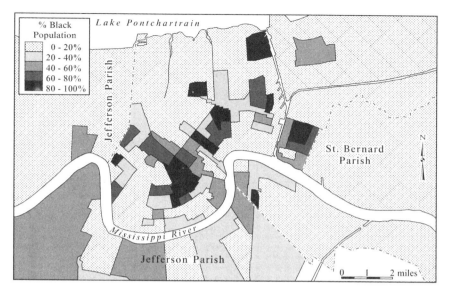

Map I.2   Percentage of black population, in census tracts, New Orleans, 1960.
Source: Social Explorer/US Census Bureau.

affluence," and 90 percent of the residents living there were black. This im-
poverished black section sliced through the heart of New Orleans's famed
crescent, its unwieldy shape mirroring the Mississippi River's serpentine cur-
vature. Its residents were among the city's least educated and least employed,
and the report documented that they had "the high birth and death rates of
the typical under-developed society."[17] While the agency issued its report at a
moment when white New Orleanians were fleeing the city following desegregation, this book highlights the ways public schools promoted separate and
unequal landscapes within New Orleans long before "white flight" took root
(see map I.2).

The story that follows is about race and power: specifically, the ways that
a public school board created and managed markets that provided benefits to
one racialized group while denying them to another. Put simply, it is a story
about the construction and institutionalization of white supremacy. Its nuts
and bolts deal with public education, urban planning, economic development,
land use, the business of real estate, and the state apparatus. But this story
is also about individual and collective aspirations and the competition those
aspirations prompted. The pages that follow show how white New Orleani-

ans manipulated the state to create the futures they desired and how African Americans exploited the limited pockets of power available to them to build and sustain communities against great odds.[18]

The local events that comprise this narrative coincided with broader shifts in the evolution of the concept of race that are examined in greater detail in the chapters that follow. For now, a brief overview will suffice. In British North America, the idea of race as a justification for slavery began to take shape during the late 1600s as wealthy planters confronted potential alliances between landless European Americans and enslaved Africans. The emergent concepts of "freedom" and "natural rights" during the Enlightenment then hastened the maturation of race as both an explanation for slavery and an indicator of fundamental human difference and hierarchy. At the turn of the nineteenth century, intellectuals such as Thomas Jefferson continued to refine ideas of race as permanent and scientifically grounded even as the Haitian Revolution gave lie to their theories.[19]

As African Americans such as Nat Turner and David Walker and white abolitionists such as William Lloyd Garrison stoked fears of widespread slave revolts during the 1830s, the link between race, education, and freedom tightened. Whites in the South and the North, who were also confronting what being "white" meant in an increasingly diverse nation, responded by assailing black schooling.[20] This repression foreshadowed the role that schools played in Reconstruction-era debates over race and citizenship, when former slaves embraced Frederick Douglass's understanding of literacy as "the pathway . . . to freedom," and southern whites responded with still more violence against black education.[21]

As Jim Crow emerged in the South during the 1890s in response to African Americans' relentless pursuit of freedom and the unsettled nature of urban life, anxious whites embraced race as a means—a dream really—for ordering all of society. Jim Crow then followed black emigres north with the Great Migration, receiving an intellectual boost from the racial pseudoscience known as eugenics.[22] The spatial reorganization of metropolises into distinct black and white residential areas over the course of the twentieth century was the latest phase in the ongoing evolution of America's racial order.[23]

The process of segregating New Orleans was more akin to colonialism than "ghetto formation."[24] Unlike "ghettos," which suggest a false sense of permanence and unilateral control, colonial metaphors and comparisons highlight the contested nature of the relationship between people imposing their power upon others and those being imposed upon. In European colonial settings, the tension between settlers and indigenous populations often created pressure for carefully managed structures of control. The hypervigilant enforcement of these controls strengthened white power even as it revealed both the tenuous nature of that power and the roles that oppressed peoples played in shaping their own futures.[25]

New Orleans began as a French colonial outpost before becoming the gateway for American empire. As the city expanded, the need to control the settlement and uses of its new land did as well. Over the long arc of this narrative, white officials strove to ensure that this new land strengthened rather than overturned the social and racial order. In this setting, schools became forts on the frontier, opening new spaces and directing the people and markets that could go there. The story of New Orleans shows that schools gave material and cultural meaning to the idea of race; by granting value to the modifiers "white" and "black," schools aided the development of inequalities based upon those fictive categories that persist to this day.

Recent scholarship has paid greater attention to public schools' impact upon twentieth-century residential segregation and metropolitan development in locales as diverse as Raleigh, North Carolina, Kansas City, Missouri, and Flint, Michigan.[26] *Race and Education in New Orleans* differs from these studies through its focus on New Orleans and its longer timeline, which highlights both the fluidity and durability of the United States' racial structure. It also emphasizes the role that public schools played in the evolution of residential segregation long before New Deal housing policies enabled the federal government to reinforce that practice. This book thus challenges the dominant periodization and characterization of metropolitan transformation. The prevailing interpretation emphasizes the ways that housing policies and markets promoted and sustained segregated schooling. But the opposite was also true: segregated schools created segregated neighborhoods.[27]

Scholars' inattention to the relationship between schools and urban change during nineteenth- and early twentieth-century history is surprising given the prevalence of school segregation throughout the country, the frequency with which school reformers promoted public education as a vehicle for urban growth, and the well-documented role that black educational institutions played in community development.[28] The lack of emphasis on the pre–World War II period is equally unfortunate given that officially sanctioned public school segregation remained common not only in the South but also in the urban North and Midwest following the Great Migration.[29] School officials in Chicago, Philadelphia, and Cleveland, among other cities, manipulated attendance districts and the pupil assignment process to create racially distinct schools during the 1920s. The number of schools in Chicago that were more than 90 percent black, for instance, leapt from one in 1916 to twenty-six in 1930, with those twenty-six educating 82 percent of the city's black students.[30] Considering the intense and often violent disputes over segregated housing that rocked many northern cities following World War I—Chicago and Cleveland in particular—it is quite possible that officials throughout the country used school locations and attendance zones to establish or strengthen residential boundaries in the decades after the war.[31]

Any examination of segregated schooling carries implications for assessing desegregation and the legacy of *Brown*.[32] On the one hand, the story told here affirms the NAACP's decision to prioritize educational inequality over other forms of discrimination and to shift its goal from the "equalization" of racially separate schools to desegregation. Schools were central to the social, political, and economic oppression of Jim Crow. By structuring race, they structured the material consequences of racial discrimination. Separate and unequal educational opportunities not only unevenly conferred the skills and credentials necessary for economic advancement; by fostering the disparate allocation of resources and protections to their surrounding neighborhoods, segregated black and white schools also influenced property values and contributed to the persistent wealth gap between whites and African Americans. Viewed in this light, segregated schools were an appropriate and necessary target.[33]

On the other hand, both the NAACP's strategic approach and the Supreme Court's decision in *Brown* permitted the continuation of the structural inequalities that segregated schools fostered.[34] Most notably, the NAACP relied on Fourteenth Amendment equal protection arguments and social scientific literature about the psychological damage that segregation inflicted upon African Americans rather than arguments emphasizing the material impacts of school segregation.[35] Until the 1960s, the organization also failed to emphasize the connections between segregated schooling and housing.[36] These strategic decisions raise intriguing questions about the alternate routes the NAACP could have traveled and what the impact of those alternatives might have been.[37]

The terms *subdivision* and *suburb* appear frequently throughout the narrative and therefore merit definition. *Subdivision* refers to a tract of land subdivided for the creation of a cohesive residential community, and *suburb* refers to a similar residential area located at a distance from the city center and often comprising multiple *subdivisions*.[38] While differentiating between a *subdivision* and *suburb* can sometimes feel like splitting hairs, this study resolves this tension by following the lead of contemporary sources. When a source refers to a section of the city as a suburb, this study does so as well. Another term that requires definition is the word *Creole*, which generally refers to Louisianians with familial roots in the francophone Atlantic world. To distinguish between Creoles who identified as white and Creoles who identified as black, the phrases white and black Creole are used, as are the synonyms Afro-Creole and Creole of color.[39]

During the nineteenth century, several suburbs (often noted by the French term *faubourg*) developed outside of the French Quarter, which was New Orleans's original city center. While separate school boards oversaw public schools in different sections of the city prior to the Civil War, these governing bodies merged during the war. Since Louisiana, like many other southern states, maintained contiguous borders for its school systems and parishes (the Louisiana equivalent of counties), the school board in New Orleans oversaw the education of students both in outlying suburbs (as they were called during the period covered here) and the inner city.[40] Since New Orleans also encompassed all of Orleans Parish, the New Orleans suburbs that receive the most attention in this book were located within the city itself. Additional suburbs eventually developed outside of Orleans Parish. But much of their growth occurred after 1960, as their racially homogenous schools attracted white residents fleeing school desegregation in the city.[41]

While every historical case study faces the challenge of justifying its broader significance, the burden is even greater when the community under examination is as seemingly distinct as New Orleans. Yet for all of the Crescent City's apparent exoticism, scholars are increasingly puncturing the myth of its exceptionalism. While its French and Spanish colonial history distinguished it from British North America, recent scholarship in the field of Atlantic history has highlighted important similarities between New Orleans and seemingly all-American cities such as Philadelphia and Baltimore during the eighteenth and early nineteenth centuries.[42] During the antebellum period, New Orleans stood apart as the South's only major city, yet its position at the nexus of slavery and capitalism arguably made it the quintessential American city—or at least a part of the United States that must be reckoned with in order to comprehend the whole.[43] Additionally, the radical egalitarian vision that New Orleans's Afro-Creoles advanced with remarkable success during Reconstruction placed them in the vanguard of American racial politics, not outside its mainstream.[44]

By 1900, New Orleans had become an even more typically American city as its racial order hardened to conform with the color lines being drawn throughout the nation.[45] Most significantly in terms of this book's focus, the trajectory of the city's urban development mirrored that of other American cities throughout the twentieth century. Neither the timing nor fact of its transformation from residential integration to segregation was unique.[46] During the nineteenth century, most African Americans in the urban North lived in predominantly white neighborhoods. This was true even for cities such as Chicago, Detroit, and New York that became "hypersegregated" during the twentieth century.[47] Thus, in important ways, the story of New Orleans and its schools sheds light on the nation and its schools more broadly.

While exclusively black residential zones developed more slowly in the urban South, where nineteenth-century levels of residential segregation were also lower, New Orleans kept pace with the rest of the country. By the start of World War II, the concentration of its black population into a single area mirrored the situation in cities outside the South.[48] New Orleans's size, age, political and economic structure, and history of black activism also provided points of comparison with northern and Midwestern cities even as regional ties to Jim Crow linked it to the emerging cities of the New South. After 1945, the "regional convergence" that bound together North and South through the shared process of postwar economic development and metropolitan stratification only enhanced New Orleans's position as a nationally representative city.[49]

New Orleanians were also attentive to national and international conversations about segregation during the early twentieth century.[50] Officials followed efforts to impose racial boundaries elsewhere, and ordinary citizens expressed a keen interest in residential settlement patterns in other cities. The race riots that affected Washington and Chicago in 1919, for example, generated a lively discussion within the *New Orleans Item* newspaper about "the Negro's place." Those riots took place as white northerners jostled for space with black migrants seeking decent jobs and schools as well as an escape from southern persecution.[51]

"In the North, and particularly in Washington," an irate reader wrote to the *Item*'s editor in July 1919, "the negro's place is wherever the white man or woman has a place. And the negro unquestionably takes advantage of his opportunity." This black "insolence," the writer continued, was largely to blame for the recent riots. "Prevented by custom from protecting themselves from the insolent self-assertiveness of the negro," he argued, "the Northern people store away their feelings, and when an opportunity to vent it does come, they make the most of it." But even as the writer ignored similar instances of violence in the South and expressed his faith in the capacity of his region's "laws and customs" to maintain its supposed racial harmony, white southerners and northerners were searching for more permanent means of regulating race relations.[52]

As the Great Migration continued, whites throughout the country clamored for greater spatial distance from blacks. In New Orleans, the public schools often provided them with the best vehicle for expressing—and realizing—those desires. This turn toward schools was not without precedent, for black and white New Orleanians had long viewed those institutions as central to the city's development and social order. Just as Ruby Bridges faced the deeply entrenched effects of this order in 1960, another young girl, Marie Justine Sirnir, had confronted its roots two centuries before.

CHAPTER ONE

AN UNSETTLED ORDER

As J. D. B. De Bow saw it, New Orleans had a reputation problem. To the outside observer, the city was little more than a swirling cesspool of foreign matter, a virtual personification of the mighty river that encircled it. "Our city has been considered a great depot of merchandise," De Bow railed in the November 1846 number of his up-and-coming monthly, "one vast warehouse in which every inhabitant is a mere transient adventurer, without any kind of local feeling or bond of union, constituting together a heterogeneous mass of material from all over the world."[1]

De Bow, a tall, shaggy-haired twenty-six-year-old who had himself arrived in New Orleans from his native Charleston only a year before, sought to refute that charge. He pointed to the bevy of new homes in the American sector, upriver from the French Quarter, as one sign that the 128-year-old city was maturing. But he also wanted to goad his new neighbors to further investment in the stabilizing infrastructure that he believed would promote commercial growth. *A society must be formed, social institutions promoted, literature encouraged and sustained, intelligence broadly disseminated, and a fixed and settled order of things secured,* he wrote. The city had already taken its first step in that direction, he argued, by "establishing a system of common schools that is unsurpassed in the Union."[2]

De Bow's hyperbolic enthusiasm for the city's public school system was understandable. Within two years of its founding in 1841, former Connecticut superintendent of education Henry Barnard was singing the New Orleans school system's praises to none other than Horace Mann, then the nation's most prominent school reformer. "They have done wonders," Barnard crowed.[3]

De Bow, who would soon become one of the South's most prominent apostles of economic modernization—and of slavery and secession—was not alone in viewing schools as central to urban development. Beginning in the 1830s,

school reformers such as Barnard and Mann pushed for the creation of cen-
tralized public school systems, especially in the nation's growing industrial
cities. These reformers believed that systems of publicly funded "common
schools," which typically served all white children in a given area, could bolster the burgeoning industrial order by transforming a city's "transient adven-
turers" into productive workers and responsible citizens.[4]

The white businessmen who founded New Orleans's public school system
"for all resident white children" similarly viewed public education as central to
community development, particularly in terms of taming the city's highly mobile population. Leaders among the city's free black population, who refused
to accept the racial exclusion that was typical of urban school systems, did
as well.[5] Yet these groups' ideas about the role that schools could play within
a city's development could not have been more different. Like De Bow and
many northern school reformers, New Orleans's white school founders believed public schools would simultaneously promote urban growth, economic
development, and a "fixed and settled" social order. The city's free black residents, meanwhile, believed public schools could and should advance a more
expansive social vision, one that would disrupt rather than strengthen the
ossifying racial order. That vision began to materialize with the final wishes
of a formerly enslaved woman named Marie Justine Sirnir Couvent.[6]

The following two sections introduce Couvent and the antebellum community she and other free people of color constructed in the downriver section of New Orleans known as the Faubourg Marigny. The subsequent section
examines the centrality of schools to antebellum debates over race and citizenship, while the fourth considers how a school for free blacks complicated
white public school officials' attempts to restrict community membership
through education. The final sections then discuss the pivotal role that schooling played in African American efforts to build a new democracy during the
Civil War and Reconstruction and the white backlash against that campaign.

I.

Along with many other New Orleanians, Marie Couvent became gravely ill
in the fall of 1832. A cholera epidemic that originated in Asia had swept into
New Orleans in late October, extending a trail of death that already stretched
from Europe to the United States' eastern seaboard. In their homes, diarrhea

and persistent vomiting wracked the disease's victims, and in many cases their hands, feet, and faces became blue and bloated in the horrific moments before they died. The scene out of doors was equally apocalyptic, as city officials burned pitch and tar and fired cannons in a desperately misguided attempt to smoke out the "miasmas" they presumed to spread the waterborne pathogen. At the city's cemeteries, bodies piled up "like corded wood," and within an eleven-day span ending on November 6 an estimated five thousand people died.[7]

Two of those unfortunates lived with the seventy-five-year-old Couvent, an enslaved male named Josué, and a recently emancipated slave named Seraphine. Couvent fell sick within days of their deaths, likely due to exposure to their illness, and on November 12, 1832, she dictated her will to a notary from what she believed to be her deathbed. As the city's board of health pronounced the epidemic over except for a handful of cases "in the lower suburbs among the poor," three free men of color gathered at Couvent's bedside to witness her final wishes. In addition to making arrangements for Seraphine's children, Couvent set aside bequests for family and friends. She then discussed the disposition of property she owned in one of the city's lower—or downriver—suburbs, the Faubourg Marigny. "I wish and ordain," she said, "that my land at the corner of Grands Hommes and Union streets be forever dedicated and employed for the establishment of a free school for the orphans of color of the Faubourg Marigny." She signed the document with an "X," which indicated that she was unable to write her own name.[8]

Couvent's bequest created a school that historians later called "the nursery for revolution in Louisiana." Her unforeseen recovery—she lived another five years after recording her will—and subsequent delays meant that the envisioned school did not open until 1848. But the school, called l'Institution Catholique des Orphelins Indigents (the Catholic Institution for Indigent Orphans), immediately established itself as a springboard for black advancement within New Orleans and as the epicenter of an unparalleled democratic vision within the United States.[9]

Banned from the city's public system of thirty-one schools, free blacks treated Couvent's school, often referred to as the Couvent School or the Catholic Institution, as though it were a public institution. The school served students from all classes in spite of its identification as an institution for orphans, and its directors regularly requested and received annual appropriations from the state legislature. They also adopted the same disciplinary procedures that the public system did, and they published their annual budget in local newspapers to ensure that "the public knows the institution's state of affairs." Benevolent associations even addressed contributions for the school to L'Ecole Publique des Orphelins indigent du Troisième district (the Public School for Indigent Orphans of the Third District), underscoring the extent to which the broader free black community shared these sentiments.[10]

By identifying their school as a public one, free blacks indirectly asserted that they, too, were part of the public and therefore deserving of the rights and privileges that accompanied membership within it. At a time of increasing racial repression in New Orleans and nationally, this overtly political act was perhaps the closest they could come to directly demanding equal citizenship rights regardless of color. Those demands would come later, with students and teachers from the Catholic Institution leading New Orleans's Reconstruction-era charge to create a new democracy without regard to caste or color.

Marie Couvent could not have foreseen all of this while dictating her will from her sickbed in 1832. But she was acutely aware of the role education had played and could play in the black community's advancement. She was also intimately familiar with the malleability of race, social status, and the line between the two. Like the free men of color she entrusted to carry out her bequest, she had experienced that fluidity firsthand.

II.

Couvent was born around 1757 in western Africa, possibly in the Gbe-speaking region along the Bight of Benin. At the age of seven, slave traders stole her from her parents and transported her to the French sugar colony of Saint-Domingue, where she eventually became the property of a resident of Cap-Français, a bustling port city on the island's northern coast. It was there she likely acquired the name Marie Justine Sirnir. While the details of Sirnir's life in Le Cap, as Cap-Français was also known, are hazy, she experienced a trauma in that city similar to the one that marred her youth.[11]

In the early 1790s, Sirnir became separated from her enslaved ten-year-old son Celestin, likely as a result of the tumult surrounding the nascent Haitian Revolution. Enslaved laborers torched plantations in the northern plain around Le Cap on August 22, 1791, transforming a year-old conflict over the political rights of free blacks into a contest over slavery. By the summer of 1793, Le Cap was in flames.

Celestin's owner was likely among the ten thousand who fled the destruction of the city that summer, skipping town with the young boy in tow. As the revolution sent shockwaves throughout the United States and wider Atlantic world, Celestin and his owner likely joined the émigrés who poured into Philadelphia, Baltimore, Boston, and New York, among other cities. A number of these refugees later hopped along the East Coast before making their way to New Orleans. With these well-known migratory patterns likely in mind, Sirnir was still searching for and attempting to secure her son's freedom twenty years later, by which time she was a well-established free woman in New Orleans.[12]

Sirnir arrived in the Crescent City as a free woman in 1804, shortly after Saint-Domingue's black rebels overthrew slavery and French colonial rule to establish the independent nation of Haiti. Her departure was part of another mass exodus from the island, as both white and black residents sought refuge in Cuba as well as in American cities such as New Orleans and Charleston in the wake of the republican victory. While it is unclear whether Sirnir secured her freedom through the revolution or other means, her migration to New Orleans carried risks because recently emancipated blacks faced reenslavement in those places where slavery remained legal. By 1806, however, she solidified her status as a free woman by exercising a right available only to those who were free: she purchased two pieces of property.[13]

In May of 1806 she bought an undeveloped lot at the corner of Grands Hommes and Union (later Dauphine and Touro) streets from Bernard Marigny, an aristocratic playboy then in the process of subdividing a large tract of inherited plantation land. Located immediately downriver from the French Quarter, the Faubourg Marigny quickly became a racially mixed suburb of strivers. Taking advantage of Marigny's willingness to sell on credit with little or no money down, many white immigrants and free people of color joined Sirnir in the neighborhood. Like her, a number of Marigny's free residents sought to advance socially and economically through the acquisition of property—both in people and land. A month after she bought her Marigny lot, for instance, Sirnir purchased a parcel of land with buildings on it on the eastern, or downriver, edge of the French Quarter, adjacent to the Faubourg Marigny (see map 1.1). By 1812, she also owned five slaves. The money for these purchases possibly came from her work as a *marchande:* a petty trader or shopkeeper. Free and enslaved black women played an outsized role in the retail trade in both Saint-Domingue and New Orleans, and Sirnir initially sold sundries.[14]

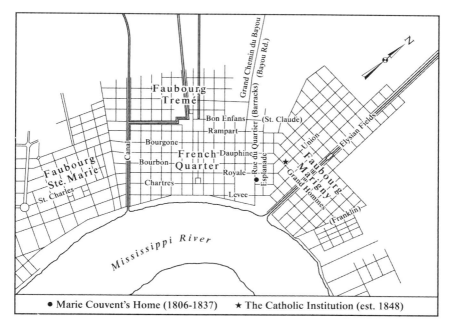

Map 1.1   Marie Couvent's New Orleans.
Map based upon *Plan of the City and Suburbs of New Orleans: From an Actual Survey Made in 1815 by J. Tanesse* (New York: Charles Del Vecchio, 1817), Library of Congress, Geography and Map Division.[15]

At the time of Sirnir's 1804 arrival, New Orleans was more a large village than a city, "a metropolis in prospect only," according to one historian. Its roughly eight thousand residents—about half as many as lived in Le Cap on the eve of the revolution—resided almost exclusively in the French Quarter, which extended a mere eleven blocks along the Mississippi River and six blocks from the river levee to the town's soupy backdoor. People of African descent were in the majority, with slaves outnumbering free people of color two-to-one.[16]

Sirnir's first years in New Orleans coincided with several developments that dramatically altered the city's trajectory. The United States' acquisition of New Orleans and the rest of the Louisiana territory from France the year before her arrival opened the floodgates to profit-seeking Americans, who had already been trickling into the city to gain access to the river. Then, in 1809–1810, the city's population more than doubled as ten thousand émigrés—two-thirds of them of African descent—arrived from Saint-Domingue via Cuba following the outbreak of hostilities between France and Cuba's Spanish overlords. That mass migration dramatically increased the number and proportion of black New Orleanians. Once the last batch of refugees disembarked, nearly two-thirds of New Orleans's residents were black, their numbers almost evenly divided between the enslaved and free. While free people of color were overrepresented and slaves underrepresented in the Faubourg Marigny, the suburb's racial demographics mirrored those of the city at large.[17]

During the first decade of the nineteenth century, New Orleans was also fast becoming the United States' primary slave market. As Chesapeake soils became exhausted after generations of tobacco harvests and cotton cultivation rapidly expanded into the South and West thanks to Eli Whitney's gin, Upper South planters increasingly sold their chattel property downriver. Congress's closure of the Atlantic slave trade in 1808 provided further impetus for the domestic market, which ripped families apart as it forcibly transferred more than one million individuals from the Upper to the Lower South in the decades preceding the Civil War. On the receiving end, slave traders, merchants, and cotton factors in New Orleans stitched together relationships with southern planters and northern and British mills and financial institutions that bolstered the development of modern global capitalism. By 1820, New Orleans was the fifth largest city in the United States, a budding metropolis whose commercial prospects looked suddenly bright. Its meteoric rise also foreshadowed the rapid urbanization that would transform scores of other communities during the antebellum era.[18]

As geopolitics altered New Orleans's course, its residents reshaped the city from the ground up. Moneyed Americans pressed into the Faubourg Ste. Marie, immediately upriver from the French Quarter, building townhouses for themselves and warehouses for the cornucopia of goods—cotton, sugar, pork, beef, and corn to name a few—that flowed into and out of the city. Free black and white Creoles (Louisianians of francophone ancestry) also moved into this area above Canal Street, which was the broad boulevard marking the French Quarter's upriver edge. But Americans so dominated the banks, brokerages, and insurance companies that sprouted up there that Ste. Marie became known as the American Sector. Much to the chagrin of the city's creole residents, by the mid-1820s the city's newspapers frequently used the terms "commercial quarter" and "American section" interchangeably.[19]

While Bernard Marigny mourned the francophone New Orleanians' loss of influence and commercial control, the Saint-Domingue migration proved a boon to his fledgling suburb. The Faubourg Marigny, in many ways, became the throbbing francophone heart of a city increasingly divided along linguistic and cultural lines. This was particularly true for the *gens de couleur libre* (free people of color), who dominated Faubourg Marigny property ownership. As Bernard Marigny lamented the shift in the city's commercial center, the faubourg's free black residents fashioned a remarkably durable community.[20]

Sirnir played a direct and emblematic role in the neighborhood's development. Although she lived the remainder of her life in the property she had purchased on Barracks Street on the edge of the French Quarter, she was among the many free blacks investing in and profiting from Faubourg Marigny real estate. According to one estimate, three-quarters of the lots in Marigny had at least one free black owner during the first half of the nineteenth century, and many of those owners were women. While many free black people owned homes in the neighborhood—at 43 percent of its population, free black residents outnumbered both whites and enslaved blacks there in 1810—a number also participated in the market as speculators, investors, developers, and landlords.[21]

Sirnir pursued the latter course. At some point after 1812, she erected "a house and several dependencies" on her Marigny lot at Grands Hommes and Union and began renting them out. The influx of refugees from Saint-Domingue in 1809–1810 had created an intense demand for housing in a city that until recently had barely more than a thousand homes for its eight thousand residents. Many émigrés rented outbuildings or other substandard residences until the uptick in Marigny construction eased the crunch. Sirnir also added another building to her Barracks Street property, which she possibly rented to immigrants from Saint-Domingue. In addition to bringing in regular income, these moves proved to be lucrative. At the time of her death in 1837, Sirnir's Barracks Street property was appraised for $3,000 and her Marigny property appraised for $12,000. She had purchased them thirty-one years before for $550 and $500, respectively.[22]

Blacks contributed to Marigny's development in other ways as well. As was the case during New Orleans's earliest eighteenth-century days as a fetid French outpost, enslaved blacks did the heavy lifting, hauling, and hewing that was necessary to transform undeveloped land into a livable suburb. After Bernard Marigny's slaves laid out lots, marked the boundaries for each block, and built roads, free blacks stepped in to create a streetscape that remains a signature of New Orleans's eclectic charm. As historian Lawrence Powell explains, the Faubourg Marigny was "where free black carpenters, masons, and joiners acquired modest competencies by constructing many of the two-bay and four-bay dormered Creole cottages, with slaves driving nails and sawing the wood." Free women like Sirnir also left their mark on the neighborhood by purchasing lots, making decisions about the type, size, and design of the buildings to be erected upon them, and directing the contractors and craftsman who carried out the work. An equivalent process unfolded in the Faubourg Tremé, the neighborhood immediately north of the French Quarter, where many free people of color settled after the city acquired and subdivided the tract following the 1809–1810 influx of Dominguan émigrés. Around this same time, free blacks in Philadelphia similarly led the charge in settling newly developed neighborhoods on that city's southwest side.[23]

Sirnir's Faubourg Marigny property was at the center of the free black community that took root during the neighborhood's early days. The fan-shaped suburb, comprising fifty-nine blocks wedged between a narrow slip of the river and the present-day Esplanade, Franklin, and St. Claude Avenues, was a racially mixed area overall in 1810. In parts of the neighborhood, white, free, and enslaved blacks were all mixed together, with whites and blacks acquiring property and living next door to each other. But free people of color primarily bought property in the suburb's northwestern quadrant. Grands Hommes Street, which ran parallel to the river and connected to Dauphine Street in the French Quarter, formed an unofficial boundary between the white- and black-owned portions of Faubourg Marigny. In fact, free black people initially purchased nearly all of the lots in the fourteen blocks between Esplanade, Grands Hommes, Français (later Frenchman), and Bons Enfans (later St. Claude), according to historian Elizabeth Neidenbach's analysis of property sales between 1805 and 1809. On the Grands Hommes Street block where Sirnir purchased her property, free blacks acquired all but one of the lots in 1806. The following year, the one white purchaser, who had acquired a lot next to Sirnir's, split it in two and sold each half to a free black woman.[24]

This clustering of free blacks in the backend of the Marigny mirrored the French Quarter's residential pattern, where so-called *libres* similarly lived further from the river on land that was both cheaper and more prone to flood. As in northern cities such as Philadelphia, Boston, New York, and New Haven, and other southern port cities such as Charleston and Baltimore, these early black enclaves prefigured the later expansion of residential segregation.[25]

The Marigny's concentration of free blacks also extended the tight internal bonds that New Orleans's *libre* population had established by the turn of the nineteenth century. While the free population dated to Louisiana's founding as a French colony, it did not blossom as a community until Louisiana's time under the Spanish flag, which ostensibly lasted from 1769 to 1803. The Spanish actively cultivated a free black class as a check against both French-speaking whites and slaves. But the Spaniards' carefully articulated corporatist ideology worked better on paper than in reality.

Once liberated, free blacks resisted their assigned place as the middle layer of a tripartite racial order. They often advanced socially and economically, particularly through service in the free black militia. *Libres* also climbed the social ladder by partnering with each other on business ventures and through strategic marriages and godparent arrangements, which enabled upwardly mobile *libres* to attach themselves to more prominent free blacks. Interracial sex also persisted unabated in spite of Spain's strict ideas regarding *limpieza de sangre* ("purity of blood"), with many free blacks inheriting wealth through their white fathers. And while *libres* aligned themselves more closely with the white governing class, as the Dons had hoped they would, the line between *libres* and slaves often blurred. They ate, drank, and prayed together—even married one another from time to time. As historian Caryn Cossé Bell noted, "The Spanish had created not so much a new fixed racial order as an unsettled racial and social flux."[26]

III.

This fluid reality clashed with the concept of race that Enlightenment thinkers were refining at that very moment, namely that "race" was a fundamental and scientifically grounded indicator of human difference. New Orleans's unsettled racial order also caused headaches for the young United States, which had fully embraced notions of immutable racial difference by the time it acquired the city and the vast Louisiana territory in 1803. The Haitian Revolution, which openly flaunted the flimsiness of the racial ideology that intellectuals such as President Thomas Jefferson pioneered, only deepened American concerns, as did the assertiveness of New Orleans's *libre* population. Shortly after the United States formally took control of New Orleans, for instance, members of the city's free black militia seized upon language in the Louisiana Purchase treaty to assert their equal standing within the American republic. "We are duly sensible that our personal and political freedom is thereby assured to us for ever, and we are also impressed with the fullest confidence in the Justice and Liberality of the Government toward every Class of Citizen which they have here taken under their Protection," they wrote in a petition.[27]

While white elites from President Thomas Jefferson to Louisiana's planter-dominated territorial legislature sought to roll back black rights, the *libres* blunted the impact of these maneuvers. The 1809–1810 influx from Saint-Domingue then reinforced their ranks, further clouding the city's already hazy lines between black and white, slavery and freedom.[28]

Sirnir's experiences and personal networks illuminated the slipperiness of New Orleans's nineteenth-century social order. This was particularly evident through her interactions with the people she owned as slaves. While she occasionally purchased slaves for purely economic reasons, her relationships with others such as a man named Bernard were quite different. Sirnir acquired Bernard, whom she had already known for some time, for $868 on February 14, 1811, by mortgaging both her French Quarter and Marigny properties. When she fell ill twenty months after purchasing Bernard, she hastily wrote a will granting him freedom upon her death. The next day, Sirnir received last rites from a priest at St. Louis Cathedral. She and Bernard then confessed to "cohabitating," received the sacrament of penance, and married. Interestingly, their marriage record described the couple as a "free black woman, who by word and mutual promise of marriage, had cohabited with Bernard, a black man *also free*, whose freedom the above-mentioned sick woman had bought." Since the Louisiana legislature had sharply limited manumission following the American takeover, Sirnir more likely lived with Bernard as though he were free without actually purchasing his freedom. With some notarial sleight of hand, however, they created a paper trail that legally documented—and protected—his freedom.[29]

Sirnir, who recovered from her 1812 illness much as she would from her cholera bout twenty years later, took Bernard's last name of Couvent, convent in English. That name was a nod to Bernard's parents, Simon Labelle and Marie Jeanne, whom the Ursuline nuns held as slaves until 1778. Sirnir also had another noteworthy connection to the Ursulines: her French Quarter home sat directly across the street from their convent.[30]

This was significant given the sisters' impact upon New Orleans's early development, particularly in the field of education. To a greater extent than any other group in the city and arguably the whole of colonial North America, the Ursulines demonstrated the capacity of schooling to subvert and shape the social and racial order.[31]

By any measure, their influence far outstripped their numbers, which generally hovered below thirty. The first twelve Ursuline nuns arrived in New Orleans in August 1727, when the French colonial capital was a squalid, sputtering outpost. Before settling into a two-story home partially surrounded by dense woods, the nuns spent their first nights camping behind palisades designed to keep alligators and snakes at bay. While colonial officials mostly wanted the sisters to tend to New Orleans's perpetually ailing population, the Ursulines doggedly pursued their primary interest in female spiritual development and education. By the spring of 1728, the convent included twenty boarders of European descent, seven enslaved boarders, and a "large number of day students and Negresses and Indian girls" who attended free afternoon catechism classes. While these day students were generally in class for only an hour and a half each day, boarding students spent about six hours per day in class studying reading, writing, spelling, figuring, needlework, and the catechism.[32]

The Ursulines' success in educating girls distinguished New Orleans from colonies in British North America. By the late 1700s, female literacy in New Orleans had reached the point where women could challenge men in civil, social, and economic matters. The nuns' interest in the education of free and enslaved black girls also contributed to the development of New Orleans's distinctly literate black population, though here their efforts were perhaps not as exceptional. The Society for the Propagation of the Gospel (SPG), for instance, undertook similar educational missions among slaves in Charleston, South Carolina, Savannah, Georgia, and New York City during the early 1700s. These institutional efforts, however, were less enduring than the Ursulines' century-long commitment to black education. They also posed less of a challenge to established social hierarchies. Unlike the SPG, the Ursulines thoroughly blurred the supposed link between race, gender, and social status by initially accepting wealthy free black girls as boarding students while relegating poor white ones to abbreviated sessions that focused only on religious education and basic literacy. They also stressed family cohesion and religious training for the individuals they held as slaves. The net impact of their efforts, historian Emily Clark concludes, "could and did create spaces for alternate interpretations of social and racial order."[33]

Marie and Bernard Couvent inhabited one of those spaces, and she enabled the construction of another by calling for her Faubourg Marigny property to be turned into a school for the neighborhood's orphaned black children. While the full extent to which the Ursulines influenced Couvent is unclear, their potential as a model for her bequest merits consideration. Couvent learned about the sisters' educational mission from Bernard and his family members, who remained their slaves, and she likely attended services regularly in the church on the convent grounds since that is where Father Constantine Maenhaut, the white Catholic priest she tapped to supervise her bequest, was stationed. Couvent also likely relished that the women living opposite her were as savvy and independent-minded as she was, and she no doubt noted the example they provided of schooling's democratic potential.[34]

As Couvent moved between her home and her Faubourg Marigny rental property, she also built relationships with the free black men who would carry out her bequest. Like Couvent, these men directly contributed to the physical development and growth of the Marigny. Also like her, they embraced her proposed school as a means of bolstering the neighborhood, their investment in it, and the community of free black men and women who lived there. This dynamic was similar to the one that unfolded in cities such as Philadelphia, where Gary Nash notes that blacks focused on strengthening community institutions such as schools in order "to create an Afro-American society within American society." In New Orleans, this reciprocal relationship between Couvent's school and the development of the city's free black community was particularly evident in the social and professional ties that bound her to the men who acted upon her bequest.[35]

At the center of these networks was Henry Fletcher, whom Couvent named as her executor. Fletcher's grandparents lived down Barracks Street from Couvent, and she likely met him there as a young boy. Fletcher grew up to become a carpenter and like Couvent was an early investor in Faubourg Marigny property, often partnering with other free men of color in the building trades. Four of the seven properties that he owned when he died in 1853 were in the Marigny, and his Marigny holdings were mostly clustered near Couvent's property. In 1812, for instance, he bought a lot across the street from Couvent's Grand Hommes Street property, and he later acquired additional lots on Histoire Street two blocks away.[36]

Many of the men who opened Couvent's school a decade after her death had biographies that mirrored Fletcher's, and they were often connected to

Couvent through either Fletcher or Bernard Couvent's son, who was also an acquaintance of Fletcher's. One of Fletcher's early business partners, for instance, was a man named Joseph Dolliole, with whom he also served in the First Battalion of Free Men of Color (New Orleans's revived black militia) during the 1815 Battle of New Orleans. Dolliole, who like Fletcher was a carpenter, also partnered with Nelson Fouché, a free black mason, to develop land in a new suburb downriver from the Faubourg Marigny. Bernard's son, who like his father was named Bernard and also was a carpenter, was among those who purchased land from Dolliole and Fouché in their new development. The younger Bernard Couvent, a probable First Battalion veteran, also sold property to Nelson Fouché on another occasion.

These men likely learned that Couvent wanted her Faubourg Marigny property turned into a school shortly after her death in 1837, when Fletcher convened a group to determine the handling of a bequest Couvent left to the minor child of her emancipated, predeceased slave Seraphine. The meeting's attendees included Joseph Dolliole, his brother Jean Louis, Nelson Fouché, and Adolphe Duhart, the son of Saint-Domingue refugees. It is possible that these men knew of Couvent's bequest for the school even sooner through either Fletcher or Joseph Camps, a witness to her 1832 will who had served in the First Battalion alongside Fletcher, the Dolliole brothers and, quite possibly, the younger Bernard Couvent.[37]

The decade-long delay in opening the school was likely due to growing concerns over the threat black education posed to the racial order in New Orleans and nationally. The 1830s marked a turning point in the evolution of race in the United States. The decade was also a turning point in the role that schools played in policing the meaning of race as white Americans confronted the threat they believed educated African Americans posed to their futures. The rapid shift to an industrial economy coupled with the equally dramatic uptick in immigration and the gradual emancipation of slaves in the North provided the backdrop for white fears about their status and socioeconomic standing. These developments untethered native-born whites by raising questions about the seemingly fixed relationship between race and citizenship. If formerly enslaved blacks could become free and polyglot foreigners could compete with the native-born for wages and resources, then what did being white really mean?

Three events that brought this racial anxiety to the fore were the publication of black abolitionist David Walker's incendiary *Appeal to the Coloured*

Citizens of the World in 1829, the introduction of William Lloyd Garrison's *Liberator* newspaper in 1831, and Nat Turner's slave revolt later that same year. In his *Appeal*, Walker called for an armed rebellion against slavery and explicitly linked the education of blacks to the institution's demise. For whites, the fact that the enslaved Nat Turner was literate confirmed Walker's theory of action and underscored the need for forceful countermeasures.[38]

In Louisiana, the legislature outlawed the education of slaves and banned language and written materials "having a tendency to produce discontent among the free coloured population . . . or insubordination among the slaves" in 1830. Like the common schools in Baltimore, whose free black population rivaled that of New Orleans, the Crescent City's public school system explicitly excluded black students from its inception in 1841. Also in the early 1840s, when New Orleans's free black population of more than nineteen thousand was the largest in the nation, city and state officials passed laws designed to keep additional free blacks from entering Louisiana. While some white New Orleanians openly opposed these new restrictions, the tide was flowing much more forcibly in the other direction. The repression reached such a level during the 1840s that half of New Orleans's free black residents simply left town or attempted to pass as white. While nearly one out of every five New Orleanians was a free person of color in 1840, free blacks comprised less than 9 percent of the total population by 1850 (see Table 1.1).[39]

Across the South multiple states passed restrictions similar to those that Louisiana adopted. Georgia, for instance, responded to Walker's tract by immediately outlawing literacy instruction for slaves and free people of color and by implementing the death penalty for anyone who distributed materials "for the purposes of exciting insurrection, conspiracy or resistance among the slaves, negroes, or free persons of color." Alabama and Virginia soon followed suit with antiliteracy laws targeting both slaves and free people of color, while North and South Carolina outlawed teaching slaves to read or write. Southern communities also cracked down on the distribution of abolitionist literature through the mail, and southern congressmen responded to the flood of antislavery petitions reaching their chamber by imposing a "gag rule" that barred all discussion of slavery. These actions underscored the extent to which both slaves and slaveholders shared Frederick Douglass's understanding of literacy as "*the* pathway from slavery to freedom."[40]

In the North, schools were also at the center of the antebellum upheaval over race, democracy, and the future. Days after news of Turner's rebellion

Table 1.1   Population of New Orleans by Race and Slave Status, 1810–1850

| | Total | White | Black | | Free Black Population as Percentage of Total |
			Free	Enslaved	
1810	17,242	6,331	4,950	5,961	29
1820	27,176	13,584	6,237	7,355	23
1830	46,082	20,044	11,562	14,476	25
1840	102,193	59,519	19,226	23,448	19
1850	116,375	89,459	9,905	17,011	9

Source: Campbell Gibson and Kay Jung, *Historical Census Statistics on Population Totals by Race, 1790 to 1990, and by Hispanic Origin, 1970 to 1990, For Large Cities and Other Urban Places in the United States*, US Census Bureau Population Division, Working Paper No. 76 (Washington, DC: US Census Bureau, 2005).

reached New Haven, Connecticut, more than seven hundred white men stormed city hall to reject the formation of the nation's first black college in that town. While the crowd vowed to "resist the establishment of the proposed college in this place, by every lawful means," Connecticut residents quickly embraced extralegal methods to undermine black education. Rioters tore through New Haven's black community following the vote, vandalizing black-owned businesses and terrorizing residents. In 1833–1834, white residents in Canterbury, Connecticut, repeatedly attacked a boarding school for African American girls that the white Quaker Prudence Crandall founded with black abolitionists James Forten, Rev. Theodore Wright, and Rev. Peter Williams. Incensed by Crandall's refusal to follow an 1833 state law that barred blacks from entering Connecticut to attend school, terrorists attempted to burn the occupied building to the ground and then ransacked it with clubs and iron bars.[41]

In the years immediately following Turner's revolt, whites similarly assailed black education in major cities such as Washington, DC, Philadelphia, Boston, and New York and in smaller towns in New Hampshire, Ohio, and Illinois. Throughout the country, white opponents of black education crafted laws, filed petitions, and took up arms. As historian Hilary Moss notes, these attacks reinforced the early nineteenth-century drive in the North to strip blacks of their right to vote—and, by extension, their citizenship—while expanding suffrage to all white men and public schooling to their children re-gardless of whether they were native- or foreign-born. "White opposition to black education," Moss writes, "became a critical component in a much larger movement to remove—figuratively, if not physically—black people from the body politic." It also clarified what being white meant for the remarkably di-verse group that sought shelter under this single racial umbrella.[42]

Back in New Orleans, the increasingly repressive environment likely dis-suaded Father Maenhaut, who was charged with overseeing Couvent's be-quest, from acting on it. In 1847, however, free black New Orleanians stepped forward to carry out Couvent's final wishes. The men who attended the 1837 meeting to discuss her affairs took the lead. Nelson Fouché, for instance, was among the ten men who successfully petitioned the state legislature for le-gal recognition of the society they formed to implement the bequest, and he and these men comprised the school's original Board of Directors. When the school opened in 1848, Adolph Duhart's wife, Françoise Palmyre Brouard, be-came one of its two instructors for female students. One of the Duharts' sons later became the school's principal, and another served on its board during the 1880s. Additionally, Joseph Camps, who had witnessed Couvent's will in 1832, had both a son and nephew, Joseph Manuel Camps and Paul Trévigne, who served as early teachers and board members.[43]

Historian Elizabeth Neidenbach points to the background of these men and their overlapping connections with Couvent in order to challenge previ-ous scholars who credited Maenhaut with reviving Couvent's otherwise un-known bequest. In shifting the credit to Couvent, Neidenbach argues that the formerly enslaved woman made calculated decisions about how she could best support her neighborhood after her death. Furthermore, Neidenbach notes that the men Couvent entrusted to carry out her wishes "were not only people who would be aware of the needs of free people of color in New Or-leans in general, but also stakeholders in the Marigny itself, optimally posi-tioned to see to it that her vision for a school was realized."[44]

Couvent, in other words, understood that these men would rally behind the school because of its capacity to advance their community as well as their personal interests. In addition to providing black children with the education they needed to safeguard their freedom at a particularly precarious moment in American history, the school would protect the financial investments that men such as Fletcher and Fouché had made in nearby property.

The founders of the city's public school system for whites were similarly interested in promoting both real estate development and communal well-being during the antebellum era. But their ideas for public education restricted, rather than expanded, community membership. And the Catholic Institution complicated those efforts.

IV.

Public education developed in antebellum New Orleans along lines that were familiar in the Northeast and Midwest. Intent to promote economic growth and stabilize diverse, transient, and often unruly populations, Protestant businessmen encouraged the formation of state-run, publicly funded school systems. Events such as an 1834 mob attack and burning of the Ursuline convent and school in Charlestown, Massachusetts, convinced Horace Mann and other reformers of the need for standardized school systems to both unify and buttress the nation's fractured social structure. But these new systems' widespread exclusion or segregation of black children, along with the constraints they placed upon independent women of the Ursuline mold, reflected the limits of the reformers' seemingly inclusive vision.[45] In this regard, New Orleans was hardly an exception.[46]

The similarities between New Orleans and other cities were not surprising given the outsized role that northeastern transplants played in the founding of New Orleans's public school system. These men did not simply look north for inspiration or peruse Horace Mann's *Common School Journal* for ideas about best practices. They unapologetically copied the model that Mann had pioneered in Massachusetts.[47]

At the time, New Orleans was the nation's third largest city, and its banking industry rivaled New York's. Like many antebellum American cities, it was also deeply divided along racial as well as gender and ethnic lines. The New Orleans Ursulines, for instance, left their French Quarter convent in 1824 for a new compound two miles downriver following a dispute partly rooted in their unwillingness to accede to male authority. By 1850, the majority of the city's free residents were also foreign-born, as New Orleans became as much a magnet for German and Irish immigrants as Boston, Philadelphia, and Chicago. Additionally, tensions between the Americans, who dominated the uptown portion of the city above Canal Street, and the French-speaking Creoles, who were concentrated below it, also had reached such a pitch that New Orleans briefly split into three semiautonomous municipalities beginning in the 1830s. The Americans in the uptown section that became the Second Municipality pushed hardest for the creation of a public school system, with Pennsylvania native Joshua Baldwin taking the lead.[48]

Baldwin, who held a post in the Second Municipality government, successfully lobbied the state legislature to pass a law on February 16, 1841, enabling each of New Orleans's three municipalities to establish independent school systems governed by their own boards of directors. The law also gave each municipality its share of state appropriations for public education and authorized the municipalities to levy taxes to support the free schools. Baldwin apparently structured the law on a plan for a public school system that he received in 1839 from Henry Barnard, then Connecticut's superintendent of education.[49]

Impressed with Mann's success establishing a system of free, publicly supported common schools in Massachusetts, Baldwin also wrote to him in April 1841, seeking information "to assist in the establishment & organization of Public Schools [in New Orleans]." By May, the council of the Second Municipality established a sixteen-member school board. Along with Baldwin, council member Samuel J. Peters, also president of the Second Municipality's Chamber of Commerce, played a key role in bringing free public schools to the upriver American sector. A decade later, the pair again joined forces in an unsuccessful campaign to promote railroad construction in New Orleans, which was fast losing ground to Midwestern states that were investing in commercial infrastructure.[50]

The First Municipality, which encompassed the French Quarter, and the downriver Third Municipality, which included Faubourg Marigny, followed the Second's lead, convening their school boards for the first time in July 1841. In August, Baldwin again wrote Mann for suggestions regarding a superintendent to "launch" the system. He stated that New Orleans "would require no more, but would not be satisfied with any less, than is required in Boston," adding that Mann should note "the impropriety of engaging any one entertaining objections to slavery." Mann, who later became an antislavery congressman, respected Baldwin's concerns since at the time he disapproved of education officials in Massachusetts promoting either abolition or integrated schooling. Like other early public school advocates, Mann also implicitly accepted the exclusion of blacks from erstwhile "common schools" since he saw little need to prepare them either for citizenship or job responsibilities that would never be available to them. After receiving Baldwin's letter, Mann recruited John Angier Shaw, a Mississippi slaveholder turned Yankee who had staunchly defended Massachusetts's nascent public school system as a state legislator. Baldwin's newly empaneled school board moved quickly to appoint Shaw to lead the Second Municipality's school system.[51]

Shaw arrived in New Orleans in December 1841, and the new system soon blossomed under his command. Registration in the Second Municipality's schools exceeded one thousand by the end of the first school year in 1842, and the board was particularly pleased that many of its students were the children of "opulent and influential citizens, who before confided their education to the private schools." By 1843, the board claimed that its system was "beginning to present a large inducement for the settlement of families within our limits." This school-inspired migration, the board gladly reported a year later, enhanced the "pecuniary prosperity of the municipality."[52]

School reformers elsewhere, particularly in up-and-coming Midwestern cities, similarly embraced public schools to promote urban growth. As historian of education David L. Angus explains, "As communities competed with one another for local and regional dominance, the stakes were high and the tactics not always ethical, but every self-respecting community with half a chance to become the next Chicago or St. Louis needed a couple of good newspapers with vigorous booster editors, an ample number of churches, paved streets, adequate fire protection, and, above all, a good system of free common schools." The immense popularity of nineteenth-century urban public school systems underscored the extent to which public schools could serve as magnets for communities on the make.[53]

As rapidly as the Second Municipality's system grew, the Third Municipality actually snagged the distinction of opening the city's first public school, taking over the private Harby's Academy in November 1841. The school was located on Victory (now Decatur) near Marigny Street, a mere six blocks from Couvent's bequeathed property. While the new public school excluded the many free black children who lived in the Marigny, several nearby private schools educated free children of color. According to Marcus Christian, an assiduous Depression-era chronicler of New Orleans's African American history, "the tradition of education which had been growing among [free blacks] for more than a century" tragically blossomed at the very moment that new legislation severely restricted their liberties.[54]

In this regard, New Orleans differed from Baltimore, a port city with a smaller slave population but an equally robust network of private and Catholic schools for free blacks. While black schools faced less resistance in Baltimore than in New Orleans, the black schools there were also less politically assertive. The Baltimore schools' attendance and literacy rates were also lower. In New Orleans, nearly 60 percent of free blacks were literate in 1850 (compared to 91 percent of whites) while in Baltimore 41 percent of free blacks were literate (compared to 93 percent of whites). Similarly, nearly one-third of New Orleans's free black school-aged children attended school in 1850 compared to less than one-sixth in Baltimore.[55]

Christian identified at least eight schools in the downtown portion of New Orleans that were open to free blacks during the 1840s and early 1850s (see map 1.2). These schools often grew out of a single teacher's work as a tutor, and these for-hire arrangements, like the schools that followed, sometimes defied the city's hardening color line. The schools included the one at 57 Bagatelle Street in the Marigny run by Joseph Bazanac, a free man of color, and Jean Louis Marciacq, a white writer who likely fled to New Orleans to escape the revolutionary tumult in France or the French Caribbean. Another free man of color, Ludger Boguille, ran a school on Grands Hommes, just a stone's throw from Couvent's property, before moving to Esplanade Avenue and Villere Street. Boguille divided teaching responsibilities with his wife, providing instruction in French while she focused on English. The free black poet Joanni Questy, who lived at No. 30 Amour Street in the Marigny, also taught school in the neighborhood, as did a man named Tuhait Louis, whose school was located at 64 Mandeville Street. Additionally, Paul Trévigne and his wife ran a school on Columbus Street near Roman in the backend of the Faubourg Marigny, while the famed writer Michel Seligny founded the Sainte-Barbe Academy on St. Philip Street in the neighboring Faubourg Tremé. Seligny's students included Victor Sejour, who became a literary sensation in France and published politically charged works in journals such as the abolitionist *Revue des Colonies*.[56]

In addition to these efforts, devout free black Catholic women embarked on a new educational venture in the 1830s that extended the legacy of the Ursulines, who stopped educating free black girls at their convent in the 1820s, apparently bowing to public pressure. Spearheaded by Henriette Delille, a prominent free woman of color, an order of free black nuns known as the Sisters of the Holy Family ministered to enslaved and free people of color,

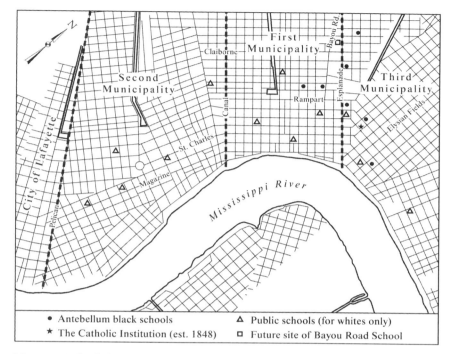

Map 1.2   Schools in antebellum New Orleans.
Map based on *Norman's Plan of New Orleans & Environs*, 1845, Library of Congress, Geography and Map Division. School data by Walter C. Stern. The map shows known school locations for white public schools as of 1845 and for black schools during the 1840s and 1850s. While a total of seventeen white public schools were open across the city's three municipalities in 1845, the frequent moves that schools made from one rented space to another complicate efforts to identify all school locations at a particular time.[57]

provided religious instruction to slaves, and operated a school for free blacks on Bayou Road in Faubourg Tremé.[58]

Delille's dedication to service developed out of her religiosity as well as her own educational experiences. She had attended a Catholic girls school in the French Quarter, which the white Sister Marthe Fontiere of the Dames Hospitalier (Ladies of Charity) established in 1823 with the financial support of free blacks. When students at Fontiere's school, Delille and her classmates engaged in charitable projects among the poor and enslaved. They expanded their philanthropic work after a trio of white French sisters, one of whom was an Ursuline nun, took over the school and moved it to a larger facility in

Tremé in 1834. Several years after church officials refused to approve the new school mistress's effort to form an interracial religious order in conjunction with Delille and several other free women of color, Delille founded the all-black Sisters of the Holy Family in 1842. As the order struggled to establish itself during the 1840s, many of the free black men who helped found the Catholic Institution came to its aid.[59]

The collaboration between the Catholic Institution and the Sisters of the Holy Family was a fitting match given their common interests and the role the former played as a hub for black leadership and advancement. From its inception, the Catholic Institution united the city's most prominent free black educators, providing them with a base from which they dramatically amplified their impact upon the community. The extent to which the school built upon existing community capital was most evident through its early faculty, which included many of the black educators and writers who were already active in the Marigny and Tremé. The five original faculty members included Ludger Boguille, who had moved his school from Grands Hommes to Esplanade Avenue and Villere, as well as Monsieur and Madame Joseph Bazanac, who previously ran the school on Bagatelle Street with Jean Louis Marciacq. When the school expanded its faculty in 1852, the esteemed poet Armand Lanusse became principal and fellow poet Joanni Questy, who previously ran a school in the Marigny, became Lanusse's assistant. Paul Trévigne, who ran the school on Columbus near Roman with his wife, also became a teacher.[60]

As public education for white students took root in New Orleans's three municipalities, the Catholic Institution's board of directors seized the opportunity to place it on an equal footing with the white schools. By convincing the state legislature to regularly set aside money for the education of poor and orphaned students, the school's directors secured what was likely the first governmental appropriation for the education of blacks in the South. In 1849, even Horace Mann's *Common School Journal* noted the school leaders' straightforward campaign for public funding: since free blacks paid their fair share of taxes to support the public schools, the school leaders argued, they should therefore benefit from their contribution. While free blacks in Baltimore, who comprised roughly 15 percent of that city's total population, put forth this same argument on three separate occasions between 1839 and 1850, they failed each time to receive either access to public schools or an exemption from school taxes. In Mobile, a city of twenty thousand with only 715 free black residents, the public school system founded in 1852 did include schools for free persons of color. But in order to attend, students had to prove that they descended from "free Colored Creoles" who lived in West Florida at the time that Spain transferred the territory to the United States.[61]

While significant, the public funding that the Catholic Institution received was neither easy to secure nor guaranteed from year to year. The school's board had to lobby the legislature for a new appropriation each year, and months sometimes passed between their initial request and the legislature's decision regarding the coming fiscal year. In 1851, for instance, the board formed a committee in December to draft a petition to the legislature seeking a new grant, and then did not receive confirmation of their $3,000 award until April 1852. Upon receiving the appropriation, the board heaped praise upon Deravine Lambert, the legislator who championed their cause, and sat aside $150 to buy Lambert a thank-you gift, not, the board carefully noted, "as compensation, but as tribute paid in recognition of his zeal." While Lambert and a legislative delegation visited the school in the spring of 1852, his patronage did not appear to speed the pace with which the school received state funding. The next allotment—of only $2,000—did not arrive until November 1853, by which point the Catholic Institution's enrollment of 240 students accounted for roughly one-quarter of the free black children who were attending school in New Orleans. The funds permitted the school to fully cover tuition for orphans in keeping with Couvent's will and to subsidize other students' tuition based on their parents' ability to pay.[62]

These students received a remarkably sound and well-rounded education, thanks to their forward-thinking teachers and school leaders. Classes were taught in French and English, and students used textbooks in both languages. The curriculum also blended academic instruction in subjects such as reading, writing, history, geography, algebra, music, logic, and rhetoric with more vocationally oriented training in areas such as drafting, bookkeeping, and applied geometry for the building trades. In the school's prospectus, the founding directors explained that they wanted students to be able to confidently apply the knowledge they acquired toward "industrial enterprises, commerce, and the arts," and they vowed to provide students with a "practical, moral, and religious education" that would give them a foundation for "material well being and moral happiness."[63]

In addition to placing students in apprenticeships when they completed the school's sixth and final grade, teachers also actively cultivated their students' political and racial consciousness, as historian Mary Niall Mitchell has

demonstrated through her careful analysis of the students' writing. By compos-
ing fictional letters to correspondents in locations such as Haiti, Mexico, and
France—where many students had real social or family ties—students "constructed a world that was navigable not only in terms of travel and communication but also in terms of capital flows and political power." Mitchell con-
tends that by "drawing transatlantic lines of communication and trade in their
letters, the free children of color at the Catholic Institution envisioned a black
Atlantic community that transcended the boundaries of individual nations
and, in the minds of the students, perhaps, transcended racial oppression."[64]

Yet while students imagined possibilities far beyond those available to
them in New Orleans, board members sometimes struggled to maintain
equally expansive visions. In July 1854, for instance, a board member named
Amand proposed using the $2,000 the school received from the state to pur-
chase property in the Tremé neighborhood for the establishment of a second
campus. When Amand proposed that the second campus "would be useful
for the poor families, who live in that part of the city," he received a haughty
response from his fellow board member, Monsieur Villard. "I don't see why
we need to buy a property near those who are in need of enlightenment," Villard said. "It is for them to walk in search of education that is given to them
for free." Villard's comment drew a quick reply from another board member,
who accused Villard of being inhumane, before the president interjected in
support of Amand's proposal. "It seems to me that this portion of our population pays taxes on their properties, and it is from these same taxes that the
Legislature allocates us two thousand dollars per year," the board president
said. "Accordingly, the property owners and poor families of Faubourg Tremé
should enjoy the benefits of the contribution we receive from the state." The
board then voted four-to-three to look for a suitable property in Tremé.[65]

While a majority of board members wanted to make the school more accessible by adding a second campus, another round of repressive measures
against free people of color apparently thwarted their plans. These restrictions followed close on the heels of the 1852 reunification of the city's three
municipalities, which concentrated political power in the hands of Anglo-
American officials who had long sought to eliminate New Orleans's blurred
racial lines. One new law limited the businesses that free blacks could own,
while another revoked the status of religious, literary, or charitable societies
such as the ones that shepherded the Catholic Institution and the Sisters of
the Holy Family into being. Were it not for the protection of the Catholic

Church, that law would have eliminated both groups. Following a slave re-volt scare in 1853, the city also called for greater police scrutiny of free black schools to ensure that they were not educating slaves, and in 1857 the state banned manumission altogether. That same year, the US Supreme Court's decision in the *Dred Scott* case stripped all blacks of their rights as American citizens. Amidst this rising tide of antiblack sentiment, the Louisiana legislature eliminated the Catholic Institution's funding in 1858.[66]

That decision prompted outrage within the school, which raised its tuition as a result. Student A. Frilot wrote in a class assignment that "the prejudice against the colored population is very strong in this part of the country." He further complained that "the white people have an Institution [public school] in every district and they are all protected very well. But we, who have but a single one, cannot be protected at all." Responding to Frilot, student Léon Dupart wrote that mothers might pull their children from the school because of the increased costs.[67]

The oppressive racial climate of the 1850s limited the extent to which the Catholic Institution's students and leaders could directly challenge this treatment. But the outbreak of the Civil War in 1861 and the Union occupation of New Orleans a year later provided them with their long sought after opportunity to establish themselves as full-fledged American citizens. In the ensuing campaign, they joined with formerly enslaved blacks to place schools at the forefront of a broader effort to build a new democracy.

V.

In New Orleans, the Union occupation brought an end to black students' exclusion from public schools as formerly free and enslaved blacks seized the opportunity to expand their antebellum educational activities. At Camp Parapet, a Union outpost along the river road just west of present-day New Orleans, black New Orleanian Robert H. Isabelle initiated one of the army's first experiments with free schools for formerly enslaved blacks. In a dispatch to the *Anglo African* newspaper, Isabelle described organizing a school in August 1862 for the roughly one thousand escaped slaves who had sought refuge at the Union camp.

Seeking to enlist the former slaves into the army, the abolitionist General John W. Phelps sanctioned and encouraged Isabelle's and other free blacks' efforts to organize schools. This move preceded President Abraham Lincoln's support, outlined in the Emancipation Proclamation, for freeing and arming slaves as a wartime expedient, and both he and Benjamin F. Butler, the Union general in charge of occupied New Orleans, did not support these actions. Lincoln, after all, was from a state that barred blacks from its public school system prior to the Civil War, and Butler, who forced Phelps out of the army over his refusal to reverse course, had openly opposed the 1855 desegregation of public schools in his native Massachusetts.[68]

But Lincoln and Butler soon changed their minds as both the need for trained black soldiers and the challenges of governing occupied New Orleans became more apparent. In July 1862, Butler established the Bureau of Education to oversee the city's existing public schools for whites, and he made the Catholic Institution a de facto public school by providing it with more than $7,500, an amount that likely covered most, if not all, of its operations. The allocation followed a request from the school's Board of Directors that mirrored those they had previously presented to the Louisiana legislature. "The colored population contributes also to the Public School fund for this Department," the board wrote in its petition to Butler, "wherefrom they derive no benefit whatsoever." By the end of 1862, black families were also trying to enroll their children in the city's white public schools, to the dismay of most white Unionists.[69]

Partly propelled by these demands—and likely eager to prevent school desegregation—Butler's successor Nathaniel P. Banks expanded black public education in October 1863 by ordering a commission to open schools for black New Orleanians. Banks went even further the following March, establishing a Board of Education "for the rudimental instruction of the freedmen of this Department [of the Gulf], placing within their reach the elements of knowledge which give intelligence to labor." The board had the power to open schools for blacks in each parish, hire teachers, set the curriculum, levy a property tax to fund the schools, and provide books, at cost, to black adults. Despite often violent opposition to black education, particularly in outlying parishes, by December 1864 the Board of Education established 95 schools with 162 teachers serving two thousand adults and nearly half the twenty thousand black children living within Union lines. In July 1865, the newly created Freedmen's Bureau assumed control of these schools.[70]

By then students, educators, and board members from the Catholic Institution had established themselves as the radical vanguard in the growing national debate over the future status of black Americans. With support from Butler, Catholic Institution leaders founded *L'Union* newspaper in September 1862 and began calling for emancipation and equal citizenship rights for blacks. Catholic Institution teacher Paul Trévigne served as the paper's editor, and Louis Nelson Fouché, the son of founding board member Nelson Fouché, contributed essays and managed the paper's subscriptions. Trévigne and Fouché's political consciousness also trickled down to students such as Lucien Lamanière, who wrote that November that he was "very glad since the Federals are here, they are telling that Gen. Butler is going to make the colored men of this city who were born free vote, if he do the colored men will be very glad to see equality reign here."[71]

Yet *L'Union* only marked the beginning of black New Orleanians' campaign for equality and their impact upon the national scene. In March 1864, wine dealer Arnold Bertonneau and plantation engineer Jean Baptiste Roudanez, black men who had both served on the Catholic Institution's board, traveled to Washington to personally present Lincoln with a petition demanding suffrage for all black men in Louisiana. The men apparently impressed the president, who articulated his shifting ideas about black voting rights in a letter to Louisiana governor Michael Hahn the following day. "I barely suggest for your private consideration," Lincoln wrote, "whether some of the colored people not be let in—as for instance, the very intelligent, and especially those who have fought gallantly in our ranks."[72]

Bertonneau and Roudanez also elaborated upon their vision for a new democracy and the role schools would play in realizing it at an abolitionist dinner in their honor following their meeting with Lincoln. Speaking to an audience that included Frederick Douglass and William Lloyd Garrison, Bertonneau explained that black New Orleanians would work to ensure that "the right to vote shall not depend upon the color of the citizen, that the colored citizens shall have and enjoy every civil, political and religious right the white citizens enjoy." He continued that, by sending their children to schools "to learn the great truth that God 'created of one blood all nations of men to dwell on the face of the earth'—so will caste, founded on prejudice against color, disappear." Then, turning to Garrison, who supported desegregation but not black suffrage, Bertonneau pointedly vowed that black New Orleanians would press for the desegregation of schools and public accommodations just as Garrison had done in Massachusetts.[73]

As was the case during the antebellum crackdown against black education, the connections African Americans such as Bertonneau drew between race, schooling, and democracy elicited violent opposition from whites. In May 1866, a racial pogrom erupted in Memphis after white police officers attempted to break up an outdoor gathering of black Union veterans, their friends, and families. After federal troops quelled the initial outburst of violence, a gang of white police officers and residents regrouped in South Memphis to launch a second attack. A federal committee later concluded that "the most intense and unjustifiable prejudice on the part of the people of Memphis seems to have been arrayed against teachers of colored schools and against preachers to colored people." During three days of violence, white terrorists torched all twelve of Memphis's black schools, burning at least eight to the ground, killed forty-eight African Americans, wounded another seventy to eighty, and raped at least five black women.[74]

Three months later in New Orleans, where Andrew Johnson's lenient Reconstruction policies enabled the antebellum mayor and police chief to return to power, police violently assaulted the constitutional convention that Louisiana's governor had reconvened to consider extending voting rights to black men. In addition to killing at least thirty-eight, the rioters burned down four black schools and attempted to ignite several others. The following spring, a new Republican supermajority in Congress responded to the violence in Memphis and New Orleans by passing the Reconstruction Act of 1867. The act divided the South into five military districts and disfranchised antebellum officeholders who had joined the Confederacy. Along with a subsequent act, it also enabled the formation of new state governments in the South that were required to ratify the Fourteenth Amendment and draft new constitutions that extended the right to vote to all men regardless of race.[75]

The new federal legislation enabled the passage of Louisiana's 1868 constitution, which was arguably Reconstruction's most radical document. Grounded in the descendants of the *gens de coleur libre*'s transatlantic notions of equal "civil, political, and public rights" regardless of race, the constitution prohibited racially segregated schools and public accommodations and proclaimed that all children in the state "shall be admitted to the public schools or other institutions of learning sustained or established by the State, in common, without distinction of race, color or previous condition." While Bertonneau was the only person affiliated with the Catholic Institution who served as a delegate to the constitutional convention, at least thirteen additional men with ties to the school were members of the select group that historian

David C. Rankin identified as "the nucleus of black leadership in New Orleans during the 1860s."[76]

Shortly before the passage of the 1868 constitution and the formation of a new biracial government, New Orleans's all-white and Confederate-sympathizing school board had incorporated the Freedmen's Bureau schools into the citywide public school system on a segregated basis. They hoped this would stave off the push for desegregation that they knew would come once blacks voted in a new municipal government. Black New Orleanians, however, did not wait for these committed white supremacists to relinquish their control of the city's schools. Within days of the 1868 constitution's passage, at least twenty-eight light-skinned black girls began attending the formerly white Bayou Road School, which was located less than a mile from the Catholic Institution on the edge of the Tremé neighborhood (see map 1.2). The group included one girl who had presented a certificate of white birth and another who was the niece of Alderman C. S. Sauvinet, an Afro-Creole activist who later won a landmark lawsuit against a white bar owner who refused to serve him.[77] The Second District School Board, which oversaw the schools between Canal Street and Esplanade Avenue after the city's 1852 reunification, had opened the Bayou Road School to white girls in the 1850s.[78]

Upon learning of the students' admission, City Superintendent William O. Rogers fired off a terse letter to Bayou Road principal Madam S. Bigot on May 7, 1868: "Please inform me if there are any children known, or generally reported, to be colored—who are now attending your school. If so, how many, when, and by what authority admitted." Bigot replied that "when these children were admitted it was never to my knowledge that they were colored." Her new students' race only came to her attention a few days later, she wrote, when "several of our pupils living in this neighborhood would report that they were not white." That response caused board member Theodore Thieneman to accuse Bigot of lying and to call for her immediate ouster.[79] By the end of May, the board passed a resolution "that all children of color, who may be found in any of the white schools of this City, shall be immediately furnished with a written transfer to the school to which they properly belong." It also called for further investigation "in the case of grave doubt as to the [racial] status of any pupil," and in a few instances asked parents to prove that their children were not racially mixed. After most parents refused to provide documentation, the board forced their children to leave the Bayou Road School.[80]

The board's display of righteous indignation notwithstanding, its members could not have been too surprised to see that blacks had pushed forward with desegregation or that they had decided to strike at Bayou Road. Several black students had, in fact, attempted to desegregate a public school near Bayou Road—and even closer to the Catholic Institution—in 1862.[81] Before absorbing Freedmen's Bureau and other black schools in 1867, the board also asked the teachers at these schools whether they supported segregation in order to determine whether it would hire them.[82] Of the twenty teachers the board questioned, the three who directly stated their opposition to segregation taught in schools located less than ten blocks from Bayou Road. Three other educators, including the Catholic Institution's Armand Lanusse and Ludger Boguille, tacitly endorsed desegregation by declining to respond to the board's inquiry. As the board reported, Lanusse "refused to give any information whatever, on the plea that he did not recognize the present Board of School Directors."[83] Quite possibly, those instructors who openly or implicitly opposed segregation taught and inspired the girls who desegregated Bayou Road.

Despite the Bayou Road students' initial setback, desegregation returned to the school and spread to others after an 1870 court decision forced the Democratic school board out of office. The desegregation of at least twenty-one of the city's schools between 1871 and 1877 likely made them the nation's closest approximations of the common school ideal. For a brief moment, these schools were *public* not simply because taxpayers funded them but because they were places where all members of the community came together. The same could not be said of New York, Baltimore, Philadelphia, or Cincinnati, all of which maintained segregated schools during the 1870s. Indeed, with one-third of its schools racially mixed, New Orleans may very well have had the most integrated system in the country.[84]

New Orleans's nineteenth-century experiment with desegregated education even overcame a violent attempt to end it in mid-December 1874. The precipitating event was the desegregation of the Upper Girls' High School, which served some of the public school system's most socially elite families. The desegregation of this Garden District preserve of white femininity coincided with congressional debate over school desegregation (the Civil Rights Act of 1875 was ultimately silent on the matter) and with the rise of the Crescent City White League. This paramilitary organization's bloody but unsuccessful attempt to overthrow the state government in September 1874 was only one of many examples of the racial terror that Confederate sympathizers perpetrated during Reconstruction. It also became a turning point in the national debate over Reconstruction, convincing many white northerners that the South was impermeable to reform and that the federal effort to maintain order through military force was woefully misguided.[85]

The backlash against school desegregation in New Orleans initially supported this interpretation. Spurred by the press and the social elites who comprised the White League, a "committee" of white teens from the city's Boys' High School launched a direct attack on desegregated schools. During three days of rioting from December 15 to 18, 1874, these "youthful regulators" expelled black students from racially mixed schools, smashed more than 350 windows, harangued teachers, attacked and threatened to kill the local superintendent, and murdered a black man and child.[86]

At the Lower Girls' High School in the French Quarter, "pupils were forcibly driven from the halls of examination and the class rooms, under the suspicion of being tainted with colored blood," City Superintendent C. W. Boothby reported. "Nor did the sets of violence cease until the 'committee' became unable to decide upon the true lineage of the young ladies, and feared that too much scrutiny would carry them upon dangerous ground."[87] During one of their attacks, the Boys' High toughs mistakenly expelled Jewish students whose complexions were as dark as some of the light-skinned Creoles of color.[88]

One of the riot's two black fatalities came after the regulators descended upon the Keller School at Magnolia and St. Andrew Streets in a racially mixed neighborhood upriver from the French Quarter. Unlike the downriver, or downtown, side of Canal Street, which was home to many francophone blacks who had been free for generations, the black men and women living in this uptown area were more likely English speakers who had only recently gained freedom. In order to protect a nearby black school from attack, between sixty and seventy black men and students gathered out in front of it armed with rocks and clubs. When the dust settled following a confrontation between this group and the Boys' High students, a black man named Eugene Duclostouge lay dead. His death sparked more fighting, and interracial street battles continued in that neighborhood into the night.[89]

The rioting forced schools to close early for the winter holidays, but desegregation continued after the break, which was longer than usual. "In New Orleans there are over seventy schools, about one-third of which are used almost exclusively by the whites, another third by the colored children, and the remainder by a mixture of all shades and colors," *Harper's Weekly* reported in February 1875.[90] At racially mixed schools such as Bayou Road and throughout the city, enrollment actually increased during desegregation, and the integrated schools were often considered the best in the city.[91] After visiting several racially mixed schools on assignment for the *Picayune,* George Washington Cable captured the ways in which these institutions were forging the new conception of citizenship envisioned in the state's 1868 constitution. "I saw, to my great and rapid edification," he wrote, "white ladies teaching Negro boys; colored women showing the graces and dignity of mental and moral refinement, ladies in everything save society's credentials; children and youth of both races standing in the same classes and giving each other peaceable, friendly, effective competition; and black classes, with black teachers, pushing intelligently up into the intricacies of high-school mathematics."[92]

VI.

But the end of Reconstruction put the brakes on New Orleans's remarkable public school success story. First, the Bourbon Democrats who came to power immediately reintroduced racial segregation in the city's schools. As the school board reassigned racial designations in the summer of 1877, its secretary recorded the formerly white, formerly integrated Bayou Road School's new status as "colored."[93] These self-styled Redeemers also slashed public funding for education. The system's budget decreased by 40 percent in 1877, and a new constitution in 1879 imposed further reductions by placing strict limitations on New Orleans's ability to levy taxes for municipal services. While the board eliminated two of its four high schools and reduced the curriculum at the remaining institutions in response to these cuts, it bucked national trends by clinging to the costly practice of sex segregation at the secondary level and even reintroducing it at the elementary level. By 1883, the system had so little money that it closed for nearly half a year to all except those who could pay tuition. When the superintendent reviewed the district's financial history in the mid-1880s, he discovered that the system's budget had declined by one-third from 1858 even though enrollment had doubled. Were it not for the bequest of John McDonogh, a wealthy slaveholder who died in 1850 and left his estate for the education of children in New Orleans and his native

Baltimore, the system may very well have collapsed. As historians Donald DeVore and Joseph Logsdon note, "Private charity, not public concern, kept the schools afloat."[94]

The Catholic Institution followed the inverse trajectory of the public schools during and following Reconstruction. As the school's students flocked to the desegregated public schools, its enrollment plummeted and by 1884 it was "almost in ruins." Rodolphe Desdunes, a former Catholic Institution student, teacher, board member, and one of its most dutiful chroniclers, attributed the school's decline partly to poor administration. A campaign to block the post-Reconstruction resegregation of the public schools also directed attention away from the institution.[95]

In 1877, former Catholic Institution teacher Paul Trévigne, former board member Arnold Bertonneau, and another Afro-Creole named August Dellande filed separate suits to block the segregation of public schools in New Orleans. The plaintiffs carefully couched their challenge as an issue of national rather than merely local significance. "This case is one of great magnitude," Trévigne argued, "involving as it does a question of civil liberty and constitutional right, with all the sacred guarantees of citizenship, and is really a test, judicially, of the status of that class termed '*colored*,' whose rights to citizenship ought to be protected." Trévigne also made plain that his case was about far more than schooling. Forcing people of color to attend separate schools, he continued, was unconstitutional because "a distinction thus made detracts from their status as citizens and consigns them to the contempt of their fellow men and citizens of this community and elsewhere."[96]

Bertonneau and Dellande made similar arguments in suits challenging their children's rejection from the Fillmore School, a formerly integrated school that was designated as white in 1877. Both men argued that the school, which was located near the intersection of St. Claude Avenue and Bourbon (now Pauger) Street, four blocks from the Catholic Institution, was the closest public school to their homes. Dellande, in fact, lived a mere 150 feet from its entrance. But neither Dellande, Bertonneau, nor Trévigne prevailed.[97]

Following these defeats, a group of Afro-Creole men, including longtime Catholic Institution supporters Nelson Fouché, Rodolphe Desdunes, and Armand Duhart, focused on reviving the struggling school. The leader of this group was Arthur Estèves, a Haitian-born sail maker who had immigrated to New Orleans at a young age. A large man with intensely dark eyes, a bushy mustache, and Vandyke beard flecked with white just below his lower lip,

Estèves joined the Catholic Institution's board in 1884 and served as its president for eighteen years.[98]

Credited with reviving the school from its doldrums, Estèves's civic activism extended beyond his involvement with the school. He was also the founding treasurer of the Justice, Protective, Educational and Social Association. Founded in September 1886, when W. E. B. Du Bois was but an eighteen-year-old Fisk student fresh off a summer teaching stint in the Tennessee hill country, the Association prefigured the great intellectual's potent, twentieth-century fusion of educational and political activism. In the preamble to its constitution, Estèves and the other founders described it as "an organization for the purpose of uniting and protecting ourselves, both socially and morally, and protecting our intellectual welfare, thereby inculcating a true sense of the importance of education, [and] uniting ourselves politically that our support and influence may be brought to bear where our interest and welfare can be advanced and our rights as citizens of this State and of the United States protected and respected."[99]

As Louisiana joined other early adopters in passing an 1890 Separate Car Law that required racially segregated train accommodations, the Association sprang into action. In September 1891, Estèves and two of his colleagues from the Justice, Protective, Educational and Social Association—Louis Joubert and the shoemaker Homer Plessy—joined with fifteen other Afro-Creole men to form a new organization, the Comité des Citoyens (Citizens' Committee), dedicated to overturning the Separate Car Law. Estèves, who served as the Committee's president, was not its only member with strong ties to the Catholic Institution. The Institution's longtime benefactor Aristide Mary was a founding member of the Committee, as were Rodolphe Desdunes and Paul Trévigne. Committee members Joubert, Eugène Luscy, and Louis A. Martinet also served on the Catholic Institution's board, and Firmin Christophe was a teacher there.[100]

The Committee tested the Separate Car Law by having Homer Plessy board a whites-only train car bound for the north shore of Lake Pontchartrain on June 7, 1892. After police arrested Plessy under the Separate Car Law, the committee filed suit on the grounds that the law violated Plessy's constitutional rights as a citizen. While the US Supreme Court ruled against him in *Plessy v. Ferguson* (1896), enshrining the concept of "separate but equal," black New Orleanians did not abandon the expansive social vision that the Catholic Institution had long fostered and which the Committee's lawsuit had embodied. One indication that that vision would persist in spite of the legal defeat came as the Citizens' Committee was disbanding. As it distributed its remaining funds to various charitable organizations, it set aside twenty dollars for the Catholic Institution. While this was no great sum, it foreshadowed the role that schools would play in the coming fight over segregation. The architects of the new racial order similarly viewed schools as a critical front in the battle to permanently fix the color line. This dynamic became particularly clear on a balmy night in January 1923.[101]

CHAPTER TWO

THE NEGRO'S PLACE

Orleans Parish School Board president James Fortier could not have been happier. Scores of his white neighbors from New Orleans's Sixth Ward had answered his call to attend the first board meeting of 1923, and the city's Municipal Building pulsed with activity. Unable to squeeze into the third-floor boardroom, attendees spilled into adjacent hallways. Above neighboring Lafayette Square, whose tree-lined walkways opened onto city hall, the US Post Office, and the *Times-Picayune*'s newsroom, the sun had already set on an unusually warm and cloudless January day. But a storm broke inside the board's chambers almost as soon as Fortier called the meeting to order. The Sixth Ward residents were upset about the construction of a new school building for blacks at the corner of Bayou Road and Derbigny Street in their neighborhood (see map 2.1). They wanted it converted to white use. "To put from eight hundred to a thousand negroes in that section almost entirely inhabited by white people would be a very serious disadvantage to both races," the delegation's leader said. "It would require that the negroes walk a great distance, or, it would cause a large number of negroes to buy or rent in the immediate vicinity of the school."[1]

Since the new building merely replaced the old Bayou Road School, which had existed as a black institution at that same Sixth Ward site since the school board adjusted its racial designation in 1877, Fortier's four board colleagues were disinclined to grant the protestors' request. The board had closed the three dilapidated houses that comprised the Bayou Road School after the 1921–1922 academic year, and many of its students stayed home while the new structure was being built. With that building scheduled to open February 1, 1923, board members were anxious to get the school's eight hundred–plus students off the streets.[2]

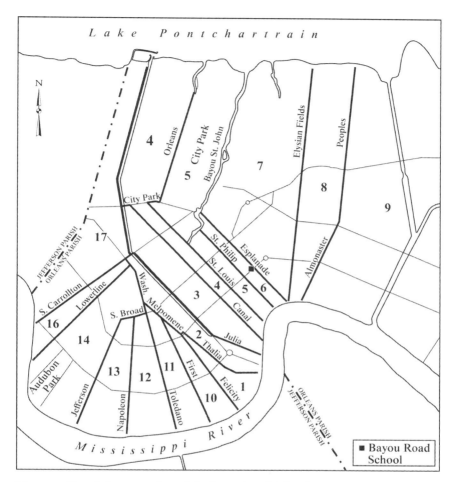

Map 2.1 New Orleans wards and the Bayou Road School.

The thirty-two-year-old board president, however, literally rose to the Sixth Ward residents' defense. Ceding his chairmanship of the meeting to board vice president Fred Zengel, Fortier asked to appear before the board as one of the dissidents. "The protestants [by which he meant protestors] would have no case if they were actuated by a selfish spirit and considered the matter simply from the standpoint of vested property rights," Fortier declared. But Fortier, a Sixth Ward resident whose professional commitments included law, banking, and real estate finance, insisted that the residents were more broad-minded. "The interests of the entire city were involved because it concerned the development and the growth of the City," he continued.[3]

To emphasize his point, Fortier recounted Louisville, Kentucky's recent failed attempt to legally require blacks and whites to live in separate areas of the city. Since the US Supreme Court had deemed Louisville's residential segregation ordinance unconstitutional in *Buchanan v. Warley* (1917), Fortier argued, the school board was the last remaining hope to preserve the racial integrity of what he called "wholly white" neighborhoods, which happened to not be true of the area surrounding the Bayou Road School. "The case of the [protestors] should make a strong appeal to the Board," he said, "since they were denied the ability by law to prevent what they would otherwise bring to pass." Removing neighborhood blight in the form of a black school, he maintained, was akin to slum clearance efforts in other cities, where millions were spent "to destroy eyesores that had existed for one hundred years."[4]

As Fortier's nod to Louisville indicated, he, the Sixth Ward residents, and the commercial elite he spoke for were hardly the only white Americans interested in residential segregation during the first decades of the twentieth century. Baltimore passed a pioneering residential segregation ordinance in 1910, and cities such as Atlanta, Richmond, Oklahoma City, and St. Louis quickly followed suit. In 1912, Louisiana approved legislation granting municipalities the authority to implement similar laws. The National Association for the Advancement of Colored People (NAACP) got these overturned in *Buchanan v. Warley*, which challenged Louisville's ordinance. But after 1917 northern and southern cities continued to use zoning and other stratagems to limit where blacks could live and under what conditions; the Crescent City even tried unsuccessfully to resurrect the Louisville ordinance nearly a decade after the court had struck it down.[5]

In New Orleans and throughout the nation, racially restrictive covenants and discriminatory lending practices privately abetted these policies, particularly as black urban populations swelled during the Great Migration. Supporters of residential segregation in the North and South also regularly resorted to violence in order to enforce existing racial boundaries or to impose new ones. In 1900, for instance, a race riot raged through racially mixed sections of New Orleans after Robert Charles, a Mississippi transplant and stout black nationalist, resisted police harassment and then shot several officers during the ensuing manhunt. In 1926 arsonists repeatedly bombed the mixed neigh-borhood that was home to some of the city's wealthiest black residents.[6]

In addition to offering a fresh perspective on these early twentieth-century developments, the evolution of residential segregation in New Orleans high-lights the role that public schools played in redrawing racial geographies and in regulating the racial order more broadly. Race was a central element of life in New Orleans at this time, as it was throughout urban America. While the city's black residents could scarcely avoid this reality, its white inhabitants were also inordinately concerned—obsessed really—with their standing vis-à-vis blacks. What W. E. B. Du Bois termed "the problem of the color-line," white New Orleanians considered a question—to use the vernacular of the day—of "the Negro's place."

As in the nineteenth century, an African American's "place" during the Jim Crow era was not a static point but remained a constantly moving target. Yet like their nineteenth-century ancestors, white residents and white business leaders such as James Fortier sought to permanently fix black people's stand-ing socially, politically, and economically, only to be forced to adjust and read-just again in the face of persistent black resistance. Herbert Cappie, an Afri-can American postal worker who came of age in New Orleans following World War I, captured this fluid reality when he recalled that "the most difficult thing about segregation was in knowing one's place. In New Orleans my place may have been over here. In Alabama it was in another place over there."[7] During the first decades of the twentieth century, this continual redefinition of the "Negro's place" became increasingly and inexorably linked with the physical space in which black and white New Orleanians lived and learned.[8]

This chapter surveys social, political, and economic conditions in New Orleans from the late nineteenth century through the immediate aftermath of World War I, with occasional glances back to the Reconstruction era to emphasize the dynamic and contested evolution of the city's racial order. The first section describes Jim Crow in New Orleans and nationally and explains when, where, why, and how this system of racial oppression came into being. The second and third sections introduce two themes that run through the re-mainder of the book: first, the conflict over land and resources that stemmed from New Orleans's inhospitable location and paltry investment in public services and, second, the tension between black demands for greater educa-tional opportunity and white residents' opposition to black schools near their homes. Before its conclusion, the chapter's penultimate section discusses the growth of private and parochial schooling within Jim Crow New Orleans and its impact upon the city's urban landscape and racial order.

I.

While the particular ways that schools gave material and cultural meaning to race in New Orleans reflected the intricacies of the city's history, the Crescent City's experience was not unique. Particularly during the decades between the world wars, New Orleans resembled major cities in the Mid-Atlantic, Midwest, and Northeast. It was within the South that it was an outlier. New Orleans was the most important city economically among the eleven states of the former Confederacy and the region's biggest by a landslide. Its bustling port and large, cosmopolitan black population continued to give it more in common with older seaboard cities such as Baltimore or Philadelphia than with nascent New South metropolises such as Atlanta, Houston, or Birmingham.[9] In 1910, New Orleans's black population was the nation's third largest, only slightly behind Washington, DC, and New York, and ahead of Baltimore and Philadelphia.[10] Atlanta, the Southeast's second-largest city by 1920, was barely half the size of New Orleans.[11] Even the enforcement of Jim Crow statutes did not distinguish New Orleans from northern and Midwestern cities since officials there explicitly endorsed school segregation in response to the wartime influx of black migrants.[12]

Jim Crow was a system of racial oppression: legally, politically, socially, and economically. Segregation, exclusion, disfranchisement, violence, and economic exploitation were key features of Jim Crow, with each of these parts contributing to the oppressive nature of the whole. After beginning to take shape around 1890 in the South, Jim Crow continued to expand and evolve as it moved north with the Great Migration twenty-five years later.[13]

As the Deep South's premier city, New Orleans showcased central elements of Jim Crow's regional variations. Louisiana's 1890 Separate Car Law, which black New Orleanians unsuccessfully challenged in *Plessy,* was an early example of southern legislation requiring segregation beyond schooling. As was the case throughout the South, African Americans rarely sat on juries by the 1890s and had long ceased serving on New Orleans's formerly integrated police force. The funding gap between black and white schools also widened significantly around the turn of the century. The state's ratio of per-pupil expenditures for black versus white students, for instance, dropped from one-half to less than one-fifth between 1890 and 1910. The job market similarly split by race, although the more fluid divisions in New Orleans mirrored the industrialized urban North more than the semifeudal rural South. Black New Orleanians, however, received no urban exemption in 1898 when Louisiana followed Mississippi and South Carolina's lead by stripping black men of their constitutional right to vote. By 1910, the remaining southern states stretching from Oklahoma to Delaware attempted to reduce black voting strength.[14]

While African American men generally retained their right to vote outside the South, rampant discrimination in employment, housing, and education largely relegated northern blacks to second-class status. Whether in Mississippi or Michigan, violence enforced the early twentieth-century color line—often with the sanction of the state. Lynchings claimed more than one hundred lives annually between 1882 and 1901, nearly 2,000 of them African American. As in New Orleans, white people in Philadelphia, Detroit, and Louisville attacked black "pioneers" who moved into new neighborhoods, often spurring these newcomers to take up arms and fire back. Scores of African Americans were also murdered during and immediately following World War I as a result of the racially motivated attacks that white mobs and officials launched against black communities in cities and towns as far flung as East St. Louis and Chicago, Illinois; Charleston, South Carolina; Elaine, Arkansas; Tulsa, Oklahoma; Washington, DC; Omaha, Nebraska; Longview, Texas; and Knoxville, Tennessee.[15]

Jim Crow first emerged in the South in response to African Americans' relentless pursuit of expanded opportunities and rewards: the very fruits of full citizenship. As black southerners remained active in political and civic life following the collapse of Reconstruction, competing white factions increasingly viewed them as a threat to their own political and economic power. This became particularly evident during the tumultuous 1890s, when black voters appeared to hold the balance of political power in the South. In New Orleans, the city's working-class, Democratic machine embraced black disfranchisement to undermine a potential alliance between the biracial Republican Party and the city's white civic and commercial elite. In North Carolina, a "Fusion" legislature that similarly united black and white Republicans and Populists during the 1890s eased voter registration requirements to allow more African Americans to vote. This enabled the already influential black professional class in Wilmington to play a larger role in running that city, its courts, and police. But in a pattern repeated with slight variations throughout the region, violence, disfranchisement, new legalized distinctions based upon race, and the race-baiting tactics of erstwhile populists undermined both real and imagined biracial alliances.[16]

Prioritizing electoral politics over principle, northern politicians largely stepped aside as the white South trampled African American civil, political, and economic rights. The Supreme Court further strengthened the legal architecture for Jim Crow through a string of decisions stretching from the *Slaughter-House Cases, United States v. Cruikshank,* and *Hall v. Decuir* in the 1870s to *Plessy v. Ferguson* in 1896. All of these cases originated in Louisiana, three of them in New Orleans. Along with the *Civil Rights Cases* (1883), they eviscerated the Fourteenth Amendment and opened the door for states to deny African Americans their citizenship rights. By no means coincidental, the disproportionate number of cases from Louisiana reflected the relative wealth of its black citizens and the fervency with which they asserted the egalitarian ideals they had enshrined in the state's 1868 Constitution.[17]

African American assertiveness also lay behind the distinctly urban character of Jim Crow, which became more pronounced as it matured and pressed northward during the second and third decades of the twentieth century. Voting with their feet, rural migrants such as Robert Charles sought better lives in the expanding towns and cities within and outside of the South. This migration, which accelerated following the turn-of-the-century influx of immigrants from southern and eastern Europe, sparked intense anxiety among urban whites over their status vis-à-vis black people in general and the space that they and African Americans inhabited in particular. The opportunities for anonymity and social mixing that the city's sidewalks, streetcars, and retail emporiums afforded were key drivers of this anxiety, as were the ethnic diversity of city life and the growing although still limited availability of jobs for African Americans in industry, business, and skilled professions. The rising popularity and institutionalization of eugenics, the pseudoscience devoted to the elimination of "inferior" racial and genetic stock, both reflected and promised a solution to racial unease. Yet nothing captured the depth of this anxiety and the white supremacist response to it more than the runaway popularity of *Birth of a Nation,* D. W. Griffith's 1915 cinematic paean to the Ku Klux Klan.[18]

This new manifestation of white supremacy also had significant transnational parallels and influences. Most notably, Jim Crow's rise coincided with the United States' expansion overseas during the late nineteenth and early twentieth centuries. As the nation pressed across the Pacific and Caribbean during the Spanish-American War and subsequent incursions, government officials and laypeople debated the status of the millions of additional people of color within the growing American empire. From the Philippines to the Panama Canal Zone, the United States restricted the rights of these new colonial subjects based upon their perceived race. The American conception of race as a means for ordering society traveled further still as officials in South Africa looked to the South for guidance on creating and maintaining segregation.[19]

As white Americans feared that their nation's supposedly fixed racial center would not hold, segregation and discrimination became enticing balms for their social, political, and economic anxieties. While white supremacy could boost even the lowliest white person's self-esteem, Jim Crow offered more significant, tangible rewards for the diverse lot deemed "white": a voice in government, the protection of the state, and the generally unimpeded ability to make and spend a dollar. Excluding black workers from unions and higher-paying industrial jobs, for instance, appealed to white workers seeking less competition and to white managers hoping to exploit racially divided workforces. Similarly, white commercial elites such as James Fortier believed that geographically isolating black residents and schools advanced the "development and the growth of the City." This was a public aspect of what Du Bois famously referred to as the "public and psychological wage" that white people received on account of their race, a set of benefits that in his estimate included access to schools that "were the best in the community, and conspicuously placed."[20]

Like Du Bois's formulation, Fortier's linking of schools and economic development underscored the material consequences of Jim Crow and the central role that schools played in maintaining them. Most significantly, Fortier recognized that in the wake of the Supreme Court's *Buchanan* decision, public schools were the most powerful means available for officially designating an area as either white or black. Embracing a widely held "racial theory of property value," he viewed black schools and residents as forms of blight that depressed nearby home prices. By moving black schools and the black families that patronized them away from white residents, Fortier and others hoped to create racially distinct residential zones. Since policymakers in New Orleans and elsewhere regularly transformed the "racial *theory* of property value" into reality through the inequitable distribution of public resources such as schools, streetlights, and sidewalks, residential segregation enhanced

white homeowners' ability to build wealth through property. Separate and unequal schools further bolstered material inequalities by unevenly conferring
the skills and credentials necessary for economic advancement.[21]

As in other cities, however, New Orleans's Jim Crow–era race relations
remained deceptively complex. As evident from their frequent appearances
in court, neither disfranchisement nor the ossification of segregation extin-
guished the egalitarian activism of the city's black Creoles. While New Orleans's culturally diverse African American residents maintained separate
civic, social, and professional organizations for Creoles and non-Creoles,
these groups often united in the years between the world wars to criticize
residential segregation, voting restrictions, and especially limited educational
opportunities—often under the auspices of the NAACP. The New Orleans
branch of that organization formed in 1915.[22]

Black and white New Orleanians also continued to live near each other,
as was the case in northern and southern cities prior to the Great Migration.
According to Arnold Hirsch, the nation's black urban population "lived in
scattered clusters" that were occasionally racially mixed and almost always
intersected with predominantly white areas around the turn of the century.[23]
Residential lines were particularly blurry in New Orleans and other older
southern cities such as Baltimore and Washington thanks to their "backyard
patterns" of black and white housing. In New Orleans, this was a product
of both urban slavery and the limited habitable space between the elevated
banks of the Mississippi River to the city's south and the soupy "backswamp"
abutting Lake Pontchartrain, less than ten miles to the river's north.[24]

II.

Struck by this near omnipotence of water, French colonizers originally called
New Orleans *l'Isle d'Orleans,* or the Isle of Orleans, when they cleared it for
settlement in 1718. Its more recent nickname, the Crescent City, similarly
reflected its perilous position on a horseshoe-shaped bend in the mighty Mississippi. Since the city's topography sloped gently downward from the river to
the lake, residents typically huddled together on the highest and driest land
near the Mississippi or along one of the natural levees that had formed as a
result of its meanderings. Bayou Road and its eponymous school sat atop one
such ridge, which Native Americans had exploited as a shortcut from the river

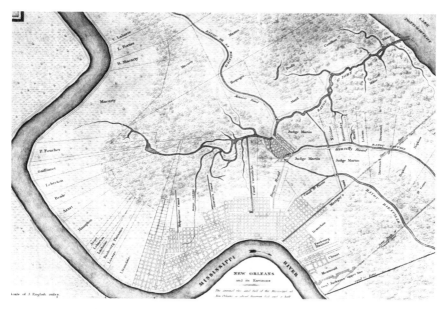

Map 2.2   Inset from Francis Barber Ogden, *Plan of the City of New Orleans,* **1829.**
Courtesy of the Norman B. Leventhal Map Center at the Boston Public Library.

to the lake and then into the Gulf of Mexico. Early New Orleanians renamed this portage Bayou Road since they used it as the primary route between their original settlement and Bayou St. John, the narrow stream that led to the lake (see map 2.2).[25]

In the eighteenth-century town center—the present-day French Quarter— whites, free blacks, and slaves lived side-by-side in what one historian described as "a patchy warren of half-concealed space and ghostly patios." As the city expanded outward during the nineteenth century, the wealthiest whites built grand homes for themselves along major boulevards such as Esplanade Avenue (which formed the downriver boundary between the French Quarter and the Faubourg Marigny) and modest quarters for their slaves along the smaller streets behind their property. Free blacks such as Marie Couvent and middling whites also bought or rented lots in these interior blocks, with many of the former settling east of the French Quarter and in the area to its north that would later house the Bayou Road School. An influx of European immigrants during the decades bracketing the Civil War helped to sustain these racially mixed housing patterns, since the new arrivals typically settled in neighborhoods with sizable black populations. New Orleans also developed an identifiable black belt along its swampy "Back of Town," where, the geographer Peirce Lewis notes, "drainage was bad, foundation material precarious, mosquitoes endemic, and flooding a recurrent hazard."[26]

But even this racially homogenous stretch overlapped with racially mixed areas, and poorer blacks were not the only New Orleanians with inadequate city services. New Orleans was the only major city in the Western world without a sewerage system at the start of the twentieth century, and it did not have a reliable water supply until 1909. The city's subtropical climate and swampy landscape only amplified these deficiencies. "You are dirty," a sanitation expert told the city in 1899. "Nature has not been kind to you in topography, and you have returned the compliment, and with interest."[27]

Despite their neighborhoods' racial heterogeneity, white New Orleanians maintained a connection between public schools and neighborhood identity. If a neighborhood had a white school, they regularly contended, it was a white neighborhood. And if a neighborhood had white residents, they believed it should only have a white school. As a result, they regularly denounced black schools near their homes, protested the proposed conversion of area schools from white to black use, or requested the relocation of white schools as blacks settled nearby.[28]

In the residentially mixed Crescent City, these demands were an attempt to draw racial boundaries around otherwise racially nondescript neighborhoods. For white residents, segregated white schools essentially became the facts on the ground that could justify their claims to territorial dominance.[29] But the limited number of black schools (as evident in map 2.3) altered the connection between school and neighborhood identity for black people. Since some black schools served more than one ward of the city, black residents focused on gaining additional buildings wherever and however they could. At times this even meant donating land for schools in isolated, heavily black areas, which amounted to a form of double taxation for African Americans. The emphasis that black New Orleanians placed upon education underscored the extent to which schools remained central to community development and economic advancement. While whites restricted black schooling in order to maintain racial supremacy, African Americans viewed schools as essential vehicles for full and equal citizenship.[30]

The narrower connection that white New Orleanians drew between neighborhoods, schools, and race reflected prevailing national norms. In the

1920s, influential city planner Clarence Perry popularized the concept of the "neighborhood unit" as the primary building block for urban development. "Schools," historian Ansley Erickson notes, "were at the literal and figurative center of Perry's and his colleagues' neighborhood unit." Perry's 1929 *Regional Plan of New York,* for instance, includes diagram after diagram of neighborhoods built around—and defined by—their schools (see figure 2.1). Prior to the publication of Perry's New York plan, many New Orleanians became familiar with the idea of neighborhood units constructed around "local centers" such as schools through the regular column that architect Milton Medary published in the city's papers from August 1920 to July 1921. The New Orleans Association of Commerce had hired Medary in 1919 as a consultant to assist with the development and promotion of a comprehensive city plan and the zoning laws that were necessary to implement it. As an attorney, bank president, homestead association director, and member of the Association of Commerce's education committee, James Fortier would have regularly interacted with the businessmen pressing for comprehensive urban planning.[31]

Rejecting the urban reality of racially mixed housing, Perry and other nationally prominent planning professionals insisted upon racially and socioeconomically homogenous neighborhoods. They believed that homogeneity would safeguard property values and ensure community cohesion. "Put like people together and give them common facilities [such as schools] to care for," Perry wrote in 1930, "and associations among them are bound to spring into existence." From Atlanta, Georgia, to Flint, Michigan, city planners followed Perry's advice by building segregated schools to anchor segregated communities.[32]

The federal government and real estate industry also promoted residential segregation at the neighborhood level as a means of protecting property values. As secretary of commerce, future president Herbert Hoover established an Advisory Committee on Zoning in 1921 that produced model legislation that thousands of cities ultimately used to implement legally permissible land use restrictions that distinguished between commercial, industrial, single-family residential, and multifamily residential areas. These were the same kinds of restrictions that New Orleans businessmen began contemplating in 1919 with the help of planning consultant Milton Medary. While the Hoover committee's "Standard State Zoning Enabling Act" did not explicitly mention race, historian David Freund notes that the authors of the 1922 document were committed to "a model of property and property rights that assumed the importance of racial hierarchies." When the US Supreme Court approved separate zones for single and multiple family housing in *Euclid v. Ambler* four years later, it essentially authorized the division of cities by class and, by extension, by race. As landscape architect Frederick Law Olmsted Jr., perhaps the most prominent member of Hoover's committee, had noted in 1918, this sort of zoning by type of residence was "more or less coincident with racial divisions."[33]

Two years before the 1962 *Euclid* decision, the 15,000-member National Association of Real Estate Boards (NAREB) had taken an equally significant stand in support of residential segregation through its revised Code of Ethics. The new code stated that "a realtor should never be introducing into a neighborhood a character of property or occupancy, members of any race or nationality, or any individuals whose presence will clearly be detrimental to property values in that neighborhood." To put teeth behind this statement, NAREB encouraged the widespread use of racially restrictive covenants and provided local real estate practitioners with model language. Since realtors could lose their NAREB membership and, effectively, their ability to ply their trade if they violated the Code of Ethics, the Association's stand carried great weight. This was the backdrop against which white New Orleanians launched their assault on black schools.[34]

III.

The Bayou Road School is the black dot near the intersection of North Claiborne and Esplanade Avenue on map 2.3, which provides a unique representation of the racial distribution of New Orleans's population and public schools in the early twentieth century. Since the US Census Bureau did not produce tract- or block-level data by race for New Orleans until 1940 and 1950, respectively, microlevel data on citywide residential settlement patterns prior to those dates is exceedingly rare.[35] Several historians have constructed vivid portraits of individual neighborhoods based upon anecdotal evidence, city directories, conveyance records, and analysis of the handwritten spreadsheets (known as "population schedules") that census takers used to record the names, races, and other characteristics of the city's residents.[36] Social scientists have also documented the city's racially mixed housing patterns in broad yet convincing strokes.[37] But the picture generally becomes hazier for

historical voyeurs interested in strolling from one section of the city to another at ground level.

Geographer Richard Campanella began to fill this gap by plotting every
black and white household in the city using the Heritage Quest database's index of the 1910 Census population schedules. Since the Heritage Quest index
permitted Campanella to isolate each household by race and enumeration
district—the multiblock area an individual census taker covered in a single
census period—his data that appear in map 2.3 provide the most detailed
approximation of the distribution of blacks and whites across the entire city.[38]
The spatial scale of Campanella's map, in fact, is about ten times more granu-
lar than previous scholars' efforts to plot residents by ward.[39] It also offers an
ideal baseline for examining the expansion of residential segregation because
the 1910 Census preceded the city's most aggressive backswamp drainage efforts, which dramatically increased both the city's habitable footprint and the
potency of schools as markers of neighborhood racial identity. Map 2.4, which
shows the racial breakdown of public schools and residential settlement patterns in 1940, highlights the increased concentration of New Orleans's black
population and black schools by the start of World War II. As the following
chapters will demonstrate, schools were often on the leading edge of this shift.

The process of segregating New Orleans, however, was still in its early
stages in 1920. At that time, the Tremé neighborhood immediately north of
the French Quarter as well as the section of the Sixth Ward that included the
Bayou Road School remained textbook examples of New Orleans's persistent
brand of residential integration. While the stretches of Bayou Road and Esplanade Avenue one block south of the school were lily white, the broader
area was a segregationist's nightmare, with white and black people living
cheek by jowl. That a majority of the area's black residents were sufficiently
light-skinned for census enumerators to identify them as mulattoes underscored the area's racially mixed character and history. For instance, in the
voting precinct containing the school (see maps 2.5 and 2.6), approximately
60 percent of households were white, 24 percent were mulatto, and 15 percent were black. The adjacent precinct was similarly mixed, with roughly 68
percent white households, 17 percent mulatto, and 14 percent black.[40] The
trapezoidal block containing the Bayou Road School included eighty-seven
whites, thirteen mulattoes, and three blacks, while the 1800 block of Governor Nicholls, located one block west of the school, provided an even closer
approximation of the city's overall racial composition. Seventy-five whites and

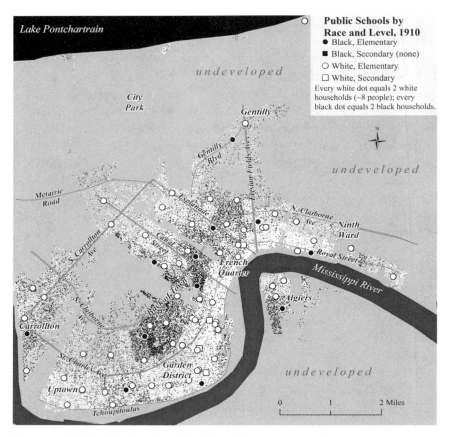

Map 2.3   Public schools and residential settlement patterns by race, 1910.

twenty-seven blacks, all but one identified as mulatto, lived along that stretch of Governor Nicholls.[41]

   During the early twentieth century, in fact, the lingering divide between Uptown and Downtown New Orleans was a more prominent spatial feature than residential segregation. As described in the previous chapter, this schism dated to the decades following the Louisiana Purchase, when American migrants shifted the city's commercial center from the French Quarter to Faubourg St. Marie, the suburb immediately upriver from it. As the Americans in the Second Municipality built new infrastructure and expanded its tax base, the downtown municipalities struggled to remain relevant. Even after railroad developers forced the city's three municipalities to reunite in 1852

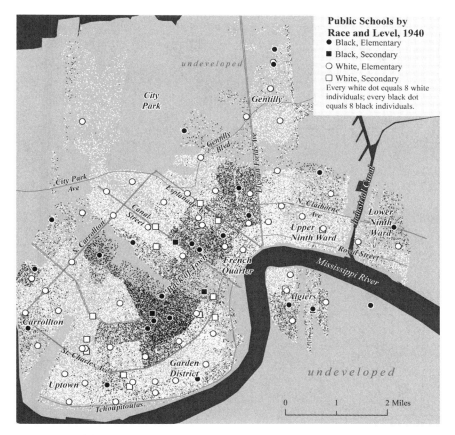

Map 2.4 Public schools and residential settlement patterns by race, 1940.

in order to save the city's moribund credit rating, Uptown and Downtown maintained distinctive identities.[42]

Downtown was the older Creole city, whose sagging economic prospects only enhanced the sense that it was stuck in time on the edge of the Atlantic world. Its early twentieth-century streetscape, fashioned largely by black Creole artisans such as Bernard Couvent, was like none other in the United States. The façades of otherwise modest shotgun houses exploded with cornucopias of wooden ornamentation; arched *porte-cochères* opened onto concealed rear courtyards; and rows of Creole cottages sat flush against the sidewalk, their high-pitched roofs sloping front to back and their multiple entrances frequently hidden behind tall wooden shutters. Black Creoles over-

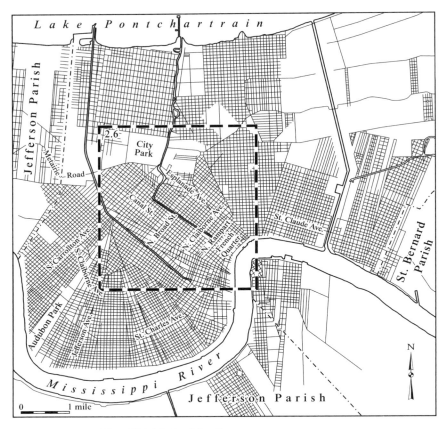

Map 2.5   Area of detail highlighted in Chapter 2.

whelmingly lived below Canal Street, and a number of Downtown blacks and whites continued to converse primarily in French after the turn of the twentieth century. The black people who lived Uptown, meanwhile, were more likely to be the Protestant descendants of slaves, many of whom arrived in New Orleans from the rural outskirts as part of a huge postemancipation migration. Additionally, Uptown was the preserve of the city's commercial and civic elite, who favored the newly developed residential parks near Audubon Park as well as the older raised center hall cottages and Italianate mansions their Anglo-Saxon ancestors had built in the Garden District (see map I.1 for neighborhood locations).[43]

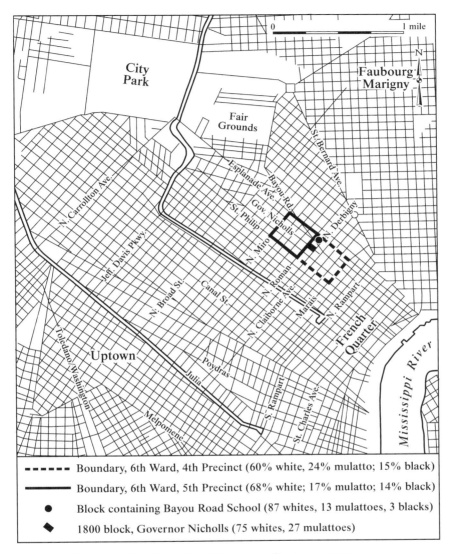

- - - - - Boundary, 6th Ward, 4th Precinct (60% white, 24% mulatto; 15% black)

—— Boundary, 6th Ward, 5th Precinct (68% white; 17% mulatto; 14% black)

● Block containing Bayou Road School (87 whites, 13 mulattoes, 3 blacks)

◆ 1800 block, Governor Nicholls (75 whites, 27 mulattoes)

Map 2.6 The Bayou Road School and its surrounding area, 1923.
Population data is from 1920 US Census, New Orleans, LA, Population, National Archives
Microfilm Series T-625, reel 620 and Heritage Quest Online.

By the first decades of the century, New Orleans's small but influential Jewish population had also settled Uptown. The wealthier, assimilated Jews who typically descended from early and mid-nineteenth-century German immigrants often lived among the civic and commercial elite. While the city's two most prominent Reform congregations built imposing, Byzantine-style temples along the oak tree–lined St. Charles Avenue, their congregants tended to choose their residences based on comfort rather than their proximity to these houses of worship. Turn-of-the-century School Board president E. B. Kruttschnitt, a successful attorney and the nephew of former US Senator and Confederate cabinet member Judah P. Benjamin, lived in a Garden District mansion with his mother, sister, and two servants. His next-door neighbor was the president of a sugar refinery; later in the century, the house across the street from his became the proving ground for the Manning football dynasty.[44]

Working-class Orthodox Jews, meanwhile, clustered within walking distance of their synagogues in the neighborhoods just above Canal Street that also attracted many rural black migrants and foreign immigrants. This allowed them to comply with religious prohibitions against mechanized travel on the Sabbath. These observant Jews were often more recent arrivals from eastern Europe, and many of them owned stores along either the twelve-block stretch of Dryades Street between Philip Street and Howard Avenue or the strip of nearby South Rampart Street that extended from Howard toward Canal Street (the geographic focus of Chapter 3). These integrated commercial districts attracted New Orleanians of nearly every race and ethnicity. Blacks shopped there, as did Sicilians, Germans, and Eastern Europeans. While Campanella argues that Dryades and Rampart Streets created a retail interface between the black back-of-town and the white front-of-town, the residential boundaries were not as distinct as this formulation suggests. Blacks and whites lived on both sides of Dryades and Rampart, and the interracial and interethnic commercial transactions upon which these streets thrived reflected the heterogeneity of the surrounding residential areas.[45]

As with New Orleans's neighborhoods, racial segregation also failed to permeate the city's labor market during the first decades of the twentieth century. Although black workers faced an economically stacked deck that disproportionately relegated them to low-wage fields such as domestic service and unskilled labor, they were significant players in what was then the South's most robust labor movement. Blacks outnumbered whites in some of the building trades, and overlapping interests encouraged intermittent biracial collaboration among the unionized dockworkers who powered the city's economy. Unlike the rural South, where white landowners depended upon black laborers and used the crop lien system to reinforce their subservient economic status, blacks and whites often competed fiercely for the same working-class jobs in the Crescent City. That competition sparked residential turf battles similar to those in the urban North and Midwest, where whites regularly used violence to expel black migrants from their neighborhoods, unions, and industrial workplaces.[46]

The 1800 block of Governor Nicholls Street near the Bayou Road School provided a glimpse of what the relative economic parity between black and white New Orleanians looked like in 1920. Although the block's white workers as a whole held higher-paying jobs than their black neighbors, a significant amount of crossover occurred between whites and blacks. A higher proportion of whites, for instance, held city jobs or were skilled laborers or lower-level professionals such as clerks, salesmen, and insurance agents. But the block's black population also included a US mail carrier.

Similarly, Donnie Cordia, a black plasterer, lived almost directly across the street from Alicade Mirabin, a white plasterer. One can imagine that Albert Buck, a fifty-year-old white man, smarted at the fact that he more or less lived and worked with Henry Lawrence, who was black. Both were low-paid laborers at a sugar refinery, and Buck could have easily seen Lawrence's home from the stoop of his rented double. White teenager Walter Englander, who lived around the corner from the 1800 block of Governor Nicholls on North Derbigny, might even have envied black father and son Louis and Frank Carter, for they were truck drivers and he was merely a trucker's helper.

The main occupational difference between the block's black and white residents was the number of black female workers. These women primarily worked as cooks and laundresses in private homes. But one neighborhood white woman, Ella Landry, also made a living by taking in other people's laundry. Forty-five-year-old white widow Ofelia Weber similarly worked as a seamstress at a factory while Aurelia Grose, a forty-six-year-old black widow, worked as a seamstress at home. Despite the better overall economic standing of the 1800 block's whites, the amount of occupational overlap likely made members of both races question the supposed immutability of Jim Crow (see table 2.1 below).[47] That creeping doubt almost certainly exacerbated tensions over the new school building on Bayou Road that was nearing completion in early 1923.

Table 2.1   Workforce Composition by Race and Job Classification, 1800 Block of Gov. Nicholls Street, 1920

	Government	Prof./Semi-Prof.	Trade	Skilled Laborer	Semi-/Unskilled Laborer	Domestic	Total
White	4	6	2	9	3	0	24
Black	1	0	2	0	5	5	13

Source: 1920 US Census, New Orleans, LA, Population, National Archives Microfilm Series T-625, reel 621. The census identified all of the black residents in the 1800 block of Governor Nicholls Street as mulatto.

While no equivalent blurring of the color lines occurred in the public schools, officials were still refining the mechanics of segregated education in the early 1920s. They had taken their boldest step toward a permanent solution in 1900, when they eliminated public education for blacks beyond the fifth grade. Reflecting a desire to reorder the city's fluid labor market, a board committee justified this move by arguing that black students' educations should "fit him and her for that sphere of labor and social position and occupation to which they are best suited and seem ordained by the proper fitness of things." The new policy also conformed with the US Supreme Court's decision the year before in *Cumming v. School Board of Richmond County, Georgia,* which sanctioned providing fewer educational offerings to blacks than whites.[48]

The wealthy Jewish attorney Ernest B. Kruttschnitt was the president of the school board at the time. A vocal advocate for public schools, Kruttschnitt also staunchly favored unequal educational opportunities for blacks and whites. As leader of the Democratic State Central Committee, Kruttschnitt had formed an alliance in the early 1890s with New Orleans mayor John Fitzpatrick's Democratic machine, which closely resembled ward-based political organizations in the urban North and Midwest. This partnership enabled Kruttschnitt to nearly double the school system's paltry budget. But little of the additional money reached black schools since he and the so-called Regular Democrats were intent on limiting black attainment. Kruttschnitt elaborated on the role schools could play in promoting white supremacy when he served as president of the constitutional convention that the state called in 1898 to strip blacks of their right to vote. Speaking to delegates in his opening address, Kruttschnitt suggested that adequate schooling for whites would ensure that even that race's poorest members could evade disfranchising provisions such as poll taxes and literacy tests. "Therefore, gentlemen," he intoned to the raucous crowd at New Orleans's Tulane Hall, "I think that the question of public education may rightly be considered a corollary of the suffrage question." While the 1898 convention ultimately pioneered the "grandfather clause" to ensure that even illiterate whites could vote, Kruttschnitt's bold attack on black education underscored the extent to which he viewed schools as pillars of a racially proscribed citizenry.[49]

Kruttschnitt passed this lesson on to his political protégé Martin Behrman, who served as mayor of New Orleans from 1904 to 1920 and again from 1924 until his death in 1926. Behrman helped revive the city's Democratic machine after a reformist slate carried municipal elections in 1896, and he was the machine's undisputed leader throughout his mayoral tenure. Intent to follow in the footsteps of the Tammany and Iroquois Clubs in New York and Chicago, the new machine considered a list of Native American names that included Natchez, Chickasaw, Tensas, and Houmas before settling on the Choctaw Club of Louisiana.[50]

The converted Catholic son of German Jewish immigrants, Behrman advanced from deputy assessor to school board member en route to becoming the Regular Democratic leader in the city's Fifteenth Ward, which encompassed the portion of New Orleans on the west bank of the Mississippi River. The stout, mustachioed politician also served alongside Kruttschnitt at the 1898 disfranchising convention, where he sat on the education committee and helped to secure free textbooks for poor New Orleanians and to ensure that the new constitution explicitly required racially segregated public schools.[51] As mayor, Behrman doubled the money the city spent on schools by passing a $200 liquor licensing fee and pushing the city's assessors to raise property assessments.[52]

Although Martin Behrman was not a member of the city's silk stocking class, his attentiveness to their role in New Orleans's public affairs was among his greatest political strengths. Like bosses in the urban North and Midwest, Behrman knew that public works projects such as school construction, drainage, and street paving would yield dividends at the ballot box by providing working-class voters with jobs and services. But unlike other machines, including its own nineteenth-century predecessor, the Choctaws were not strictly wedded to working-class immigrants or the unions that represented them. In addition to striking accords with commercial leaders, the Choctaws pursued an economic modernization program that often benefited capital more than labor. The construction of a city-run Public Belt Railway to connect major trunk railroad lines to waterfront terminals, for instance, ultimately strengthened local business magnates' influence over the docks.[53]

Some of Behrman's development projects also favored wealthy residents. In the Ninth Ward, which encompassed the city's swampy eastern edge, his administration began constructing the Industrial Canal in 1918 to provide access between the river and the lake. While the city drained the area alongside the canal for the construction of shipbuilding plants, it did not provide sufficient sewerage, drainage, or water facilities to the black and immigrant workers who moved to the Ninth Ward to staff the factories. The administration's most ambitious drainage project, meanwhile, involved reclaiming the equivalent of 2,000 acres from Lake Pontchartrain for the construction of a high-end white suburb. The *Times-Picayune* touted that project as "paradise without cost" since the government planned to fund it through the sale of the additional land it created. But officials also assured businessmen that the public entity in charge of the venture would "provide everything necessary in the way of conveniences and ornamentation" to make the community an attractive place to live and "a civic asset to New Orleans." The project became a boon to private landowners and developers, who acquired about half of the reclaimed land.[54]

Business and real estate interests similarly permeated the Behrman-era school board, especially following its 1912 shift from a seventeen-member, ward-based body to a five-member board elected citywide. While self-proclaimed "good government" reformers lobbied for this change in hopes of undermining Behrman's machine, he artfully managed to maintain control of the board until his own defeat in 1920.[55]

Half of the fourteen school board members who served between 1912 and 1920 had deep professional ties to the real estate industry. Two were real estate lawyers, two headed mortgage-lending homestead associations, one was the president of a realty company, another an executive at one of the city's largest banks, and one other headed a fire insurance company. The remaining members included a lawyer who occasionally handled real estate transactions, three businessmen, and a salesman, a baker, and a court reporter.[56] While eight of the twenty-three men elected to the ward-based board between 1908 and 1912 were professionally connected to the real estate industry, that group included a mix of professionals (e.g., two physicians, five lawyers, and a cotton factor), tradesmen (e.g., a machinist, a pattern maker, and a foreman), and municipal employees.[57]

At the time Behrman took office in 1904, both the city and its school system had nowhere to go but up. One historian tartly described turn-of-the-century New Orleans as "a foul and unsightly pesthole." In addition to the drainage canals full of "garbage and excrement" and the mosquitoes that bred like mad in trash-clogged gutters, street maintenance was nearly unthinkable on account of the regular floods.[58]

In 1905 a shortage of school buildings also prevented nearly 70 percent of school-aged children from attending school, an extreme version of a problem that other growing cities such as Detroit faced. While the new revenue Behrman generated from the liquor fee permitted the district to raise teachers' salaries and construct much-needed school buildings, the disparate investment in black and white schools bolstered racial inequality and left a physical legacy that persisted for decades. As enrollment jumped by more than 22,000 students between 1900 and 1920 (see table 2.2), the New Orleans school board built thirty-nine additional schools. But less than one-sixth of those schools were for black students even though they accounted for one-third of the in-

Table 2.2. Public School Enrollment, by Race, 1900–1940

Year	Black	White	Total Students	Black Students (%)	% Change (black)	% Change (white)	White Schools (#)	Black Schools (#)
1900	5,509	26,038	31,547	17	—	—	55	11
1910	7,674	38,151	45,825	17	39	47	66	13
1920	12,997	40,923	53,920	24	69	7	70	16
1930	22,572	56,834	79,406	28	74	39	78	23
1940	27,787	53,657	81,444	34	23	-6	70	30

Source: Louisiana Department of Education, *Annual and Biennial Reports,* 1900, 1910, available at www2.state .lib.la.us/doeafsr/; New Orleans Public School Directories, 1900, 1910, 1920, 1930, 1940, boxes 1 and 4, School Directories, Orleans Parish School Board Collection (Mss 147), Louisiana and Special Collections Department, Earl K. Long Library, University of New Orleans; *Annual Report of the New Orleans Public Schools,* 1920–21 and *Statistical Report of the New Orleans Public Schools of the Parish of Orleans,* 1930–31 and 1939–40, boxes 9 and 10, Annual Reports, Orleans Parish School Board Collection. Separate boys' and girls' elementary schools located within the same building are counted as one school while separate high schools and elementary schools located within the same building are counted as two schools.

creased enrollment. New black schools were also rarely as large or as well-designed as the buildings for whites. As a result, black children faced severe overcrowding.[59]

At the Bayou Road School in 1920, fifteen teachers attempted to teach seven hundred students in three "unsanitary, dark, rented dwelling houses." Persistent leaks caused plaster to drop from the ceilings and the walls, and an inadequate heating system meant many teachers and students stayed home on cold and rainy days. Crowding was even worse at the uptown Thomy Lafon School, where thirty-three teachers were responsible for 1,750 students.[60] By 1927, Lafon's enrollment of 2,700 students and forty-one teachers made it "the largest elementary Negro school in the world," according to a black newspaper editor.[61] The district often addressed overcrowding by running double sessions, with one group of students attending in the morning and another in the afternoon. This practice, which decreased the time students spent in school to as little as two and one-half hours per day, disproportionately affected blacks. In 1922, more than 5,000 black students attended school part-time compared with fewer than two hundred whites.[62]

In the long run, however, Kruttschnitt, Behrman, and the Democrats had more success eliminating the black vote than solidifying educational inequalities. Relentless protest from black New Orleanians led to the reinstatement of the grammar school grades (sixth through eighth) by 1914 and to the addition of a black high school by 1917 (the topic of Chapter 3). Pressure from black residents also contributed to the board's 1916 decision to remove the remaining white teachers from black schools, which meant black educators could at least turn their substandard facilities into their own educational realms.[63]

Bayou Road's principal Mary Coghill was one of many black educators who did just that. A no-nonsense leader, Coghill cultivated a disciplined teaching corps to support her students' individual and collective advancement. Under Coghill's tutelage, a former student recalled, "that's when I really was able to feel that . . . there was nothing better than your teacher." Like black churches, businesses, and civic organizations, black-run public schools sustained New Orleans's black community and provided a base for civil rights activism.[64]

The extra money Kruttschnitt and Behrman secured for the schools also failed to counteract a legacy of municipal parsimony that left some white students with lower educational attainment than blacks. A 1909 national study, for instance, found that only one-quarter of New Orleans's white students finished elementary school. That rate was lower than the completion percentages for black students from Richmond, Virginia, and Wilmington, Delaware, and the second-lowest among the study's surveyed cities.[65]

Some of New Orleans's school buildings for whites were also nearly as bad as those available to blacks. "There is an immediate need," Superintendent John Gwinn wrote in 1920, "for more than two hundred new school rooms in order to abandon rented buildings, basement rooms, part time plan and double classes and to make space for reduction of the number of pupils per teacher in some of the crowded schools." Of the school system's eighty-eight buildings, Gwinn noted that close to half were wooden, ten were more than sixty years old, nineteen more than forty years old, and the majority still heated by stoves. Gwinn estimated "that some five million dollars would be required to add the necessary new rooms and to remodel and repair the present buildings."[66]

As in most US cities, World War I had exacerbated the district's capital needs. Wartime restrictions on building materials brought school construction to a near standstill nationally at a time when enrollments were rapidly rising. The situation was particularly acute in New Orleans as a result of its limited prior investment in educational infrastructure. And New Orleans continued to spend far less than other cities despite Kruttschnitt's and Behrman's efforts to boost revenues. In 1913–1914, the $24.70 per year that New Orleans spent for each pupil was less than two-thirds the amount spent per public school student across the nation's largest cities. Chicago spent close to thirty-six dollars per student.[67]

The system's fiscal situation worsened after a massive hurricane damaged nearly all of the city's school buildings in 1915. When the costs of repairing schools cut into other parts of the municipal budget and threatened the city's credit rating, the business leaders on the Board of City Debt and Liquidation pushed through state constitutional amendments that severed the school board from the city government. While these changes gave the school board its own dedicated property tax, the schools' budget decreased with the elimination of city funding, and the board lost the political capital it had gained through its relationship with city hall.[68] In 1918–1919, for instance, the system spent about eight dollars less per student than it had in 1913–1914 in inflation-adjusted dollars. A pair of tax increases following World War I finally pushed the system above its pre-hurricane funding level, but the postwar recession and then the Great Depression eroded its fleeting fiscal recovery. School budgeting was essentially a zero sum game in the Crescent City throughout the interwar period: whites viewed funds for black education as money taken away from their schools; the board cut teachers' salaries to pay for new buildings; and residents competed for resources before the board like Mardi Gras parade goers jostling with each other for the sparkly beads and doubloons that well-heeled riders parsimoniously tossed from passing floats.[69]

IV.

New Orleans's limited investment in public services dated to the Redeemers' post-Reconstruction retrenchment, and those cuts fueled the growth of the city's sizable private school sector. Despite its Catholic majority, New Orleans had at most a dozen parochial schools when radical Reconstruction began in 1867. That number approached fifty by 1874 as students sought refuge from desegregated public schools, but declining enrollments after that year led the editor of the city's Catholic weekly to conclude that "parochial schools on the pay system are virtually a failure." Catholic and other private schools rebounded, however, as the Democrats gutted the public system after 1877. The parochial system grew to about sixty schools by the decade's end, and the total number of religiously affiliated schools reached ninety-five by the mid-1880s. By then the city had 205 private schools (compared to 54 public ones), which registered an estimated 16,399 students, or 40 percent of all children who were enrolled in school.[70] That reflected as much as an 11 percentage point increase from the 1869–1870 school year, which was the year before the public schools desegregated.[71] While the Catholic schools served the bulk of those students, nonsectarian private schools likely enrolled as much as one-fifth of the city's schoolchildren. In the years leading up to World War II, private and parochial schools consistently accounted for about one-third of New Orleans's school population (see table 2.3).[72]

The expansion of private schooling in New Orleans corresponded with the growth of parochial school systems in the nation's largest cities during the decades following the Civil War. In the Northeast and Midwest, parochial systems blossomed largely as a result of late nineteenth- and early twentieth-century urbanization and industrialization. As more and more immigrants moved to cities to work in factories, they frequently enrolled their children in Catholic schools. In 1880, for instance, the proportion of students at parochial schools in Cleveland, Pittsburgh, Cincinnati, Milwaukee, and Buffalo either rivaled or exceeded that of New Orleans. By 1930, Boston, Philadelphia, St. Louis, and Baltimore had joined New Orleans among the cities with the nation's highest rates of parochial school enrollment (see table 2.4).

Like its public schools, New Orleans's parochial schools profoundly influenced the city's urban landscape and evolving racial order during the early twentieth century. This was most evident through the role that schools played in the Catholic Church's contested creation of racially separate parishes. Unlike most American cities, New Orleans maintained interracial parishes and churches from the colonial period through the post-Reconstruction era. While the church segregated organizations and activities such as parish societies, catechetical instruction, and processions, black and white Catholics worshiped together in the same churches and—until the 1890s—the same pews. At the turn of the century, New Orleans was home to tens of thousands of black Catholics, more than any other diocese in the country.[73]

When Archbishop Francis Janssens established the city's first segregated parish for African Americans in 1895, he faced stiff resistance from rank-and-file black parishioners as well as the activists who were challenging the Separate Car Law and other segregationist statutes in court. Black opposition was so widespread that church leaders did not even attempt to create another black parish until 1909. They faced less opposition then and followed the establishment of this second black parish with an additional six over the following decade. Black Catholics acceded to this heightened level of segregation largely because of one inducement: schools.[74]

Prior to the late 1880s, black Catholic schooling in New Orleans was an ad hoc venture; its availability largely depended upon the initiative of groups such as the Ursulines, the Sisters of the Holy Family, and the Catholic Institution. Following the Third Plenary Council of Baltimore in 1884, which called for a nationwide expansion of parochial schools to check the growing influence and organization of public school systems, the Archdiocese of New Orleans established a network of segregated black schools within its otherwise integrated parishes. Since the expansion of black Catholic education came as the public school system faced withering cuts, the segregated parochial system expanded educational opportunity for African Americans. But the new system also served as a springboard for further segregation within the church and the city as a whole.[75]

Between 1906 and 1916, nine parishes that operated separate schools for

Table 2.3   Public vs. Private School Enrollment in New Orleans, Selected Years, 1869–1940

Year	Public School Enrollment	Private School Enrollment	Total Number Enrolled in School (Private and Public)	Percentage of Enrolled Students in Private School
1850	5,946	5,668	11,614	49
1869	24,000	10,000	34,000	29
1871	19,091	19,401	38,492	50
1877	19,507	12,000	31,507	38
1890	23,209	16,610	39,819	42
1915	41,076	20,847	61,923	34
1920	53,920	24,000	77,920	31
1930	79,406	30,653	110,059	28
1940	81,444	28,537	109,981	26

Sources: Social Explorer Dataset (SE), Census 1850, digitally transcribed by Inter-university Consortium for Political and Social Research, edited and verified by Michael Haines, compiled, edited, and verified by Social Explorer; *Report of the Chief Superintendent of the Public Schools of the City of New Orleans, LA, to the State Board of Education,* January 1886, 241, 266–267 (the report is included in *Biennial Report of the State Superintendent of Public Education of the State of Louisiana, 1884–1885), available at* www2.state.lib.la.us/doeafsr/; Donald E. DeVore and Joseph Logsdon, *Crescent City Schools: Public Education in New Orleans, 1841–1991* (Lafayette: University of Southwestern Louisiana Press, 1991), 70, 91, 102, 128; Louis R. Harlan, "Desegregation in New Orleans Public Schools During Reconstruction," *American Historical Review* 67, no. 3 (April 1962): 669, 669 n. 33; *Annual Report of the New Orleans Public Schools,* 1920–21 and *Statistical Report of the New Orleans Public Schools of the Parish of Orleans,* 1930–31 and 1939–40, boxes 9 and 10, Annual Reports, Orleans Parish School Board Collection (Mss 147), Louisiana and Special Collections Department, Earl K. Long Library, University of New Orleans; Louisiana Department of Education, *Annual and Biennial Reports,* 1900, 1910, 1930, 1940, *available at* www2.state.lib.la.us/doeafsr/. This chart reflects locally reported numbers in those regular instances when the state reported wildly different public school enrollment numbers than the local district did.

Table 2.4   Catholic School Enrollments as Estimated Proportion of Total Enrollments for Large US Cities, 1880 and 1930 (ranked by 1930 rates)

City	Catholic School Enrollment (%)	
	1880	*1890*
Pittsburgh	34	46
Cincinnati	42	44
Boston	14	41
Buffalo	39	41
Milwaukee	48	39
New Orleans	**34**	**37**
St. Louis	25	35
Baltimore	25	33
Cleveland	47	33
Philadelphia	17	31
Chicago	28	29
San Francisco	19	29
Detroit	26	28
New York	12	9

Source: Adapted from David P. Baker, "All the Masses: Reconsidering the Origins of American Schooling in the Postbellum Era," *Sociology of Education* 72, no. 4 (October 1999), Table 1, p. 204.

Note: Baker developed his estimates based on Catholic school enrollment data published in the *Official Catholic Directory* (New York: P. J. Kennedy & Sons, 1880 and 1930) and public school enrollment data from US Bureau of Education, *Report of the Commissioner of Education for the Year 1888–89* (Washington: Government Printing Office, 1894) and US Bureau of Education, *Biennial Survey of Education* (Washington: Government Printing Office, 1930). He calculated the proportions by dividing Catholic school enrollment by the total of Catholic and public school enrollment. While this method inflates the proportion of Catholic school attendance by excluding other private schools, it provides a reasonably reliable snapshot of nonpublic school attendance for major cities. The Louisiana State Department of Education regularly (though not annually) reported private and public school enrollment by parish, and the department's numbers roughly align with Baker's. In 1885, for instance, New Orleans's percentage of private school enrollment was 40% (versus the 34% Catholic enrollment Baker reported for 1880), and its private school enrollment rate was 32% in 1929–30 (versus Baker's 37% for 1930), according to the Department's reports. (The Department did not report private school enrollment for 1880–81 or 1930–31.) See State Department of Education of Louisiana, *Eighty-First Annual Report for the Session 1929–30,* October 1930, 67, 71, 81; *Biennial Report of the State Superintendent of Public Education of the State of Louisiana, 1884–1885,* 241, 266–67, available www2.state.lib.la.us/doeafsr/. As Baker notes, the federal government's estimates for private school attendance appear quite low when compared with Catholic records.

white as well as black children closed their schools for blacks. Church leaders correctly guessed that the closures would force African Americans into their own parishes. While Catholic officials had historically created "national parishes" for different immigrant groups by first building a church and then adding a school, the process worked in reverse for black Catholics in New Orleans and elsewhere. Schools drew black parishioners away from the integrated churches they had long attended and into separate congregations. The approach was so successful that church leaders from Cleveland, Los Angeles, and St. Louis looked to New Orleans, which had long defined Catholic interracialism, as a model for the creation of racially separate parishes.[76]

The creation of segregated Catholic parishes and schools directly affected New Orleans's urban landscape and built environment. As with public schools, white hostility to black parochial schools often pushed those institutions into less desirable neighborhoods and facilities. Samuel Kelly, the white priest in charge of the black Corpus Christi parish, reported that "nobody wanted 'Father Kelly and his little niggers' in their buildings." Additionally, the church repeatedly built grand new structures on major thoroughfares for its white parishes while pushing black parishioners into abandoned and decrepit buildings on interior streets. Adding insult to injury, church leaders used contributions from their exiled black parishioners to pay for the new and more elaborate white cathedrals.[77]

While this shifting of resources from African American to white hands mirrored public school practices, parochial schools diverged from public ones in terms of their impact on residential settlement patterns. Whereas public schools encouraged the reshuffling of the population through the creation of geographically distinct black and white neighborhoods (as discussed in Chapters 3–6), parochial schools often reinforced existing residential arrangements. This was likely due to the fact that segregated Catholic parishes shared territorially defined and overlapping borders. That meant that each neighborhood had a white as well as a black church and—unlike the public system—a white and a black school. The availability and geographic permanence of these valued community resources likely discouraged black and white parishioners from moving. The uptown neighborhood surrounding the black St. Dominic Church and School (later renamed Joan of Arc), for instance, was predominantly white when the school opened in 1909 and remained so decades later. For the white residents who lived near St. Dominic, which was located in the parish's formerly integrated and multiethnic Mater Dolorosa

Church building, moving would mean abandoning their parish and the newly constructed whites-only Mater Dolorosa a few blocks away. By emphasizing racial rather than ethnic differences and by placing white priests in charge of black parishes, church leaders also reassured St. Dominic's white neighbors of their unique and superior status vis-à-vis their black Catholic neighbors.[78]

Segregated parochial schools influenced New Orleans's racial order in one other important way. Like public schools, black Catholic schools became centers of resistance to Jim Crow. Once again, the leaders of the Catholic Institution were in the vanguard. Following the disastrous hurricane in 1915, the school came under the supervision of a white priest and religious order as a condition of the funding it received to support its rebuilding. But the renamed St. Louis School retained its all-black board of directors, which refused to fully relinquish the independence Marie Couvent had insisted upon in her will. When the archbishop sought to gain full control over the school in 1920 by withholding a three-hundred-dollar bequest, the board decided the school's autonomy was more important than the money. Its members voted unanimously to "not surrender their rights" because of their "duty [to] . . . their race." Other black Catholic schools similarly fostered racial pride and leadership to undermine Jim Crow.[79]

V.

To a certain extent, New Orleans's lower levels of late nineteenth-century immigration and industrialization as well as its unique experience with Reconstruction distinguished the growth of its private school sector from those in the North and Midwest. In New Orleans, the proliferation of private schools and the steep divestment in public education were simultaneous and mutually reinforcing. As residents left the public system in response to its dwindling post-Reconstruction budget, they lost interest in supporting it financially, which further undermined the system's quality and desirability and encouraged still more residents to switch to private schools. The city's high rate of nonsectarian private school enrollment also suggested that education outside the public system was more than a Catholic working-class phenomenon. The city's Catholic and Protestant elite, the latter having pioneered the public school system before the Civil War, had little appetite for an expansive public sphere by the 1870s. These men—or their descendants—hungered instead for a diet of low taxes, low property assessments, and renewed social standing.[80]

Private schools fit nicely onto this menu, and statistics indicated that the city's commercial and civic elite overwhelmingly favored them over public ones. In 1901, for instance, just 122 white public school students were the children of physicians and 118 the children of attorneys in a city that boasted nearly 400 white doctors and 570 white lawyers. Children whose parents fell into the more ambiguously titled occupational category of "broker" were also sparsely represented. Fewer than 140 white public school students were the sons and daughters of brokers in a city where close to 500 men earned their living as either brokers or bankers. Conservatively assuming an average of just one school-aged child for every white doctor, lawyer, and broker in the city, an estimated three-quarters of these children attended private rather than public schools.[81] Consider it a protean form of white flight.

It is tempting to conclude that this preference for the private over the public sector reflected something more deeply engrained within the culture of white New Orleans or the South as a whole. Members of New Orleans's white elite, after all, founded both the White League and a set of exclusive Carnival organizations during the height of Reconstruction. Both organizations allowed white men to create shadow power structures at a time when they were largely barred from holding public office. While less menacing than the White League, the so-called Mardi Gras "krewes" sought to restore the city's former social hierarchy by imposing order upon an inherently disorderly celebration. Their meticulously stage-managed parades, which created a previously nonexistent distinction between the participants and the audience, became the public face of Carnival. But the organizations placed equal or even greater weight upon the private balls they held in the evenings. Like the elite white men who led the violent disfranchising campaigns throughout the region, New Orleans's White League, Carnival, and commercial leaders (who were generally one and the same) made little distinction between their private interests and the public good. If private schools could effectively train their children to succeed them as the city's social and financial pillars, then they believed that everyone benefited, the social and economic consequences of an underfunded public school system notwithstanding. Nothing captured this attitude better than the unintentionally ironic motto of Rex, the exclusive organization which anointed itself King of Carnival in 1872. The krewe existed, its motto proclaimed, "pro bono publico," for the good of the public.[82]

The Carnival elites' penchant for playing dress-up, however, might have exaggerated a difference between New Orleans and northern and Midwestern cities that was a matter of degree more than kind. New Orleans was not the only city whose schools suffered from upper-class divestment during the early twentieth century. By 1911, for instance, the majority of Boston's lawyers lived, paid taxes, and sent their children to school outside the city. In 1925, 40 percent of the attorneys who worked in Newark lived in the suburbs, and by 1932 nearly 90 percent of that city's Chamber of Commerce officers and board members lived in Newark's suburbs.[83] Wealthier New Orleanians differentiated themselves primarily by creating their own private spheres within the city proper, a development that possibly had as much to do with the city's swampy surroundings as anything else.

As New Orleans stepped up the draining of its watery periphery following World War I, its development trajectory increasingly mirrored that of other cities: affluent whites migrated away from the areas closest to the city center, which then became contested terrain for the lower-income blacks and whites who remained behind. The similarities between New Orleans and the nation's other major cities did not stop there, however. Despite New Orleans's limited manufacturing sector, the port maintained the Crescent City's status as an economic engine of national significance. Machine politics in New Orleans also mirrored those in other big cities, as did the civic and commercial elite's preference for private rather than public interests. Nor was New Orleans's high rate of private school attendance unique.

Most significantly, during the Great Migration race became as prescient and complex an issue in northern cities as it was in New Orleans. White and black workers competed for jobs—albeit on a patently uneven playing field—in the factories and stockyards of Chicago just as they did along the docks in New Orleans. They also jostled for recreational, educational, and living space, with powerful white voices in the North and South insisting upon segregation in all of these areas.[84] The history and activism of New Orleans's Creoles of color distinguished the city from other places. But the many ways in which these individuals gave lie to the myth of race highlighted the impossibility of a totally fixed color line, whether in law or fact, in New Orleans, New York, Chicago, or Philadelphia. In all of these cities, a central question of the post–World War I era was that of the "Negro's place." As the following chapters highlight, the relationship in the Crescent City between schools, race, and the future of the city was also not unique.

In New Orleans, as the question of the "Negro's place" became increasingly intertwined with the physical space in which black and white people lived, schools emerged as the primary vehicle for reinforcing the racial order. James Fortier, the civic and commercial elite he represented, and his Sixth Ward neighbors focused on schools as a means of promoting residential segregation. When they defended the racial sanctity of their neighborhoods, they did so by talking about the future of their schools. Schools also played a key role in drawing white residents to the new neighborhoods on the city's recently drained periphery, and they were focal points in the conflicts between the black and white residents who continued to live in the city's older sections. As the next chapter shows, the spark for these battles often came from black residents who challenged the inequities of Jim Crow by demanding better school facilities.

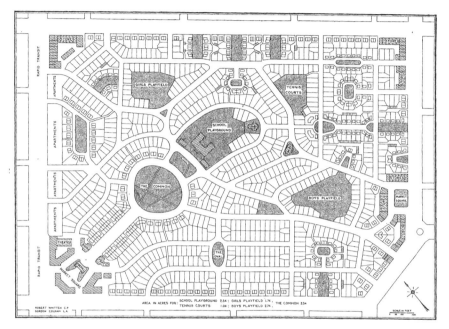

Figure 2.1   An example of a neighborhood unit organized around a school.
Clarence Arthur Perry, *The Neighborhood Unit*, in *Regional Survey of New York and Its Environs*, vol. 7 (New York: Regional Plan of New York and its Environs, 1929).

Figure 3.1 Walter L. Cohen.
A. E. Perkins, ed., *Who's Who in Colored Louisiana* (Baton Rouge: Douglas Loan Co., 1930).

Figure 3.2 McDonogh No. 35 High School, Corner S. Rampart and Girod Street in New Orleans.
The Charles L. Franck Studio Collection at The Historic New Orleans Collection, Acc. No. 1979.325.1870.

JAMES J. A. FORTIER
Attorney at Law

Figure 4.1

This 1917 caricature of James Fortier highlights his numerous civic and commercial activities. The stack of mortgages on the table as well as the reference in the upper left of the image to his service as president and attorney for the Pyramid Homestead Association highlights his ties to the real estate industry. W. K. Patrick, *Club Men of Louisiana in Caricature, Nineteen Hundred Seventeen* (East Aurora, NY: The Roycrofters, 1917).

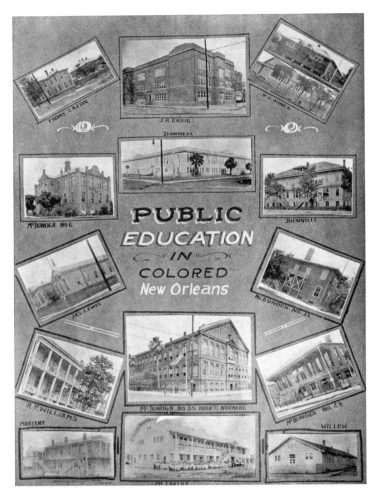

Figure 4.2
O. C. W. Taylor, *The Crescent City Pictorial* (New Orleans: O. C. W. Taylor, 1926), Amistad Research Center.

The $70,000 Grammar and High School is now in the course of construction in

Jefferson Heights Subdivision

Take a look at the picture—the foundation is already there—the uprights are there, too. There is no need to look at the signboard where the school was to be built—that time is past—the school is there. It will soon be completed, offering that one chief asset to any section that is to grow—a place where children can receive the proper education.

LOTS ARE SELLING FAST
You Can Buy Them
With Schillinger Sidewalks and Gravelled Streets for

$200 to $365—On Terms
10 Per Cent Cash—3 Per Cent Monthly
NO INTEREST
Titles Guaranteed by Union Title Guarantee Company

JAS. F. TURNBULL
REALty Developer
332 Baronne St   Main 2139

Ride Out Today—On Jefferson Highway
2 1-2 Miles Above City Limits
SEE THE LOTS OR MAIL THE COUPON TODAY

JAS. F. TURNBULL,
332 Baronne St., Corner Union St.
Kindly send me full particulars regarding Jefferson Heights without obligation on my part.
Name ....
Address ....

Figure 5.1   Advertisement for Jefferson Heights subdivision, 1923.

Times-Picayune, 26 August 1923. © 2017 NOLA Media Group, L.L.C. All rights reserved. Used with permission of The Times-Picayune and NOLA.com. The lots in Jefferson Heights were about one-third to one-half the cost of lots in neighboring Crestmont Park, which meant the new public school would likely serve both upper- and middle-income students.

Figure 6.1   Gentilly, looking north toward Lake Pontchartrain, 1949.
A Planning and Building Program for New Orleans' Schools, 1952. The Historic New Orleans Collection, Acc. No. 90–560-RL, Gift of Orleans Parish Public Schools. While some development had taken place in Gentilly by the time of this photograph, it was almost exclusively limited to the area east of the London Avenue Canal. The canal is partially visible in the upper left of the above image. Charles Colbert lived southeast of the canal in a section of Gentilly not visible in this image.

Figure 6.2   Gentilly, looking north toward Lake Pontchartrain, 1951.
A Planning and Building Program for New Orleans' Schools, 1952. The Historic New Orleans Collection, Acc. No. 90–560-RL, Gift of Orleans Parish Public Schools. Despite rapid growth since 1949, the area along the left side of the above figure remained undeveloped at the time of this photograph. This undeveloped area was separated from the built-up portions of Gentilly by the London Avenue Canal, which is barely visible along the left edge of the above image. Charles Colbert lived south of the undeveloped area, outside the lower left corner of the frame.

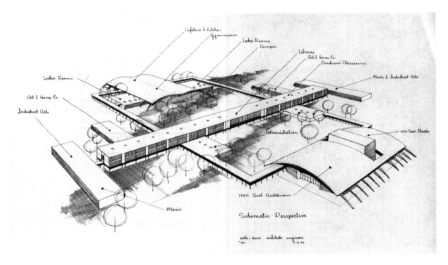

Figure 6.3 "Schematic Perspective," George Washington Carver Junior-Senior High School, 1954.
Curtis & Davis, *The Architectural Report to the Orleans Parish School Board: George Washington Carver Junior-Senior High School, Basic Design Drawings, Analysis and Solution* (New Orleans: Curtis & Davis, 1955), folder 10, box 3, Charles Roussève Collection, Amistad Research Center.

CHAPTER THREE

BLACKS AND JEWS

On New Year's Eve 1912, police arrested an eleven-year-old black boy in New Orleans's Third Ward for firing six shots into the air from a .38 caliber revolver. The boy had been walking down South Rampart Street, hustling tips with the three other members of his vocal quartet: lead singer Little Mack, bass Big Nose Sidney, and baritone Redhead Happy Bolton. The eleven-year-old sang tenor. As the group reached the corner of South Rampart and Perdido Streets, a boy on the opposite side of the street rattled off several shots from an old six-shooter. The eleven-year-old replied in kind, reloaded, and was preparing to shoot again when a tall white police officer grabbed him from behind. After a fitful night in a Juvenile Court jail cell, the youth was shipped to the Colored Waif's Home for Boys on the rural outskirts of the city. On New Year's Day 1913, a New Orleans newspaper reported the incident, printing the boy's name for the first of what would be many times. It was Louis Armstrong.[1]

Since Armstrong first picked up a cornet during his stay at the Waif's Home, his arrest became a critical component in the origin story of one of America's most celebrated art forms. But the anecdote also provides a window into New Orleans's complex turn-of-the-century racial and cultural geography and how that geography influenced debates over urban development and residential segregation. During the first decades of the century, Armstrong's neighborhood was among the more diverse and vibrant in the city. It was home to blacks and whites, natives and immigrants, residences and retailers, schools and rail yards, honky-tonks and houses of worship. As segregation became more entrenched, however, the neighborhood became the site of contentious struggles over the future of New Orleans's racially and spatially heterogeneous landscape.

The area's public schools assumed a central role in these battles as whites responded to black demands for secondary education and better school facilities. In particular, the school board's decision in 1917 to convert the neighborhood's white elementary school into a black elementary and high school spurred the area's white residents, particularly its Jewish immigrants, to launch a spirited defense of their neighborhood. They worried that the school conversion would turn what they considered to be a white area into a black one and that this new racial designation would affect future public and private investment in the neighborhood. Pointing to the area's black residents and its questionable character, school officials countered that their decision merely ratified its black identity. While Armstrong's neighborhood, like so many others in the city, defied such easy categorization, the debates over its racial identity highlighted the increased prominence of race in matters of urban development. The creation of the black high school marked the climax of those debates. By giving the neighborhood a black identity, the school validated the Jews' fears and prefigured the area's destruction. As a result, what blacks gained in expanded educational opportunity, they lost in residential stability and quality.

The first section that follows provides an overview of Louis Armstrong's boyhood neighborhood while the second and third examine the African American campaign for greater educational opportunities through the lens of civic leader Walter L. Cohen. The fourth section then focuses on the Jewish immigrants' protest against the proposed black high school in their neighborhood, and the fifth situates that protest within the broader challenges confronting the neighborhood and others like it. The chapter's final section charts the redevelopment of the area and the displacement of its residents in the years after it secured a black high school.

I.

Armstrong's rendezvous with the police began when he surreptitiously retrieved the .38 from the bottom of an old cedar trunk that his mother kept in the single room they shared with her boyfriends and his sister at Perdido and South Liberty Streets (adjacent to New Orleans's present-day city hall). Armstrong's boyhood home was nestled among the many "cribs" within the four-

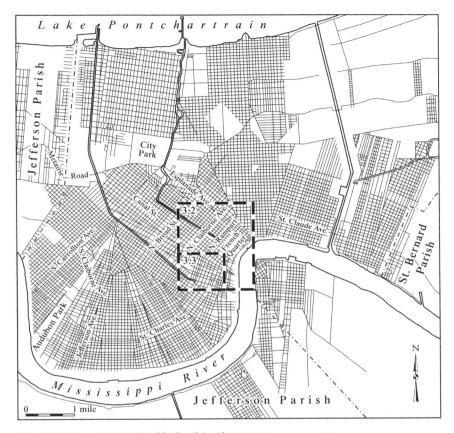

Map 3.1 Area of detail highlighted in Chapter 3.

block area between Perdido, Gravier, Franklin, and Locust Streets that comprised the smaller of the city's two legalized vice districts. (See maps 3.1 and
3.2; Franklin and Locust later became Loyola Avenue and South Robertson
Street, respectively.) Armstrong's mother May Ann occasionally worked as a
prostitute, and these shallow, wood-framed cribs, which typically had common
walls and sat flush against the sidewalk, provided the lowest barrier to entry
for women looking to make ends meet in the sex trade. This secondary district
earned a reputation as "black Storyville" since its bars, dance halls, and prostitutes served the black men who were not welcome at the higher-end brothels
in the larger, better-known Storyville on the downtown side of Canal Street.[2]

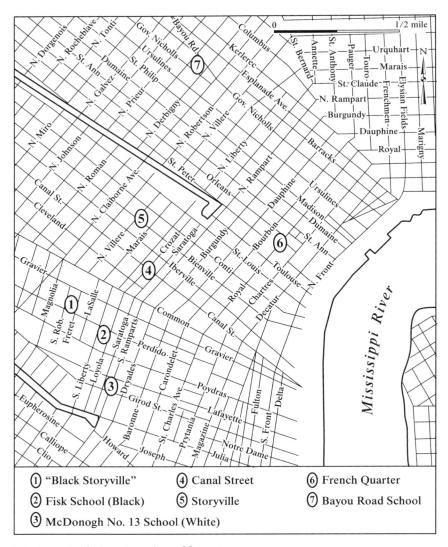

Map 3.2 Louis Armstrong's world, 1912.

As Armstrong and his buddies walked the three blocks along Perdido Street's cobblestones from South Liberty to South Rampart, they passed the Fisk School.[3] Armstrong attended Fisk intermittently before heading to the Waif's Home. But by 1912 he had possibly finished his education there since it, like the city's twelve other black public schools, did not continue beyond the sixth grade. The boys also passed the Odd Fellows and Masonic Hall, where black prostitutes often ended their nights by dancing to bands that played the blues, quadrilles, and slow drag into the early hours of the morning.[4]

While nearly all of the residents along this stretch of Perdido Street were black, the people who lived on the streets that Armstrong's quartet crossed were a far more diverse lot. The 500 block of South Franklin (Loyola) between Poydras and Perdido, where the Fisk School was located, was home to black railroad workers, laundresses, and cooks as well as Italian fruit peddlers, banana ship laborers, and homemakers. The 400 block of South Franklin (Loyola), between Perdido and Gravier, also housed a mix of blacks and Italians. Black residents were in the minority on Saratoga, the next street the gang crossed. But here many Eastern European Jews with names such as Marskovichtz and Finkelstein lived alongside black migrants from Mississippi, Georgia, and Alabama as well as Italians like grocer John Segretta. Armstrong, in fact, later became familiar with Segretta's son Joe, who managed a grocery store that doubled as a saloon and honky-tonk.[5] The residential mixture that Armstrong observed as he strolled down Perdido Street also held true for the area as a whole. A sample of more than two thousand individuals living in the fifteen square blocks bounded by Julia, Gravier, South Liberty, and South Rampart Streets, for example, revealed an almost identical number of black and white residents.[6]

The character of the neighborhood changed from residential to commercial when Armstrong's quartet reached the pavement of South Rampart Street. Today, that street sits in the shadow of the Mercedes Benz Superdome and the Central Business District.[7] But a 1938 city guide called South Rampart "the Harlem of New Orleans." "For a distance of several blocks it teems with a great variety of shops catering largely to the Negro population," the guidebook continued. "Countless cafés and refreshment stands are in evidence." One Depression-era black teenager offered a similar assessment. "*Everything* black was on Rampart Street," he recalled. "We had a couple of black drugstores where you could go in and have a soda. . . . And we had one excellent black restaurant called the Astoria. White table clothes and everything."[8]

South Rampart's reputation as a primarily, if not exclusively, black shopping and pleasure palace was already well established in Armstrong's day. The six-block stretch of South Rampart between Gravier and Howard Avenue featured a host of establishments exclusively for blacks: thirteen barrooms, twelve barber shops, seven rooming houses, the two drug stores, and the famed Astoria Hotel. But it also boasted a pair of whites-only bars, a handful of restaurants that served whites and blacks, and many Jewish- and immigrant-owned businesses with integrated customer bases. The white Mc-Donogh No. 13 School was at the intersection of South Rampart and Girod, three blocks from where Armstrong shot his revolver and a short five-block walk from the Fisk School.[9] While the area below, or on the riverside, of Rampart Street was more heavily white than the area above it, nearly one-quarter of the residents in the nine-block area directly below McDonogh No. 13 were black (see map 3.3).[10]

Quite often, Rampart Street's jewelers, tailors, and clothing store proprietors lived in small, residential quarters behind or above their shops. Shoe store owner M. Schneider, for instance, lived with his wife, three sons, and daughter on the 400 block of South Rampart, which was immediately uptown from where Armstrong fired the gun. That block was also home to the Russian Jewish Davidson family, the French butcher Louis Braquet, the Belgian-Flemish drug store owner George Thomas, the Italian restaurateur Strata Sideri, and the married black migrants N. J. and Carrie Jones, who worked as a carpenter and laundress, respectively. The block also included several blacks who boarded with white families, including hod carrier Frank Rose and odd-job laborer Clinton Van Dyer, who lived with jewelry store owners Frank and Mary Maur. After his stint in the Waif's Home, Armstrong collected junk and hauled coal for the Karnofsky family, Russian Jews who also owned a clothing and variety store in that block of South Rampart. Morris Karnofsky later converted the family business into a record shop, which became popular among black jazz musicians.[11]

Armstrong spoke fondly of the Karnofskys, who were possibly the only whites he really knew as a boy. They offered him meals in their home, introduced him to Russian folk music, and encouraged him to say "this" and "that" instead of "dis" and "dat."[12] Like many southern black children, New Orleanians especially, Armstrong played with whites as a young boy.[13] But the time and space that whites and blacks shared in Armstrong's wondrously diverse neighborhood never transformed into comity because they understood their lives and relations with each other through distinct prisms. As music historian Thomas Brothers argues, Armstrong and his black peers were immersed in a vernacular black culture in which few whites participated. The Sanctified Church, brass band street parades, late-night honky-tonks, and a collective ethic were key elements of that culture. Jim Crow and the ever-present threat

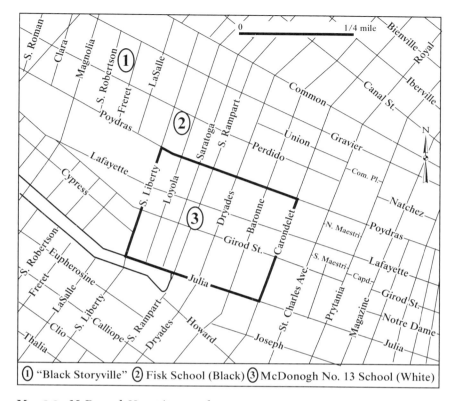

① "Black Storyville" ② Fisk School (Black) ③ McDonogh No. 13 School (White)

Map 3.3   McDonogh No. 13/35 sample area, 1910.
The 1910 US Census recorded 2,796 individuals living in the bounded area. The census identified 69 percent of these residents as white, 31 percent as black or mulatto. For the nine blocks above Rampart, 47 percent were identified as black or mulatto versus 22 percent in the blocks below Rampart. Source: 1910 US Census, New Orleans, LA, Population, National Archives Microfilm Series T-624, reel 520.

of violence reinforced Third Ward blacks' interest in cultural autonomy. From their experiences living with whites, they knew that freedom from oppression mattered much more than integration.

The neighborhood's white residents also had little interest in residential integration, albeit for quite different reasons. The Jews in particular were engaged in an assimilative quest to succeed in the American mainstream and to solidify their standing as white Americans.[14] As part of that project, they often disavowed their close connection with the black neighbors and customers with whom they interacted daily. Those disavowals became particularly intense on those occasions when public officials and developers discussed the future of their neighborhood. Race was the central topic whenever those discussions arose: was this a white area that deserved future investment and protection, or was it a black one that simply needed second-rate accommodations for that race? In the name of self-preservation, the Rampart area Jews ignored reality and claimed that they lived in a white neighborhood. Blacks, meanwhile, refused to disappear into the woodwork and demanded additional services, particularly in the areas where they lived. These competing visions collided when blacks stepped up their campaign for expanded educational opportunities.

II.

Black demands for better public schools often bubbled up from the school-based "Mothers' Clubs" who focused their energies on supplementing the district's meager offerings.[15] But these requests often failed to gain traction until they received support from black men such as Walter L. Cohen, whose priorities did not always gel with those of the black masses. Cohen became the leader of the state's "Black-and-Tan" Republicans and served as registrar of the US Land Office in New Orleans under Presidents McKinley and Roosevelt. One interwar observer of black New Orleans considered him "one of the three Negroes of political consequence anywhere in the South." Regardless of whether that assessment exaggerated Cohen's regional clout, he was undoubtedly the most influential black New Orleanian of his day.[16]

Cohen joined the Third Ward black residents' fight for better public schools in 1914 when he presented a petition on behalf of the Colored Educational Alliance to the Orleans Parish School Board. The Association's demands included a new building to replace the wooden framed Fisk School and the rented cottage that functioned as its annex. Together these schools served more than nine hundred students, and Fisk had "dump closets" in lieu of sanitary toilets connected to a sewer line.[17] The Alliance's other demands included the introduction of black night schools for youths and adults who worked during the day, a beefed-up industrial training program, the creation of an industrial training high school that included a teacher training program, and new buildings for several schools, including the one on Bayou

Road.[18] That school's student-teacher ratio was pushing fifty-five-to-one, and the district's inspector had acknowledged its deplorable shape in a report he had submitted to the board the previous month. "Rented buildings. Very bad condition. New school needed," he bluntly noted.[19]

Two politically likeminded black professionals accompanied Cohen (see figure 3.1) before the board: the Congregational minister Henderson H. Dunn, a founder of the Educational Alliance, and Robert E. Jones, another licensed preacher and the editor of the *Southwestern Christian Advocate*, the regional newspaper affiliated with the Methodist Episcopal Church. Jones was particularly familiar with Louis Armstrong's boyhood neighborhood, since the *Advocate*'s Baronne Street office was blocks from Fisk and the white McDonogh No. 13 School.[20]

According to historian Donald DeVore, clergymen such as Jones melded the philosophies of Booker T. Washington and W. E. B. Du Bois to provide "black New Orleans with a theology and ideology that stressed individual initiative, community development, and black liberation." Walter Cohen similarly promoted individual as well as collective advancement in the face of Jim Crow. His background also gave him a unique perspective on the relations between the Rampart Street area's black and Jewish residents.[21]

Born in 1860, Cohen's father was Jewish and his mother was a free woman of color. Bernard Cohen owned a clothing store at 33 Front Street, which was on the downtown side of Canal Street near the Mississippi River in the heart of the city's nineteenth-century Jewish enclave.[22] Cohen's mother Amelia Bingaman, born around 1835 in Natchez, Mississippi, was the daughter of Col. A. L. Bingaman, a white slave owner and celebrated "turfman," or horseracing aficionado. Amelia's mother was likely one of the colonel's slaves, and she possibly began her life as his enslaved property as well. Although Cohen was sufficiently light-skinned for census takers to occasionally identify him as white, he fully embraced his mother's racial identity. He also adopted her Catholicism.[23]

Residential proximity likely contributed to Amelia and Bernard's courtship since they lived a few blocks from each other before they moved into Bernard's home in the neighborhood that became Storyville.[24] Since European immigrants and free blacks continued to interact fairly freely in Downtown New Orleans during the 1830s and 1840s, their relationship would have previously generated little notice within that racially mixed area. But the repressive campaign the city launched against free blacks during the 1850s caused many to seek either temporary exile abroad or solace within local black organizations such as the Prince Hall Masons, which was closely aligned with the African Methodist Episcopal (AME) Church. For historians Joseph Logsdon and Caryn Cossé Bell, these different reactions prefigured the Reconstruction-era split between New Orleans's French- and English-speaking blacks. While the former often drew upon Haitian and French revolutionary traditions to demand a complete obliteration of the color line, the latter more frequently favored accommodation and racial solidarity.[25] The Cohens' decision to ride out the storm at home suggested a willingness to accept the color line, if only for the sake of survival. Even as war, occupation, and Reconstruction dramatically altered prospects for Crescent City blacks, Amelia Cohen's response to the racial repression of the 1850s almost certainly influenced her son's ideas about race.

Walter Cohen likely gleaned political lessons from his father as well since Bernard was a vocal Lincoln and Union supporter. His political education began in earnest, however, when he served as a teenaged page in the Reconstruction state legislature. P. B. S. Pinchback, a black politician and former army officer who served as Louisiana's governor from 1872 to 1873, was one of his primary mentors. A native Mississippian, the light-skinned Pinchback regularly tangled with the more radical black Creole politicians. These idealistic Creoles wanted nothing less than a social revolution: full political and civil equality for blacks and the elimination of all racial discrimination. While not afraid to take principled stands on behalf of blacks, Pinchback was more of a realist. As a delegate to the Louisiana constitutional convention in 1867, for instance, he initially opposed an equal accommodations provision on the grounds that it required forced integration.[26]

Pinchback further distanced himself from radical Creole leaders when he accepted the Compromise of 1877, which ended Republican rule in Louisiana, in order to receive political patronage. He then solidified his standing as the Creoles' black Judas by supporting the Democrats' new state constitution in 1879. That document eliminated the 1868 constitution's prohibitions against segregated schools and public accommodations, but Pinchback endorsed it in exchange for the creation of the all-black Southern University. As the national Republican Party gave up on black southerners, Pinchback believed his course was the most reasonable way forward. "I have learned to look at things as they are and not as I would have them," he said. "This country, at least so far as the South is concerned, is a white man's country. . . . What I wish to impress upon my people, is that no change is likely to take place in our day and generation that will reverse this order of things."[27]

Believing otherwise, the Creoles continued to fight. They sued unsuccessfully to overturn first the 1877 resegregation of New Orleans public schools (as discussed in Chapter 1), and then the 1879 constitutional provisions that permitted segregation. The *Plessy* generation of Creole activists based their campaign for equal rights upon the lessons they learned directly from their radical elders. But their success in bringing their cause all the way to the US Supreme Court unintentionally codified their failure.[28]

Walter Cohen, meanwhile, applied Pinchback's Bismarckian approach to politics in order to advance himself and his people within a patently unjust system. Like his white contemporary Martin Behrman, who also embraced Catholicism over his native Judaism, he possessed an affability that served him well in both politics and business. New Orleanians of all stripes affectionately referred to him as "Captain Cohen" despite his lack of military experience. Even the Rev. Robert E. Jones, one of Cohen's less approving black peers on account of the latter's penchant for drinking and gambling, described him as "a fine man; congenial, big hearted and princely in many of his ways." But neither Cohen's peccadilloes nor his rivals' attempts to exaggerate them for political gain slowed Cohen, who could find humor in even the darkest topics. When the Ku Klux Klan reemerged following World War I, he joked that he could be its primary target since he embodied the three groups it hated the most: the Negro, the Jew, and the Catholic.[29]

By the 1890s, Cohen's prominence within the state Republican Party allowed him to stake a claim to federal patronage. After he supported William McKinley in the 1896 presidential race, McKinley appointed him registrar of lands. He remained in that post during Theodore Roosevelt's administration—largely thanks to the support he received from Booker T. Washington and influential white Republicans such as Mark Hanna. For the rest of his life, Cohen spent a good deal of time fending off Louisiana's "Lily White" Republicans, who sought to expel blacks from the party leadership. Despite Washington's entreaties to protect Cohen's "Black and Tans," Roosevelt favored paternalism and white supremacy, arguing that blacks would be best served through a white-controlled party.[30]

Despite being politically toothless in Louisiana after the 1890s, the Republican Party nevertheless gave Cohen entrée into the upper echelons of New Orleans's white power structure. His membership in numerous black benevolent associations and his founding of an insurance company in 1910, meanwhile, solidified his position vis-à-vis the black masses. Organizations such as the Odd Fellows, Knights of Pythias, San Jacinto, and Autocrat Club offered Cohen and other blacks solace from Jim Crow as well as the institutional bases for attacking it. Insurance companies served as even more significant sources of black political leadership since successful owners developed vast networks of black clients while gaining financial independence from whites. By the mid-1920s, Cohen's People's Industrial Life Insurance Company employed roughly three hundred agents, maintained customers across the state, and brought Cohen a handsome annual salary of $20,000 ($283,000 in 2017 dollars).[31]

Cohen's connections up and down the social ladder made him New Orleans's most sought after racial interlocutor. Quite often, he was the best vehicle for blacks to present their grievances to white officials. He regularly intervened with judges and politicians, for instance, in cases of police brutality against blacks. But while these intercessions might help individual suspects, Cohen's approach was incapable of spurring systemic change. As historian Arnold Hirsch notes, it was "a brand of politics that emphasized patron-client relationships both in Cohen's connections to the outside world and in his dominance within the black community." The businessman and Republican appointee's political and financial life also reflected the extent to which the elites among the oppressed in colonial systems of apartheid often had vested interests in the inequitable structures they sought to reform.[32]

Cohen's August 1914 visit to the school board with the Colored Educational Alliance fit this pattern. Although he hoped to lessen Jim Crow's impact upon blacks, he was willing to accept greater residential segregation if necessary. When requesting new school facilities, for instance, Cohen, Dunn, and Jones specifically asked the board to transfer black students from the McCarthy School, which was located in a racially mixed neighborhood, to "the colored section of the Ninth Ward." The school later moved to an area that was more heavily black. The men also did not raise any objections when the board recommended they scout alternate locations for the Fisk School deeper in the "back-of-town," in an area further removed from the more heavily white sections below Rampart Street.[33]

Cohen, Dunn, and Jones were similarly pragmatic when requesting public secondary education for blacks, and their approach here differed slightly from that of the parents of black schoolchildren. While the professional men asked the board to establish an industrial high school that included a teachers' training program, the umbrella organization for the city's black parents' clubs did not specify that the high school and accompanying teachers education department needed to have a vocational focus. This difference mirrored the national debate over black higher education that was then playing out between liberal arts proponents such as W. E. B. Du Bois and advocates of industrial training such as Booker T. Washington and his northern philanthropic allies. Historian James D. Anderson argues that the Hampton-Tuskegee model ran counter to the black masses' long-standing attempts to challenge the social order through education, since it aimed to cultivate a conservative corps of black teachers and leaders. But the debate over black secondary education in New Orleans suggested the situation was more complex. In 1914, the board was unwilling to support any high school for blacks, regardless of its focus. By requesting a vocational high school, the Colored Educational Alliance likely hoped to pry open a door that was then firmly shut. A significant number of black leaders and educators in New Orleans also supported vocational *and* classical schooling throughout the first decades of the twentieth century, a point Anderson overlooks in his discussion of black secondary education in the Crescent City. Cohen's position on the appropriate kind of secondary education for blacks also shifted according to political realities.[34]

III.

The drive for a black high school had gained momentum when the state legislature moved Southern University from New Orleans to Baton Rouge in 1913. Like Leland and New Orleans University—two of the city's three private black universities—Southern offered grammar, secondary, and postsecondary training to compensate for the school board's failure to provide middle and high school education for blacks. (Straight University, which offered degrees in medicine and law, was the third and perhaps most prestigious of the city's private black universities.) White state officials wanted to relocate Southern because they believed its urban location impeded its mission to provide vocational and particularly agricultural training to blacks. As whites began to move into the uptown neighborhood surrounding Southern's campus, they fully agreed. Several black leaders from outside of New Orleans favored the move as well since the Crescent City already had the three private colleges in addition to Southern. Joseph S. Clark, the president of Baton Rouge College and later of Southern, also wanted Louisiana to have a centrally located public black university. Trained at Leland, Howard, and the University of Chicago, Clark was a devout Washingtonian who frequently urged blacks to "live a God-fearing life, work unselfishly, do your best, and you will reap what you sow." Black New Orleanians, however, vigorously protested Southern's move and unsuccessfully took a lawsuit to the state Supreme Court in hopes of blocking it. The Orleans Parish School Board also opposed the school's relocation since it correctly anticipated that blacks would use Southern's departure to pressure it to provide black public education beyond the sixth grade.[35]

Black mothers led that charge. In July 1913, the mothers of secondary school pupils at Southern petitioned the board to "make arrangements for a colored high school, as the pupils formerly attending the Southern University are now deprived of the State High School by the decision of the Supreme Court closing the Southern University in this city."[36] The following month, the Mothers' Club from McDonogh No. 6, a black elementary school located a half-mile from the University's shuttered campus, demanded the addition of seventh grade since their children previously continued their education at Southern.[37]

After the board honored that request for 1913–1914 and then restored eighth grade the following year, black people continued to press for a high school. The city's recent focus on white secondary education partly fueled their demands. Between 1912 and 1913, the board had opened four new high school buildings for whites at a cost of nearly one million dollars. These grand facilities replaced overcrowded, makeshift structures and comprised the city's most significant investments in public education in years.[38] While blacks did not necessarily expect equivalent support for secondary education, they sought to capitalize on the city's renewed interest in high schools. New Orleans University president Charles Melden, for instance, cited these new buildings when he argued that a black high school could stem the flow of northbound migrants. If nothing else, he hoped to shame the board into action by noting that in recent years it had spent fifty times as much on white school buildings as on black ones.[39]

Grassroots activists also refused to fold in the face of these vast inequalities. In early 1915, for instance, the Parents' Club from the Bienville School, located two blocks north of Storyville, petitioned the board for a black high school.[40] The next year, the Louisiana Freedmen Baptist Association established a private high school in a black residential enclave on the city's western edge to compensate for the loss of Leland University.[41] Damage from a powerful hurricane along with pressure from white neighbors and the city government had caused Leland to abandon its campus next to Tulane University in 1915, a move that opened the door for a developer to convert the prime real estate into a whites-only residential park.[42] The Colored Educational Alliance also continued to emphasize the need for a public black high school.[43]

The closure of Southern University and the growing white demand for segregated worship prompted the Catholic Church to create its first high school for blacks in 1915. After purchasing the shuttered Southern University building on Magazine Street, the archdiocese simultaneously founded Xavier High School and the city's third racially separate parish for African Americans. Underscoring the link between segregated Catholic churches and schools, the archdiocese built the new Blessed Sacrament Church directly behind Xavier. White residents who lived nearby petitioned the city council to oppose the building's continued use "for Negro educational purposes," and they later sought to take over Blessed Sacrament Church on the grounds that the new structure was "too good for the 'niggers.'"[44]

Both of these efforts failed, however, while Xavier became a resounding success. Catholic and non-Catholic black students traveled from across the city to attend Xavier, and enrollment in Catholic middle schools swelled as families sought to prepare their children for admission to the high school. As was the case with the neighborhood surrounding the black St. Dominic Church and school, which the archdiocese had established in 1909, Xavier's neighborhood remained overwhelmingly white long after the school opened. Some of the neighborhood's white Catholics even attended Mass at Blessed Sacrament, angering black parishioners by seeking to establish segregated seating at the church expressly set aside for African Americans.[45]

When the Orleans Parish school board continued to drag its feet into 1917, Walter Cohen, Rev. Robert Jones, and Rev. Henderson Dunn returned in May of that year with a large group of black professionals and educators to demand that the board take action. Mary D. Coghill, the Bayou Road School principal, was among those to sign a petition outlining the group's numerous requests. As had been the case three years earlier, these black leaders presented the high school as one plank in a larger platform of demands that included the creation of night schools, industrial training for boys, and additional facilities to accommodate the swelling enrollments at the Bienville, Miro, and Fisk

Schools, among others. In a subtle shift from their 1914 position, they asked for the inclusion of industrial and teachers' training courses within a regular high school instead of a strictly industrial high school that also trained teachers. As the black Interdenominational Ministers' Alliance made clear in a separate resolution supporting the drive for the high school, black New Orleanians wanted a secondary institution that would "serve *to the largest extent* our people in this great city."[46]

IV.

The school board finally bent to the accumulated pressure from civic leaders and the growing number of black grammar school graduates in July 1917, when it announced that its budget for the upcoming academic year would include money for a black high school. The *Times-Picayune* applauded the move, noting blacks' lengthy campaign for the school and the growing consensus among black and white leaders that better school facilities could improve race relations and slow the Great Migration. Yet the initial proposal was quite modest: the board intended to locate the new school within an existing one, providing only those funds necessary to pay the handful of instructors who would teach secondary courses.[47] A recently passed municipal ordinance pertaining to prostitutes, however, inadvertently strengthened blacks' hand. That legislation, which historian Alecia Long identified as "the city's first residential segregation ordinance based primarily on racial criteria," required black prostitutes to live in the Uptown vice district where Louis Armstrong grew up. Fisk Elementary School sat directly across the street from this area.[48]

Blacks complained that an area designated for prostitute housing was not the appropriate location for a school, and the school board agreed.[49] Stating that Fisk was "no longer suitable for school purposes," the board voted on August 24, 1917, to close Fisk and transfer its black students to the McDonogh No. 13 School on South Rampart Street (see figure 3.2). To enable that transition to take place, the board decided that it would reassign the white students who had attended McDonogh No. 13 to "other schools in the immediate neighborhood." Additionally, the board announced that part of the McDonogh No. 13 building would "be rearranged and converted into a Colored High School."[50]

Since McDonogh No. 13 was significantly larger and sturdier than Fisk's already overcrowded facility, the board's decision was a notable success for black New Orleanians.[51] White residents, however, considered it a coup and quickly mounted a counteroffensive. Sophia Jacobson, a McDonogh No. 13 parent who lived directly across South Rampart Street from the school, spearheaded the protest. She hurriedly corralled her white neighbors to attend a meeting on Monday, August 27, where twenty-four mothers of McDonogh students initially joined her in signing a petition opposing the school's conversion from white to black. About forty men and women presented that petition to the school board the following evening, and the number of petition signatories swelled to 645 white adults and 584 white children by the time the residents appeared before the board again on September 7.[52] Protest leaders also filed a lawsuit against the school board in civil district court in hopes of blocking the conversion.[53]

The most vocal protestors were overwhelmingly Jewish immigrants whose families lived and owned retail and service shops along South Rampart Street. All but one of the petition's initial signers lived on South Rampart Street, and nearly all of them had recognizably Jewish surnames.[54] Like Jacobson, whose husband was a German-born tailor, most of these women were immigrants whose families owned their own stores. Rosa Rubenstein, for instance, was an Austrian-American mother of four school-aged children whose Russian-born husband was a dry goods merchant. The eldest son of Carrie Dulitz, a widowed mother of six, owned a clothing store, as did the husband of Fannie Gordon, another Russian immigrant. Lecia Woshastrom's husband Abraham repaired shoes. The petition's initial signatories also included Tillie Karnofsky. Like other South Rampart Street Jews, the Karnofskys' clothing and variety store was only one of the family's several businesses. They also ran a junk wagon and delivered coal, employing the teenaged Louis Armstrong for both ventures. The aspiring musician played a tin horn to entice children to deposit recyclable rags and bottles on the junk wagon he rode with Tillie's son Alex, and his coal distribution route brought him into the jazz hotbed of Storyville for the first time.[55]

The Jewish protestors raised several objections to McDonogh No. 13's conversion from white to black. They worried that their children would have to travel too far to reach their new schools and that they would have to cross dangerous streetcar and railroad tracks to get there. They complained that the school board should not abandon a "suitable" school building such as Fisk when education funding was insufficient and facilities were in such great demand. They also incorrectly claimed that John McDonogh, the millionaire slaveholder whose bequest to New Orleans paid for the construction of Mc-Donogh No. 13 and many of the city's other public schools bearing his name, left money only for the education of white children. McDonogh's will, in fact, explicitly directed funds toward the education of poor children "of both sexes and of all Classes and Castes or Color."[56]

The protestors' overriding concern, however, was the future of their neighborhood, which they considered to be directly linked to the racial identity that McDonogh No. 13 conferred upon it. The white residents' lawsuit, along with their other statements opposing the conversion, highlighted the connections that they believed existed between schools, race, and urban development. The men who filed the lawsuit, all of whom owned property fronting South Rampart, plainly stated that McDonogh No. 13's continuation as a white school was central to their twin goals of "maintaining the identity of South Rampart Street as a business thoroughfare and excluding therefrom large numbers of people of the colored race." The plaintiffs also noted that some of them bought real estate near McDonogh No. 13 "with the knowledge that said school was being used for the education of white children," and they argued that South Rampart Street became "a business thoroughfare rivaling in extent and in importance the busiest thoroughfares in this or other cities" partly because white merchants owned its shops. The conversion of McDonogh No. 13 into a black school, the suit alleged, "will destroy the efficiency and adaptability of the said South Rampart Street as one of the business thoroughfares of this city by creating a congestion, and the gathering thereon, of large numbers of people of the colored race." The petitioners worried that this would cause property values to plummet.[57]

These arguments mirrored those that white residents in West Baltimore marshalled in 1901 to protest the proposed conversion of the under-enrolled English-German School into that city's first high school for blacks, the Colored High School and Polytechnic Institute. "We are not actuated by race prejudice," one conversion opponent said. "But we desire to preserve the value of our property, which has taken some of us a lifetime of hard work to accumulate." Nine years later, another white resident in Baltimore, whose racially mixed residential patterns closely resembled those in New Orleans, similarly complained that the conversion of a white school to black use would draw blacks to that city's Northwest Side. These claims had earlier antecedents as well, most notably in antebellum Boston, where white residents opposed the location of a black school in their Beacon Hill neighborhood for fear that it would decrease property values and spur social decay. Speaking in support of the protestors, former Boston mayor Harrison Gray Otis argued that "the respectable citizens who are now building and improving that part of the city will be . . . forced to desert it."[58]

To bolster their arguments, the Jewish protestors in New Orleans repeatedly—and preposterously—claimed that their neighborhood was lily white. "This neighborhood is inhabited by white people," they stated in their petition.[59] "Very few colored people reside in that neighborhood," Sophia Jacobson wrote to the editor of the *Daily States* newspaper.[60] "The neighborhood is 90 per cent white," Rampart Street grain dealer Ira Weingrun told the school board.[61]

To a certain extent, they knew they were stretching the truth. In 1910, for instance, a light-skinned black woman named Gibb lived with her four children on the other side of the rented double that housed the Jacobsons' home and tailor shop. The black druggist George Hart lived next door to Ms. Gibb. It is hard to imagine that the Gibbs and Jacobsons never interacted given that Gibb's son Edward and Jacobson's son Abraham were the exact same age. Weingrun could not avoid the neighborhood's black residents either. His hay and feed shop stood directly across Rampart from Hart's drug store. Like Jacobson and Weingrun, Hart was still in the same spot in 1920. But by that time Coleman Brown, a black warehouse laborer, and his wife Louisa, a chambermaid, lived next door with their seven children, Coleman's sister Elizabeth, and her daughter Myrtle. Adolph and Annie Polmer, who were particularly active opponents of McDonogh No. 13's conversion, lived next to the Browns.[62] Even the Jewish merchants' claim in their lawsuit that they wanted to exclude blacks from South Rampart Street strained credulity since they largely depended upon black customers for their livelihood.[63]

What, then, explained the white protestors' seemingly bold-faced dishonesty? Quite possibly, their mendacity was the product of a Jim Crow–induced cognitive dissonance. Since their daily proximity to blacks defied the idea of a clearly demarcated racial hierarchy, they viewed and described their neighborhood as they believed it to be rather than as it actually was. Most likely, they did not recognize their dishonesty, for while they lived adjacent to and depended upon black people as customers, they did not socialize with them and they certainly did not consider them to be members of their community.[64]

More significantly, however, the protestors' false claims about the area's racial composition reflected their understanding that they and their neighborhood faced an uncertain future. Few doubted South Rampart Street's vitality as a retail corridor. But at a time when cities were increasingly exploring physical and statutory distinctions between both residential and commercial zones as well as different types of residential areas (as discussed in Chapter 2), the neighborhood's continuation as a place for respectable (i.e., white) people to live was very much in doubt. Demonstrating their understanding of the racial calculus that devalued property located near African Americans, the Jewish protestors made a play to protect their future. By distorting the area's demographics, they hoped to preserve the white school that they believed would cement their neighborhood's white status. In doing so, they asserted that they deserved special material privileges and protections because they were white.[65]

To recognize their precarious position within New Orleans's social and economic order, South Rampart Street's Jewish merchants needed only to consider the noisy, cramped, and increasingly industrial space surrounding McDonogh No. 13. Scrap metal, coal, and lumber yards dotted several neighborhood corners, and foundries fouled the air. The New Basin Canal and a tangle of train tracks had long blocked the area's western edge. In 1911, the construction of four railroad terminals, each 80 feet wide and 550 feet long, created an additional boundary immediately north of the school. That project obliterated the seven residential blocks between Girod, Poydras, Saratoga, and North Robertson that were directly above McDonogh No. 13 and necessitated the closure of another white elementary school, Samuel J. Peters. Many of the houses that remained in McDonogh No. 13's neighborhood were dilapidated, and its numerous barrooms benefited from their proximity to "black Storyville." McDonogh No. 13's enrollment was declining, and crime was also a problem. In the previous three years, police had arrested 1,410 people in the three blocks immediately below the school.[66]

Given these conditions and the city's demonstrated reluctance to support areas with large black populations, the white protestors were understandably concerned about the impact McDonogh No. 13's conversion would have upon their neighborhood. Several months earlier, in fact, the character and fate of the South Rampart Street corridor had generated a significant amount of public discussion when a railroad company proposed building a new passenger terminal there. During that debate, as would be the case with the fight over McDonogh No. 13, public officials repeatedly pointed to the presence of black residents as a sign of the entire area's depravity. City leaders, however, divided over the best way to respond to this situation. Some supported the passenger terminal because it would reduce the area's black population while others argued that no degree of redevelopment could save the area from its black menace. Faced with these alternatives, the McDonogh No. 13's supporters attempted to define the area as a white neighborhood. By stating that fiction publicly, they believed that they could make it reality and preserve the one institution that gave it substance. But the debate surrounding the passenger terminal suggested their chances of success were slim.

V.

In March 1917 the Louisiana Railway and Navigation Company (L. R. & N.) sought permission from the city's legislative body (known as the Commission Council) to build a new passenger station directly across the street from McDonogh No. 13. L. R. & N.'s plan called for its acquisition of the properties lining the uptown side of Girod Street along the three blocks from South Rampart to South Liberty. By late March, the railroad company had acquired all but seven of the roughly thirty-five properties it hoped to purchase.[67]

The L. R. & N.'s permit application appeared headed for approval until the city's commissioner of public utilities issued a report that was critical of the project. That report reached its conclusions based on opposition to the project from the public school district as well as the owners of properties that would abut either the new station or the tracks leading to it. After the company provided school officials with more details, the superintendent and school board withdrew their opposition and, in L.R. & N.'s words, "admitted that the tearing down of the dilapidated residences and eating and drinking places for negroes on Girod Street from Rampart to Liberty would greatly improve the neighborhood and would be to the advantage of the school." But the dissident property owners, including the Killeen Foundry two blocks north of McDonogh No. 13, remained opposed. Although the Commission Council followed the public utilities commissioner's recommendation and voted down the L. R. & N.'s application, it agreed to reconsider the matter following a hearing.[68]

As would be the case in the fight over McDonogh No. 13, the debate over the passenger terminal revolved around competing perceptions of the Rampart Street neighborhood. Proponents of the terminal trumpeted it as an up-

and-coming commercial district while opponents characterized it as a nuisance zone. In both battles, the neighborhood's critics pointed to the presence of black residents and the businesses catering to them as evidence of the area's blight. Commissioner of Public Utilities E. J. Glenny opposed the project, in part, because the surrounding area included many "second-hand shops, negro barrooms and cook shops and is generally undesirable for a passenger depot, which would have to be used by ladies and children who would perchance wish to travel on the Louisiana Railway & Navigation Company's trains."[69] Glenny's implication that the neighborhood was suitable for the white women who already lived there but not for traveling "ladies" likely offended Rampart Street's Jewish merchants, who owned many of the second-hand shops to which the commissioner referred.

The railroad company responded to Glenny's critique by stating that its proposed station would eliminate the neighborhood's "only really objectionable features" by razing "the last of the dilapidated residence buildings in the three blocks of Girod Street" between Rampart and Liberty. It also pointed out that the Rampart Street neighborhood compared favorably with the location of its existing passenger terminal, which faced the brothels along the Basin Street entrance to Storyville. Business groups shared the L. R. & N.'s enthusiasm that South Rampart Street was "rapidly improving and this improvement will be hastened by the erection of the depot."[70] The terminal's supporters included the Contractors' and Dealers' Exchange, the Board of Trade, and the New Orleans Real Estate Board, which contended that the new station would boost travel and industry in the Crescent City. New Orleans's powerful mayor Martin Behrman also offered his support for the project, provided L. R. & N. acquired additional property in the neighborhood to provide trains with a wider passageway into the new station. "I do not think it consistent with public interest to allow the L. R. & N. into the city through a narrow chute in Rampart Street," the mayor said. "Let the L. R. & N. be *white*, and buy sufficient property for their right of way."[71]

Behrman likely meant that the rail line should be *wide*, not that it should be "white," by eliminating the black tenements that stood in its three-block path along Girod Street. But regardless of the mayor's intended meaning, Glenny focused his criticism on those buildings and others like them. Much of the commissioner's unfavorable report on the project, in fact, hinged on the number of blacks living in or frequenting the neighborhood. In particular, Glenny would dispute L. R. & N.'s claim that "the only really objectionable features of the neighborhood will be removed" when it demolished the Girod Street residential structures. He also challenged the company's and business leaders' claims that South Rampart Street was rapidly improving "since immediately adjacent to the upper line of the Louisiana Railway and Navigation Company's property is a row of six or seven tenement negro dwellings, one of which is apparently built upon the party line and overlooking the depot, and in, what will remain of the said 'three blocks' there are presently twenty houses in which negroes live and upon one of which a raid was made last week resulting in seven or eight arrests."[72]

Based on his correspondence with L. R. & N. president William Edenborn, Glenny doubted the company would buy any additional property "to remove any of the remaining 'objectionable features.'" He also questioned the boosters' contention that the proposed station would, in his words, "change the character of a long established neighborhood." Passenger terminals, he wrote, were more likely to encourage the establishment of rooming houses than single family homes and were unlikely to "appeal to manufacturing establishments, since they offer no great facilities for the movement of freight." In the conclusion to his report, Glenny castigated Edenborn for claiming that the existing passenger terminal's proximity to Storyville, not its cost, was the reason he wanted a new depot. It was better for visitors to enter New Orleans opposite a prostitution district, Glenny contended, than through a black neighborhood. "My suggestion that [Edenborn] remain where he is was born of a desire to prevent him from subjecting the public to contact with the denizens of a neighborhood both darker as to the color of its habitués as well as to the crimes therein committed," he wrote.[73] Ultimately, L. R. & N.'s bid for the new station collapsed when the railroad company was unable to come to terms with a property owner who feared that the trains scheduled to run past his building would damage it. Glenny backed the property owners who were concerned about potential damage, refusing even to consider a letter Edenborn wrote to him seeking reconsideration of the L. R. & N. proposal.[74]

Three months later, Glenny's characterization of the South Rampart Street neighborhood appeared to inform the Jewish merchants' tactics as they fought to preserve McDonogh No. 13 as a white school. In addition to rebutting the commissioner's claims about the area's racial composition, they also countered his depiction of the neighborhood's depravity. Speaking before the school board on August 28, Ira Weingrun "referred to several improved places and said there was one place where $17,000 had been spent recently to make one store one of the finest in the city." As the protestors constructed their alternate narrative of a hard-scrabble neighborhood on the rise, they received a welcome assist from Captain John Fitzpatrick, who became the lead plaintiff in their lawsuit against the school board. The Third Ward's longtime political boss, the seventy-three-year-old Fitzpatrick served as mayor from 1892 to 1896. He was a large, garrulous man who had refereed bareknuckle boxing matches and courted organized labor as well as black voters before the machine strayed from those constituencies. Although his advancing age was evident in the halting signature he affixed to the lawsuit, he remained a powerful spokesman for the Third Ward's ambitious immigrants.[75]

After Weingrun addressed the school board on August 28, Fitzpatrick argued "that the citizens surrounding the school are good citizens and taxpayers."[76] In a later appearance before the board, he again touted the improvements made along Rampart Street "and referred to the $1,200,000 assessed valuation of property in Rampart between Canal and Julia streets." He and other speakers at that meeting prophesied that Rampart Street would become "a business street the peer of any in the city."[77]

The woman who ignited the challenge to McDonogh No. 13's conversion also challenged the portrait of neighborhood dereliction that Glenny had painted before the Commission Council. The men and women, however, couched their protest in gendered terms. Unlike the men, who emphasized the money residents had pumped into neighborhood businesses and the potential for diminished property values, women like Jacobson and McDonogh No. 13 Mothers' Club president Esther Blumenthal stressed both their duty as mothers to protect their children and their previous work to improve the school. The women, for instance, filed a separate petition of intervention to accompany the men's lawsuit in order to highlight the danger their children would face if they had to cross streetcar and railroad tracks to reach other white schools.[78] Building upon the men's argument that their investment in the neighborhood deserved to be rewarded, the women suggested that their commitment to the school also deserved recognition. "The board knows the Mothers' Club of McDonogh 13 has worked for the benefit of that school," one mother wrote to the *Picayune* editor, "and have done all they could within the last year to lessen the expense, by buying books for the school."[79] Jacobson continued in a similar vein: "We are constantly doing something to improve or aid the school, and it should be permitted to remain."[80] Blumenthal even offered "a prayer from the mothers" in hopes of swaying the all-male school board: "If you are fathers do not forsake us," she said, "let us have our old school."[81]

While black residents mostly stayed away from the school board meetings where their white neighbors aired their grievances about McDonogh No. 13's conversion, they did not remain silent about the high school they had been promised.[82] F. P. Ricard, a well-known black educator, likely spoke for many black residents when he loosed a torrent of criticism upon the protestors. "What! Mr. Editor, Messrs. School Board, Mr. and Mrs. General Public," he wrote in a letter to the *Item*, "is the tardy act of justice to the hundred thousand negroes of this city, the purpose of the authorities to open a high school for them this fall to be frustrated for the poorest and meanest of reasons?" Ricard continued by calling the protestors' objections a sham, particularly their claim that 90 percent of the neighborhood's residents were white:

> Despite the most patent evidence to the contrary, what a miserable excuse for a reason, especially since these whites are there engaged in business, and most likely no less than 90 per cent of their customers are negroes. That a people should be welcome in hordes to buy second-hand clothes, shoes, hats and pistols, feast on cheap food, soak in grog and etc., but objected to when they come in quest of education may be perfectly consistent but assuredly not appealing to the right-minded.

Ricard also impugned the protestors' arguments that their investment in the neighborhood entitled them to keep McDonogh No. 13. "Are we then to be humiliated with the dictum that wherever 'so much has been spent' on the improvement of property that it is too good for the improvement of human beings if they happen to be black?" he wrote. He then concluded with a bold threat leveled directly at the protestors: "Permit the suggestion that it is the very step you are taking instead of the presence of a negro high school that is fraught with harm to your precious property and the prosperity of the community. Some of the negroes are going to begin right now to withhold from you the patronage that has enabled you to make your vicinity too good for a school for their sons and daughters."[83] While Ricard correctly predicted that most blacks would not boycott the Rampart Street shops, his warning prefigured the mass action that blacks took against the city's Jewish merchants forty-three years later.[84]

The protest against McDonogh No. 13's conversion reached its climax on September 14, when a large delegation from the school's Parents' Club packed the school board's Friday evening meeting. Accompanied "by the applause and appeals of more than two hundred lusty-lunged youngsters," the white protestors again complained that changing the school's racial designation would degrade neighborhood property values and endanger their children. One particularly agitated woman warned the school board that its move could spark a race riot on the scale of the so-called Battle of Liberty Place, which took place forty-three years earlier to the day.[85] During that Reconstruction-era fight, originally known as the Battle of September Fourteenth, the Crescent White League made a failed attempt to violently overthrow the state's ruling biracial coalition.[86]

But the protestors failed to sway the board, whose Committee on Teachers and Instruction had prepared a lengthy report on the school conversion in advance of the meeting. The committee began the report by emphasizing the time and care it took before making a decision. In particular, its author J. Zach Spearing, a leading real estate attorney, noted the committee's two visits to the neighborhood to assess its conditions and the validity of the protestors' claims. The report offered several justifications for the conversion. First, it noted that the "increasing encroachment of commercial houses of various, numerous, and sundry characters into the territory adjacent to McDonogh No. 13" had contributed to the drop in white enrollment at the school. Just as the construction of the Illinois Central rail sheds had forced the relocation of the Samuel J. Peters School, the report noted, the spread of commercial activity surrounding McDonogh No. 13 necessitated its closure. Second, the report reiterated the need to relocate black students from Fisk in light of the restricted district for black prostitutes. Finally, and most importantly, the board rejected the protestors' claim that its decision would turn the area into a black neighborhood.[87]

Instead, it argued that its decision merely affirmed the neighborhood's existing identity as a black area. Believing that its decision could not create what already existed, the committee wrote that there was no "justification for the suggestion that by locating the colored pupils in the building of McDonogh No. 13 this board is converting a white district into a negro one; certainly such was not the intention of the Board nor do we think such will be the result of this action." The report went on to catalogue the numerous buildings that already marked the neighborhood as black in its mind. These included the "negro tenement house immediately adjacent to McDonogh No. 13 on Girod Street end" and the "twenty-three negro barrooms and twenty negro barber shops" near the school.[88]

Before concluding his report, Spearing took a subtle swipe at the white protestors. Noting that the establishment of bars required approval from a majority of the residents and property owners within three hundred feet of the proposed location, Spearing interpreted the presence of so many drinking establishments as a sign of the white residents' tolerance for their neighborhood's less refined features. He wrote:

> The conclusion is irresistible that a majority of the present residents and property holders of the area referred to either consented to the establishment of the negro barrooms within that area or that such residents and property holders moved into or acquired their holdings within that area after the negro barrooms were established.

Given the number of black businesses in the neighborhood, Spearing wrapped up, "it can hardly be contended that the location of a negro school in the building of McDonogh No. 13 . . . can or will have any effect upon the locality." As a sop to McDonogh No. 13's former white patrons and "to avoid confusion in the future," the committee recommended the school's name change from McDonogh No. 13 to McDonogh No. 35.[89]

On the surface, the board's contention that it did not seek to change the Rampart Street corridor from a white to a black district appeared to absolve it from any involvement with residential segregation. But the board's rationale did not contradict its interest in using public schools to strengthen distinctions between black and white neighborhoods. Spearing, after all, argued that the very features that made the area unsuitable for white residents and a white school, namely its increasingly decadent, commercial character, made it the appropriate place for blacks to live and learn. This thinking both reflected and perpetuated a vicious cycle in which officials steered blacks toward the least hospitable neighborhoods, which in turn received limited protections because they were considered black.

The board's claims to the contrary notwithstanding, the neighborhood's demographics, the white parents' protest, and the earlier battle over the railroad terminal demonstrated that the area's future and racial identity were anything but settled questions in 1917. Yet just as the Jewish residents myopically claimed that their neighborhood was white, the school board ignored the area's actual composition and history to label it black. The Jewish residents fought the conversion of McDonogh No. 13 so vociferously because they feared the change would formalize the school board's assessment of their neighborhood, which was precisely what Spearing aimed to do. The entire episode revealed a significant shift in the Crescent City's racial order. After two hundred years of racially heterogeneous housing patterns, white residents and officials were ready for a change. Affixing labels to the old, racially mixed neighborhoods was the first step in the sorting process, and it invariably involved winners and losers.

VI.

The character, composition, and racial identity of the area surrounding McDonogh No. 13 changed dramatically following its conversion to McDonogh No. 35. Whereas white high schools often served as anchors that encouraged residential development, public investment, and zoning protections (the topic of Chapter Five), the opposite happened around McDonogh 35. Rather than build up the residential area surrounding the school, developers and city leaders slowly tore it down. The area's transformation into a disposable neighborhood was all the more dramatic considering that 35 (as it is often known today) was among New Orleans's preeminent educational institutions. Its high school enrollment leapt from a modest 143 in its first year of operation to more than 2,000 by 1930.[90] Its early faculty also included some of the city's most distinguished and erudite black residents. Lionel Hoffman, the school's founding principal, was a former college professor who had worked as a marine biologist in Florence, Italy, and as the director of agriculture for the British colonial administration in Nigeria. O. C. W. Taylor, later editor of the *Louisiana Weekly*, taught math. Charles Rousséve, whose 1937 study of black Louisiana's history and literature continues to receive scholarly attention today, taught English, and George Longe, a noted bibliophile and Louisiana Federation of Teachers stalwart, taught geometry. McDonogh 35 also educated many of the men and women who later provided leadership within the local Civil Rights Movement and black political structure.[91]

Like African American students who attended underfunded and overcrowded segregated schools elsewhere, students contrasted McDonogh 35's ramshackle building with the caliber of its teachers. While this and other black schools in New Orleans were not free from the class- or culture-based inequities that plagued white schools, it nevertheless earned its reputation for excellence. "The building [was] so old it was crumbling. It was old and gloomy and dark," recalled Ruth Cappie, who graduated from the school in the 1930s. "And they had classrooms in the basement part and they were dark and the basement was dark. . . . [But] we had very good teachers and we had a principal, he was eccentric but he had the good of the students at heart."[92]

In the decades following McDonogh No. 35's creation, however, perhaps no section of New Orleans experienced as much demolition, residential displacement, and redevelopment as this one.[93] The destruction followed close on the heels of the white residents' unsuccessful effort to block the transformation of McDonogh No. 13 into McDonogh 35. In 1924, for instance, a new passenger terminal opened on the site across Girod Street from McDonogh 35 that the Louisiana Railway and Navigation Company had eyed seven years earlier. The construction of the station and the tracks leading to it required the demolition of roughly four dozen residential properties on the three blocks between Julia, Girod, South Rampart, and South Liberty. Similarly, Charity Hospital's 1929 construction of a tuberculosis ward at the corner of LaSalle (formerly Howard) and Gravier swallowed up much of the housing on one of the blocks that formerly comprised "black Storyville." The city's comprehensive zoning ordinance, also dating to 1929, aided these changes since it gave the area the lowest level of residential protection.[94]

The pace of destruction then accelerated after World War II, when the city targeted much of the property lining South Saratoga between Julia and Gravier for demolition and expropriation to accommodate street widening and the construction of a municipal government complex that included the present-day city hall. That complex and other redevelopment projects eventually devoured most of black Storyville's remaining housing stock, and parking lots quickly proliferated between that area and McDonogh 35. Some of the black residents whom the municipal complex displaced resettled in the segregated Magnolia and Calliope Housing Projects, which were located further uptown and deeper in the city's traditional back of town.[95] But many were not as fortunate. "Hundreds of Negro families are being rendered homeless by the City of New Orleans in its modernization program and by the Housing Authority of New Orleans in its expansion program," the black journalist John E. Rousseau vented to Mayor DeLesseps "Chep" Morrison in 1952. A similar process of "Negro removal" packaged as "urban renewal" transpired in cities across the country as white policymakers and businessmen razed black neighborhoods near central business districts in hopes of boosting downtown property values.[96]

The school board contributed to the area's rapidly declining *tout ensemble* by minimizing its investment in the McDonogh 35 building. By 1921, the school had already outgrown the building it inherited from McDonogh No. 13 four years earlier. The building's 565 high school students reflected a four-fold increase from the 1917–1918 school year, and they continued to share the space with hundreds of elementary students.[97] Another thirteen hundred used the buildings at night as an evening school. To resolve the space crunch, the board spent $6,000 in the spring of 1921 to return the twelve-room Fisk building adjacent to the former black Storyville to "satisfactory condition" for use as an annex to McDonogh No. 35.[98] Soon after, the board renamed Fisk the A. P. Williams School and reestablished it as an elementary school independent from McDonogh No. 35, which continued solely as a high school.[99]

But these moves only shifted the problem three blocks deeper into the more blighted and more heavily black back of town. While prostitution persisted near the Fisk/Williams site despite the city's official elimination of its vice districts in 1917, school officials no longer expressed concern over the school's proximity to brothels. When black petitioners asked the board in 1924 to either move the school or eliminate the vice district surrounding it, the board failed to act.[100] The removal of elementary students from McDonogh No. 35 also did little to ameliorate that building's inadequacy. As the high school's enrollment approached eight hundred in 1922, one board member reported "that conditions existing at McDonogh No. 35 were the worst in the City." Concerned that the use of the basement for manual training could spark a fire, the board member recommended moving that department to another building and converting the basement into three additional classrooms to ease the school's overcrowding. The superintendent responded by suggesting that the board transfer McDonogh No. 35's manual training department to another black school, which already ran a double session to accommodate its numerous elementary students.[101] While it is unclear whether the board acted on the superintendent's recommendation, its relative neglect of black facilities reinforced the blight that its predecessors believed suited certain neighborhoods for black students.

Table 3.1 Population in the McDonogh No. 13/35 Sample Area, 1910–1930

Year	Total Population (#)	Black Population (%)
1910	2,796	31
1920	2,132	45
1930	987	53

Source: US Census, New Orleans, LA, Population, 1910–1930, National Archives Microfilm Series (NAMS) T-624, reel 520, NAMS T-625, reel 618, and NAMS 5163, Reel 21. Compilation and analysis by the author.

A noticeable demographic shift also accompanied the area's physical changes. As evident in table 3.1, seven years before McDonogh No. 13's conversion, nearly one-third of the residents in the eighteen-square-block area surrounding the school were black. (This is the area blocked off in map 3.3.) While Rampart Street had long served as an unofficial division between the white "front of town" closer to the river and the black "back of town," that line was fairly porous. In 1910, for instance, nearly half the residents living in the back of town above Rampart (closer to S. Liberty Street) were black versus slightly more than a fifth below Rampart Street (closer to Carondelet Street). By 1920, blacks comprised close to half the overall area's population of 2,132 men, women, and children, but the black population was more evenly divided between the section above and below Rampart. By 1930, however, more than half the area's residents were black and the black population was particularly concentrated in the back of town. The total population had also dropped sharply to 987, which reflected the decrease in the area's housing stock as a result of demolition and redevelopment. The changes on McDonogh No.13/35's block were perhaps most pronounced. While 39 percent of its 187 residents were black in 1920, 72 percent of its 126 residents were black in 1930.[102]

As these demographic shifts unfolded, public officials, bankers, and real estate agents increasingly characterized the areas near McDonogh 35 as black neighborhoods. Like Glenny and Spearing before them, they too deemed black areas inherently undesirable. The federal Home Owners' Loan Corporation's residential security maps and accompanying surveys provided particularly vivid examples of the durability of this line of thinking. These maps famously rated and color-coded the residential sections of the nation's major cities according to their investment risk. Like the Federal Housing Administration's more influential lending guidelines, they portrayed areas with black residents as unwise investments. The areas shaded in green on the maps were the "best," those in blue were "still desirable," the yellow sections were "definitely declining," and the red ones were "hazardous." Both the 1936 and 1939 New Orleans maps shaded the residential areas nearest McDonogh 35 red.[103]

To justify the grade, the report accompanying the 1936 map noted the three railroad tracks that cut through the area, two of which happened to terminate on blocks opposite McDonogh 35. The report also explained that "there is a heavy concentration of negro population and many of the cheaper type of double cottages and very poorly maintained. . . . Population consists largely of negroes of low class with some whites living in the southern part of the area." While at least one scholar has questioned the extent to which the HOLC maps and reports—as opposed to other federal policies—actually influenced lending practices and perpetuated residential segregation, they nevertheless provide a reliable snapshot of local attitudes since New Orleans real estate agents and bankers signed off on them. In 1936, for instance, five local real estate agents and the head of real estate sales at the Whitney National Bank, which was one of the city's most influential financial institutions, approved the HOLC's neighborhood classifications. In 1939, an even larger number of local real estate luminaries collaborated with the HOLC's field agents to generate the map and area descriptions.[104] That year's survey also explicitly linked certain neighborhoods' "hazardous" ratings and black identities to the presence of black schools, which its authors assumed to be of lower quality than white ones. The survey's brief description of one black enclave began with the following: "An area of predominantly cheaply constructed cottages occupied by Negroes. Large Negro school in area. Most all streets are gravel." In cities across the country, HOLC surveyors similarly gave low ratings to neighborhoods with inadequate municipal services and schools that they deemed second-rate.[105]

As the destruction of the McDonogh 35 area's housing stock attests, the connection that local powerbrokers made between race, schools, and blight was anything but incidental. At the very least, the city's willingness to destroy black neighborhoods, which were often recognized as such because they had black schools, revealed its blatant disregard for black residential stability. It also stood in marked contrast to the services and protections lavished upon white neighborhoods.

- - - - - - - - - - - - - - - - -

It would be foolish to single out the conversion of McDonogh No. 13 from white to black as the sole cause of its neighborhood's physical and demographic changes. The area, after all, was already teetering on the brink in 1917. But the conversion was a turning point for the neighborhood since it both formally marked it as a black area and established the rationale that would justify its later destruction. Examining the school's genesis within the context of New Orleans's shifting race relations also highlights two significant developments within southern and urban history. First, it reveals segregation's evolution from a means of maintaining social order to a system of social as well as spatial control. Second, it shows the prominent role public schools played in that shift.

Public schools became an even more powerful tool for promoting residential segregation after a slate of business-friendly reformers gained control of the school board during the early 1920s. While Martin Behrman's machine was generally as willing as business leaders to conflate private benefits with public welfare, the political scientist George Reynolds wryly noted in 1936 that its support for business was not absolute. "In most cases involving the simple choice of public versus private interest," Reynolds wrote, "the Machine supported private interest except when its own political welfare was involved."[106]

Since the machine's opponents typically emphasized private interests over political exigency, they struggled to overcome Behrman's superior political operation. The mayor's Choctaw Club relied on patronage, strict control of elections, and a disciplined system of ward and precinct captains to block challenges from self-styled reformers. While machine opponents twice changed the structure of the New Orleans school board in hopes of wresting it from Behrman's control, the artful mayor outflanked them each time. In 1912, for instance, reformers convinced the legislature to replace New Orleans's seventeen-member, ward-based board with a five-member body elected at large—a strategy similar to that which Progressive-era reformers successfully pursued in numerous cities, including New York, Detroit, and Philadelphia. But Behrman parried by pushing through legislation that called for the almost immediate election of the new school board. When voters went to the polls in the fall of 1912, Behrman's candidates won all five seats.[107]

Reformers finally outfoxed the Choctaws in 1920, however. After a falling out with Behrman, outgoing Governor Rufus Pleasant lubricated reformist candidate John M. Parker Jr.'s path to the statehouse by doling out thousands of jobs to antimachine voters. Parker's equally liberal distribution of patronage, coupled with an aggressive smear campaign and the passage of women's suffrage, secured Andrew J. McShane's victory over Behrman in the 1920 mayoral election. Antimachine candidates Percy Moise and Fannie Baumgartner, the first woman to win elective office in Louisiana, also secured six-year terms on the Orleans Parish School Board that year. With Fred Zengel's and James Fortier's election to the board in 1922, the reformers gained control of the schools.[108]

As in other cities, the reform board in New Orleans was closely aligned with local business interests, particularly in real estate.[109] Zengel worked as a real estate attorney while the jack-of-all-commercial-trades Fortier practiced law, ran the Commercial Credit Co. bank, and was a director, attorney, and past president for the mortgage-issuing Pyramid Homestead Association.[110] Fellow reformer Percy Moise managed credit for a company that imported tons of coffee annually through the Port of New Orleans, and the husband of Fannie Baumgartner, who was a homemaker, worked for a grain dealer.[111] Daniel J. Murphy, the lone machine ally to remain on the board, boasted similarly strong business and real estate credentials. A lawyer and notary, Murphy was president of the Panama Realty Company. He also maintained a long-standing relationship with the Orleans Homestead Association, on whose board he had served alongside his former school board colleague and machine stalwart Joseph Reuther, who was a baker.[112]

As Murphy demonstrated, the antimachine coalition's professional ties were not exceptional within the broader history of New Orleans's at-large school board. While the older and larger ward-based board included a mix of businessmen, professionals, skilled tradesmen, and municipal employees, commercial elites—most notably real estate professionals—dominated the five-member citywide board.[113] From its creation in 1912 until the United States' entry into World War II, at least thirteen of the twenty-seven people who served on the at-large board had direct connections to the local real estate industry. Those thirteen included three real estate attorneys, three executives and three board members for mortgage lenders, one realty company president (Murphy), an executive at one of the city's largest banks, a building contractor, and the head of a fire insurance company. In addition to these men, two others were attorneys who occasionally handled property transactions, and at least one other (a prominent restaurateur) served as a director for a homestead association prior to joining the school board. The members without clear real estate ties included company chiefs, accountants, and salesmen.[114]

Beyond their opposition to Behrman's machine, the diverse lot of reformers who gained control of the school board in the 1920s hoped to create a more orderly and economically productive society by expanding the system of segregation. Housing and education figured prominently in this vision of social and economic reform. The replacement facility for the Bayou Road School provided the new 1922 board majority with an early opportunity to tackle both of these fronts at the same time. Despite internal divisions and black protests, they managed to snatch victory from the jaws of defeat.

- - - - - - - - - - - - - - - - -

CHAPTER FOUR

BAYOU ROAD

When James Fortier joined the Orleans Parish School Board in December 1922, the school system was rocketing toward a fiscal crisis. Under pressure from business leaders wary of the postwar recession, reform mayor Andrew McShane slashed the taxes that property owners paid to fund schools. The resultant dip in the system's revenues placed the school board at the center of multiple storms. Its largely female teacher corps, which had formed the Deep South's first teachers union in 1919, challenged it to preserve wartime pay raises and to eliminate the disparity between male and female salaries. White and black parents also continued to pester the board to address their children's overcrowded and inadequate school facilities. Yet the best the board could do was to shift funds from one constituency to another. As Fortier conceded shortly after his election, the board could not safeguard any of its future expenses. He urged his colleagues to consider every part of the system's budget—salaries, construction, academics—as potential targets for cuts.[1]

This widening gap between the system's needs and its resources quickly exacerbated the long-standing tensions over the presence of black schools in racially mixed neighborhoods. The board's dwindling budget made school buildings particularly prized commodities, and white residents were loath to see black New Orleanians gain access to additional facilities before they did. The fiercest fight on this front involved the new structure for the black Bayou Road School. The school's black patrons had been lobbying for better accommodations since 1910, and the three-story brick building they were slated to receive was the first black school built on the same scale as a white one since Reconstruction. That structure was nearing completion as the board's fiscal forecast worsened and James Fortier assumed the board's presidency.[2]

While white residents from the Sixth Ward sparked the debate over the replacement building, Fortier fanned the flames. Like the residents, he presented his stance as a defense of white supremacy. He considered it unfathomable to give a modern school facility to black students when whites were also in need. Fortier also shared the Sixth Ward residents' concerns about the impact a new black school building would have upon their neighborhood. In addition to attracting additional black inhabitants, he and the residents feared the structure would mark the area as a black district. Like the white Third Ward residents who opposed McDonogh No. 13's conversion, they suggested that such a label would inhibit the area's growth and lower property values. They also boldly urged the school board to convert the new building on Bayou Road to white use and to find an alternate location for the black school in an area that was already run-down or overwhelmingly black.

The political resurgence of antimachine candidates such as Fortier aided the white, grassroots desire for the enhanced appearance and reality of residential segregation. While ex-mayor Martin Behrman and his political allies supported residential segregation as heartily as their opponents, creating new distinctions between white and black neighborhoods fit particularly well with the reformers' vision for New Orleans. A rather diffuse lot, the reformers, or "New Regulars" as they sometimes called themselves, rarely developed consensus on issues other than their opposition to Behrman's "Old Regular" Democratic machine (also known as the Choctaw Club). While Fortier and other white reformers often distinguished their interest in "good government" from "politics," they were hardly apolitical. Support for "progressive" causes such as equal pay for female teachers, minimum wage and maximum hour laws, and expanded educational opportunities for black children similarly belied their faith in the status quo. Rather than question society's organization along racial and class lines, the reformers eagerly sought to perfect it. To an even greater extent than Behrman's Choctaws, they favored the interests of the city's civic and commercial elite, to which they often belonged.[3] In this regard, they mirrored progressive school reformers in other big cities.[4] No one better embodied the conservative nature of reform activism in New Orleans than James Fortier (see figure 4.1). He embraced its impulses as though they were his birthright, which to a certain extent they were.

This chapter's first section investigates the origins of Fortier's support for white supremacy, followed by a second section that chronicles African Americans' long campaign for better educational facilities at Bayou Road. The third section examines white opposition to the construction of a $110,000 replacement building for the dilapidated and overcrowded school, while the fourth explores the role that seemingly moderate white actors played in the dispute. The chapter concludes with an assessment of this conflict's resolution and how that resolution expanded black educational opportunity even as it tightened residential segregation, white supremacy, and the material distinctions between white and black neighborhoods. In Jim Crow New Orleans, asymmetrical compromise was the closest that African American residents and activists could come to victory as their aspirations collided with those of white residents, policymakers, and reformers.

I.

Fortier's credentials as a reformer were as established as his lineage, which he cherished as a badge of honor. Fortier was a sixth generation New Orleanian whose forebears arrived from Brittany around 1720, before colonial authorities had even laid out the French Quarter's grid. Although the Fortier family would later suggest otherwise, the town was little more than a squalid outpost at the time. By many accounts, the numerous convicts, deserters, and prostitutes whom France deported to Louisiana between 1717 and 1720 influenced New Orleans's daily life to a greater extent than its handful of wealthy concessionnaires and colonial officials. Without its enslaved African majority, the colony never would have extricated itself from the muck.[5]

The Fortiers, however, prospered in New Orleans's improvisational environment, joining an emerging merchant and planter class that was fiercely committed to its independence and self-aggrandizement. The family in many ways became the Forrest Gumps of early New Orleans, popping up at almost every key moment in the city's lively history. Shortly after Spain assumed control of Louisiana in 1766, for instance, Michel Fortier signed on to the municipal Superior Council's protest against changes in trade policy. When France formally regained control of Louisiana in November 1803, Michel Fortier's son, Michel II, joined the caretaker government that handed the colony off to the United States the following month. By that time, Fortier and his partner Alexo Réaud had established a healthy business exporting skins and pelts to Bordeaux and lumber products to Caribbean ports. In 1814–1815, Michel Fortier II commanded the Corps of Free Men of Color during the Battle of New Orleans. That service earned him the praise of Louisiana's governor, who wrote a commendatory letter to Andrew Jackson. That same governor had selected Fortier to replace the free black militia's black officers more than a decade before, firing the opening shot in the Americans' campaign to restrict the rights of free black New Orleanians.[6]

By the middle of the nineteenth century, Michel Fortier's grandson Valcour Aimé had amassed a fortune as a sugar planter and refiner in St. James Parish, about fifty miles upriver from New Orleans. On the backs of 215 enslaved laborers, his 9,000-acre St. James Sugar Refinery pioneered the large-scale production of the sweetener in Louisiana. The plantation's showpiece was a fifteen-arpent garden, which one visitor likened to Versailles. A man-made river snaked in and around the garden's carefully manicured parterres, and "an unbroken mass of blooming violets" lined a portion of the river's banks. An octagonal pagoda with stained glass windows and small, tinkling bells sat atop one hill. Aimé's great-grandson James Fortier undoubtedly relished memoirist Eliza Ripley's 1912 recollection of Aimé as her "(romantic) ideal of a French marquis."[7]

While Aimé solidified the family's wealth, James Fortier's father Alcée (b. 1856) cemented its legacy. A celebrated writer and historian, Fortier served as a professor of Romance languages and an administrator at Tulane University for the thirty-five years preceding his death in 1914. His publications in English and French included folktale collections, a novel, literary criticism, and histories of France, Mexico, and Louisiana. In addition to his long presidency of the Louisiana Historical Society, Fortier served as president of the Modern Language Association in 1898 and chaired the history jury at the 1904 St. Louis World's Fair; the French government named him a Chevalier de la Legion d'Honneur, its highest recognition. Much like the elder Creole statesman and writer Charles Gayarré, Fortier fiercely defended the mythologized nobility and whiteness of New Orleans's Creole population. "The Creoles of Louisiana, and I mean by that expression the white descendants of the French and Spanish colonists, have always occupied a high standing in the community," Fortier once wrote before ticking off a list of Creole accomplishments. "The Creoles are, in short, men of energy, in spite of the calumnious assertions to the contrary, and, as a rule, speak very good French." James Fortier maintained his father's interest in a whites-only definition of "Creole," carefully adding a 1922 article on the word's "real meaning" to the scrapbook he kept during his tenure on the Orleans Parish School Board.[8]

The effort Alcée Fortier and others poured into this myth stemmed from the francophone population's contradictory response to the American onslaught that followed the Louisiana Purchase. On the one hand, French-speaking whites assimilated to the racial dualism of the American South by dissociating themselves from their black Creole relatives and rejecting their own three-caste system. On the other hand, they asserted their distinctive identity and history as Creoles as though it were a cri de coeur. As New Orleans became more thoroughly Americanized over the course of the nineteenth century, Creole intellectuals placed even greater emphasis on their allegedly white, heraldic past. During Reconstruction, white Creoles loosed a volley of celebratory literary and historical works. This doubling down came partly in response to new English-only policies that threatened their French identity. More significantly, they sought to assert their status as whites in the face of the era's Afro-Creole resurgence. With blacks and whites equal in the eyes of the law and black Creoles holding prominent positions in state and local government, white Creoles elevated themselves through historical flights of fancy. They ramped up their efforts even further after George Washington Cable gained national prominence in the 1880s for his fictionalized portrayals of the Creoles' life, culture, and, most notably, racially mixed origins.[9]

Following Gayarré's lead, Fortier repeatedly attacked Cable's portrayal of Creole indolence, placing the white "Creole race" at "the very head and front of [Louisiana] history." When he presented a paper on Louisiana's black French dialect to a largely northeastern audience at the Modern Language Association in 1885, Fortier avoided even using the word *Creole* to describe black speech patterns lest he lend credence to Cable's descriptions. "It was my purpose," he later explained to New Orleanians, "to prove that the Louisiana Creoles did not speak the absurd jargon which Mr. Cable attributes to them." Fortier would later contrast white Creoles' refined French with black French that was "sometimes quaint, and always simple." A rumor eventually circulated that Fortier's disdain for Cable, who advocated for African American civil rights in a famous 1885 essay, was so great that friends had to separate them when they nearly came to blows at a crowded New Orleans restaurant. The professor allegedly admonished the novelist never to speak to him in public again.[10]

Ironically, Fortier's and other Creoles' defensiveness reflected the extent to which they had adopted American norms, particularly in terms of race. Alcée Fortier was, in fact, a paragon of postbellum white southern American manhood. As with many of New Orleans's turn-of-the-century elites, a pivotal experience from his youth was his participation in the Battle of September Fourteenth—later rechristened the Battle of Liberty Place—the unsuccessful coup d'état that the Democratic White League launched against the state's Republican government in 1874. On the afternoon of September 14, more than eight thousand White Leaguers overran a severely outnumbered, racially mixed force of metropolitan police and state militiamen in Downtown New Orleans. In addition to Fortier, the White League's troops included future Democratic state leader E. B. Kruttschnitt, future U.S. Supreme Court justice Edward Douglass White, who joined the 1896 majority in *Plessy,* and the fathers of future "good government" and business leaders such as *Picayune* publisher Ashton Phelps and Governor John M. Parker Jr. The arrival of federal troops later that day quickly quelled the rebellion. But as one historian noted, the battle persisted in popular memory as an emblem of white supremacy, male dominance, "upper-class political entitlement . . . and, most of all, the legitimization of establishment violence in the name of good government."[11]

The Battle of Liberty Place provided Alcée and James Fortier, like other participants and their offspring, with a point of reference—and justification— for later reform activism, however bare-knuckled it might be. Alcée, for instance, took up arms alongside other battle veterans as a member of the Young Men's Democratic Association (YMDA), whose paramilitary squads monitored the polls and guarded ballot boxes during the 1888 municipal elections. The *Times-Democrat* referred to YMDA's victory over the city's working-class political machine that year as "a bloodless Fourteenth of September . . . whose result was just as great and equally as necessary to the substantial prosperity not only of the Crescent City, but likewise to the cause of reform and good government." Alcée Fortier also contributed to another silk stocking victory over the machine in 1896, when the son of a White League veteran was elected mayor.[12]

Alcée passed the lessons of Liberty Place on to James, who recalled studying alongside his father at the dining room table in the family's Esplanade Avenue home, which was located a mere six blocks from the Bayou Road School. The mosquitoes that buzzed around the dining room's large oil lamp and the overflowing bookcases, "handhewn by the slaves of Valcour Aimé's plantation," provided the backdrop for these nighttime sessions. The elder Fortier often continued writing at the table after his children finished their lessons. "What a furious activity he had!" James Fortier recalled years later. "His energy was so tremendous that the table used to quiver and shake under the driving power of his pen as it crashed over the paper."[13]

The impact of the father's teachings was evident in the political activities of the son. While "reform" was frequently Crescent City shorthand for the restoration of white upper-class rule, both father and son championed a slew of other ostensibly progressive causes. As a state legislator, for instance, James Fortier went toe-to-toe with Behrman during a failed attempt to pass a minimum wage and maximum hour bill for women and minors. Similarly, Alcée had pushed for compulsory education, higher teachers' salaries, and better school facilities as a member of the Public School Alliance. Like other well-heeled members of the Alliance, however, Alcée's support for public education had its limits: he sent James to the private Jesuit College for grammar and high school.[14]

The strongest evidence that James embraced his father's teachings came from the Louisiana State Museum's 1938 official history of Reconstruction, which the younger Fortier edited while serving as president of the museum's board. Titled *Carpet-Bag Misrule in Louisiana,* the pamphlet placed the White League and the Battle of Liberty Place at the center of a valiant and ultimately successful effort to restore white dominance in the Pelican State. Viewed in this context, James Fortier's comment during the January 1923 debate over the Bayou Road School "that he was unwilling to do anything that would affect the white man's supremacy [and] that he was ready to deny the negro political equality and if necessary *resort to force* to do so" appeared to be more than overheated rhetoric.[15]

Between World War I and World War II, neither Fortier's interest in the supposed horrors of Reconstruction nor his commitment to the armed defense of white supremacy were unique to New Orleans. As evidenced by the widespread popularity of the 1915 cinematic epic *Birth of a Nation*, which valorized a patriotic Ku Klux Klan's eradication of post–Civil War "Negro rule," a broad swath of white Americans shared Fortier's beliefs. Academic historians in the North and South similarly characterized Reconstruction as a sordid time marked by the dominion "of the uncivilized Negroes over the whites of the South" and as an era "to be remembered, shuddered at, and execrated." In these retellings, which were standard fare in elementary and high school textbooks, white terrorist organizations became the heroes of the age.[16]

From *Birth of a Nation* to *Gone With the Wind*, published two years before Fortier's pamphlet, the reimagining of the Civil War and its aftermath as a tale of white gallantry, regrettable political conflict, and shared suffering enabled white southerners and northerners to reconcile their differences. In the process, they erased the war's relation to slavery and black liberation. For W. E. B. Du Bois, the consequences of this sort of rewriting of history were clear. "It is not only part foundation of present lawlessness and loss of democratic ideals," he wrote in 1935, "it has, more than that, led the world to worship the color bar as social salvation." Against these great odds, black New Orleanians sought to lessen their degradation at the hands of the state.[17]

II.

The black Bayou Road Parents' Club began complaining about the school's conditions as early as 1910, when it occupied a single, overcrowded rented building that was on the verge of collapse. At the time, the city provided seventy-one public schools for whites and just twelve for blacks. That meant African Americans had access to less than 15 percent of the city's school facilities despite comprising more than one-quarter of its population.[18]

The school board responded to the Parents' Club's request for more space by renting an additional structure as a school annex. When Bayou Road's white neighbors protested that addition, the board told them it would proceed with the annex since it had already signed a lease and the "Bayou Road Colored School has been established there for a number of years." While the annex reduced the school's overcrowding, this second rented building was in no better condition than the first. By 1914, the deplorable state of the buildings elicited a condemnatory letter from the City Board of Health. School board member John X. Wegmann, who was the president of a fire insurance company, disputed some of the health inspector's findings but concluded after a visit to Bayou Road that "there is no doubt but that the main building and annex are not at all suitable for school purposes." He informed the board that a new building was the only viable solution, and it soon compiled a list of seventeen possible locations.[19]

Walter Cohen was the head of the Bayou Road Parents' Club when the board began scouting the potential sites. He lived less than a mile from the school with his wife, adult daughters, and one grandchild, and his seven-year-old granddaughter Yolanda Bell likely attended Bayou Road in 1914.[20] True to form, Cohen urged the board to pursue the middle path when selecting a location for Bayou Road's new building. He told board members that all blacks "wanted was for the school not to be located where it would cause protests and disturbances." Although white neighbors had in fact objected in 1910 when the board rented the second building, Cohen informed the board that black parents "were more than satisfied with the school where it is now." He even offered to contribute $2,000 through the Colored Civic League toward the purchase of a lot adjacent to the existing school site, providing an example of the double taxation that African Americans were willing to endure simply to secure basic educational opportunities.[21]

Cohen's endorsement made an impression on board president and bank executive Sol Wexler, who convinced the board to stick with the existing site partly since, he mistakenly asserted, "the school has been located on it for so many years without protest." But students languished in their rented quarters for several more years after the 1915 hurricane and then World War I delayed construction. The new Bayou Road building then returned to the board's agenda in 1921, when Superintendent John M. Gwinn included it in his long-term plan for black education. Following more pressure from the school's patrons, the board voted on July 14, 1922, to authorize the construction of a $110,000 brick structure.[22]

Toward the end of July 1922, a delegation of white Sixth Ward residents appeared before the board to protest "against the creation of a negro school at Bayou Road and Derbigny Street." S. P. Pierce spoke first. Striking a pose typical of these disputes over schools, race, and the future of the city, Pierce played with time and space as he would an accordion, expanding and collapsing it to suit his needs. He ignored the racially mixed character of the area surrounding the Bayou Road School by focusing on the slivers within it that were not mixed. He similarly dismissed black residents' historical claims to the area. As recorded in the school board's minutes, Pierce stated that "the site was not the logical place for a negro school; that the section was not a negro neighborhood; that a large percentage of the pupils of the Bayou Road School came from a great distance to the school and that he had understood that the Bayou Road School was only a temporary affair." Other speakers echoed Pierce's statements, with one adding that as a result of the construction "negroes would move into the neighborhood and that such a condition would prove obnoxious to the residents of that section." Another suggested the board reserve the new Bayou Road building for whites and either build a school deeper into the back of town or convert the nearby Parham School from white to black since it was located "in a negro neighborhood."[23]

The protestors at the July 1922 meeting initially failed to sway the board.

Daniel Murphy, a Behrman ally who preceded Fortier as board president, quickly corrected Pierce's claim that the existing school was intended as "a temporary affair." "The Bayou Road School had been in existence for fifty years," he said before noting "that the predecessors of the present Board had threshed out the matter of the location of this school upon other occasions." Murphy, an attorney and president of the Panama Realty Company, also appeared genuinely sympathetic to black students' needs, as did other board members. "The negroes of that section must be provided with school facilities," Murphy told the delegation. He added that protests would result wherever the board chose to locate the school. Percy Moise, a reformist member of the board and a credit manager for a large import company, also lashed out at the white residents for appearing with "destructive criticism and without any constructive plan."[24]

While Moise said he was willing to suspend a decision about the new building's racial designation until the protestors returned with viable alternatives, the board nevertheless pressed forward with the construction of the new facility. In November of 1922, the board voted to name the new Bayou Road school building after Joseph A. Craig, one of four black men who joined the post-Reconstruction school board in 1877. When the school's patrons approved of the name, graybeards such as Cohen would have likely recalled that Craig was the only black member to vote in favor of resegregating the city's schools.[25]

For the moment, the construction of the Craig building took precedence over other concerns in the increasingly cash-strapped district, including the crowded conditions at Warren Easton, the city's only high school for white males. The board responded to Easton's rising enrollment on December 22, 1922, by appointing seven additional teachers and converting a vacant library and parts of the basement into classrooms. But when a representative from the Easton High School Association asked for a more permanent solution, Fortier snapped that the board "was not in a position to do anything more than to offer general terms of encouragement and to express its appreciation of the interest of the parents."[26]

As construction of Craig neared completion, however, Fortier changed his tune. Prior to the board's first meeting of 1923 on January 12, he issued his call to white Sixth Ward residents to show up to protest the building's scheduled opening as a black school on February 1.[27] While the delegation trotted out many of the same complaints they had lodged six months earlier, the scale of the newly constructed school building inflamed their protest. A Dr. Pierce, likely the S. P. Pierce who had led the July protest, noted that the last petition "had been presented before the present handsome building had been erected." He suggested that the building's grandeur would lure new black residents to the neighborhood. Another protestor argued that the school's location was as much a hardship for blacks as whites, claiming "that there were vested rights involved and that it was an injustice to the negroes to force them to come a great distance to the school located in a white section." However, under questioning from board member Fred Zengel, a prominent real estate attorney, the speaker acknowledged that he was not a representative for area blacks. When an equally skeptical Percy Moise asked where the protestors proposed sending the eight hundred to one thousand black students slated to attend Craig, one woman suggested the board convert the nearby McDonogh No. 9 school from white to black. "It was wrong," the woman stated, "to house white children in McDonogh No. 9, which building was stated to be in a hazardous condition, while the negroes would be given a school that was really a monument."[28]

The school board had in fact considered converting McDonogh No. 9 to a black school ten years earlier. But the board backed off after white residents protested. The residents' anger at the prospect of losing No. 9 showed the extent to which white residents viewed public schools as markers of a neighborhood's racial character and overall quality. Converting McDonogh No. 9 from white to black, one white protestor alleged in 1913, would "change the district that we have all been trying to build back into a negro neighborhood, the same as it was before that school was erected about thirty years ago."[29] The significance whites attached to a school's racial designation was probably a salve even when facilities were inadequate. After the board maintained McDonogh No. 9 as a white school in 1913, it largely ignored residents' persistent complaints about overcrowding. While residents were displeased that their neighborhood did not have an adequate school building, they likely took comfort in the fact that the building—and by extension, their neighborhood—remained white.[30]

The Sixth Ward residents who appeared before the board in January 1923 were essentially making the same argument the McDonogh No. 9 and McDonogh No. 13 delegations had made years before: a new black school building in their neighborhood would turn it into a black neighborhood, which would lead to its inevitable decline. Fortier's frustration with his colleagues' unwillingness to listen to this argument led him to take a stand in the residents' defense. But Fortier also believed more was at stake than the future of the neighborhood where he grew up.

The board president viewed white supremacy, residential segregation, urban growth, and black education as inextricably intertwined issues. Like his board forebears who eliminated black schooling beyond grade five in 1900, he understood that Jim Crow was an economic as well as a political and social system whose success depended upon unequal educational opportunities for blacks and whites.[31] He feared that providing black children with a modern school building was a first step toward providing them with a modern curriculum on par with the one available to whites, a dangerous move that would allow black people to compete for nonmenial jobs. To this end, Fortier was particularly displeased that the new building did not have industrial training facilities. As a result, he said the "building was inadequately equipped to give these people the kind of training which they required." It was absurd, he declared, "to follow any plan for the education of the negro which involved anything beyond reading and writing and the teaching of a trade."[32] To provide a more appropriate industrial education for blacks, Fortier said he hoped to interest Julius Rosenwald, the Sears & Roebuck chief whose philanthropic foundation had begun shifting its support from black schools in the rural South to trade high schools in urban areas.[33]

Dismissing Superintendent Gwinn's contention that there were no viable alternatives for turning Bayou Road into a white school, Fortier suggested the school serve as either an annex to one of the existing—and overcrowded—white girls' high schools or as a second industrial high school for whites. The future of the Bayou Road neighborhood and of the city itself, he dramatically concluded, hung in the balance. "To put negroes in the Bayou Road School would prevent the growth and development of that section," he said. By contrast, "if the school were made a white school it would permit the real estate people of the city to sell values in that section." He moved that the school board postpone opening the school for blacks to permit a more comprehensive study of the situation.[34]

At the January 12 meeting, the other four board members agreed to consider a postponement only if they received an alternate plan for the 850 black students slated to attend Craig beginning February 1. Percy Moise also suggested that the board borrow money to build another school for blacks in a more agreeable neighborhood and then transfer the Craig students to that building upon its completion.[35] Less than a week later, on January 18, Fortier used the opening his colleagues provided to suggest that other schools could accommodate prospective Craig students if they adopted double sessions, with one group attending in the morning and another in the afternoon. "No great violence would be done the cause of negro education," Fortier declared, "if these children were deprived of approximately one and one-quarter hours daily for the next five months."

Moise quashed the discussion by objecting to "depriving the pupils in question of a minute's time of education." But Fortier revived the issue at a January 26 board meeting. He again urged the board to delay the opening of Craig until he presented a comprehensive plan for black education, reminding members of his ongoing efforts to secure money from the Rosenwald Fund. Daniel Murphy joined Moise in opposing a postponement "since this was the first move on the part of the Board to give the negroes a real substantial building."[36]

Fannie Baumgartner, however, shared Fortier's interest in reevaluating black education from the ground up. She and the board president even urged a reconsideration of the curriculum at McDonogh 35 High School, which had featured a college preparatory program with credits awarded "on [the] same basis as in the White High Schools" since its inception in 1917.[37] The board's initial adoption of 35's liberal arts curriculum was not an honest attempt to provide separate yet equal education to black and white students. Rather, the board hoped to train the small corps of black teachers, doctors, and lawyers who were vital in a completely segregated society. But Baumgartner agreed with Fortier at the January 26, 1923, meeting "that it was unwise, in order to qualify one negro for a teaching position to give chemistry, botany, physics, and other high school subjects, to the great mass of negro pupils" who were attending the city's lone black high school.[38]

Like Fortier, Baumgartner also seamlessly linked her curricular concerns to the issues of schools, race, and the future of the city at the heart of the Bayou Road debate. The black McDonogh No. 6 School in Uptown New Orleans, she casually noted at the January 26 board meeting, "was badly located in that it was situated in a strictly white section."[39] The last black school built on par with white buildings, McDonogh No. 6 was "a solid, substantial and very elegant building of brick" that had opened in 1876. It was located several blocks from the Mississippi River on Napoleon Avenue, a wide boulevard with many large homes and wealthy white residents.[40] Baumgartner's comment about No. 6's location was surprising since she had agreed in 1921 to build a four-room addition to better accommodate the school's crowded black populace. But Fortier did not consider her reference to McDonogh No. 6 a non sequitur. "The location of the negro schools," he readily agreed, "was a matter to be discussed in connection with the general plan of negro education."[41]

The board followed up on Baumgartner's concerns about McDonogh No. 6 eighteen months later in July 1924 by voting to turn it into a commercial high school for white girls. That move reduced crowding at the white Sophie B. Wright High School, located five blocks up Napoleon from McDonogh No. 6, while pushing No. 6's former students into a smaller, formerly white building (McDonogh Memorial) in a more racially mixed interior neighborhood. Whites who lived near McDonogh Memorial trotted out familiar arguments to protest its conversion from white to black, and the black members of the McDonogh No. 6 Co-Operative Club asked the board to reconsider their ejection from their Napoleon Avenue schoolhouse. But by then the board had already committed to renovating the fifty-year-old McDonogh No. 6 building for white use. In preparation for McDonogh Memorial's conversion from white to black, that school's former Mothers' Club also redistributed the materials it had previously donated to the school lest they fall into black hands. The regifted items included playground equipment, assorted athletic gear, and a five-hundred-volume library.[42]

Baumgartner foreshadowed these later actions at the January 26, 1923, meeting when she moved that the board postpone the opening of the new school building at Bayou Road until Fortier presented his comprehensive plan for black education.[43] Zengel, who worried that opening the Craig School to blacks would prevent Fortier from completing the plan, sided with Fortier and Baumgartner, and the motion carried 3–2 with Moise and Murphy in the minority.[44] The move effectively closed the brand new Bayou Road building for the remainder of the school year and placed four other black schools on double sessions to accommodate Craig's would-be students.[45]

The board's decision also reflected the central role that schools had assumed in the nationwide movement to officially distinguish between white and black urban zones. As Fortier noted at the outset of the Bayou Road debate two weeks earlier, the Supreme Court's rejection of residential segregation laws in *Buchanan v. Warley* meant that the power to redraw racial boundaries largely rested in his and his school board colleagues' hands.

III.

Fortier's apparent victory at the January 26, 1923, board meeting initially backfired. Black New Orleanians quickly mobilized in response to the closure of the newly constructed Craig School building on Bayou Road, holding a pair of mass meetings on January 31.[46] Representatives from the National Association for the Advancement of Colored People, the Colored Educational Alliance, the National Progressive Association of Negroes, several school-based parents' clubs, and labor unions attended the meetings. At the gatherings, the protestors appointed businessman Emile LaBranche, book dealer and Republican activist James E. Gayle, and physicians B. F. Easter and George W. Lucas to bring their protest before the school board.[47] These organizations and men represented the institutional backbone of the city's incipient civil rights movement, whose roots stretched deepest in the city's downtown wards.[48]

Yet the Craig School controversy elicited outrage among black people from a range of backgrounds and neighborhoods. The *Times-Picayune,* for instance, published letters opposing the building's closure from black writers living in the downtown Ninth Ward as well as the uptown Third and Twelfth Wards. While Henry E. Braden, who owned the Astoria Hotel on Rampart Street, and school founder Frances Joseph Gaudet were light-skinned Creoles, porter Charles Levy and laundress Mrs. C. E. Gates Phillips likely were not. Levy, who lived along a racially mixed stretch of Louisiana Avenue in Uptown New Orleans, argued that Craig should remain black since "the negro is an integral part of this great city and . . . should not be denied opportunity."[49] Phillips, from the city's Third Ward, used her letter to urge the school board to not only open the new Craig school building but also to make good on its previous plan to increase educational capacity for blacks by converting the McDonogh No. 30 School in her ward from white to black use.[50] In August 1921, the board had decided against converting McDonogh No. 30 after white residents protested that "the neighborhood was almost entirely white."[51]

Several fixtures within the city's white establishment also demanded the board open Craig to blacks. Most significantly, the city's three white-owned daily papers opposed its closure. The *Times-Picayune* considered the board's stance "glaringly unfair and unjust" and believed that "so flagrant an injustice ought to provoke vigorous protest from all fair-minded folk."[52] The Association of Commerce, the Public School Alliance, and the President's Cooperative Club, an umbrella organization of white school-based parent clubs that

Baumgartner previously led, joined the newspaper in siding with the black protestors.[53] The Building Trades Council, which represented labor unions, also opposed the closing "based on the fact that many of the children of negro members of the organization are being deprived of school advantages through the closing of the school."[54]

The *Picayune*'s editorial stance proved particularly influential. Two days after the paper criticized the board's position, board members Zengel and Baumgartner visited three of the schools slated to receive the black students previously assigned to the new Craig building.[55] On that cold and rainy Monday, Zengel and Baumgartner saw rooms so crowded that as many as four students shared a desk. At the Valena C. Jones School, classes met in dark rooms in cottages the board had rented years before to provide extra space. Baumgartner worried that the crowding was so bad that an epidemic of smallpox, diphtheria, or scarlet fever could easily spread throughout the entire school. "The condition at the Valena C. Jones School is simply awful," she reported. The Bienville [School] is worse."[56] These observations led Zengel and Baumgartner to question Fortier's plan.

When the school board reconvened on February 9, the president's wavering colleagues were the least of his troubles. Members of the various groups who wanted the new Joseph A. Craig School to be opened to black students turned out en masse, as did many white residents who opposed the school. During a particularly raucous meeting, audience members repeatedly interrupted speakers with "cat calls, hoots, and applause," and board members sniped at one another and district administrators.[57] After Fortier invited the assembled delegations to speak, Walter Cohen announced that Emile LaBranche, chairman of the black mass meetings, would speak on behalf of black New Orleanians. La Branche began by summarizing the decade's old complaint of the Bayou Road Parents' Club about the school's "deplorable . . . and unhealthy conditions" and the board's as yet unmet promise to provide a new building. "We now come to you and ask that you open to the colored children this school which has been built for them," he said. LaBranche, who attended the Bayou Road School in the 1890s, told the board that no section of the city had a greater need for a school than the area Craig would serve. "In the vast area existing from Bienville to Allen and from the river to the woods," he said in reference to a swath encompassing all of the Fifth and Sixth Wards and significant portions of the Fourth and Seventh—"there is only one school—the Joseph A. Craig School."[58]

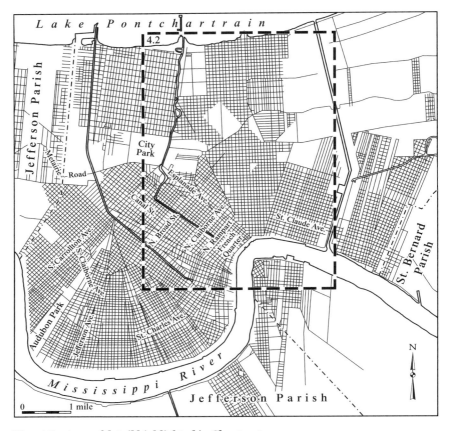

Map 4.1   Area of detail highlighted in Chapter 4.

LaBranche's comment reflected white and black New Orleanians' divergent understandings of the Crescent City's racial geography (see maps 4.1 and 4.2). While whites often viewed a school as a neighborhood's defining characteristic—as evidenced by their opposition to black schools near their homes—blacks focused on access, not proximity. Simply put, there were not enough black schools. Creating attendance zones that would send the Bayou Road School's former students to other schools, LaBranche said, "does not make the schools any larger, nor nearer our homes."[59] He noted that black students had traveled great distances for years to attend the Bayou Road School, and redistricting would merely reduce the number of available seats for black students without easing their commutes.

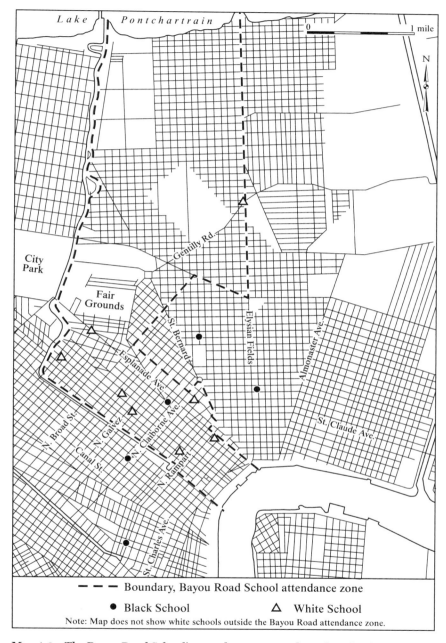

Lake Pontchartrain

City Park

Fair Grounds

Gentilly Rd.

N. St. Bernard

Esplanade Ave.

Elysian Fields

Almonaster Ave.

N. Broad St.

N. Galvez

N. Claiborne Ave.

Canal St.

N. Rampart

St. Claude Ave.

St. Charles Ave.

0   1 mile

N

– – – Boundary, Bayou Road School attendance zone

● Black School   △ White School

Note: Map does not show white schools outside the Bayou Road attendance zone.

Map 4.2   The Bayou Road School's attendance zone and nearby schools, 1920.
School data by Walter C. Stern. Source: *School Directory*, 1920–1921, box 1, School Directories, Orleans Parish School Board Collection (MSS 147), Louisiana and Special Collections Department, Earl K. Long Library, University of New Orleans.

LaBranche's straightforward plea failed to sway the white residents who continued to oppose the school. Following Fortier's earlier argument, a Dr. Swords said that the issue was about more than property rights and values. Following a familiar New Orleans refrain, he told the board that his thinking was influenced by values he learned from his father, a Battle of Liberty Place veteran. "The two principles which give us most concern are white supremacy and race segregation," Swords said. "While these two principles of white supremacy and race segregation must be maintained, the white race must do it with magnanimity, with fairness and with justice to the colored race." Equitably upholding white supremacy and segregation, Swords maintained, involved respecting—but not extending—those rights black people already possessed.

"We have not come here and petitioned this Board to destroy a school in existence as it had existed," Swords stated. "But when that school is enlarged and made a permanent structure, when you accord the people of that race *additional rights* which you seek to invest them with, we enter our protest and ask that it not be opened. They have not acquired any vested rights to additional facilities." To open the school to blacks, Swords continued, would set a dangerous precedent that blacks could "come into a white settlement and build a permanent structure."[60] Like proponents of residential segregation from St. Louis to South Africa, Swords raised the specter of racial violence and social equality.[61] The school board, therefore, had one option for permanently settling the question of black schooling. "Put the facilities for their education in the section inhabited by them," Swords concluded. "Keep them out and segregated from the section of that inhabited by the white race."[62]

As Swords ceded the floor, the sixty-three-year-old Walter Cohen attempted to lower the meeting's emotional intensity. "We recognize that this is a white man's country and we are at your mercy," he announced. "We are not desirous of social equality." But an argument between a white and a black audience member interrupted Cohen before he could continue. Fortier then seized the opportunity to second Sword's argument. How could the board give Craig to blacks, Fortier asked, when the system's white high schools were over capacity? He said the situation was particularly dire at Warren Easton High School, where nearly 1,500 students squeezed into a building intended for 800. "Fifteen hundred of our white boys to prepare to go to the university, to become business men, to get the advantages of education," Fortier railed. "Our white boys of the Warren Easton High School are crowded and put in basements. A surplus of seven hundred boys who might comfortably learn their lessons on full time in the Craig School." The situation, Fortier said, was no better at the downtown girls' high school. "The students at the Esplanade Avenue School are overflowing and overcrowded, and they cannot make use of these rooms because it was dedicated to the memory of a negro teacher."

Fortier then blamed Superintendent Gwinn for mishandling black education. While Fortier acknowledged Gwinn's 1921 plan for black school construction, he incorrectly claimed that "the only recommendation that was carried out was the objectionable one in regard to the Bayou Road School." The superintendent, Fortier suggested, could have easily identified a more suitable location for a new black school. "If he had walked four blocks to Claiborne and St. Philip, he would have found Little Africa itself," he said. Fortier contrasted St. Philip Street with Ursulines Avenue, located one block downriver from St. Philip. The three-block strip between Ursulines and Esplanade Avenues, from Claiborne Avenue to Bayou St. John, was a "thoroughly white section," he said. The new school building was in the southeastern corner of that area (see map 2.6 for a detailed view of this area).[63]

Perhaps unwittingly, Fortier's reference to the intersection of Claiborne and St. Philip St. as "Little Africa" acknowledged that geographic area's centrality to the history of slavery in New Orleans. During the eighteenth century, that intersection was part of a stretch of land known as "Congo Plains." "Congo Plains" also encompassed the smaller area known as "Place des Nègres" and, eventually, as "Congo Square," where nineteenth-century slaves and free blacks gathered to dance, sing, and trade goods. By the time Fortier suggested locating a school for black students within blocks of this historic spot, it appeared on maps as Beauregard Square since the Commission Council had renamed it to honor Confederate general P. G. T. Beauregard in 1893.[64] But regardless of his understanding of history, Fortier was off base when identifying St. Philip Street as "Little Africa," the heart of which he placed at the intersection of St. Philip and North Claiborne. A bare majority of residents in the block of St. Philip on either side of that intersection were in fact black or mulatto.[65] While this reflected a higher proportion of black people than in the city at large, white residents had no trouble blending in.

But Fortier did not cite historical precedent to support his claims about the city's racial geography. Instead, he held up a population map that a New York engineering firm had created as part of a city-commissioned study of New Orleans's streetcar system (see map 4.3). Ironically, the map included

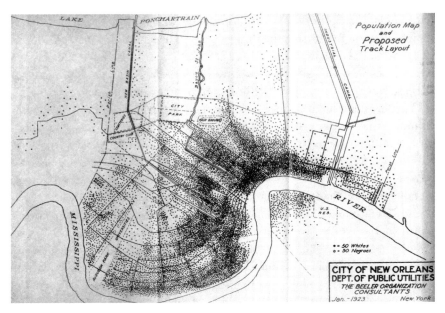

Map 4.3   Population and proposed streetcar track layout, New Orleans, 1923.
John A. Beeler, Report to the Commissioner of Public Utilities, City of New Orleans, on the
Street Railway Situation. New York, 1923. "Population Map and Proposed Track Layout,"
Exhibit 2-B, Louisiana Research Collection, Tulane University.

one black circle for every fifty white residents and one white circle for every
fifty black residents. "St. Philip Street is almost thoroughly black except from
Rampart Street to the river," Fortier said. "These white circles are absolutely
interwoven, fifty to the circle, continuously on St. Philip Street four blocks
away from the school." Fortier maintained that locating a school for blacks
on St. Philip or in another area with a concentrated black population would
support the city's campaign to increase the spatial separation of the races. As
Fortier told the board, the New York engineers were complicit in this plan:

> These people talking to me this afternoon said: "In your plan for negro
> education, be sure it will serve the best interests of the people to place the
> negro schools in negro sections. We are surveying to redistrict to give more
> service on one [streetcar] line to the black people."

The transit engineers, Fortier told his colleagues, "are ready to cooperate in the segregation of the negroes."[66]

The engineers' report, which was incomplete at the time of the February 9 school board meeting, did not explicitly endorse residential segregation. But the distinctions it made between the service needs of a "high class residential district" such as the white area along the stately Napoleon Avenue and a contiguous "negro district" demonstrated the ways civic improvements such as rail lines could reinforce both residential boundaries and the link between racial designations and neighborhood quality.[67] As the sociologist H. W. Gilmore noted in 1944, streetcars did in fact contribute to greater residential segregation in New Orleans during the early twentieth century. Since streetcars eliminated the need to live within walking distance of work, many black people left the "Negro residential fringe" adjacent to white residential areas for more concentrated and distinct black sections located between white neighborhoods. Picking up on the reflexive relationship between schools and residential segregation during the interwar period, Gilmore wrote that "this concentration has in turn attracted to these areas schools and other facilities for Negroes which are an incentive for more Negroes to move there."[68]

IV.

As the February 9, 1923, meeting came to a close, neither Fortier's histrionics nor the white residents' fury convinced the board to continue to deny black students access to the newly constructed Craig School. With Fortier the lone dissenter, the board voted four-to-one to open Craig to blacks the coming Wednesday, February 14. Fortier's defeat, however, did not signal a significant break between him, his colleagues, and the members of the white establishment who wanted Craig opened. Fortier's white opponents merely favored a more humane approach to segregation than he did. While he wanted to pump additional black students into overcrowded schools and to reduce the amount of time they spent there in order to immediately tighten residential boundaries, they were willing to wait until they could implement a more permanent solution.[69]

The involvement of Mrs. George P. Thompson from the white Presidents' Cooperative Club reflected this. "In the estimation of the Club," Thompson told Fortier during the February 9 meeting, "it is a matter of justice, of obedience to the constituted law and a matter of patriotism that the colored boys and girls of that district be supplied with a school that they can go to under regulations that any other children are expected to go to school." She considered it unjust that Bayou Road's students had been without a school since September. Yet Thompson's call for fair play was not an indicator of wavering support for white supremacy. Rather, she worried that the board's failure to provide black children with a school would undermine white expectations that blacks obey the laws of segregation. Thompson was also as interested as Fortier in establishing tighter distinctions between black and white residential districts. Six years earlier, for instance, she had joined the Rampart Street Jews' protest against McDonogh No. 13's conversion.[70]

Like progressive reformers in other American cities, Thompson and the business leaders in the Association of Commerce who broke with Fortier viewed segregation as a rational mechanism for promoting social cohesion. In Flint, Michigan, for instance, white reformers drew upon the Progressive era writings of city planner Clarence Perry and others to promote a community schools initiative that strengthened the distinctions between black and white neighborhoods in the name of urban unity. According to historian Andrew Highsmith, "school attendance zones created neighborhood boundaries and established the rules of membership in [Flint's] rigidly segregated public sphere." While James Fortier was more militant in his support for white supremacy than either Thompson or the Flint city builders, he shared their faith that segregation and white racial dominance served the greater good.[71]

Fortier's forceful attacks against Superintendent Gwinn also concealed the extent to which the two men agreed with Fortier's contention that "the location of the negro schools was a matter to be discussed in connection with the general plan of negro education."[72] In his 1921 plan for black education, for instance, Gwinn had linked curricular curtailments and geographic isolation as the twin means for expanding educational opportunity without promoting black advancement.[73] While Gwinn argued that schools and curriculum could be "much alike or quite the same for the two races through the grades necessary for learning the fundamentals of education or for the instruction in the elements of good citizenship," he suggested that "after this point there needs to be considerable differentiation in the courses for differing classes and a still wider differentiation in the instruction provided for the two races." Specifically, he proposed providing blacks with basic instruction on par with white elementary schools through the sixth grade followed by three years of junior high school focused on vocational and industrial education. "The democratic doctrine, fundamental in our theory of government, that there must be equal educational opportunities for all children of all people has led into many errors in providing schools and courses of instruction of the same kind and extent for children of different races, mental, physical, and social traits and qualities; and social and economic conditions," Gwinn said. "The errors have been due to a mistake in translating *equal* into the *same*." A similar logic lay behind the National Education Association's influential 1918 "Cardinal Principles of Secondary Education" report. That document called for a high school curriculum that offered students different academic and nonacademic tracks within comprehensive high schools that were socially, if not racially, heterogeneous.[74]

Gwinn's 1921 plan, like Fortier's opposition to a black school at Bayou Road and Derbigny, also reflected school officials' interest in restricting black schools to existing black neighborhoods. The superintendent, for instance, recommended constructing at least five additional schools for blacks, five annexes for existing schools, and three replacement buildings for dilapidated structures. Gwinn specified the location for each of his proposed construction projects, flagging five majority black neighborhoods as his preferred sites for the new schools (see table 4.1). While Gwinn recommended erecting Bayou Road's replacement building on its existing site, he favored moving the McCarthy School from its predominantly white location in the present-day Bywater area to the more isolated and racially mixed Lower Ninth Ward.[75]

Constructing new black schools in areas where blacks were already concentrated enhanced access for the children living in those neighborhoods. But there was nothing inevitable about the specific locations Gwinn chose since each was integrated into more mixed or predominantly white areas. For instance, while blacks headed 61 percent of the households in the twenty-plus-square-block voting precinct on the downtown side of St. Bernard Avenue and North Roman Street which Gwinn recommended as the site for a new junior high school, they headed only 44 percent of the households in the slightly larger precinct on the uptown side of that intersection.[76] As Emile LaBranche noted during the 1923 Bayou Road debate, the city's inadequate number of black schools and the geographic dispersal of its black population meant that blacks generally had to travel to reach schools regardless of where the board located them.[77] By recommending the construction of black schools in exist-

Table 4.1 **Proposed New Black School Construction and Black Residential Concentration, by Voting Precinct, 1921**

Location	Recommendation	Ward/Precinct	Black Population (%)
St. Bernard Avenue and North Roman Street	New junior high school	Seventh Ward/ Sixth Precinct	61.5
In the vicinity of Bienville and Claiborne	New junior high school	Fourth Ward/ Third Precinct	80.8
Area bounded by Carondelet, Louisiana Avenue, Freret, and Sixth Streets	New junior high school	Eleventh Ward/ Ninth Precinct	82.4
Spruce and Monroe Streets	New elementary school	Seventeenth Ward/Third Precinct	51.3
Back Claiborne not more than four squares, and in the neighborhood of Third Street	New elementary school	Eleventh Ward/ Eleventh Precinct	77.7

Source: Orleans Parish School Board Minutes, 24 June 1921, Orleans Parish School Board Collection (Mss 147), Louisiana and Special Collections Department, Earl K. Long Library, University of New Orleans; US Census, 1920, New Orleans, LA, Population, National Archives Microfilm Series T-625, reel 620, via Heritage Quest Online for demographic data. Voting precinct boundaries are described in *New Orleans Item*, 28 October 1920, 18.

ing black enclaves, Gwinn likely sought to avoid the sort of controversy that surrounded the McDonogh No. 13 conversion. This approach also formalized these enclaves' status as black neighborhoods, which likely appealed to businessmen who were increasingly focused on developing newly drained parts of the city for whites only.

A similar dynamic unfolded in cities such as Raleigh, where future North Carolina governor J. M. Broughton successfully dismissed black opposition to a 1926 plan to construct a new school in the city's southeastern quadrant rather than in a black middle-class suburb in the northeast. "Obviously a school ought to be built somewhere near the children it is to serve," wrote

Broughton, then a member of Raleigh's school board. "Nearly ninety percent of the colored population live in the southern and southeastern sections of the city. Accordingly, this is where their schools ought to be, and their churches, too, for that matter."[78]

Like McDonogh No. 13's conversion, Gwinn's recommendations for the area presently known as Central City, which at the time was considered part of the broader back of town, bolstered its transformation into a racially homogenous and largely neglected black residential zone. The new junior high school he wanted to build in the swath of Central City bounded by Carondelet, Louisiana Avenue, Freret, and Sixth Street made sense since it would reduce the severe overcrowding at the nearby Thomy Lafon School, located at Seventh Street between Freret and Magnolia (see map 6.4 for a detailed view of this area). But even though blacks comprised the overwhelming majority of residents in that immediate area, more whites than blacks lived in one of its adjacent voting precincts. Similarly, while blacks grossly outnumbered whites on the lake side of Claiborne Avenue near Third Street, where Gwinn hoped to build a new elementary school for black children, enough whites lived on the opposite, or river, side of Claiborne to support the white Judah P. Benjamin elementary school.[79]

The board's 1923 decision to build a black school on the riverside of Claiborne Avenue at Third Street, three blocks from Judah P. Benjamin, preceded the area's transformation into a thoroughly black neighborhood. In 1920, for instance, 77 percent of households were black in Benjamin's voting precinct.[80] By the late 1930s, however, more than 90 percent of households were black on most nearby blocks. In 1939, the Home Owners' Loan Corporation's surveyors referred to this section of New Orleans as "the largest area of concentrated negro population in the City," and they noted that two sections of it were slated for slum clearance.[81] The school board responded to this transition by converting Benjamin from white to black in 1936 and later renaming it after Fortunatus P. Ricard, the black educator who had lambasted the white opponents of McDonogh No. 13's transformation into McDonogh 35.[82]

Some of Gwinn's other recommendations that the board eventually implemented also foreshadowed those areas' transformations into more solidly black neighborhoods.[83] Comparing maps 2.3 and 2.4 helps illuminate this reality. The one proposal listed in table 4.1 that the board resisted was Gwinn's suggestion to build a junior high school closer to Thomy Lafon. The board's failure to follow through on this recommendation allowed that school's enrollment to approach three thousand by 1930 as the surrounding area's black population swelled.[84]

The conclusion of the Bayou Road saga provided still more evidence that James Fortier was not a racial outlier. Within minutes of its vote to open Craig to blacks, the board agreed to borrow $250,000 to build a replacement building in an area less offensive to whites. This was precisely what Moise had recommended to the board a month earlier. Board members made clear that they hoped to move black students out of the new building on Bayou Road and Derbigny as soon as possible. "You could buy a piece of property in what the protest[ors] call the black belt," Moise suggested. "[You] could give notice that it would be a negro school and then use this school [on Bayou Road] for something else. That is not any new plan. I always told them that I would be willing to do that." None of the whites who had prodded Fortier to open the newly constructed building on Bayou Road to blacks protested this move either.[85]

Four months after the new building on Bayou Road opened to black students, the board took its first step toward the school's relocation by paying $48,300 for property on St. Philip Street between Marais and North Villere, along the strip Fortier had previously fingered as "Little Africa" and in the heart of the Tremé neighborhood.[86] The proposed site sat several blocks north of the historic Congo Square. In selecting this particular block, the board was apparently more attentive to residential nuances than Fortier had been during his February 9 tirade, since this stretch of St. Philip had a significantly higher concentration of blacks than the area closer to Claiborne Avenue. That a number of the white residents in these lower blocks of St. Philip closer to the river were from Italy might have also influenced the board's thinking, given Italian immigrants' generally low standing compared to that of other white New Orleanians.[87]

Black residents were notably silent about the proposed relocation, which reflected their tendency to prioritize access to schools over their locations. Just as black Catholics ultimately lessened their opposition to racially distinct parishes to gain access to additional parochial schools, black families often tolerated residential isolation as the cost of securing a public school and sustaining a community.[88] At times, blacks even led the charge for locating black schools in heavily black neighborhoods. In 1914, for instance, Walter Cohen and the Colored Educational Alliance had encouraged the school board to move McCarthy to the Ninth Ward's "colored section."[89]

Black New Orleanians also purchased land in largely black neighborhoods and then donated it to the school board to boost their chances of securing additional schools. Between 1907 and 1910, black Seventh Ward residents pooled their money and bought six lots in the block bounded by Annette, St. Anthony, Miro, and Galvez Streets for the construction of a public school. Cohen and Bayou Road principal Mary Coghill were among the roughly 2,500 African Americans who rallied at the site in November 1910 to show support for the project. Similarly, black residents on the west bank of the Mississippi River held fish fries, picnics, and other fund-raising dinners to purchase land for a school on Algiers's isolated "lower coast," an area Gwinn later discussed in his 1921 facilities plan. According to the black-owned *Cleveland Gazette*, this practice was the norm throughout Louisiana. The paper reported in 1911 that African Americans donated the land for nearly 60 percent of the one thousand black public schools in the state while white residents provided land for only 22 percent of the state's nearly two thousand white public schools.[90]

Even with the free land—another example of the "double taxation" blacks often paid in order to access public education—the board was slow to create additional black schools.[91] Several years passed before it erected a wooden framed structure to house Miro Elementary School (later renamed Valena C. Jones) on the site that the Seventh Ward residents donated (see figure 4.2). Recall that this was the school whose "simply awful" conditions in 1923 convinced board member Fannie Baumgartner of the need to open the new facility on Bayou Road to black students. When the board finally replaced the overcrowded Jones building with a modern brick facility in 1929, a crowd of thousands again turned out to celebrate the occasion. (Jones is the black school located between St. Bernard and Elysian Fields Avenue on map 4.2.)[92]

The creation and expansion of Valena C. Jones marked the culmination of years of lobbying by individuals such as Joseph Hardin and Fannie C. Williams and organizations such as the Seventh Ward Educational League and Seventh Ward Civic League. Hardin, a medical doctor and businessman who shared Walter Cohen's engagement in Republican politics, cofounded the Seventh Ward Civic League and supported the creation of similar ward-based associations elsewhere in the city. As in other cities, the Seventh Ward league and the citywide Federation of Civic Leagues, which Hardin also helped establish, pressed city officials to provide the neglected neighborhoods where black residents lived with such basic services as streetlights. The campaign to replace the dangerously inadequate Valena C. Jones building fit this nationwide pattern of black, community-based investment and activism. Decades later, Hardin's peers continued to celebrate him as "a pioneer leader in the organization of a group of interested and civic-minded citizens, who succeeded in getting the Orleans Parish School Board to replace the ancient dilapidated Miro Street School building in the Seventh Ward with a modern adequate brick and concrete structure, the Valena C. Jones School for children of the Seventh Ward."[93]

Under the thirty-three-year leadership of principal Fannie C. Williams, the 2,000-student Jones School became the lifeblood of the Seventh Ward. Williams, who earned her master's degree from the University of Michigan and served as president of the National Association of Teachers in Colored Schools, established a health clinic at the school that enabled students to receive free dental care and other services. She also oversaw the formation of the city's first black Girl Scouts troop and added a nursery school and kindergarten to Jones before the school board provided those opportunities in black schools. Additionally, Williams incorporated African American history and civic education into the Jones curriculum, organizing each classroom into a state with an elected governor and legislative body. The future civil rights leader and United Nations ambassador Andrew Young, who attended Jones in the late 1930s, remembered Williams as "a handsome, dark-skinned woman with pressed, white hair, [who] believed in strict discipline and patrolled the halls of the three-story structure observing classes and seeing for herself that everything was in order." The seasoned educator, Young continued, "went about the task of uplifting the race with great gusto and almost legendary determination."[94]

Despite the school's success, real estate analysts concluded in the late 1930s that the area surrounding Jones "present[ed] a very bad picture" on account of its racially mixed population and poorly maintained houses.[95] A similar dynamic developed between the Joseph Craig School and its Sixth Ward neighborhood. In January 1927, the school board completed construction of the new building on St. Philip Street and transferred Craig's students and the Craig name from Bayou Road to the new location on St. Philip between North Villere and Marais (see map 3.2 for a view of this area). "This school will be remembered as the one erected to replace the new Craig School, which created such a storm when President Fortier, of the School Board, tried to block the entrance of the Negro children [in 1923]," the black-owned *Louisiana Weekly* informed its readers. Yet the 1927 opening of this replacement facility only underscored the Pyrrhic nature of blacks' victory over Fortier four years earlier since it had little net impact on black schooling.[96]

By 1927, the black demand for education already exceeded the capacity of both the building on Bayou Road and the larger school on St. Philip that replaced it. When the four-year-old facility on Bayou Road closed, it ran half-day sessions for students up to the fifth grade to accommodate its oversubscribed enrollment. While the larger St. Philip Street structure reduced the number of students in half-day shifts, it did not eliminate this draconian practice. Even before the building opened, officials expected Craig students through the second grade to attend school for only a morning or afternoon session.[97]

Like the area surrounding McDonogh 35, the St. Philip Street neighborhood also experienced successive waves of demolition and residential displacement *after* it gained a black school. The city began readying the wrecking balls almost as soon as the new school opened. In 1928, Mayor Arthur J. O'Keefe announced plans for the construction of a municipal auditorium at Beauregard (i.e., Congo) Square, bounded by North Rampart, St. Claude, St. Peter, and St. Ann, and by the following year the project had consumed the two residential blocks immediately north of the plaza. During the 1930s, the city also knocked down the nearby Tremé Market, which occupied the wide median along Orleans Avenue between Marais and North Robertson and was the fourth largest public market in the city. In 1940, the federal government began demolishing the fifteen square blocks that had comprised Storyville, the neighborhood adjacent to Tremé that poor black residents had inhabited almost exclusively since the vice district closed in 1917.[98]

The government tore down the old Storyville in order to build the Iberville Housing Project under the US Housing Act of 1937. While that Act required the government to build as many new units as it razed, Iberville was designated for whites, understandably generating considerable resentment among the neighborhood's black residents. Within four months, the last of the area's 817 displaced families were relocated, with a number of the former vice district's black residents resettling in the Lafitte Housing Project immediately north of both Iberville and Tremé and within walking distance of the relocated Craig School. The government completed construction of Lafitte as a blacks-only development in 1941, building it atop a partially vacant, triangular strip of land nestled between a pair of railroad tracks, Orleans Avenue, and Claiborne Avenues. Residents loved Lafitte's well-constructed, red brick apartments, and the project brought stability to the neighborhood.[99]

But realtors and government officials were never bullish about the broader area's future, and they rarely stopped thinking about ways to tear it down. In the mid-1950s, city officials quickly zeroed in on Tremé as they considered building a new cultural center. The neighborhood ultimately sacrificed the nine blocks directly south of Craig between St. Ann and St. Phillip Streets for what became Louis Armstrong Park. By the end of the 1960s the government also cleared the four rows of live oak trees that lined the Claiborne Avenue median through Tremé in order to accommodate an elevated section of Interstate-10.[100]

The tree-lined neutral ground had been a cultural touchstone of Tremé's black community, a spot to watch Mardi Gras parades and to shoot the breeze with friends and neighbors. But in a scene that played out throughout the country, "the highway builders," in historian's Raymond Mohl's words, "rammed an elevated expressway through the neighborhood before anyone could organize or protest." The city's Office of Policy Planning later wrote that "Tremé was considered a blighted area and thus an obvious target for rehabilitation." But with the broader area remaining almost evenly divided between white and black residents until World War II, Craig's location on St. Philip Street likely contributed to the perception that Tremé was black and therefore run-down. The Home Owners' Loan Corporation's 1939 residential survey of New Orleans provided evidence that local realtors believed this to be the case. When explaining why Tremé was a "hazardous" investment, the surveyors noted the area's black residents and its black school: Joseph A. Craig. They pretended as if the neighborhood's lone white school, a small facility occupying a corner opposite Beauregard Square, did not even exist.[101] While this demonstrated that urban renewal in Tremé affected whites as well as blacks, the neighborhood's white residents could more easily relocate to other areas of the city.

The link that the HOLC surveyors made between black schools and poor investments mirrored the logic James Fortier applied in 1923 when he argued that a white school on Bayou Road "would permit the real estate people of the city to sell values in that section." By kicking black students out of the building on Bayou Road, the school board granted Fortier his wish and ensured that white students would not face the kind of overcrowding that continued to plague black schools. After sitting idle during the 1927 spring semester, the Bayou Road facility became the temporary home for the district's commercial high school for white boys. This saved the superintendent from having to implement an earlier plan for those students, which involved housing them in makeshift quarters on the median opposite an existing white school. The following school year, the board shifted the overflow population of white boys from Warren Easton High School to Bayou Road, just as Fortier had encouraged it to do in 1923. After initially calling the school the Warren Easton Annex, the board honored a request from the Daughters of the Confederacy by renaming the building after Liberty Place veteran and *Plessy v. Ferguson* jurist Edward Douglass White.[102]

On the surface, the fact that the conflict over Bayou Road resulted in a new school building for black students seemed to validate the late Booker T. Washington's strategy of emphasizing the mutual obligations that black and white southerners owed one another. But there was nothing mutual about this apparent African American victory. The modern facility that originally opened to black students in February 1923 only came to fruition after more than a decade of pleading from African Americans, whose educational opportunities the school board already sharply limited. The new building also failed to satisfy the long-standing debt the board owed African Americans since it lacked sufficient space to meet the educational demand. The 1927 transfer of black students from Bayou Road to the second new building on St. Philip Street, coupled with the subsequent redevelopment of that neighborhood, further revealed white residents' and policymakers' willingness to permit black advancement exclusively on their terms. As with the Valena C. Jones School, the ordeal highlighted black New Orleanians' commitment to building strong institutions to challenge Jim Crow. Yet it also underscored the persistence and adaptability of white supremacy. Confronted with black demands for more and better school facilities, anxious whites successfully pursued a new racial and spatial order to promote their own social, political, and economic mobility at African Americans' expense.

The Bayou Road saga laid bare the growing consensus among white New Orleanians that black schools did not belong near white homes, even if the surrounding area was racially mixed. While white intolerance for black schools predated even the McDonogh No. 13–35 conversion, it became more firmly entrenched within official policy during the 1920s. But the battle over the racial future of mixed neighborhoods such as the one surrounding the former Bayou Road School quickly became of secondary importance to school officials and upwardly mobile whites. Massive drainage projects in the city's former hinterlands back of Claiborne Avenue were opening up a new frontier for white settlement. As interested as Fortier and others were in saving some of the city's older, racially mixed areas for whites while relegating others to blacks, these incipient subdivisions offered even greater promise for a spatially segregated future. Fortier and his board colleagues eagerly embraced public school construction as the best means available for establishing residential beachheads for whites only. In fact, the dust had barely settled from the Bayou Road saga before the board began scouting properties for a new white high school in Uptown New Orleans.

CHAPTER FIVE

THE MOST ATTRACTIVE
PARTS OF THE MODERN
COMMUNITY

Bernard Fellman considered it an insurance policy. Others derided it as Fellman's folly, joking that the successful dry goods merchant had "buried his money in the mud."[1] Regardless of one's perspective, the narrow spit of land that Fellman purchased for about $4,000 between 1885 and 1887 was not much to behold. The tract sat on the backside of Uptown New Orleans, running nearly two miles toward a navigation canal that emptied into Lake Pontchartrain (see maps 5.1 and 5.2). Development petered out several blocks below the property's southern border, and the land turned swampy on the lakeside of the Claiborne Canal (now Claiborne Avenue). While surveyors subdivided these wilds into a Cartesian grid of named streets as early as the 1850s, those plans were purely aspirational. More people passed through the area aboard the Louisville, New Orleans & Texas Railroad, whose tracks crossed Fellman's property, than lived anywhere nearby. Without the technological means to keep it dry, the Fellman tract seemed destined to remain part of New Orleans's dank, muddy outskirts.[2]

Even after the introduction of a citywide drainage system around the turn of the century, the surrounding area developed slowly. Through the first two decades of the twentieth century, a smattering of black and white truck farmers and dairymen were its only inhabitants. When Fellman's son Leo, who managed Bernard's estate after his death, drew up plans for a residential subdivision on the family's land in 1915, he limited his vision to the fourteen blocks on the riverside of Claiborne. Homebuilders began buying parcels there in the early 1920s, and by the summer of 1923 Fellman had sold seventy-seven of his nearly two hundred lots. The city aided Fellman's

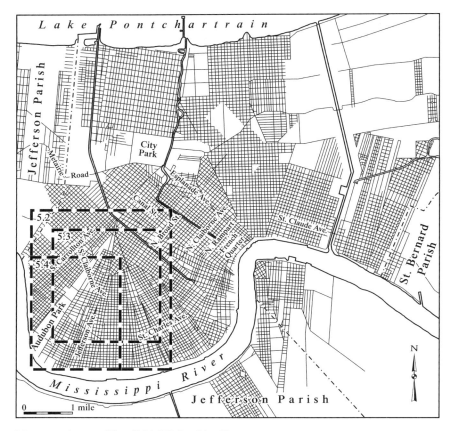

Map 5.1   Areas of detail highlighted in Chapter 5.

efforts to create a refined, residential milieu by passing a zoning ordinance in 1922 that prohibited nearly every type of commercial establishment from the surrounding area. Fellman additionally required purchasers to agree to racially restrictive covenants stating "that there shall not be erected any house, residence, or other structure in which persons of the African race will reside or congregate except as servants employed on the premises." As prices within the subdivision doubled, real estate boosters gushed. "There is virtually a new city growing up," the *Times-Picayune* wrote in June 1923, "and it already is one of the most attractive parts of the modern community."[3]

Although more than half of Fellman's riverside lots were unsold and the twenty-plus blocks of his tract on the lakeside of Claiborne remained un-

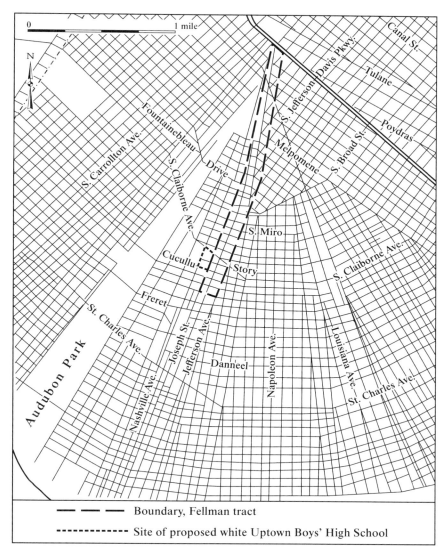

Map 5.2   Uptown New Orleans, the Fellman tract, and proposed white high school site, 1923.

Sources: "Succession of Bernard Fellman," 4 November 1892, COB 145/490, Conveyance Division, Orleans Parish Civil District Court, New Orleans, LA; Orleans Parish School Board Minutes, 13 August 1923, Orleans Parish School Board Collection (MSS 147), Louisiana and Special Collections Department, Earl K. Long Library, University of New Orleans.

touched, the school board agreed with the *Picayune*'s sanguine assessment. Within months of resolving the Bayou Road saga, the board purchased three city blocks adjacent to the Fellman tract in August 1923 as the site for a new high school for white males (see map 5.2).[4] The board intended this additional high school to relieve overcrowding at Warren Easton High, where, President James Fortier had reminded them during the Bayou Road debate, "our white boys . . . are crowded and put in basements." The move also underscored the role that public school—particularly high schools—would play in promoting the disparate development of white and black neighborhoods. As postwar drainage projects dramatically increased the city's habitable footprint, white public schools became "one of the most attractive parts of the modern community," capable of luring residents, boosting public investment, and widening the gap between black and white educational access, residential accommodations, and personal wealth. For white residents, the school board's repeated early investment in nascent subdivisions on the former urban fringe offered welcome relief from the city's older racially mixed neighborhoods, where turf battles continued to rage.

The following section describes the early moves the school board made to support the Fellman tract's development as a whites-only residential subdivision. The chapter's second section then considers how the construction of a new white school in the Broadmoor neighborhood bolstered the spatial reorganization of the city even as African Americans successfully challenged a municipal residential segregation ordinance. The third and final section examines how the creation of multiple white schools near the Fellman tract encouraged municipal and federal efforts to tighten the link between race, education, neighborhood quality, and property values in the segregated city.

I.

The land Bernard Fellman purchased in 1885 was not even part of New Orleans when he migrated to the city in the early 1850s. It was in the separate municipality of Jefferson City, which was still in its infancy as the German native established a dry goods shop on Rampart Street. Jefferson City originated as seven privately developed faubourgs squeezed between the downriver city of Lafayette, which became part of New Orleans in 1852, and the upriver town of Carrollton, which became part of New Orleans in 1874. The 1835 completion of a New Orleans-to-Carrollton passenger rail line bisecting this area (the still active St. Charles streetcar) as well as the Crescent City's growing demand for building materials, waste disposal, meat, and dairy products provided the impetus for these independent suburbs to unite to form Jefferson City.[5]

Dozens of slaughterhouses proliferated near the stock landing at the foot of Louisiana Avenue, and dairy farmers found ample space to pasture cattle upriver from Napoleon Avenue. While Faubourg Plaisance, along Louisiana Avenue, and Faubourg Bouligny, which ran parallel to Napoleon, were established communities by the mid-nineteenth century, the remaining suburbs further upriver were nearly empty. Rickerville, which included the tract Fellman would later buy, contained only an old plantation house near the river and undivided pastureland extending for miles behind it.[6]

That suburb took its name from its primary owner, Samuel J. Ricker Jr. Ricker was a chronic schemer who manipulated his children's portions of his deceased wife's estate to expand his land holdings and personal profits. In the 1840s, he struck up a partnership with John H. Pearson & Co., a freight forwarding firm out of Boston. But Pearson sued Ricker after he failed to explain what happened to $32,000 worth of goods that Pearson had paid him for but never received. Pearson won the lawsuit, and he secured a portion of Ricker's land as his compensation for the unpaid debt.[7]

That land remained in the Pearson family longer than Jefferson City existed as an autonomous entity. New Orleans annexed the town in 1870, after Republican governor Henry Clay Warmoth forcibly removed a conservative municipal government bent on resisting the federal government's plan for Reconstruction. The Reconstruction legislature also undercut Jefferson City's economic base by mandating that all animal slaughtering take place downriver from New Orleans proper, at the facilities of the Crescent City Livestock and Slaughtering Company. The move was intended as both a public health measure and a means of challenging Texas for dominance in the cattle industry. But it also cost the Jefferson City butchers their livelihood, and their lawsuit against the state-sanctioned monopoly provided the US Supreme Court with its first test of the newly passed Fourteenth Amendment. By narrowly interpreting the rights that the amendment protected, the court's decision against the butchers in the *Slaughter-House Cases* laid the legal groundwork for Jim Crow's rise. It had the additional unintended consequence of lighting Jefferson City's path from hardscrabble industrial area to high-end residential district since it effectively eliminated the area's primary trade.[8]

Reconstruction proved more propitious for Bernard Fellman, however, than for Jefferson City's working-class butchers. In 1873, Fellman dissolved his dry goods partnership with Henry Kern to strike up a new partnership with his brother Leon. The switch enabled him to move his storefront operations from Baronne and Rampart Streets to Canal Street, which was the city's premier commercial avenue. When he married Anna Dreyfous the following year at Temple Sinai, one of two congregations favored by the city's wealthier Reform Jews, the *Picayune* referred to him as "one of our most enterprising Canal street merchants, a useful citizen, and an estimable man." Although his partnership with his brother was even more short-lived than his joint venture with Kern, his business continued to thrive after he established his own four-story shop on Canal.[9]

When the Pearsons decided to sell their former Jefferson City swampland in 1885, Fellman bought nearly all of it for about an eighth of the $32,000 it was worth to John Pearson in 1853. The loss did not appear to hurt the well-connected Pearsons, however. When a notary signed off on the sale, Benjamin F. Butler, the Union general who ruled New Orleans with an iron fist during the army's Civil War occupation of the city, stood in as the guardian for two of the family's children. At the time, Butler had recently completed a term as governor of Massachusetts and an unsuccessful run for president. The record was silent regarding Fellman's opinion of the man many New Orleanians referred to as "Beast."[10]

Fellman quickly expanded his Rickerville holdings through additional purchases. He paid $145 for another undeveloped block on the same day that he bought the Pearson land, and a month later he bought three more blocks at tax sales for a total of $35. In 1887, he then paid just $125 for a nearly mile-long stretch of land that had already passed from John Pearson's estate to an intermediary owner. These property acquisitions were often family affairs for Fellman since his brother-in-law Felix J. Dreyfous regularly served as his attorney, and his father-in-law, the well-known notary Abel Dreyfous, occasionally formalized the deals. Despite the speed and regularity with which Fellman bought property, he was much slower to do anything with it. His Rickerville tract remained in abeyance when he died seven years later, as did the farmland he purchased at the northern end of Manhattan. He likely made that purchase after he and his family moved to New York toward the end of the nineteenth century.[11]

Following Bernard's death, his widow Anna Dreyfous Fellman and their son Leo returned to New Orleans, and they maintained this cautious yet calculating course with the family's real estate portfolio. Anna, whose brother Felix was a rising star within reform political circles, remained in the dry goods business while also carefully guarding Bernard's estate.[12] After a fire destroyed the family's Canal Street building in 1901, Anna and Leo rebuilt it while she pursued a largely unsuccessful, decade-long lawsuit in federal court to secure a larger insurance payout. Her attorney when she first filed suit in 1902 was none other than E. B. Kruttschnitt, the school board president and state Democratic chief who spearheaded black disfranchisement in Louisiana. Anna similarly did not hesitate to go to court in 1908 when a man put a fence across what she believed to be the back end of her untended Rickerville property.[13]

Leo Fellman, the only of Anna and Bernard's eight children to return permanently to New Orleans after Bernard's death, used his inheritance to build one of the most successful real estate practices in the city. Nineteen at the time of Bernard's death in 1892, Leo immersed himself in the property side of the family business. He orchestrated his first major development deal shortly after the turn of the century, acquiring property for the construction of a theater and office building in the heart of the city's growing business district. Although Leo became a member of the tony New Orleans Country Club, he favored intellectual pursuits more than golf, tennis, or locker room bull sessions. His social reticence, however, belied the insistent confidence he displayed when doing business.[14]

Nowhere was this more on display than in his handling of the tract that took his family name. In 1909, for instance, the City Engineer's Office produced a map of Rickerville, where Fellman's property was situated, that showed several east-west streets stopping abruptly at Rickerville's downriver edge, effectively cutting it off from the rest of the city. Fellman responded by publishing a pamphlet that lambasted the proposal. "To put it bluntly," Fellman wrote of the city engineer's map, "the result is a making of blind alleys of all the longitudinal streets in that neighborhood, and a material inconvenience to the public and depreciation of property values in that section."[15]

Fellman's argument carried the day, and by 1915 he crafted plans for a subdivision on the portion of the family tract on the riverside of Claiborne. But even as the city extended streets and sewerage, gas, and electrical mains into the proposed subdivision, the area failed to shake its rural feel. It looked, the *Times-Picayune* noted, "like a parkway for homes without the homes."[16]

As World War I wound down, however, Leo Fellman ambitiously took steps to realize his vision for the riverside development. After Bernard's estate passed from Anna to their seven surviving children upon her death in 1919, Leo readied the family tract for development. He first purchased his sister Rose's one-seventh stake in the estate for $95,000. Then the development firm he had named after his father, Bernard Company, acquired his and the five other siblings' shares for $685,000 ($9.96 million in 2017 dollars). Fellman's Bernard Company also paid to widen Peters Avenue (now known as Jefferson Avenue) and to plant palm trees along its median. Additionally, he restricted construction to certain models of single-family homes, each set back from the property line with a minimum lot width of forty feet to avoid crowding. Fellman's racially restrictive covenants as well as the city zoning ordinance that prohibited most businesses from the area further primed the area for the city's growing white, professional class. By 1923, the former cow pasture was in the midst of a dramatic transformation.[17]

The quickening pace of sales and construction within the riverside portion of the Fellman tract coincided with the school board's search for land for an uptown high school for white boys. (The city's extant high school for white males, Warren Easton, was technically neither uptown nor downtown since the school board opened its new building on Canal Street in 1913 in order to satisfy the competing demands of civic leaders from both sections of the city.)[18] The board began discussing possible locations for the uptown high school as early as May 1923, at the same time that it was searching for a property on St. Philip Street that would provide the Craig School with a more racially suitable location. By August, the board settled on an uptown site: three undeveloped blocks adjacent to Fellman's incipient riverside subdivision.

The scale of the purchase distinguished it from previous property acquisitions. While the board paid $42,000 for an entire uptown block for a white elementary school in March 1922 and $48,300 for the St. Philip Street property for Craig in June 1923, it doled out $72,500 for the high school property bounded by South Claiborne and Nashville Avenues and Joseph and Cucullu Streets (see map 5.2). The board unanimously signed off on the purchase even though it was already borrowing millions of dollars and preparing to reduce teachers' salaries to cover an anticipated revenue shortfall.[19]

Immediately after the board approved the purchase, board president James

Fortier ceded the gavel to Vice President Fred Zengel, just as he had done six months before when he spoke against opening the new school building on Bayou Road to blacks. This time, however, he did not have any complaints. Rather, he stepped aside at Zengel's request so his colleagues could vote on a name for the proposed boys' high school. With Fortier abstaining, the board unanimously agreed to name the new school in honor of his father, the deceased professor of romance languages, Creole mythologizer, and Liberty Place veteran Alcée Fortier. After the board members and superintendent eulogized the late professor, James Fortier resumed his chairmanship of the meeting and offered the "sincere appreciation of himself and family for the action of the Board just taken."[20]

Although the board did not plan to build the school for another five years, there was nothing inevitable about the location it selected for the proposed Alcée Fortier High School. A recent flurry of residential construction and what the boosterish *Picayune* called the "insistent demand for vacant lots" reflected the surrounding area's growth.[21] But it remained one of the least densely populated sections of the city. That barrenness was particularly evident in the population map James Fortier had flaunted to incorrectly claim that the area surrounding Bayou Road and Derbigny was entirely white (see map 4.3).[22] Wide swaths of blocks near the proposed school site were not subdivided and numerous lots were empty.[23] On the lakeside of Claiborne Avenue, which was then an unpaved east-west arterial with an open drainage canal running down its center, several tracts near Fellman's were as undeveloped as his. These areas did not have subsurface drainage, and the city had not yet opened their streets.[24]

The section's major attraction was the Ursuline Convent, a massive religious and educational complex of gray brick buildings designed in an English-Gothic style. The convent sat directly across Nashville Avenue from the proposed high school site. The Ursuline nuns, who had run a school for girls since 1727, moved from the rural Ninth Ward to their roughly eight-acre Claiborne Avenue campus in 1912 after the city expropriated their downriver property in order to build new levees and the Industrial Canal.[25] By this time, the Ursulines had long since ceased educating black girls, focusing exclusively on whites instead. When the nuns moved their convent in 1912, their uptown environs were nearly as undeveloped as the Ninth Ward home they left behind. But even as the adjacent area experienced a significant amount of residential growth in the decade following the convent's move, developers could still select from their vacant lot or block of choice in 1923. This was especially true on the lakeside of Claiborne. As with the public schools, the Ursulines' advance into the uptown hinterland helped establish it as white-occupied territory.[26]

Despite the area's relative absence of inhabitants, school board members, the city government, and real estate developers were committed to its development. Soon after the school board purchased the Claiborne Avenue site for the high school, it began negotiations with the city and Fellman over the widening of Joseph Street and the construction of sidewalks along it. Joseph Street ran between the school board's newly acquired property and Fellman's riverside subdivision, although the twenty Joseph Street lots opposite the school site were empty. When Fellman balked at ceding five feet from his side of Joseph Street because it would make his lots too shallow, schools superintendent Nicholas Bauer reminded him that they had a mutual interest in the proposed enhancements. "The additional footage that seemed to be essential to Mr. Fellman's property for the building of bungalows," Bauer tartly noted, "was just as essential to the School Board for the building of a high school."[27] The two sides eventually reached an agreement when the board allowed Fellman to give up four feet in exchange for its eleven.[28] While Fellman drove a hard bargain, he likely recognized that the combination of a high school, a wider street, and sidewalks would raise the sale price for his lots.

Other developers also followed the school board's lead in investing in this section of Uptown. Two months after the board purchased the three blocks on the riverside of Claiborne for the high school, a firm known for its development of high-end, whites-only residential parks paid a reported $80,000 for a two-and-one-half-mile tract on that avenue's lakeside.[29] A few months after that, the *Picayune* noted that developers would extend an existing residential park into that area and that the city would open and pave streets on the lakeside of Claiborne, "affording the much needed and talked of short cut to the commercial center of the city."[30]

Fellman, however, continued to wait patiently. True to his family's form, he held on to the vast majority of the lakeside tract until the city and school board invested even more heavily in the area.[31] As he considered the timing of his next move, he likely paid close attention to the rapid development of the nearby Broadmoor neighborhood. That area's emergence showed that nothing spurred neighborhood growth like a brand new white public school.

II.

For as keen an observer of real estate trends as Fellman, no neighborhood provided a better guide for his own ambitions than Broadmoor, which overlapped with the undeveloped lakeside section of his tract. This area bounded roughly by Claiborne Avenue, Toledano, Octavia, and Melpomene (see map 5.3) was originally a twelve-acre lake that connected to Bayou St. John through a narrow tributary. Alligators and herons were once its chief inhabitants. The introduction of drainage canals in 1885, followed by the construction of a nearby pumping station in 1903, enabled a small number of mostly black settlers to trickle into the area. The Napoleon and South Claiborne Avenue streetcar lines connected Broadmoor's periphery to the rest of the city, and the population gradually increased as drainage improved. When Albert Baldwin Wood, an engineer with the city's Sewerage and Water Board, devised a screw pump in 1913 that was capable of lifting water from below sea level to higher elevation outflow canals, Broadmoor and other watery outskirts appeared poised to explode. But budget shortfalls and restrictions on building materials during World War I stalled both the city's ambitious plans for swampland reclamation and Broadmoor's growth.[32]

Once the federal government lifted its wartime limitations, developers and the school system prepared for a bonanza of construction activity. As with Miami Beach, which emerged Venus-like from Florida's mangrove swamps following the war, mastering an inhospitable environment was a precondition for the Crescent City's growth. By 1925, the city's "Wood pumps" helped drain 27,000 acres of land that had been uninhabitable at the turn of the century. This newly dried land enabled New Orleans to maintain its position as the South's largest metropolis even as Miami and Houston joined Los Angeles and San Diego as the nation's fastest growing metropolitan areas. After writing just 552 building permits in 1918, New Orleans granted more than three thousand in 1923, largely in the former swamps back of Claiborne Avenue.[33]

Before the recession set in a few years later, the flush economic times that immediately followed the war enabled the city to invest in public education as never before. By raising the basis for collecting property taxes for 1920 from 75 percent to 90 percent of assessed value, the Commission Council provided the school system with the much-needed opportunities to grow alongside the city and to modernize its antiquated facilities. When Schools Superintendent

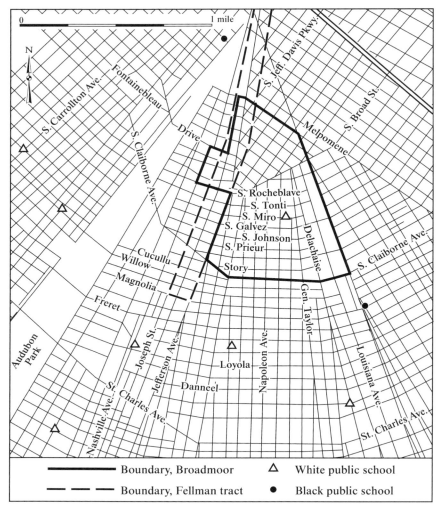

Map 5.3 Broadmoor, the Fellman tract, and area public schools, 1922.

Sources: *School Directory*, 1920–1921, box 1, School Directories, Orleans Parish School Board Collection (MSS 147), Louisiana and Special Collections Department, Earl K. Long Library, University of New Orleans; Sanborn Map Company, *Insurance Maps of New Orleans*, vol. 5, additional sheet 532, September 1922; "Succession of Bernard Fellman," 4 November 1892, COB 145/490, Conveyance Division, Orleans Parish Civil District Court, New Orleans, LA; Greater New Orleans Community Data Center.

John Gwinn outlined the district's capital needs following the council vote, he noted the reflexive relationship between the school system's and the city's expansion. The district's building program, he wrote in the summer of 1920, needed to consider "the [current] distribution of population and present and probably future directions of growth of population."[34]

While forecasts about the city's growth were a necessary if imprecise part of the planning process, Broadmoor provided Gwinn and the school board with an opportunity to put their fingers on the scale. The area was poised for a building boom, and its recently drained tracts offered developers and city leaders an opportunity to claim it for whites only. The only problem was that many black residents already lived in its older, established sections.[35]

The family of John Boucree, who was born in 1923, was among those early black settlers. As he recalled, "There was a portion like my father and his father [that] bought property in that area before I was born when it was swamp and wilderness and whatnot, and they built in that particular area." Boucree's father, who was a carpenter, built his family's single shotgun house at South Galvez near Delachaise. His grandfather, who was a contractor, built a larger two-story house down the street.[36]

White officials, however, were loath to let history—or black families like the Boucrees—interfere with their vision of progress, and in 1921 the school board committed to building a white elementary school in the neighborhood. The board's gambit was the opening move in a far-reaching campaign to establish Broadmoor's whites-only bona fides. As Leo Fellman surely recognized, the strategy worked.

By the end of World War I, Broadmoor's mixture of empty lots, houses under construction, and yet-to-be-platted blocks provided a glimpse of what Fellman's riverside development would look like a few years later. The Sanborn Map Company, which mapped structures in the nation's cities in order to assess fire insurance risk, did not include the largely uninhabited Broadmoor neighborhood in its 1908–1909 survey of New Orleans. But Broadmoor's uptown edge, the area between Claiborne, Peters (later Jefferson), Napoleon, and South Rocheblave, experienced enough construction by September 1920 that the company issued a new page to document its growth. The map underscored the extent to which Broadmoor was in the process of being born. Six of the thirty-four blocks in this section of the neighborhood were not subdivided, and another four contained only empty lots. Nearly all the blocks with homes also replicated in miniature the jack-o'-lantern appearance of the area as a whole, with uninhabited spaces next to inhabited ones. Maps of city-wide construction activity and the fact that Sanborn did not survey the rest of Broadmoor for another two years indicated that this pattern predominated throughout the neighborhood.[37]

Despite Broadmoor's uneven development, Gwinn urged the board in the summer of 1921 to purchase land for a white school in this "rapidly developing area back of Claiborne intermediate above and below Napoleon Avenue."[38] The board acted quickly: in September 1921 it closed on a vacant block in that section for $15,500.[39] The Andrew Wilson School, named for a recently deceased former school board member, opened a year later on South Miro Street between Milan and General Pershing.[40] The board acquired the land that spurred Broadmoor's growth as a white enclave from C. C. Dejoie, a prominent black Creole insurance executive who later founded the *Louisiana Weekly* in 1925. Considering the number of black people who had already settled in Broadmoor, Dejoie's early toehold in the area was not an anomaly. Black residents such as the Boucrees, in fact, dominated the two built-up blocks bounded by South Tonti, South Galvez, General Taylor, and Delachaise Streets immediately east of the Wilson school site.[41]

While Broadmoor was already expanding when the board committed to building the school, residential construction intensified after the board acquired the property from Dejoie. Builders erected scores of homes during the year the school was under construction, and the area still had plenty of room to grow after Wilson opened in September 1922.[42] Sanborn, in fact, did not even map the area surrounding Wilson until the month the school opened, and even then dozens of lots remained vacant and Napoleon Avenue was the only paved street nearby.[43] Not surprisingly, real estate agents were quick to highlight Wilson's proximity when attempting to sell lots in Broadmoor. The phrase "near Wilson School," for instance, appeared in at least forty-five real estate advertisements in the *Times-Picayune* in 1923 and 1924.[44] The racially restrictive covenants placed on massive developments such as Louisiana Avenue Parkway, which ran along Broadmoor's eastern edge and was virtually uninhabited when the school opened, also boosted sales and aided the area's growth as a white enclave. By 1925, the school district was already looking for additional space to accommodate the white students who had flocked to the three-year-old Wilson School.[45]

Broadmoor's experience was not unique, either. In 1923, the board agreed to build a white school in a new subdivision on the West Bank of the Mississippi River after its developer offered to donate the land. As with Broadmoor, the board built the school before the neighborhood was fully inhabited.[46] The board was also an early investor in the lily-white Lakeview subdivision as it was taking shape in the mid-1920s.[47]

A school's perceived ability to enhance a neighborhood's quality and racial character also extended beyond the New Orleans city limits. In addition to touting a new $600-per-lot residential development in neighboring Jefferson Parish as "a strictly white place of residence," a 1923 newspaper advertisement for the Crestmont Park neighborhood highlighted the nearby public school that was under construction. Jefferson Heights, a more modestly priced subdivision adjacent to Crestmont Park, also sought to cash in on this same school's construction (see figure 5.1). The fact that Jefferson Heights' owners had donated the land for the school to the parish government underscored the perceived importance of schools to suburban development.[48] These early Jefferson subdivisions also laid the foundation for the parish's explosive growth following World War II, which the federal government further fueled through the construction of Interstate 10 and the backing of low-interest loans for whites who bought homes in racially homogenous communities. Outside of the New Orleans metropolitan area, school officials in Raleigh, North Carolina, also relocated white schools to racially restrictive suburbs during the 1920s with the understanding that housing construction would soon follow.[49]

In addition to highlighting white residents' interest in education and racial homogeneity, the public schools' ability to draw them to newly developed neighborhoods reflected the prominent role white children, or at least concerns about their welfare, played in early twentieth-century urban development. The crown jewel of New Orleans's reclaimed lakefront, for instance, was a subdivision that featured dead-end streets specifically intended to offer "sanctuaries" for youths.[50] Removing their children from the unavoidable interracial contact of the inner city, many white parents seemed to think, was best for their safety, health, and future.

To a certain extent, however, Wilson's popularity exacerbated rather than alleviated tensions over race and space. The pressure mounted as Wilson and other uptown white schools pressed the school board for annexes toward the end of 1925. The Parents' Club from the E. B. Kruttschnitt School, located at Dryades and Foucher, presented its case before the board that December. Like the old McDonogh No. 13, Kruttschnitt served a significant number of Jewish students, a demographic fact that the school board indirectly acknowledged when naming it after the prominent Jewish lawyer and politician who had died the year before the school opened in 1907.[51]

After the Kruttschnitt Parents' Club asked for an annex at the school board meeting on December 11, 1925, Superintendent Nicholas Bauer, who had replaced Gwinn, noted the similar requests the board had already received from Wilson and Merrick, another uptown white school. "The matter called for serious thought," Bauer said, "as all requests were linked together in order to provide for the rapidly growing area back of Napoleon Avenue." Board president James Fortier agreed. "The situation would be solved in some way," he said. The difficulty, he acknowledged, lay in determining how many annexes the board should build, where it should build them, or whether it should build an entirely new school in lieu of or even in addition to the annexes. But he assured parents that "the matter would be taken under advisement at once."[52]

The Kruttschnitt parents' confidence that the board would promptly address their petition likely waned after they heard Fortier's response to the next request the board received. Jacob Hoffman, a white jeweler who lived in the Ninth Ward, encouraged the board to buy land for a school near the Industrial Canal since property values were rapidly rising there. Fortier replied that "the Board may build a school this year or the next, but it would make no promises." The president then showcased the irascibility that had marked his opposition to the Craig School's Bayou Road location two years earlier. Fortier told Hoffman that the board recognized that children in his and other outlying areas walked great distances to reach school. But, Fortier continued, the board "would wait until it was definitely decided what kind of section this would be [since] it wanted to be sure of the trend of the population as the improper locating of a school would be as wrong as not building any school at all." While Hoffman's Ninth Ward neighborhood was not very densely populated, Sanborn maps showed that it was nearly as built up in 1908 as Broadmoor was in the early 1920s. Since the area was almost exclusively residential, Fortier's unwillingness to build a school there until the board knew "what kind of section" it would become likely reflected his concern that it would become a black neighborhood. While the board believed that the Wilson School and the white homebuyers it attracted could beat back the early black advances into Broadmoor, it had less confidence that a school could preserve the racial sanctity of a working-class area like the Ninth Ward.[53]

That logic did not bode well for the Kruttschnitt parents' petition for more space because the area surrounding the school was already racially and socioeconomically mixed. After the board failed to act on their December 1925 petition, the school's boosters renewed their request a year later. By then, however, Bauer concluded "that the enrollment in the Kruttschnitt School is falling off because of negroes coming into the neighborhood [and] that additional accommodations are needed in this vicinity but not on the present site of the Kruttschnitt School, which is becoming a negro neighborhood."[54]

Three weeks later, arsonists ignited the first in a series of bombs targeting black property near Kruttschnitt. The first blast went off October 30 about seven blocks from the school, causing no injuries. The target appeared to be the black Lincoln Theater on the corner of Howard (later La Salle) and Louisiana Avenue. Shortly before 11 p.m. two nights later, a stick of dynamite or small bomb exploded on the steps of Henry E. Braden's nearby home in the 2000 block of Louisiana Avenue. Located three blocks from Kruttschnitt between South Saratoga and Danneel Streets, Braden's house was valued at more than $20,000. The explosion resonated for more than a mile, tore through Braden's concrete front steps, and shattered his home's front windows. Braden, an insurance executive who also owned the black Astoria Hotel near McDonogh 35 High School, was among the prominent African Americans who had pushed for black children to gain access to the new school building on Bayou Road three years before. His neighbors also included influential black residents such as Fortunatus P. Ricard, the educator who had pilloried the white opponents of McDonogh No. 13's conversion into the black McDonogh 35 in 1917.[55]

By mid-November a third bomb went off near black homes at Eighth Street and Carondelet, which was within blocks of Kruttschnitt School and Braden's home. This time, the attackers dropped their explosive from a speeding car, shattering several windows in the area. Bombers then returned to Braden's home late in the evening of November 13. Witnesses said five white youths or men lobbed an incendiary from a passing car and drove by the house again to inspect the damage, which was minimal.[56] While it is impossible to say whether Bauer's comment about Kruttschnitt's environs "becoming a negro neighborhood" instigated the bombings, the superintendent's remark was certainly not what the school's patrons wanted to hear. They likely interpreted it as a death sentence for their school and neighborhood; quite possibly, Bauer's words inspired them to fight back.

African Americans in cities such as Philadelphia and Louisville faced similarly violent reactions during the 1910s and 1920s when they moved into supposedly white neighborhoods, and they often responded in kind. The most famous example involved Ossian Sweet, a black doctor in Detroit whose new home came under attack from several hundred white residents in September 1924. The violence against Sweet's home followed a white mob's eviction of two other black Detroiters who had purchased homes in the city. In one of those cases, the mob destroyed Dr. A. L. Turner's house and stole his furniture. Sweet faced a murder charge after he fired into the crowd that surrounded his family home, but he ultimately secured an acquittal. The summer after the attack on Sweet's house, as many as 4,000 rock-throwing whites surrounded another black family's home in Detroit, dispersing only after the family fired back.[57]

In New Orleans, Superintendent Bauer's comment and the bombings that followed occurred at a moment when friction over racially mixed housing was at its highest level since Robert Charles's standoff with police twenty-six years before. The Commission Council had stoked these tensions two years earlier by approving a residential segregation ordinance. The September 1924 ordinance, which prohibited black people from moving into majority white neighborhoods and vice versa, built upon the grassroots fervor for residential segregation that had surrounded debates about public school locations for more than a decade. The act defined "white community" and "negro community" to "embrace every residence fronting on either side of any street within three hundred feet of the location of the property involved, measured along the middle of the street in any and all directions." While the ordinance did not require members of the community's existing racial minority to leave, it barred any new minority inhabitants from moving into the neighborhood without the express approval of its racial majority.[58]

Council members took only ten seconds to adopt the ordinance, and white boosters crowded the council's chambers to cheer the measure's passage. If Mrs. L. E. Stephens's congratulatory comments to the council provided any indication, school- and youth-related issues were particularly relevant to the ordinance's supporters. "You may be sure that not only myself but every other mother of white children in New Orleans sincerely appreciates this restriction that will prevent negro children coming into our communities and mixing with our children," she told the council. Stephens lived down the street from the black Boucree family and one block from the Wilson School, which her children presumably attended. Like many of the houses in the area, her duplex on South Galvez Street was built after Broadmoor's white public school opened.[59]

Broadmoor and the Kruttschnitt School neighborhood immediately south of it quickly became ground zero for the new segregation law. Two days after the council passed the measure, whites living along the 2700 and 2800 blocks of Louisiana Avenue between Willow and Magnolia Streets—roughly nine blocks north of Kruttschnitt—posted large placards declaring that the area was strictly "for white people." One sign in the 2700 block read, "Under the new law—Act 119 of 1924—this block is for white only. Anyone destroying this sign will be dealt with according to law."[60]

The signs went up after word spread that a black doctor named J. E. Simms planned to move to a duplex in the 2700 block of Louisiana, six blocks from Henry Braden's house. Residents also believed that another black man planned to move to the 2800 block. While blacks already owned and occupied two homes in the 2700 block, the *Picayune* reported that white neighbors viewed those residents "with disfavor" but not "antagonism" since they believed blacks would voluntarily leave the neighborhood once the city enforced the new ordinance. Seeking to stay away from a hostile area, Simms sought a release from his purchase agreement. When the bombings riddled this area two years later, the *Louisiana Weekly* noted that the explosions took place "in the section where the bitter segregation fight was begun."[61]

While Dr. Simms's decision to vacate his purchase likely delayed the violent showdown south of Claiborne Avenue, the Broadmoor neighborhood north of Claiborne became the city's first target when it began enforcing the ordinance. The city scored its first conviction under the act in the spring of 1925, ordering a black woman named Anna Beck either to pay a $50 fine or serve sixty days in jail. Under the law, Beck also had to find a new place to live or face additional penalties. The court determined that Beck had violated the ordinance by moving into a home in the 3400 block of Milan Street between South Johnson and South Galvez, which it said was a white neighborhood.

Beck's home was two blocks south of Wilson School and roughly one block from the homes of ordinance supporter Mrs. L. E. Stephens and early Broadmoor settlers the Boucrees. Her case highlighted the aggression with which white officials sought to erase Broadmoor's black past. It also underscored the role that private real estate practices as well as school and housing policies played in encouraging white settlement. Like most of Milan Street between Wilson and South Johnson Street, Beck's home did not exist when the school opened in 1922. To the extent that the built-up area around Wilson then had a racial identity, it was decidedly black. Yet the homebuilding that followed the school's construction quickly tipped the balance in favor of white people, bolstering their claims to territorial dominance under the residential segregation ordinance.[62]

The police did more than enforce the ordinance. Officers stopped John Boucree twice as a teenager on the presumption that he did not belong in the neighborhood his family had long inhabited. Once, police pulled him off of his own porch on the suspicion that he had robbed a nearby house. In that instance, a white neighbor came to his defense and chewed out the officer for detaining him. Another time, two police officers stopped him as he walked from the Napoleon Avenue streetcar to his house at dusk. When Boucree told the officers that he lived nearby, one replied, "Well then nigger, move to another area." Dumbfounded, Boucree continued the three blocks toward his home as the police trailed him in their patrol car.[63]

As in other cities, African Americans in New Orleans fiercely resisted the city's expanded effort to restrict where they could live. Boucree, for instance, recalled his mother fielding aggressive calls from white realtors seeking to buy his family's home. "They wanted to clear this area out of blacks who were living in there and they couldn't do it unless they bought the property owned by blacks," he said. "One day I happened to be listening, my mother answered the telephone and somebody was offering her and she said, 'No, my house is not up for sale.' She said, 'Now, if I sell you my house what am I going to do?' He said, 'Oh, you can go and shack up with somebody else until you find another place.' She said, 'Well, you go and shack up with whoever that person is,' and hung up the telephone."[64]

In addition to these individual acts of resistance, black New Orleanians launched an organized campaign against the residential segregation ordinance. In October 1925, Rev. Robert E. Jones, editor of the *Southwestern Christian Advocate,* headed a group of black businessmen and property owners that presented a petition opposing the ordinance to the New Orleans Association of Commerce. They emphasized the ordinance's economic consequences as well as its arbitrariness. "We are doubtful," they wrote, "of the safety of the investment of homes for our people, as it is an easy matter to declare any part of the city a white community or it is an easy matter to turn any part of the city into a white community by forcing out a sufficient number of our people from that community." Since black homeowners often lived in one half of a double while renting out the other half, the petitioners noted that police enforcement of the ordinance scared away prospective tenants, which jeopardized their ability to pay their mortgages. That argument gained the support of the white City Homestead League, which sought a solution that, in the *Picayune*'s words, would "accomplish the aims of segregation without injury to property and human rights."[65]

At a subsequent meeting with city officials and white real estate and business leaders, Joseph Hardin, the Seventh Ward Civic League cofounder, emphasized the limited scope of his group's demands. "There has never been a case where Negroes have tried to force themselves upon such sections as Rosa Park or Audubon [Place]," Hardin said, citing two upscale, exclusively white developments in Uptown New Orleans. "They do want to move out of districts unpaved and unimproved and enjoy facilities the same as any other people." While city officials vowed to eliminate the hardships the ordinance created for blacks, they nevertheless continued to enforce it. Police officers finally stopped harassing blacks under the ordinance in February 1926, after black residents and a real estate company joined forces to secure an injunction. By then, however, a black homeowner's challenge to the law was winding its way toward the US Supreme Court.[66]

The local branch of the NAACP prepared its legal challenge to the segregation ordinance soon after the mayor signed it into law. The group found a plaintiff after a white man named Joseph Tyler secured an injunction blocking black homeowner Benjamin Harmon from converting his single cottage into a double. Harmon intended to rent one-half of the converted double to black tenants, and Tyler received the injunction on the grounds that the segregation ordinance barred Harmon from doing so. When the NAACP challenged the injunction, a civil district court judge ruled in its favor, stating that New Orleans's ordinance was no different from the Louisville segregation statute that the US Supreme Court struck down in *Buchanan v. Warley* in 1917. In that case, which the national NAACP spearheaded, the court found that Louisville's ordinance violated the Fourteenth Amendment's prohibition against the deprivation of property without due process of law. Louisville, the court ruled, could not prevent the sale of a property strictly because the person who intended to buy and inhabit it was black.[67]

Despite this apparent precedent aligned against him, Tyler appealed to the Louisiana Supreme Court with the support of New Orleans's city attorney. The justices there accepted the city's contention that its ordinance was constitutional because it merely regulated the occupancy, but not the sale, of property. "To say that such a law takes away the freedom of contract," Justice C. J. O'Niell wrote in his March 1925 decision, "would be the same as to say that the so-called zoning ordinances—by which, in many cities, business establishments are forbidden in residence districts—take away the freedom of contract because they forbid an owner of property in such district to sell it to a grocer who is willing and ready to buy it only on condition that he may use it for his grocery store." But the US Supreme Court found O'Niell's logic to be too clever by half. Harmon's case had reached the high court in April 1926 after black New Orleanians raised $10,000 to fund the appeal, and the court heard arguments in the spring of 1927. In a per curium decision, the court rejected the Crescent City's residential segregation ordinance on the authority of *Buchanan v. Warley,* which had explicitly stated that the right to own property was meaningless without the accompanying right to occupy it.[68]

By underscoring the combined potential of collective action and the federal judiciary to address racial inequities, Harmon's triumph lighted a path for New Orleans's nascent civil rights movement. Seizing upon the decision's significance, DeJoie's *Louisiana Weekly* immediately issued a call for further action. "Let us determine that we shall contend with every legal and right effort for those things that should be ours and are denied us," the *Weekly* announced. "We have won a signal victory. And every victory that is won for us must be won by us."[69]

White developers and officials, however, quickly proved that they did not need a segregation ordinance either to kick blacks out of neighborhoods where they already lived or to bar them from new ones. In Broadmoor, the combined force of a white public school, racially restrictive covenants, the potential for violence, and rising home prices made it all but impossible for black people to live there. By 1940, the neighborhood's population of more than seven thousand included just 389 black residents, John Boucree's family of six among them.[70] Leo Fellman, whose interest in the bottom line fueled his embrace of white supremacy, applied Broadmoor's lessons to the development of the remainder of his tract. As the school board expanded its plans for the uptown white high school it had committed to in 1923, Fellman and his associates seized an opportunity to build and sell even more homes.

III.

Within two years of buying the Claiborne Avenue property intended to house Alcée Fortier High School, school officials began considering building a second white high school nearby. The idea may have come from Mayor Martin Behrman. In August 1925, Behrman sent Superintendent Bauer a brief note stating that he wanted Bauer to talk with the city attorney about a square of land that the city owned several blocks closer to the river from the proposed Fortier High site.[71] The land was part of the Touro-Shakespeare Alms House's spacious and mostly unused grounds, which ran between Nashville Avenue and Joseph Street from South Rampart (later Danneel) toward the southern boundary of Leo Fellman's riverside subdivision (see map 5.4).[72]

The Alms House received its initial funding in 1882 from professional gamblers who preferred to donate to charity rather than pay licensing fees. Allen Elementary School, which opened in 1904, was located on the Alms House's property at the corner of Nashville and Franklin (later Loyola) in a building that previously served as the Boys' House of Refuge. But Allen catered more to the affluent than the indigent. Many wealthy, white New Orleanians had started moving to this section of Uptown toward the end of the nineteenth century, and the school board created Allen partly to serve them. Noting the lack of nearby sidewalks and paved streets when Allen opened, the *Picayune* predicted that "the school may have some influence on the building up of that area back of St. Charles Avenue, increase the value of property and improve it generally."[73]

The otherwise financially disastrous Cotton Centennial Exposition of 1884, which took place in the present-day Audubon Park, had provided the initial spark for the area's development. After well-heeled New Orleanians built houses near the shuttered Exposition site, their investment and lobbying contributed to Audubon's eventual transformation from untamed swamp to landscaped park. Beginning in the 1890s, developers also began carving up nearby property to create private "residential parks," which attracted still more affluent, white residents. Frederick Law Olmsted Sr., whose son John Charles Olmsted spearheaded Audubon Park's makeover, had pioneered the use of British-inspired deed restrictions to create the United States' first park-like suburb in Riverside, Illinois. Olmsted's other son, the landscape architect and zoning advocate Frederick Jr., later refined this practice to create

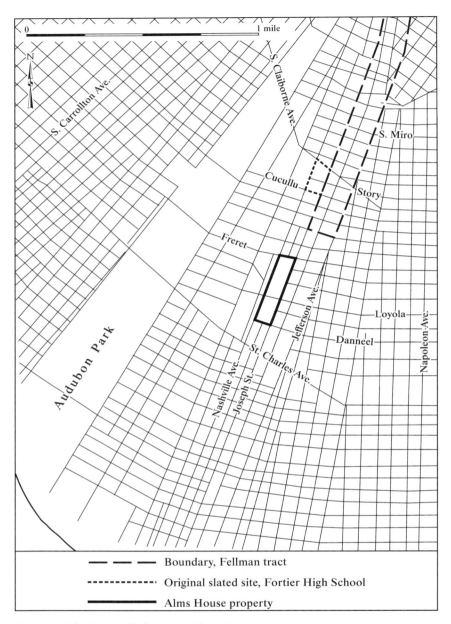

Map 5.4 The Touro-Shakespeare Alms House property, 1924.
Sources: "Succession of Bernard Fellman," 4 November 1892, COB 145/490, Conveyance
Division, Orleans Parish Civil District Court, New Orleans, LA; Orleans Parish School
Board Minutes, 13 August 1923, Orleans Parish School Board Collection (MSS 147), Louisiana and Special Collections Department, Earl K. Long Library, University of New Orleans; Sanborn Map Company, *Insurance Maps of New Orleans*, vol. 5, 1909, sheets 507,
509, 510.

the exclusive Roland Park subdivision outside Baltimore. In New Orleans, development began on two additional residential parks opposite the Allen School—Richmond and Everett Place—shortly after the school opened.[74]

Tulane University was also in the vanguard of this upriver migration, moving its campus from the edge of the French Quarter to its current spot on St. Charles Avenue opposite Audubon Park in the early 1890s. Loyola College soon followed Tulane to St. Charles, building its present-day campus on an adjacent lot beginning in 1909. The black Leland University, whose St. Charles Avenue campus predated the Cotton Expo and Loyola's and Tulane's moves uptown, soon fell victim to the surrounding section's growth. The new residents complained about their black neighbors, and the city pressured the school to make upgrades to its physical plant that it could scarcely afford. When Leland abandoned its campus in 1915 after suffering extensive hurricane damage, a developer quickly converted it to a whites-only residential park named Newcomb Boulevard.[75] The stately yet secluded nature of developments such as Everett Place and Newcomb Boulevard meant the broader area remained bucolic. Lawrence Fabacher, a brewery president who built a large St. Charles Avenue residence and estate near the Alms House, maintained a private casino, poultry house, conservatory, and stables on his property.[76] His cows reportedly grazed on the Alms House grounds throughout the 1920s.[77]

Several months after Behrman contacted Bauer about the Alms House property, the school board set its sights on acquiring a portion of it. In a closed-door session in April 1926, the board instructed a district administrator to meet with the Commission Council to gauge its interest in donating the block immediately behind Allen as the site for long-discussed Fortier High.[78] By then, uptown residents were increasingly pressuring the board to build the boys' high school it had first discussed and purchased property for three years before.

Fannie Baumgartner even made the construction of the school one of her top priorities during her 1926 school board reelection campaign. The silk stocking composition of her campaign committee underscored the extent to which her platform reflected the interests of the city's white uptown establishment. In addition to Mrs. George P. Thompson, the president of the Parents' Cooperative Club and perennial school board gadfly, the committee included Ida Weiss Friend, a Public School Alliance veteran who had complained for years about overcrowded conditions at Allen.[79] Ironically, Allen's crowding stemmed partly from the fact that the school board allowed students who lived near Wilson to attend Allen due to the lack of sidewalks on the lakeside of Claiborne.[80] This turn of events provided another reminder of the precipitating role Wilson played in Broadmoor's development and of the unintended consequences of building schools in advance of other city services.

Parental and community demand for the uptown boys' high school grew throughout 1927 and 1928, but the school board lacked the funds to build the school. Leo Fellman, meanwhile, began planning for the opening of the lakeside portion of his tract, which faced the originally proposed school site on Claiborne Avenue. The developer's first task was to lobby the Commission Council for a street that would connect his land to the lakeside portion of Canal Street via Jefferson Davis Parkway, which would provide future residents with a speedier, backend route to the city's business district. In February 1929, the Council voted to close a four-block stretch of Joseph Street and open a new street through Fellman's property from Fontainebleau Drive to Melpomene. In exchange, it asked Fellman to donate the land for the new road, which he later named Vendome Place, and to pay to pave it and install subsurface drainage and sewerage pipes beneath it. The Council also agreed to pave Octavia Street in order to connect it with Jefferson Davis.[81]

Shortly before the Council green-lighted Fellman's new boulevard, the school board also took steps that dramatically increased Uptown's cachet as the city's premier residential area. In November 1927, the board opened a new, nearly $400,000 building for Allen on the Loyola Avenue end of the Alms House property. While the building primarily served elementary school students, it also provided space for high school girls taking secretarial courses. A year after this new structure opened, the board struck a $258,000 deal with the city to acquire the three-block portion of the Alms House grounds stretching from Allen's Loyola Avenue site to Freret Street. W. A. Kernaghan, known locally as the "dean of real estate men," aided the purchase by conducting a pro bono appraisal of the property and advising the board on how much it should pay.[82]

In early 1930, the board then allocated more than one-third of a three-million-dollar bond issue to build Fortier High for boys and a separate academic high school for white girls. The board decided to erect Fortier on the Freret Street side of the Alms House property and the girls' high school on the Claiborne Avenue property purchased in 1923. Its plan also called for the construction of an additional $200,000 building for Allen along the Joseph Street side of that property, which would permit the school to serve its commercial and elementary students in separate facilities.[83] The *Picayune* marveled at the "great educational center rising in [this] small uptown area." Noting the proposed buildings' proximity to Tulane, Loyola, and the Ursuline Convent, the paper wrote that "those fortunate seekers after knowledge who live in this section will, in a very few years, be within walking distance of schools offering elementary, intermediate and high school work, commercial courses, Catholic parochial instruction and college and graduate courses leading from freshman composition to anything you want for the reaching of a Ph.D."[84]

Even as the board moved forward with the construction of Fortier and the girls' high school, which it named after settlement house stalwart Eleanor McMain, portions of the surrounding area remained unimproved. Nashville Avenue, which ran alongside both high school properties, was unpaved. A three-block stretch of Nashville was also impassable since it served as an unofficial "dumping ground for all kind of trash."[85] Yet the fact that the board spent more than three times as much for the Freret Street site in 1928 as it had for the similarly sized plot on Claiborne five years before spoke to the neighborhood's rapidly rising prospects.

The city also took steps to preserve the Uptown real estate market's great expectations. In 1929, it adopted a comprehensive zoning ordinance that permitted only single and double residential units, churches, and schools in that area. Cities throughout the nation took similar measures during the 1920s as civic and commercial leaders embraced city planning as a single-shot approach to boosting economic growth, social order, and their own residential and business investments. Recall that bans on multifamily housing like the one New Orleans applied to Uptown effectively barred poor and black residents under the cover of preserving property values in higher-end neighborhoods. Developers such as Fellman, who had already limited construction in his riverside subdivision to singles and duplexes through restrictive covenants, understood and appreciated this dynamic. He would have also recognized that the concentration of so many white public schools in a single section of the city further protected the neighborhood's property values and racial purity, along with his subdivision's racially restrictive covenants.[86] While rarely acknowledged by historians, school construction strongly bolstered the city planning movement.[87]

Even though the Depression sent the local real estate market into a tailspin, white school construction and residential development proceeded apace uptown. By the time Fortier High opened in February 1931, McMain High School for girls was on track to open the following year and the city was in the process of paving both the lakeside extension of Octavia Street and Vendome Place, the new boulevard it had cut through the Fellman tract between Fontainebleau Drive and Melpomene Avenue.

While neighborhood protests scuttled the school board's plan for a second Allen building—parents disliked the idea of upwards of six thousand students sharing a campus with limited playground space—the uptown educational center was well on its way. As the city neared the end of its Octavia Street and Vendome Place paving jobs in March 1931, Leo Fellman announced his intentions to subdivide and sell the portion of his tract on the far side of Claiborne Avenue. But he died in 1934 at the age of 59 before he could carry that plan to fruition.[88]

Following Fellman's death, his longtime business associate Stanley LeMarie stepped up to fulfill his mentor's vision. LeMarie had started working with Fellman in 1920 when he was thirty years old, very likely cutting his teeth selling lots in Fellman's subdivision on the riverside of Claiborne Avenue. Beginning in 1935, LeMarie marketed the subdivided lakeside portion of the Fellman tract much as his deceased boss had sold the riverside subdivision a decade before. Between Claiborne Avenue and Fontainebleau Drive, a winding tree-covered boulevard that connected with Broad Street as it sliced through the center of Broadmoor, LeMarie restricted purchasers to the construction of single residences that cost at least $7,000. Duplex apartments were only permitted on certain streets. LeMarie implemented similar restrictions along Vendome Place, except that the houses there had to be slightly larger, the minimum construction cost was higher, and no duplexes were allowed. Just as Fellman had done with his riverside subdivision, LeMarie adopted restrictive covenants to exclude black people from property ownership. They were barred from living or congregating in any of the subdivision's houses on the lakeside of Claiborne unless they were employed as servants.[89]

LeMarie started selling the lots at an inauspicious time. With the Depression deepening, prices for existing homes dropped and the cost of building new ones rose. The $7,000 minimum required for homes built in the subdivision was also twice the average value of new single-family homes in New Orleans in 1938 and beyond the reach of most of the city's workers. By 1939, however, LeMarie managed to sell about 60 percent of the area's lots at prices ranging from $2,000 to $5,500 apiece. All but one of the purchasers paid in full in cash, and the one buyer who relied upon a mortgage paid off that loan within a year. Based upon the number of homes constructed by 1940, the lots closest to McMain's Claiborne Avenue campus appeared to be the most popular, followed by those on Vendome.[90]

McMain's presence also appeared to spur construction within Fellman's original riverside development. In 1933, for instance, the section of the subdivision nearest McMain was the least built up. By 1951, however, the four blocks adjacent to the girls' high school contained an additional twenty-seven homes. The city also paved Nashville and eliminated the dump that had previously blocked traffic heading to the far side of Claiborne Avenue.[91]

Similar activity took place outside of the Fellman tract near Fortier High. In the late 1930s, real estate broker F. Poche Waguespack and his associates paid the city $70,000 for the remaining block of the Alms House grounds, located across Loyola Avenue from the Allen-Fortier complex. In 1939, Waguespack said he planned to subdivide the tract into about fifteen lots, several of which he had already sold. His expectation that construction costs for the subdivision's first three homes would be about $40,000 apiece indicated that it would be a luxury development on par with the nearby residential parks. But Fortier's opening also preceded the construction of more modest homes. A block next to the school that was devoid of houses when the school opened, for instance, soon filled in with modern bungalows similar to those in Fellman's riverside subdivision.[92]

Although the school board purchased the final parcel for its uptown educational complex shortly before the bottom fell out of the local real estate market, the neighborhoods nearby weathered the Depression better than any other section of the city.[93] For local bankers and real estate brokers, the link between the schools and the surrounding area's stability was by no means incidental. They said as much when assisting the federal field agents who produced the map and area descriptions included in the Home Owners' Loan Corporation's 1939 survey of New Orleans's real estate market. LeMarie and Waguespack were among the local real estate heavyweights who helped produce those documents.[94]

On the HOLC's color-coded map of New Orleans, surveyors labeled just three public elementary and secondary schools: Allen, Fortier, and McMain. The descriptions of the three areas nearest the schools also identified the schools as positive aspects of the neighborhoods along with their access to major transportation routes, the newness of their housing stock, and their lack of black residents. The lakeside portion of the Fellman tract even received the HOLC's highest rating. "This area was the last vacant tract of any size in the fully developed 'Uptown Section' of the city and development was only started about 3 yrs. ago," the HOLC's description of the Fellman tract began. In addition to the restrictions LeMarie placed upon construction, the report noted that the area was "in easy walking distance to Tulane, Sophie Newcomb and Loyola Universities. Large girls high school, boys high school and grade school located almost adjoining on south."[95]

HOLC surveys for other cities also drew connections between schools and neighborhood quality. Surveyors in Madison, Wisconsin, for instance, explained the grade they gave one of the city's highest-rated neighborhoods by noting that it was a "comparatively new section" with "good transportation, schools." HOLC surveyors in Philadelphia and Atlanta similarly noted schools and transportation as favorable features of those cities' top-rated neighborhoods.[96]

At the very least, LeMarie and Waguespack's contributions to the HOLC maps of New Orleans indicated the extent to which those documents reflected perceptions that were already widespread among the Crescent City's real estate professionals. In many ways, these perceptions became self-fulfilling prophesies: brokers and bankers rated areas based on their racial homogeneity and access to schools, transportation, and other services, and then made lending and sales decisions to turn those ratings into reality. Newly developed areas with new white schools were the most striking examples of this since developers like Fellman and LeMarie often decided who could live there and the types of homes they could build. All they had to do next was sell lots, at which both men proved particularly adept.

Perhaps most significantly in terms of understanding the evolution of residential segregation in urban America, these racially homogenous communities took shape prior to the impact of influential programs like the Federal Housing Administration (FHA), which enabled white homebuyers to secure low-interest, long-term loans with little money down. A confidential 1939 federal report, for instance, noted that the FHA's program for insuring loans for home purchases "has not been an important factor in New Orleans." While the FHA had insured about 600 loans worth $300 million, many of these loans supported the construction of new homes in areas deemed of lesser quality than the neighborhoods near Fortier and McMain.[97]

Particularly as the FHA and other federal home loan programs expanded during the 1940s, white homebuyers likely used them to buy and build homes near Fortier and McMain. An undated promotional brochure for the lakeside portion of the Fellman tract, for instance, noted that the FHA "has made it possible for you to borrow money with terms of repayment to fit practically any income." Yet that same document also called attention to the development's proximity to Fortier and McMain, even including the latter school on the brochure's plan of the subdivision. The fact that the schools marked the neighborhood as white before buyers took full advantage of federally backed loans underscored that the FHA and other programs aided rather than initiated the process of government-sponsored residential segregation within New Orleans.[98]

As in Broadmoor, the construction of new white public schools was so deeply entangled in the Fellman tract's development and growth that it is impossible to differentiate the extent to which schools versus zoning, restrictive covenants, federal programs, or municipal investment caused the area to become an exclusively white, middle- and upper-middle-class community. More important than apportioning causation, however, is the recognition that the new schools tightened the link between race, neighborhood quality, and property value.

This dynamic had tangible benefits for white New Orleanians. In addition to expanded academic opportunities, the new schools and the subdivisions whose growth they promoted provided white New Orleanians with residential stability and personal wealth as well as the false sense that they had earned these advantages through their own efforts. As the whites who lived near the former McDonogh No. 13 left their Third Ward neighborhood—responding perhaps to the loss of their school, the influx of black residents, or the near omnipotence of the wrecking ball—many of them were able to make soft landings in these newly developed white neighborhoods. Morris Gerber, whose mother Rose was one of the white opponents of McDonogh No. 13's conversion into the black McDonogh 35 High School, became one of the first students to graduate from Fortier High School in the winter of 1932. His family joined the white migration further uptown, buying a home in 1925 at 1810 State Street, only a few blocks from both the boys' and girls' high school sites.[99]

The move offered white families such as the Gerbers meaningful financial rewards. By 1940, the average owner-occupied home value in the census tract that included Fortier and McMain reached $7,566. In the tracts that contained Fellman's lakeside subdivision, where development was only just getting started, the average home value was well over $8,000, more than double the citywide average. The Gerber family home was worth $25,000 in 1940, and they ultimately sold it for $56,500 in 1964. Fellow McDonogh 35 opponents Samuel and Lena Ball also benefited financially from the spread of racially exclusionary housing. The home they purchased in Broadmoor was valued at $10,000 by 1930.[100]

In McDonogh 35's census tract, by contrast, decades of demolition and unevenly applied zoning left fifteen hundred rental units but only twenty owner-occupied ones by 1940. Only three of that area's homeowners were not white, and the most expensive of their homes was valued at less than $3,000. Like other white Third Ward migrants, however, the Gerbers and the Balls maintained their shops on Rampart Street for many years following their moves uptown. The money these white shop owners made off their black patrons provided another example of the profitability of segregation.[101]

As public and private investment flowed to the areas surrounding new white public schools, black residents also tried to leverage their schools to secure additional support for their neighborhoods. But these efforts were often nonstarters. The smaller, more cheaply constructed black schools were not intended to be civic monuments the way Fortier and McMain were. The $525,985 the school board paid for McMain's construction, for instance, was more than the combined cost of the two black schools the board built during the 1920s—the new Craig School on St. Philip and the brick replacement structure for Valena C. Jones in the Seventh Ward.[102] Black schools were also often tucked away in isolated sections of the city, and officials' neglect of these schools and their surrounding neighborhoods was mutually reinforcing. In 1924, for example, the superintendent told the school board "that it was not advisable to reopen the evening school in the Valena Jones building as this school was inaccessible in wet weather on account of the bad condition of the sidewalks and streets."[103]

The improvements that black schools attracted to their surrounding areas were usually second-rate. Principal A. E. Perkins of the Danneel Colored School, which was located between a pair of railroad tracks west of the Fellman tract's lakeside terminus, went before the school board in 1924 to request "that sidewalks and streets about the school be repaired, that electric lights be placed at corners of streets upon which school is located, and the erection of a fence around the building" to prevent loiterers from bothering students and teachers.[104] Three years later, Perkins and the Colored Civic League of New Orleans followed up on that request, adding that another four black schools faced similar circumstances.[105] In a series of letters in 1927, Perkins pleaded with the city to simply gravel, not pave, an inaccessible street in front of the school in order to "give us a route through Foutaine Bleau Drive and the river; thus saving the Community nearly a half mile in distance around."[106] While the city eventually addressed that problem, another street two blocks north of the school remained impassable as late as 1940.[107]

By then the imbalance between black and white schools, particularly at the high school level, had reached the point where the system of segregation threatened to collapse under its own weight. On the eve of World War II, New Orleans's more than 16,000 white secondary students attended thirteen different high schools, where they had the option of attending either an academic, commercial, or vocational institution. The city's nearly 5,000 black high school students, meanwhile, attended one of three schools for the first two years of high school depending upon where they lived. But any black student who wanted to actually graduate from high school had but one option: McDonogh 35, the only high school in the city that offered courses beyond the tenth grade.[108]

The board's failure to provide adequate secondary school options for blacks proved to be the tipping point as the civil rights movement heated up following World War II. In June 1948, A. P. Tureaud, the attorney for the New Orleans branch of the NAACP, filed a lawsuit in federal district court seeking the equalization of black and white public schools. The black Creole lawyer devoted a significant portion of his initial filing to the high school situation. While he acknowledged the four high schools for blacks, he argued that none were accredited or "equal in any respect" to the high schools for whites. Additionally, he wrote, "students residing in the uptown section of Orleans Parish . . . are compelled to transfer to McDonogh No. 35 High School in order that they may obtain the preparation necessary to pursue a college course." Yet the nineteenth-century structure that McDonogh 35 inherited from whites in 1917, Tureaud continued, was old, dilapidated, and "completely devoid of . . . facilities necessary to provide a proper and adequate high school training for Negro children."[109] As the school board scrambled to respond to the lawsuit, it launched an unprecedented drive to open additional black schools. The process of selecting locations for these new schools, however, reignited neighborhood battles for racial superiority that had been smoldering since the 1920s. It also provided the board with new opportunities to build racial inequality into the city's urban landscape even as the campaign to end segregation intensified.

CHAPTER SIX

AN EDUCATIONAL
SOWETO

Once again, the school building on Bayou Road became a focal point in the struggle over race, education, and the future of New Orleans. In 1949, black students regained access to the facility they had been kicked out of more than two decades before. Although the structure known then as the Edward D. White School was vacant, its white neighbors dusted off the arguments they had successfully marshaled in the 1920s. "If the building is given over to the use of colored pupils," one white Sixth Ward resident claimed in June 1948, "white people would move and the entire neighborhood would become colored."[1]

A former New Orleans mayor turned state senator aided the residents' cause by pushing through legislation to deny African Americans access to the school. The law prohibited the conversion of a school from white to black without approval from a super-majority of nearby property owners. But the school board, unwilling to pay for new black facilities even as it faced the NAACP's equalization lawsuit, chose to open the building to black students. When white residents sued the school board under the state's anti-conversion legislation, a judge sided with the board and declared that law unconstitutional.[2]

With unintended irony, the board turned the Bayou Road complex into a high school and renamed it after former Southern University president Joseph S. Clark. Thirty-five years earlier, Clark's willingness to relocate the university and its high school department to Baton Rouge had eliminated public secondary education for black New Orleanians. While black activism contributed to the creation of McDonogh 35 in 1917, and the school board later added some high school grades to other black facilities, the high school bearing Clark's name initially made a mockery of secondary education. When Clark High's first campus opened in 1947 in a formerly white elementary school six blocks from the Bayou Road building, the board intended it to serve every black high school student living below Canal Street. But Clark High only offered ninth and tenth grade, and its building could not even contain those students. During its second year of operation in 1948–1949, the school relied on a "platoon" system that accommodated students in three staggered four-hour shifts.[3]

Even as Clark High gained its second campus on Bayou Road in 1949 and the upper grades the following year, the shortened school day remained in effect. In October 1950, representatives from the school's Parent Teachers Association beseeched the school board for more black school buildings. Its petition focused on the "vicious platoon system" and noted that Clark's truncated schedule required some students to rise at 5:30 a.m. to head to school, only to return home at midday. Others left school so late they walked home in the dark. The parents were outraged at the board's willingness to invest heavily in white suburbs not yet built while stonewalling black requests. They paid particular attention to Gentilly, a roughly eight-square-mile area between City Park and the Industrial Canal (see maps 6.1 and 6.2).[4] As in the older Lakeview neighborhood on the western side of City Park, the federal government's racially proscriptive housing programs were fueling a mass migration of white residents to that suburban part of the city.[5] The Clark petitioners recognized that the construction of schools only aided the growth of these exclusively white, in-town suburbs. "The new schools promised the colored remain on the planning board," the petition read, "while one white building in the Gentilly section is under construction and on July 26, the ground was broken for another in the same Gentilly section."[6]

The PTA prepared its October 1950 petition at a heady time in the black struggle for educational equity. Two days before the group approached the school board, the NAACP Legal Defense and Educational Fund's Thurgood Marshall had written to local NAACP attorney A. P. Tureaud to recommend amending the equalization lawsuit in order to "attack segregation head on." Marshall's note followed the national NAACP's decision several months earlier to abandon school equalization in favor of a frontal assault on school segregation. The organization made this shift in the wake of its recent Supreme Court victories in a pair of cases relating to segregation at the graduate school level. When Tureaud replied enthusiastically to Marshall, he included

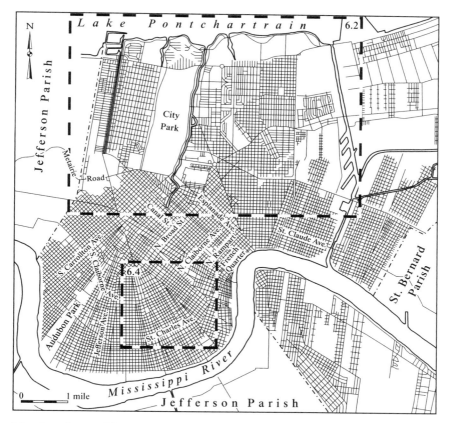

Map 6.1   Areas of detail highlighted in Chapter 6.

the Clark petition as evidence of the grassroots agitation in New Orleans for directly attacking Jim Crow.[7]

This fight also unfolded against the backdrop of a huge wartime and post-war black migration to New Orleans and other cities. Nearly 35,000 new black residents streamed into New Orleans during the 1940s. This marked a 23 percent increase in the black population versus a 14 percent increase for whites; by 1950, blacks comprised nearly one-third of the city's 570,000 residents. The prospect of better jobs and schools attracted blacks to the city, just as mechanization and stifling levels of racial subordination encouraged them to flee the plantations of the rural South.[8]

The influx strained New Orleans's already inadequate black school and

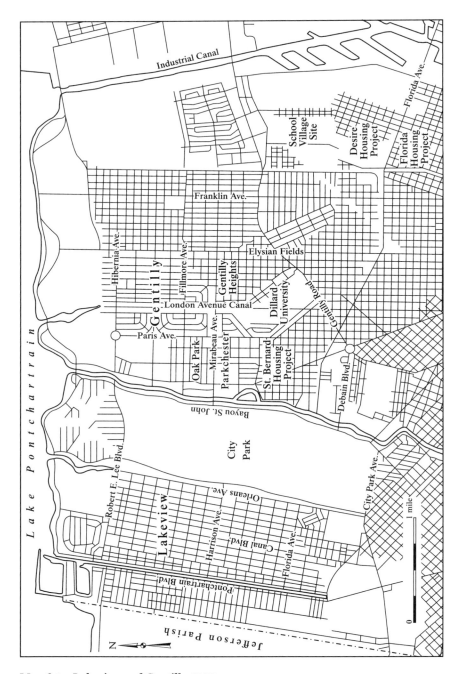

Map 6.2   Lakeview and Gentilly, 1952.

housing facilities, and white officials and tax-wary residents permitted these shortages to reach crisis proportions. With few vacancies in public housing, families doubled or even tripled up in tiny apartments. The school board, meanwhile, failed to build any black schools between 1941 and 1951 even though it knew *before* the war that most black school facilities were overcrowded and woefully deficient. As a result, the city's 30,000 black public school students—a 34 percent increase from 1940—had access to barely one-third of the system's buildings even though they comprised nearly half of its enrollment. The school system's white population, meanwhile, declined 15 percent during the 1940s as students left the poorly performing public system for private and parochial schools. By 1950, the number of white students in private schools nearly equaled the number enrolled in public ones.[9]

As the NAACP and black parents stepped up their attack on segregation, school officials parried by inscribing racial inequalities more deeply into the Crescent City's urban landscape. They found willing collaborators among the real estate developers and local and federal officials who sought to address the significant postwar housing shortage. As had been the case during the 1920s, the construction of new white schools lured residents to suburbs such as Gentilly as these areas were being born. This time, however, developers and city planners worked even more closely with the school board, thanks in part to the encouragement they received from the federal government. Acknowledging the significance of this new, collaborative ethic, the school board's top planner predicted in 1952 that "New Orleans can be assured that the school system will become, in actuality, an integral part of the over-all physical development of the city."[10]

The planner's prediction came true in ways even he may not have imagined. As the new suburban schools pulled the white population further from an increasingly black inner city, school and municipal officials worked with the federal government to build the city's "second ghetto": a massive "school village" and housing project located in a swampy section of the Ninth Ward that was cut off from the rest of New Orleans by train tracks and drainage canals.[11] The scheme was akin to an educational Soweto, and officials hatched plans for it as they confronted the consequences of their earlier success in building the city's "first ghetto" in the former back of town.[12]

The following section describes the role that schools played in transforming the present-day Central City neighborhood into an exclusively black residential area. The next section charts the collaboration between school, municipal, and federal officials to construct all-white suburbs on New Orleans's northeastern edge. The final section then details how similar cooperation resulted in a racially isolated school and housing complex for African Americans that ensured the persistence of segregation well beyond its legal demise.

I.

By 1950, New Orleans's checkerboard pattern of residential integration was fast becoming a historical relic, most notably in the area now known as Central City (see maps 6.1, 6.3, and 6.4). At the time, school officials called this section the Back of Town, and in doing so affixed boundaries to a phrase that had previously referred more generally to New Orleans's less socially and topographically appealing hinterlands. The area was also known colloquially as St. Monica after its black Catholic parish and school.[13] Regardless of its name, this area's racial heterogeneity was among its most notable and volatile characteristics during the late nineteenth and early twentieth centuries. Its schools were often at the center of these hostilities. When the White League spurred teenaged "regulators" to violently disrupt the city's racially mixed public schools in 1874, for instance, some of the fiercest fighting took place in the present-day Central City. Here, too, the black gunman Robert Charles took his violent stand against police and white rioters in 1900; during that riot, a white mob burned the area's only black school, Thomy Lafon, to the ground. The twelve-block stretch of Dryades Street that ran through the Back of Town nevertheless thrived as a commercial district because of its neighborhood's ethnic and racial diversity. This strip was essentially a continuation of the adjacent Rampart Street corridor, where blacks and Jews sparred over McDonogh No. 13 in 1917.[14]

Despite its racially and ethnically mixed past, Central City was uniformly black by the middle of the twentieth century—the only such section of the city. The area counted eight of the city's nine census tracts that were more than 90 percent black, and fewer than 3,000 of its 43,000 residents were white. The only other tract with a similar proportion of black residents was the small, semi-industrial neighborhood behind the Fellman tract where A. E. Perkins's Danneel Colored School was located.[15] The Gert Town neighborhood, where more than three-quarters of the residents were black, linked Central City with

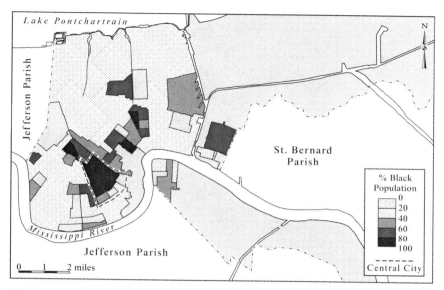

Map 6.3   Percentage of black population, in census tracts, New Orleans, 1950.
Sources: Social Explorer/US Census Bureau; "Central City Neighborhood," The Data Center, http://www.gnocdc.org/orleans/2/61/index.html.

the Danneel neighborhood, and together these areas formed a pie-shaped black belt in the heart of the city.

While the stretch of Louisiana Avenue near LaSalle Street and the black Flint-Goodridge Hospital featured a number of fine homes, including hotel proprietor Henry Braden's $20,000 residence, conditions were spottier throughout the rest of Central City.[16] A 1952 school board report noted that "the total capacity of the schools is inadequate to accommodate the children, and in most cases the buildings before renovation were obsolete and insanitary." That assessment, however, suffered from bureaucratic understatement. In 1948, for instance, a local newspaper had written of black students injured by falling plaster and of black schools that lacked electricity in most of their classrooms. Central City's Sylvanie Williams School, which served one thousand students, only had electric lights in two rooms. Postulating on how students learned in the dark, the district administrator in charge of black education guessed that they "used their imagination."[17]

Public schools had in fact bolstered Central City's transformation into New

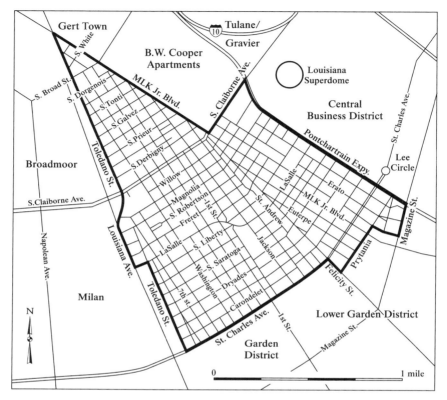

Map 6.4   Central City and surrounding neighborhoods, 2002.
Map based upon map by The Data Center (formerly the Greater New Orleans Community Data Center), http://www.gnocdc.org/orleans/2/61/index.html. The B. W. Cooper Apartments in the upper portion of the map is the more recent name for the Calliope Housing Project.

Orleans's first black ghetto during the 1920s and 1930s. Partly to relieve overcrowding at the rebuilt Thomy Lafon—"the largest elementary Negro school in the world," the *Louisiana Weekly* claimed in 1927—the school board added two black schools to the area during the twenties and another two the following decade. Since two of these black schools replaced white ones, the only schools for whites that remained in the general area by 1940 hung around its periphery.[18]

One of those remaining white schools on the edge of Central City was Kruttschnitt Elementary. Shortly after the superintendent recommended converting Kruttschnitt from white to black in 1926, white residents launched a rash of bombings that targeted Braden's home and other black-owned property nearby. The board dropped the proposed conversion following the bombings, deciding instead to add an annex to accommodate Kruttshchnitt's overflow white population.[19]

But the board invested more heavily in black schools in Central City, and both the number and percentage of blacks living there increased after the board added black schools to the area. While the relationship between Central City's black schools and its large black population was reciprocal, the board's decision to concentrate black schools there was part of its broader effort to create new boundaries between white and black sections of the city. After all, New Orleans's dispersed black population would have justified the construction of black schools in multiple areas throughout the city. But school officials regularly argued that black schools should be located "as near as possible to the center of the present negro population." As the incidents involving Kruttschnitt, McDonogh No. 13, and Bayou Road demonstrated, white residents also repeatedly opposed black schools near their homes. Since the US Supreme Court repeatedly rejected attempts to distinguish between black and white neighborhoods by law, public schools became the most powerful means available for officially designating an area as either black or white. Schools, in fact, were the largest racially specific public expenditure in New Orleans prior to the construction of the city's first segregated housing projects between 1938 and 1940.[20]

Public housing dramatically accelerated residential segregation, particularly in Central City, where the city's housing administration built two of its first four projects for black people. New Orleans was the first city in the country to receive funding under the federal Housing Act of 1937, also known as the Wagner Act after its chief sponsor, Senator Robert F. Wagner of New York. The Act encouraged slum clearance and the construction of affordable, low-income housing, and unlike most of the New Deal housing reforms that preceded it, the law did not focus on prospective homebuyers. Rather, it provided significant federal financing for the construction of housing projects as well as rent subsidies for their low-income residents. The Wagner Act created a decentralized approach to public housing, leaving decisions on issues such as separate projects for blacks and whites up to local housing administrations. Throughout the South and in northern cities such as Trenton, New Jersey, and Harrisburg, Pennsylvania, officials opted to build explicitly segregated projects. As historian Arnold Hirsch notes, the requirement that federal projects respect existing racial boundaries meant that public housing generally "offered little challenge to prevailing residential practices and was used more fully to confine blacks in the postwar period."[21]

The 1937 housing law also contained an "equivalent elimination" clause, which mandated that local housing administrations build at least one new housing unit for every slum unit they cleared to make way for the projects. Since the law required the projects to be located in the same city or general area (but not the same neighborhood) as the cleared slums, these new developments shifted population within some cities. In New Orleans, the provision helped push more black residents into Central City. One of the area's projects, Magnolia, was built on the same site as the slum it replaced; another one, known as Calliope and later as B. W. Cooper, was built on previously vacant land. The Housing Authority of New Orleans (HANO) selected Calliope's uninhabited thirty-two-acre site, which until then had been one of the city's main trash dumps, to offset the units it demolished for the construction of two downtown projects, the white Iberville and black Lafitte developments. New Orleanians called the dump Old Silver City because "it shone like silver" from the discarded tin cans that filled it. Before building Calliope (pronounced Cal-ee-ope in New Orleans despite deriving its name from the classical Greek muse of poetry), workers hauled the waste to the city's lakefront to create infill for the construction of a municipal yacht harbor.[22]

Since black residents bore the brunt of HANO's project-related slum clearance efforts and generally lived in the worst conditions, the 690-unit Calliope development provided much-needed assistance to displaced and other low-income blacks. In 1939, for instance, the majority of New Orleans's black families lived without bathing facilities, inside flush toilets, electricity, gas, and cooking facilities, and one-third of black households did not have any water. The demolition that preceded construction of the first public housing projects only added to the number of African Americans in need of adequate housing. The white Iberville project, for instance, replaced the former Storyville neighborhood, whose residents were almost all black at the time it was razed. Similarly, blacks comprised roughly half of the residents living in the area that was cleared for the white St. Thomas Housing Project in the Irish Channel neighborhood. While many former Storyville residents resettled in the adjacent Lafitte Housing Project, others eventually moved into one of the

Central City projects along with some of the St. Thomas migrants. As the city demolished much of Louis Armstrong's former neighborhood after World War II to make way for a municipal government complex, many of its former residents also resettled in Calliope and Magnolia.[23]

Public schools were also essential to the success of the projects and the role they played in transforming Central City into an exclusively black residential zone. HANO officials understood that re-creating a neighborhood in the case of Magnolia or creating a brand new one in the case of Calliope required schools, and they worked closely with the school board to locate black schools within or next to these new projects. HANO, for instance, initiated conversations with the Orleans Parish School Board regarding the location of the black school that would serve Magnolia's residents almost immediately after the federal government approved funding for the project. Rather than erect a new school, housing officials ultimately built Magnolia around the existing 2,500-student Thomy Lafon School, which was the school board's preferred spot. The school, in fact, was the project's most prominent feature on architectural site plans. By constructing Magnolia as a "superblock," with streets routed around rather than through the complex, HANO isolated both the housing project and the school from the rest of the city.[24]

The school board also supported the creation of Calliope, acquiring four blocks on the riverside of the proposed project site for the construction of a large black vocational high school. The board's decision to build the facility followed decades of agitation from black leaders such as Walter Cohen and Henderson H. Dunn, who first requested a trade school in 1914. The board began seeking money from the Rosenwald Fund in 1923 to support the construction of a vocational school, but it dropped the project several years later to pay for a new central office. Only funding from the federal Works Progress Administration, not newfound sympathy for black demands, permitted the school to become a reality. The inclusion of a large auditorium as part of the school, which the board named after Booker T. Washington, made it a center of the Calliope community. For HANO, the board's plans for Booker T. Washington were also an indicator of its role in supporting segregation as the housing authority cleared local slums. HANO's executive director, Alvin Fromherz, captured that sentiment when he wrote to School Board architect E. A. Christy shortly after the board announced its intentions to build the trade high school in 1939. "Undoubtedly the cooperation and coordination which will exist between the Orleans Parish School Board and the Housing Authority of New Orleans *will increase* concerning our respective activities," Fromherz said.[25]

Fromherz's prediction soon came true as the school board readily complied with HANO's requests regarding the school facilities that were needed in other proposed slum clearance areas. In April 1941, for instance, the board agreed to conduct a needs assessment for a flood-prone, largely vacant tract of land near the Industrial Canal that HANO eyed for a potential white housing project. While World War II delayed this development's construction, the 500-unit Florida Housing Project opened in 1946. Its initial residents were largely rural white migrants who came to New Orleans to work in war-related industries, only to become financially untethered after V-J Day. These residents were poorer than those living in the city's other white project, and parents often struggled to feed and properly clothe their children. At HANO's request, the school board directed the white children who lived in Florida to attend Frantz Elementary School, which had opened a few blocks from the project site in 1937. The school board also erected a school to serve the black St. Bernard Housing Project shortly before that development opened in an isolated section of the city north of the Fairgrounds racetrack. School and housing officials in Nashville similarly bolstered segregation after World War II by constructing new schools to serve segregated public housing projects.[26]

By the time the Florida Housing Project opened in New Orleans, the NAACP and black residents had placed increased pressure on the school board to improve facilities, particularly at the high school level. The black Citizens Committee on Equal Education, for instance, complained in 1946 that the city had no accredited high school for blacks despite maintaining seven such high schools for whites. The Committee found the fact that McDonogh 35 was the only black school offering a college preparatory curriculum especially galling. "McDonogh #35 High School is old, dilapidated, has never been the proper type of building for a High School, is located in a neighborhood not conducive to study and the building and facilities do not in any sense compare with the buildings and facilities of any of the White High Schools," the Committee wrote to the school board. By frequently referencing the Equal Protection Clause of the Fourteenth Amendment, the Committee telegraphed that it would not accept half measures.[27]

Yet half measures were exactly what the board took. In addition to creating Clark High School for students living on the downtown side of Canal Street, school officials attempted to assuage black demands by creating an additional high school Uptown. To secure a spot for this school, the superintendent recommended converting the underutilized Kruttschnitt Elementary School from white to black use. As with Clark High's expansion into the vacant E. D. White building on Bayou Road, white residents reprised their 1920s antics to protest Kruttschnitt's conversion. But neither their appearances before the board nor the lawsuit they filed in civil district court was successful. In September 1949, the board opened Kruttschnitt to black secondary students. It also changed the school's name. With black students walking its corridors, the building would no longer bear the name of the deceased corporate attorney who championed black disfranchisement and educational inequality as the twin pillars of white supremacy. Instead, board members renamed it after a late black leader whose racial gradualism they likely pined for: Walter L. Cohen.[28]

The creation of Clark and Cohen High Schools, however, did little to address educational inequality, a fact even white school officials acknowledged. The problem was particularly acute in Central City, where schools were straining under the weight of their shoddy construction and the area's booming black population. Barred from living in many other parts of the city by restrictive covenants and federal lending guidelines, an additional seven thousand black residents moved into the area between 1940 and 1950.[29] In 1952, Charles Colbert, the school board's recently appointed supervising architect for planning and construction, estimated that the section had five thousand more students than its schools could properly accommodate. Discussing Central City's six elementary schools, Colbert wrote that "all of these schools are old and inadequate." Two in particular, he noted, were "beyond hope of renovation and rehabilitation."[30]

Superintendent Lionel J. Bourgeois also readily discussed the inadequacy of the system's black school facilities. Born on a sugar cane plantation in Convent, Louisiana in 1890, Bourgeois spent three years as Haiti's superintendent of education during the United States military's lengthy occupation of the country. He moved to New Orleans upon leaving that post in 1920, working his way up the ranks from teacher to central office administrator. When he became superintendent in 1946, he quickly initiated a series of studies to enable the district to build the "kind of educational institution, which in my judgment, can meet the challenge of the survival of democracy." These early reports paid particular attention to the system's need for more and better facilities, and Bourgeois frankly discussed the shortage of black schools.[31] "At no time in the history of public education in New Orleans," he wrote in his 1948 school facilities plan, "has there been even a semblance of adequate housing for Negro children."[32]

Bourgeois's 1948 plan called for $40 million in school construction and renovation, with $25 million going toward black schools. Of the fifteen new school buildings the superintendent proposed for blacks, he recommended locating seven in Central City. He wanted three of those to replace existing facilities and the other four to be brand new buildings.[33]

Bourgeois's proposal paralleled those in other southern communities, where officials also hoped that heavy spending to "equalize" black and white schools would stave off challenges to segregation. These investments came in response to a legal strategy that the NAACP initiated in the 1930s as part of its long-term plan to topple Jim Crow. Largely prioritizing discrimination in schools and housing over labor and employment concerns, the NAACP filed suits attacking racially restrictive covenants, inequitable school funding, and unequal salaries for black and white teachers. In addition to establishing actionable judicial precedents regarding the meaning of "equal protection of the laws," the organization stated in 1930 that cases calling for equalization of black and white schools would "make the costs of a dual system so prohibitive as to speed the abolishment of segregated schooling." Similarly, the cases to equalize black and white teachers' salaries helped the NAACP mobilize local communities and attract additional dues-paying members by offering the prospect of meaningful financial rewards for black professionals.[34]

The NAACP's strategy, however, presented southern black teachers with a dilemma. They were beholden to white-run school boards, which meant any overt move they made against Jim Crow could cost them their livelihood. The question of whether to boldly call for desegregation, to press for equalization, or to simply keep their heads down and do their best within the current system proved more vexing still. Many teachers were reluctant to support desegregation. Some feared—quite rightly—that black teachers would lose their jobs if schools integrated. Others shared W. E. B. Du Bois's concern that "a mixed school with poor and unsympathetic teachers, with hostile public opinion, and no teaching of truth concerning black folk, is bad." Yet throughout the South many black teachers challenged Jim Crow through their pedagogy as well as more direct forms of political action. The African American teachers in New Orleans were no exception.[35]

Led by George Longe, an early McDonogh 35 faculty member, black teachers in the Crescent City launched a salary equalization campaign in 1938. On the heels of NAACP victories in Maryland and Virginia, the New Orleans teachers prevailed in federal court in 1942. New Orleans–based NAACP attorney A. P. Tureaud then initiated similar salary suits in other Louisiana parishes before filing the state's first school equalization suit in St. Charles Parish in the spring of 1948. The Louisiana legislature immediately increased school funding and black teachers' salaries, mirroring the response to equalization lawsuits throughout the region. In South Carolina, Governor James Byrnes, a former US secretary of state and Supreme Court justice, launched a $75 million school building program in hopes of blunting the impact of the school equalization suit pending in his state. That lawsuit, *Briggs v. Elliott*, became one of the four cases the Supreme Court ultimately consolidated under *Brown v. Board of Education*.[36] In New Orleans, the politically savvy Bourgeois released his $40 million facilities plan several months before Tureaud filed an equalization suit there. The superintendent actually welcomed the litigation, which he hoped would prod his recalcitrant school board into action.[37]

To a certain extent, Bourgeois's decision to concentrate black schools in Central City reflected the mutually reinforcing roles of schools and housing in segregating the city. The school board's effort to cluster black schools in that section after World War I, for instance, had bolstered its status as a black neighborhood, which in turn attracted additional black residents and exacerbated its already inadequate housing conditions. Local and federal officials then targeted Central City as the site for the much-needed black projects, necessitating the construction of additional schools and drawing still more black residents to the area. By 1948, it therefore seemed as though Bourgeois had no choice but to reinforce the institutional strength of the Central City ghetto by building more black schools in that area.

But his plan's numerous ties to the Home Owners' Loan Corporation's residential security maps suggested that the process was considerably less organic than that. First, Bourgeois's plan developed from the recommendations of a citizens' advisory committee, which the former HOLC state director Paul Habans chaired. Habans's familiarity with the HOLC's residential security maps made him particularly aware of the public and private interest both in expanding residential segregation and linking neighborhood value to race. Second, at the urging of Brooke H. Duncan, director of the City Planning and Zoning Commission, Bourgeois tapped Stanley LeMarie to spearhead the acquisition of property for schools in "the congested areas [i.e., Central City] and the areas in the Uptown section."[38]

Both Duncan and LeMarie, the late Leo Fellman's top deputy and successor, had helped the HOLC develop its 1939 residential security map. Since the Central City black belt ran alongside the lily-white Broadmoor neighborhood and extended toward the Fellman tract, there is little doubt that LeMarie hoped to locate black schools in areas that both respected and strengthened existing racial boundaries. At the very least, Habans's, Duncan's, and LeMarie's involvement with Bourgeois's facilities plan revealed the extent to which it depended upon the same assumptions that drove the HOLC's neighborhood classifications. Put simply, Bourgeois accepted residential segregation as the sine qua non of school construction and urban development, and he took steps to ensure its persistence. While the five members of the post–World War II school board had fewer ties to the real estate business than their predecessors, the superintendent's advisory committee preserved the school system and the industry's close relationship.[39]

New Orleans was not the only city where overlapping school and real estate interests fortified the boundaries between white and black residential zones. In northern cities that lacked laws requiring school segregation, officials regularly used school locations and attendance policies to create and preserve segregation within schools and neighborhoods. Rather than allow black students to attend under-enrolled schools in nearby white neighborhoods, the Chicago Board of Education added hundreds of new school buildings and mobile classroom trailers to black neighborhoods during the 1950s. Residents dubbed these mobile units "Willis Wagons" after Superintendent Benjamin Willis, who enjoyed strong support from Chicago business leaders.[40]

School officials in Detroit and Boston also embraced temporary solutions to overcrowding within predominantly black schools rather than permitting black students to attend schools in white neighborhoods. In the Eight Mile–Wyoming section of Detroit, an area whose black population increased significantly following World War II, the school board considered reopening a long-shuttered, antiquated building to accommodate black students who were already enrolled in a racially mixed school. While a 1947 parent protest blocked this move, the board continued to manipulate school boundaries to tighten the distinction between black and white neighborhoods and schools. More than a decade later, the Boston School Committee similarly agreed to spend nearly $200,000 to purchase and renovate an abandoned Jewish school building in a Dorchester neighborhood with a growing black population. Although the site lacked sufficient space for students to congregate before and after school, during recess, or for fire drills, the Committee preferred it to allowing black students into white neighborhoods and schools.[41]

In New Orleans, Bourgeois's building program proceeded slowly. By the time he revisited his facilities plan in 1950, the board had converted Kruttschnitt, White, and two other schools (one of which was in Central City) from white to black use, allocated funds for additions at seven schools, including two in Central City, and set aside money to build three new schools, all in Central City. Yet Bourgeois recognized that this was not enough. "Despite the above list of notable accomplishments within the past two years, a great deal remains to be done to equalize educational opportunities between the white and the Negro divisions," he wrote in his 1950 facilities plan. In particular, Bourgeois noted the school system's need to build or convert "additional buildings to house the Negro students in attendance in many overcrowded buildings."[42]

White residents' opposition to additional black schools was the main impediment to Bourgeois's progress. In 1948, for instance, the superintendent lobbied hard for the passage of a state constitutional amendment that permitted the board to levy additional property taxes for school construction. While the measure passed statewide, New Orleans's overwhelmingly white voters rejected it by a 24,000-vote margin. With a majority of school board members committed to honoring that local opposition, another year passed before Bourgeois was able to convince them to levy the constitutionally authorized tax hike. On several occasions, Bourgeois also postponed proposed conversions of schools from white to black in the face of white opposition.[43]

Even after the board raised property taxes, school and housing officials' earlier success in isolating black residents within Central City complicated the system's building program. By 1952, for instance, the school board was on track to open three new elementary schools and one junior high in Central City by the 1954–1955 school year. But Charles Colbert, who updated the district's building plan the year after he became the head of its planning division in 1951, predicted that the district would still need to build an additional three elementary schools almost immediately after those opened, followed by another two before the end of the decade. He estimated that by 1969, the area would need at least one more junior high school as well as a senior high, partly because the Cohen building (the former Kruttschnitt Elementary) was not big enough to be a proper high school. Cohen, in fact, was so crowded during its first year of operation in 1949 that it could only accommodate ninth graders. If more desirable smaller schools were built, Colbert said, the number of schools Central City needed would rise to eight elementary, two junior high, and one high school.[44]

The problem, however, was that there was very little vacant land within Central City and the land that was available was quite expensive. According to Colbert, land prices ranged from $68,000 to $99,000 per acre in that part of the city, which meant that site acquisition would cost the district between $3.9 and $15.5 million, depending upon whether it followed national recommendations for school acreage or built according to lower, locally accepted standards. The limited amont of land underscored one of the economic ironies that sustained residential segregation in New Orleans and other cities. The restrictions that barred blacks from living in other parts of the city (often under the cover of protecting property values) inflated rental prices and congestion within Central City. As a result, the high rents private landlords could charge black tenants made black neighborhoods so crowded and profitable that public agencies such as the school board struggled to buy land for the services these areas so desperately needed.[45]

In his 1952 plan, Colbert explained that this reality led the school district to explore numerous options for reducing its land costs. The board slated Central City's new junior high, for instance, for a site next to an existing park, which would save money by doubling as the school's play area. The board selected that site only after it rejected an earlier proposal to build the school atop a graveyard, a fact that Colbert cited in order to emphasize the extent of the board's challenge when it came to Central City's building needs. "The problem of obtaining adequate sites for such facilities is so urgent and difficult that unusual measures are in order," Colbert wrote.[46]

To solve this conundrum, Colbert developed a plan that he believed could provide a national model for school construction. "In this era of rapid transit, of commuting between suburb and city, it seems logical that the schools should follow the general pattern and relocate on the periphery of the city," he wrote. The architect's proposal called for the creation of a suburban "school village" that could eventually house as many as ten schools serving up to 10,000 students, most of whom would be bused to the site from Central City. The location Colbert had in mind was an isolated ninety-acre tract in the city's

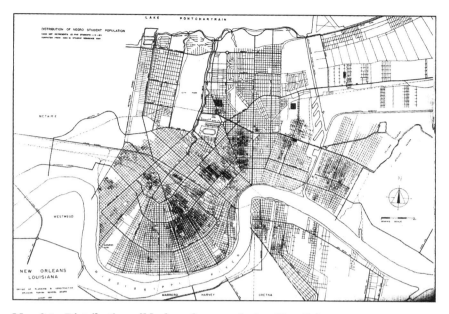

Map 6.5   Distribution of black student population, New Orleans, 1952.
Colbert's school village plan called for busing black students concentrated in the pie-slice-shaped Central City area to the undeveloped area marked by a black square in the upper-right quadrant of the map. Orleans Parish School Board—Office of Planning and Construction, *A Planning and Building Program for New Orleans' Schools*, 1952. The Historic New Orleans Collection, Acc. No. 90–560-RL, Gift of Orleans Parish Public Schools. Map edited by Mary Lee Eggart.

Ninth Ward, roughly six miles from Central City. A double layer of drainage canals and railroad tracks flanked its eastern and western sides, while a third rail line formed its northern border. Several blocks south of the site, another drainage canal and rail line separated the area from the Florida Housing Project, which had opened to poor white residents in 1946 (see maps 6.5 and 6.6). The school board had purchased this tract in September 1952 for $300,000, which was roughly six to eight million less than the equivalent amount of land would have cost in Central City, according to Colbert's estimates.[47]

This land in New Orleans's mostly undeveloped eastern fringe was so much cheaper than in Central City that Colbert predicted in 1953 that the board would save enough money to "provide the children with the finest of bus transportation to the village site, at today's prices, for more than a century." (He believed the board could save even more if it hired retired house-

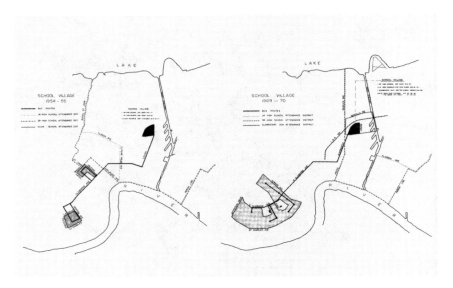

Map 6.6   The School Village.
Orleans Parish School Board—Office of Planning and Construction, *A Planning and Building Program for New Orleans' Schools,* 1952. The Historic New Orleans Collection, Acc. No. 90–560-RL, Gift of Orleans Parish Public Schools. The above maps do not show the drainage canals and railroad tracks that ran parallel to Peoples and Florida Avenues to the west and south of the proposed village. The city's 1951 street plan also called for the addition of an expressway parallel to the train tracks north of the site.

wives and teachers to drive buses at nonunion wages rather than rely on the city's unionized bus drivers.) By concentrating so many black children and schools together in one location, Colbert also contended, the system would be able to provide better and more specialized services, all while removing students from what he considered their unhealthy slum surroundings in the uptown Central City neighborhood. Additionally, the high school Colbert planned for the village would relieve overcrowding at the downtown Clark High School, whose inadequacies had become a focal point in the black campaign to topple segregated education.

By the time Colbert unveiled his plan for the "school village" in 1952, *Brown* was pending before the Supreme Court and other cases attacking school segregation were making their way there. Black New Orleanians had also petitioned the Orleans Parish School Board to end segregated schooling in November 1951 in advance of filing their own desegregation lawsuit.

Meanwhile, in South Africa, the Group Areas Act of 1950 sought to establish an impermeable color line by forcibly relocating black, Indian, and colored people from inner-city Johannesburg to the outlying southwestern townships that became Soweto. While Colbert's plan reflected the magical thinking—prominent among white Americans and South Africans—that segregation would last forever, it also provided a framework for turning those dreams into reality.[48]

Ironically, the school village defied one of the guiding principles for determining school sites that Colbert laid out in his 1952 facilities plan. "The attendance district should encompass a homogeneous community," he and his associates wrote in a clear nod to Progressive-era planners such as Clarence Perry, "and the school should be so located that it can serve the neighborhood as a natural community center." Despite this apparent contradiction, Colbert crowed to a national architectural magazine in November 1953 that the village proposal was "perhaps the first major new concept in city school planning since the introduction of the neighborhood school."[49]

At the same time that Colbert outlined his vision for the school village, education officials and developers were also looking to New Orleans's eastern edge as the potential location for additional white schools and homes, albeit in more pleasing surroundings than the proposed village site. As was the case during the 1920s and 1930s, the school board took the lead in investing in areas slated for development. This time, however, the collaboration between the board and developers was even greater, largely because of the federal government's encouragement to build new schools for exclusively white subdivisions. For Colbert, this was a project that hit particularly close to home.

II.

Colbert was a nationally recognized authority on school planning and design when he became the school board's supervising architect in 1951. As an assistant professor of architecture at Tulane University in the late 1940s, he was a staunch advocate of what came to be known as the International Style. In place of architectural ornamentation, this idiom embraced new building materials such as aluminum and lightweight concrete, and it featured uninterrupted bands of windows as well as steel or concrete piers that elevated structures off the ground. Along with architects such as Nathaniel Curtis and

Arthur Q. Davis, who later designed the Louisiana Superdome, Colbert's or-
ganizational and promotional talents ensured that the International Style became more than academic fodder in New Orleans. In 1948, for instance, he attracted 30,000 spectators to an event he organized to showcase his students'
modern school designs. Colbert initiated that project after Schools Superintendent Bourgeois kicked off his proposed $40 million building program by
unveiling a more traditional model for a white elementary school in Gentilly.[50]

In league with school board member Jacqueline McCullough, who fought
Superintendent Bourgeois's efforts to fund black school construction even as
she called for additional white schools in the city's suburban outskirts, the
professor successfully pushed the board to abandon what he considered to
be an "outdated" and "obsolete" school plan. But after the board returned
to a traditional design in 1949 by proposing a two-story, granite structure
for the Gentilly school, Colbert and McCullough teamed up to deliver eighty
speeches over a two-month period to promote a more modern approach. Colbert again corralled his students to prepare an exhibit, and this time 50,000
people viewed the displays they set up in a large downtown department store.
Since Colbert chaired the National Committee on School Buildings for the
American Institute of Architects (AIA), his opinion on these matters carried
a good deal of weight. In addition to convincing the board to consult with the
local chapter of the AIA on the Gentilly school, he and McCullough secured a
commitment that only practicing AIA members could design future schools.
While conversations about the Gentilly school noted the area's growth and
"crowded" conditions, the situation in that rapidly expanding suburb paled in
comparison to the space crunch at the city's black schools, where the district's
building program was ill suited to meet existing, let alone prospective, needs.[51]

Like many white residents, Colbert also had a vested interest in Gentilly's
future. When he became the school board's chief planner in 1951, the thirty-
four-year-old architect lived with his wife and daughter on the outer edge of
that section's developed landscape. The Colberts' neighborhood was known
as Parkchester Apartments, and it consisted mostly of single-story, ranch-
style duplexes and triplexes, a total of 1,256 family units in all, many of them
inhabited by war veterans such as Colbert. Gentilly experienced a flurry of
residential development and construction following World War II (see figures 6.1 and 6.2). But in 1951, the section north of Mirabeau Avenue between
Bayou St. John and the London Avenue Canal (the area partially visible along
the left side of figure 6.2) was virtually uninhabited. By walking two blocks

north from his home to Mirabeau, Colbert could gaze across green space that was a mile wide and more than a mile and a half long, extending without interruption toward Lake Pontchartrain. As he examined this vast expanse, his head must have filled with plans for realizing its great expectations.[52]

Colbert and his Parkchester neighbors likely viewed the verdant plains' eventual development as an inevitable extension of Gentilly's remarkable postwar growth. While just over 8,000 people lived in Gentilly before the war, its population mushroomed to more than 30,000 by 1950. With the exception of the black St. Bernard Housing Project and the adjacent area near Dillard University in Gentilly's southwestern corner, nearly everyone living there was white.[53]

As in other parts of the country, the federal government subsidized this transformation. By backing long-term, low-interest mortgages that required nominal down payments, the Federal Housing Administration's (FHA) and related efforts all but guaranteed a customer base for residential developers and homebuilders. Buying a home, in fact, often became cheaper than renting thanks to the FHA. As a result, developers designed homes and subdivisions according to the FHA's guidelines, which placed a premium on the construction of new, suburban homes for middle-class white residents. The FHA essentially shut blacks out of its process by refusing to insure nearly all loans in poorly rated neighborhoods (the agency's equivalent of the yellow and red areas on the HOLC's Residential Security Maps) and denying applications from black people seeking to live in higher-rated neighborhoods. The FHA based these decisions on the long-standing assumption that black residents eroded property values.[54]

As numerous scholars have noted, the FHA articulated its racialized vision for metropolitan development most clearly and influentially in its *Underwriting Manual,* which fair housing advocate Charles Abrams famously likened to "a chapter from Hitler's Nuremberg Laws."[55] Few scholars, however, have fully acknowledged the role that schools played in the FHA-backed development of white suburbs.[56] In addition to detailing specifications for evaluating construction and design standards, neighborhood quality, and a borrower's creditworthiness, the *Underwriting Manual* included guidelines for assessing the quality and accessibility of schools. The 1938 edition of the *Manual,* for instance, noted that if children living in an otherwise pleasant neighborhood were "compelled to attend school where the majority or a considerable number of the pupils represent a far lower level of society or an incompatible racial element, the neighborhood under consideration will prove far less stable and desirable than if this condition did not exist." The 1947 *Manual* similarly emphasized that schools with high-quality facilities and instruction helped to maintain an area's desirability. While the 1947 *Manual* discouraged the development of tracts that were not already near community facilities such as schools, it nevertheless supported new school construction for particularly large subdivisions and in those cases where there was "a definite need for the installation of new community facilities to open additional areas for residential use."[57]

Given the FHA's predilection for racial and socioeconomic homogeneity, these guidelines implicitly encouraged the creation of segregated schools across the country.[58] If you construct a large subdivision for whites in an outlying area, the *Manual* essentially advised developers, then you better build a white school to go along with it. Yet the FHA's guidelines also underscored the reciprocal nature of the relationship between school construction and residential development. As was the case in Broadmoor and the Fellman tract during the 1920s and 1930s, public schools for white students often functioned as preconditions for the creation of new, racially segregated subdivisions. The difference during the postwar building boom, however, was that the expansion of segregated schooling was national in scope and occurred at the urging of the federal government. As David M. P. Freund argues about the broader impact of the FHA, the federal government's interventions were not simply accepting the housing market's inherent racial biases, they were "inventing a new market for residence, subsidizing that market, and dictating the distribution of its resources to some people but not others."[59] The development of the vacant swath of land north of Charles Colbert's home illustrated the role that schools played in that process of market creation.

On the eve of World War II, the area encompassing and surrounding Colbert's future neighborhood consisted mostly of vacant fields and a handful of milk dairies. The nearest residential area was a collection of shacks originally known as Boscoville but recently rechristened Gentilly Heights. That neighborhood sat east of the London Avenue Canal just below Mirabeau Avenue, covering the area visible at the very bottom of figures 6.1 and 6.2. (The Parkchester neighborhood where Colbert later settled was built on the opposite side of the London Avenue Canal and is not visible in figures 6.1 and 6.2; for a view of Gentilly Heights and Parkchester, see map 6.2.) In 1939, the Home

Owners' Loan Corporation referred to Gentilly Heights as "an isolated community of negroes." It had no gas, electricity, or sewerage, and few of its homes were connected to city water mains. But the HOLC's surveyors also reported a rumor of a projected development in the uninhabited section north of what would become the Parkchester Apartments. According to a local real estate broker who fed information to the HOLC, one man owned the sizable tract between the London Avenue Canal, Bayou St. John, Mirabeau, and Fillmore Avenue, and he planned to "develop 2 sub-divisions in this area, one in the higher price bracket and one in the medium." The owner, George Dreyfous, was one of the late Leo Fellman's first cousins.[60]

The anticipated development of Dreyfous's bayou-side tract took off following the wartime slowdown in residential construction. In the summer of 1948, an outfit known as the Parkview Development Corporation, which had acquired Dreyfous's property as well as some additional land adjacent to it the year before, revealed its intention to invest millions in the nearly 300-acre tract. As with so many other postwar suburban developments, the company shaped its plans according to the FHA's financing guidelines.[61]

Almost immediately after announcing its vision for the tract, the company also took steps to secure a public school within its proposed development, which it called Oak Park. School and city officials were equally receptive to the developers' offer to donate ten acres of land for a school so long as the city footed the bill for subsurface draining, paving, and sidewalks surrounding the school site. "This site is badly needed for this fast developing area and the opportunity to acquire a ten acre site should not be lost from lack of foresight and wisdom in future planning," the chairman of the city's Planning and Zoning Commission wrote to the mayor and Commission Council. On behalf of the school district, Bourgeois also offered to contribute $30,000 toward the city's costs. By the end of the year, the Commission Council signed off on the deal, with the city and the school district agreeing to split the cost of the sidewalks, drainage, and paving. This cooperation between the city and the school district underscored another key component of the role that schools played in New Orleans's postwar development. Even when turf battles incited testy exchanges between municipal and school officials, the two sides shared and often acted on a vision of unified city and school planning.[62]

While another two years passed before the school board moved forward with the planning and construction of the school in Oak Park, the board's work still preceded housing construction and the movement of residents into Oak Park. Colbert was well aware of this since a pair of maps included in his 1952 school facilities plan clearly showed that no one then lived in this section of Gentilly.[63]

The role that Oak Park's school played in its development was also not unique to New Orleans. The Supreme Court, for instance, acknowledged the considerable role schools played in shaping urban landscapes in its 1971 decision in *Swann v. Charlotte-Mecklenburg,* which authorized busing to achieve desegregation. "People gravitate toward school facilities, just as schools are located in response to the needs of people," Justice Warren Burger wrote in the majority opinion. "The location of schools may thus influence the patterns of residential development of a metropolitan area."[64]

In the eastern section of Davidson County, Tennessee, just outside Nashville, real estate developer H. G. Hill Jr. also donated land for two schools to serve the suburban communities he was constructing during the 1940s. Real estate agents then touted the developments' proximity to the schools in newspaper advertisements. As historian Ansley T. Erickson noted in her study of suburbanization in Nashville, school location guidelines that the federal Department of Health, Education, and Welfare (HEW) published in 1958 reinforced prior federal and local policies that supported the development of white suburbs. Erickson and other scholars have also documented the ways that schools contributed to suburban growth outside the South. Erickson and Andrew Highsmith write that in Flint, Michigan, for instance, "on several occasions, members of the [school] board formally collaborated with local builders and representatives of the Federal Housing Administration in the planning and construction of new schools at the center of racially restricted neighborhoods." In the southern Los Angeles suburb of Southgate, meanwhile, school attendance zones reinforced residential segregation while ensuring that blacks and whites also went to separate schools. Similarly, the postwar construction of dozens of schools in Columbus, Ohio's northern perimeter bolstered that city's burgeoning white suburbs, just as separate schools for blacks and whites in Kansas City, Missouri, strengthened residential segregation there.[65] New Orleans's proposed black school village also reflected the national contours of the division of metropolitan areas along racial lines. The federal Housing Act of 1949, in fact, provided the spark that enabled Charles Colbert's vision for that village to become a reality.

III.

Faced with an intense shortage of low-rent housing, New Orleans officials moved nearly as quickly following the passage of the 1949 Housing Act as they had when the federal government began offering money for the creation of public housing projects in 1937. Shortly after President Harry S. Truman signed the 1949 law, the Housing Authority of New Orleans (HANO) received approval for the construction of 5,000 additional low-income housing units. But opposition from local real estate interests, who worried that proximity to projects would undermine property values, led HANO to concentrate on expanding its existing projects rather than building new ones. In Central City, for instance, HANO added 680 units to the Magnolia project's original 723 and 860 to Calliope's original 690. A similar dynamic guided the expansion of public housing in Chicago under the 1949 Act.[66]

Several features of the 1949 legislation also limited its effectiveness. In addition to requiring that "economy will be promoted both in construction and administration" of housing projects, the new legislation stressed the erad-ication of blighted areas more than their improvement. As a result, the new public housing units were more cheaply constructed and less architecturally pleasing than the older ones, and the dramatic growth of the projects eroded their connections to surrounding neighborhoods. This was most evident in Central City, where the Magnolia expansion eliminated the middle-class black housing that formerly abutted the project and the Flint-Goodridge Hospital.[67] These intraracial class divisions later became institutionalized when many black middle-class residents resettled in Pontchartrain Park, a 1,000-home subdivision for African Americans that opened in the northeastern corner of Gentilly in 1955 (see map I.1). As early as 1952, the school district began planning a black elementary school for Pontchartrain Park, which received support from the Federal Housing Administration, white investors, black pro-fessionals, and the City of New Orleans.[68]

In the summer of 1951, HANO received a nearly $24 million commit-ment from the federal government under the 1949 Act for the construction of a new, 1,860-unit black project in a sparsely inhabited area west of the Industrial Canal. The location HANO had in mind sat between Charles Col-bert's proposed school village site to the north and the white Florida Housing Project to the south, with the train tracks and drainage canal along Florida

Avenue providing a buffer between the existing white and proposed black developments. HANO eventually named the black housing project Desire, after one of the streets that cut across the property and along which Tennessee Williams's famed streetcar had run. That both the streetcar and the bus that replaced it ended their routes south of the proposed project did little to diminish the name's cachet. Elia Kazan's film adaptation of Williams's play, after all, was one of the most notable releases the year HANO acquired the property for the black project it named Desire.[69]

School and housing officials had simultaneously set their sights on this land in the city's undeveloped eastern edge.[70] Two weeks before the federal government signed off on the proposed project's location in July 1951, for instance, Colbert's planning division presented a report to the school board on the potential size and location of a proposed downtown black high school. Colbert's team began investigating locations for the high school in May, and they favored building the school "further out in this newer section," where he said land was considerably cheaper than in "the present crowded area." But the board failed to reach a consensus about the proposed school's location at that meeting.[71]

The board then renewed its consideration of Colbert's proposal shortly after HANO selected its site for the Desire Housing Project. During an hour-long discussion at the board's July 23 meeting, Ernest O. Becker, the assistant superintendent in charge of black education, sharply critiqued Colbert's recommendation of an outlying site adjacent to the proposed Desire project. In addition to arguing that Colbert was too heavily favoring future rather than immediate needs, he charged that the architect's plan contradicted previous commitments the board had made to blacks living on the downtown side of Canal Street. "Mr. Becker pointed out that the Negro population in this area had been promised a high school as soon as funds were available and that Clark High and Annex would be discontinued and a new comprehensive high school built," the board's secretary recorded in the meeting minutes. "He added he was not opposed to a school in the future in the area suggested by Mr. Colbert as he felt the need would develop; however, the need in this congested downtown area was pressing now." To bolster his argument, Becker pointed out that nearly 1,500 black high school students lived in the more centrally located area he favored versus the 82 who lived in Colbert's preferred peripheral section.[72]

Colbert, however, pressed the board to prepare for the future rather than focus solely on the present. "The population of New Orleans was moving in the direction of the Industrial Canal and the Negro population outward," he told board members. "Twenty-five years hence these areas would be the center of the population in New Orleans. The price of real estate in this outlying section, being so much less than that proposed for the congested downtown area, would enable the Board to give the Negroes a school with facilities such as they had never had before—a football field, gymnasium, track space, etc." While he conceded that the school's distance from the center of the city might create frustratingly long commutes for blacks, he argued that "they would be compensated by the quality of construction and the building once they arrived at school." Much like James Fortier, who had spoken decades before about the public schools' capacity to reshape the Crescent City's racial geography, Colbert also stressed that his plan would enable the board to make his vision for New Orleans's future development a reality. "One of the opportunities the School Board would have," he said, "would be to assist in city planning by helping to direct population."[73]

Thanks in part to board member Jacqueline McCullough's expanded influence, Colbert's proposal carried the day. McCullough, who changed her last name to Leonhard after marrying, became the board's president following the election of two more Bourgeois critics in the 1950 elections. This new board majority, which disapproved of Bourgeois's handling of several school incidents, quickly moved to oust the superintendent. It then proceeded to discredit much of the work he had done to meet the school system's many postwar needs.[74]

The new board, for instance, embraced Colbert's recommendation to locate the new black high school by the Industrial Canal partly because he presented it as part of a broader, long-term plan for school construction. But its elation over Colbert's vision disregarded the plans that Bourgeois had formulated years before and that Leonhard had delayed through her opposition to higher property taxes. While Leonhard talked of a board that "had been stumbling around on a building program" before Colbert came along with "a definite plan," the previous board never lacked a clearly articulated strategy for school facilities. Rather, Bourgeois's proposals struck more of a balance between the growing white suburbs and the already overcrowded black inner city than this new board considered necessary. For Colbert and Leonhard, the Industrial Canal site provided an opportunity to leave the decaying inner city behind while taking a bold—and economical—step into the metropolitan future.[75]

Yet the area Colbert favored for the black high school and which HANO had already selected as the site for Desire suffered from one significant deficiency: it was hardly suitable for large-scale human habitation. Becker tried to convey this point at the July 23 board meeting. In addition to noting that public transportation did not serve that part of the city, he highlighted other shortcomings in relation to the three potential Desire-area school locations that Colbert identified as Sites A, B, and C. "Site A," Becker said, "is in part a public dump and the remaining part mostly swamp land. In addition it borders on a largely White community [the Florida Housing Project]. There are no streets running through Site A. Sites B and C can be reached by only one street, Louisa-Piety."[76]

Even with its tangle of train tracks and nearby industrial activity, the greater Desire area belonged more to the country than the city in 1951. As in early black suburbs elsewhere in the country, many residents built and owned their own homes. These inhabitants, many of whom hailed from the rural South, also made use of the abundant land, raising gardens as well as domesticated animals. Charlena Matthews, whose father purchased a home in the nearby area while the project was under construction, recalled the shock of moving from the Seventh Ward to the city's eastern edge. "It was country," Matthews said. "The streets wasn't even paved then. People had chickens, ducks, goats. And we looked at this and said, 'Well, damn Daddy. What is this about?' We said, 'Whoa! Mommy, Daddy bought a house in the country.'" Even the music that Matthews heard in her new neighborhood was different. "I'd never heard any kind of blues before," Matthews said. "Not living in the inner city of New Orleans. Not that kind of blues. It's like a rural Mississippi kind of music."[77]

While Colbert responded to Becker by acknowledging the lack of public transportation and roads, he expressed confidence that the city would build additional streets according to the Planning and Zoning Commission's recently approved master plan. He also contended that "population increase will demand [transportation] service by the time the proposed school is ready for occupancy." Like Colbert, HANO also accepted the Desire area's isolation and soggy soil largely because it was so much cheaper than more centrally located land. Federal officials contributed to this decision since they rejected the local housing authority's initial proposal to build the new project near one of its existing developments on the grounds that the property was too expensive.[78]

During the summer of 1952, as Colbert was finalizing the facilities plan that outlined his vision for the school village, the school board acquired the ninety-acre tract north of the Desire Housing Project site. At the same time, Colbert, the city's Planning and Zoning Commission, and HANO were also working on a plan to provide public schools for housing projects, Desire in particular. These conversations resulted in a resolution the board passed in June 1952 vowing to cooperate with HANO and the planning commission. In a letter to the commission's chairman, Planning and Zoning Director Louis Bisso explained how the interagency collaboration unfolded. "As you know, we have been working very closely with Mr. Charles Colbert, Supervising Architect of the Planning and Construction Office and he and I more or less drafted the Resolution," Bisso wrote. "The main purpose of the Resolution is to make sure that the Housing Authority does not go too far off the Master Plan in its Urban Redevelopment Program, particularly with respect to future locations of schools."[79]

Bisso's stratagem apparently worked, because in November 1952, one month before the Supreme Court heard oral arguments in *Brown*, HANO and the school board revealed plans to include two elementary schools within the Desire project site itself. The announcement came before HANO had even advertised for bids for Desire's construction, and Colbert clearly reveled in the role the school system was playing in the project's development. He considered the plan "precedent shattering," stating that it would "consolidate the benefits of public housing and public education," not to mention segregation.[80]

As school and housing officials hashed out the details for the proposed elementary schools, Colbert also pressed forward with his plan for the downtown black high school. In keeping with the school village proposal, the board decided in June 1953 to simultaneously build a junior and senior high school on the ninety-acre tract adjacent to Desire. The board named these schools, each intended to serve 1,500 students, after George Washington Carver. In June 1954, a month after the US Supreme Court declared segregated education "inherently unequal" in its *Brown* decision, the board approved an architectural contract for Carver Junior and Senior High and prepared to clear the school site. The architects who received the contract were Nathaniel Curtis and Arthur Q. Davis, whose embrace of the International Style soon disrupted New Orleans's architectural establishment.[81]

Curtis and Davis effected considerable savings by designing the schools as a single project with a shared cafeteria, auditorium, and gymnasium. By arranging the schools with a common wall along a central axis, the architects essentially created two schools that were mirror images of each other (see figure 6.3). The original plans called for the junior and senior high classrooms to be on either side of the complex's long central building, the libraries in the center of this structure, and the noisier music and industrial arts buildings perpendicular to it. The architects placed the shared auditorium at one end of the campus and the shared gym and cafeteria, which bore a striking resemblance to the dining hall at the Louisiana State Penitentiary at Angola, at the other. Covered walkways protected students from the elements as they moved about the campus and provided informal gathering spots along with the spaces beneath the complex's elevated buildings. While some black educators questioned the wisdom of putting so many students together in one space, the architects and school officials reassured them that the complex's design provided each school with sufficient autonomy.[82]

While retaining the basic layout, the board dropped the auditorium in 1956 after the superintendent recommended it use the money "for purchase of school sites in new residential areas where delay in acquiring sites would cause much greater expenditures in the future." In place of the auditorium, the contractor built a large, sheltered play area. Before the complex opened in 1958, the board also commissioned Curtis and Davis to add a 935-student elementary school to the complex. That school's buildings ultimately flanked the covered play area. This elementary school replaced one of the two schools the board originally planned to build within the Desire Housing Project, and the board received kudos for keeping the construction costs for both elementary schools exceedingly low. The board budgeted the school that was part of the Carver complex at eleven dollars per square foot, and it built the other elementary school that was in Desire for even less. In 1957, *Progressive Architecture* magazine awarded Curtis and Davis its top design prize for the Carver complex, helping to cement the young firm's national reputation.[83]

But the school board's cost-cutting undermined the Desire school village's functionality. The windowless hallways and cement floors in the Curtis and Davis–designed elementary school, for instance, fared poorly in New Orleans's subtropical climate, and students often slipped when the floors became slick from the humidity. The board closed the other Desire elementary school, which another architectural firm designed, twenty-five years after it opened because chunks of its ceiling were plummeting onto students' desks.[84]

Even the land itself posed problems. The soil quality was so poor that the Carver Complex required seventy-foot-long piling instead of the forty-foot piling used to support a school the board built in Central City. Even the concrete walkways needed to be built atop pilings lest they fall into the earth. Given the complex's isolated location, providing it with water, sewerage, and drainage services also proved difficult and costly. When Jacqueline Leonard learned that constructing a water main to serve the site could cost as much as $400,000, she suffered an apparent bout of selective amnesia pertaining to the complex's troublesome location and the willingness with which the board had covered similar costs for suburban white schools. Word of the probable expense caused her "to grow indignant, pound the table and say that it was 'disgraceful' that the school board with its meager funds should always be called on to 'pave streets and put in utilities,'" the *Picayune* reported. The board ultimately split the expense with the city, HANO, and a contractor who was developing an industrial site adjacent to the Carver complex. Such was the cost of relying upon schools to create the new urban frontier.[85]

The Desire Housing Project, which opened to residents in 1956, suffered from similar deficiencies, and city and federal officials knew it from the beginning. The brick veneer on the project's 262 buildings made them appear as sturdy as HANO's earlier developments. But that exterior merely covered wood and plaster frames that succumbed to termites and rot over time. Unlike in the city's other projects, contractors did not reinforce Desire's wooden floors with concrete. The buildings also began sinking even before residents moved in. "Porches fell away from buildings. Sidewalks cracked. Gas, water and sewer lines twisted and ruptured," one history of the project noted. With train traffic often cutting off access to the development, fire and police stations at either end of the project had to handle emergency calls to ensure access by responders. The tenants' association tried to draw attention to these failings, firing off a peremptory report in April 1956. "A proper investigation, we feel, will reveal the Desire project as a real scandal and a blight on public housing in New Orleans," the association stated.[86]

This call, however, went unheeded, and by May 1957 all of Desire's units were full. With nearly 14,000 residents, it was one of the largest projects in the country built with federal funds. The federal Public Housing Administration contributed to Desire's heft since it had offered HANO unused money from other southern projects on the condition that it expand—but not enhance—Desire. The project also proved attractive to the rural migrants who continued to stream into the city. Desire, in fact, accommodated much of the black population increase in New Orleans during the 1950s. Ironically, it also provided blacks displaced by the expansion of the Calliope and Magnolia projects in Central City with a place to land. Much as Charles Colbert had hoped, Desire and its school village drew black residents to New Orleans's edge. But the schools at first proved incapable of handling the load. More than 10,000 of Desire's 14,000 initial residents were children, and crowding at its new schools forced them to immediately adopt platoon schedules. As a result, thousands of children filled the neighborhood throughout the day, and adults struggled to know which of them were supposed to be in school.[87]

In July 1953, shortly after moving forward with its plans for Carver Junior and Senior High, the school board and its new superintendent abandoned the phase of Colbert's school village proposal that involved busing students from Central City. By this time Colbert had returned to private practice, and several years later he became dean of Columbia University's School of Architecture. When he left that post after three stormy years, the university hailed him as "one of the nation's best known architects and planning experts."[88]

The school village came into being alongside three of the most significant developments in post–World War II America: the Second Great Migration of African Americans from the rural South to cities, the government-subsidized movement of white residents to racially homogenous suburbs, and the NAACP's victory in *Brown v. Board of Education*. As African Americans in New Orleans and nationally tested the limits Jim Crow placed upon their freedom, officials at every level of government deepened the grooves of racial inequality within the metropolitan landscape.

As during the critical interwar period, schools aided the transformation of race into a concept directly tied to physical space. In New Orleans, school and housing officials made Central City into an exclusively black residential area by concentrating segregated black schools and housing projects there. These officials also collaborated with the federal government to support the growth of all-white suburbs such as Oak Park, and a similar constellation of policymakers addressed overcrowding within Central City through the creation of the isolated and exclusively black Carver and Desire complexes. Confronted with black challenges to segregation, whites used their power to create more of it.

Even without its headline-grabbing busing component, New Orleans's educational Soweto maintained its significance. The three-school, five-thousand-student Carver complex became an anchor for a new black home-land that was out of sight and mind for most city dwellers. While Desire residents turned their neighborhood's schools into strong community insti-tutions, they had few doubts about the motivations that drove white officials' decisions about the project and school complex's location and design. As one of Carver's early students explained, "They knew integration would eventu-ally come and they would need somewhere for all these black kids to go. You know, this integration thing, they wasn't all for that."[89]

Desire residents soon discovered the extent of white New Orleanians' opposition to integration when the school board selected the nearby Frantz Elementary School as one of the first white schools to desegregate in 1960. That school, on the edge of the white Florida Housing Project, became the scene of the next great battle over schools, race, and the future of the city, and white residents fought it along the lines that their forebears had established decades before.

EPILOGUE

CRISIS AND CONTINUITY

The crowd began to gather outside Frantz Elementary in New Orleans's Ninth Ward around 8 a.m. on Monday, November 14, 1960. It was a warm, gray, and humid day.[1]

Three months earlier, federal judge J. Skelly Wright had selected November 14 as the date for the start of school desegregation in New Orleans. While the move followed more than a decade of black activism targeting segregated education, white resistance remained strong. Having already threatened to close schools rather than permit their desegregation, state officials continued to hatch plans to preserve segregation until the deadline approached. Spurred by the local NAACP, Wright beat back each segregationist stratagem, even issuing a restraining order against the governor and every member of the legislature for good measure late in the evening on November 13.[2]

The Orleans Parish School Board, meanwhile, had sought to minimize the extent of desegregation even as it accepted Wright's deadline. Accordingly, they whittled the number of black students scheduled to transfer to formerly white schools down to five. Then four, after one of the students removed her name from consideration. To avoid a Little Rock–style showdown, officials withheld the names of the schools that would desegregate. But the sizable police presence around Frantz that morning alerted nearby residents that it was on the list.[3]

At roughly 9:25 a.m., two cars pulled up in front of the school, which served many students from the nearby Florida Housing Project. Six-year-old Ruby Bridges and her mother Lucille exited the first vehicle, joined by three US marshals from the second. As the group walked toward the school's entrance, the white onlookers hurled unthinkable invectives. "If my mother was for integration, I'd string her up," one of them shouted. Others chanted, "Two,

230

four, six, eight. We don't want to integrate" and sang "Glory, glory segregation" to the tune of "Battle Hymn of the Republic." After the Bridges entered the building, the white parents who had not already kept their children at home rushed to the school to retrieve them. By the end of the day only fifty white students remained at Frantz, and the crowd outside had swelled to at least five hundred. A similar scene unfolded on the far side of the Industrial Canal in the Lower Ninth Ward, where three other black girls desegregated the formerly white McDonogh No. 19 Elementary.[4]

While that Monday ended without violence, the ensuing days were less peaceful. One thousand spectators greeted Bridges outside of Frantz as she returned to school on Tuesday. "You wanna be white, we'll make you white!" one woman shouted from the crowd. "We're gonna throw acid in your face!" Another threatened to poison her food. In a throwback to the 1874 school riots, hundreds of white high school students took to the streets and threatened to break into Frantz and McDonogh 19. That evening more than five thousand rallied on behalf of the White Citizens' Council at the city's Municipal Auditorium, where Plaquemines Parish political boss Leander Perez bellowed, "Don't wait for your daughter to be raped by these Congolese. Don't wait until the burr-heads are forced into your schools. Do something about it now!"[5]

On Wednesday, roughly two thousand white teenagers heeded Perez's call. They stormed city hall and the school board's downtown offices and pelted black motorists and pedestrians with rocks and bottles. Blacks fired back with their own projectiles, including Molotov cocktails. By the end of the day, one black man had been stabbed and one white man shot. Even after the number of white students attending Frantz and McDonogh No. 19 dropped to two and zero, respectively, protestors maintained their vigil outside the schools. (With Perez's aid, the majority of the schools' white students transferred to neighboring St. Bernard Parish.) When white moderates organized a "carlift" in December to safely transport white students to Frantz, the mob attacked the vehicles and then published the names and phone numbers of their owners. Observing the scene outside the school in late 1960, the novelist John Steinbeck likened it to a carnival freak show. "In the New Orleans show," Steinbeck wrote, "I felt all the amusement of the improbable abnormal, but also a kind of horror that it could be so."[6]

A broad range of writers have offered interpretations of what came to be known as the New Orleans School Crisis. Several have focused on the political underpinnings of the crisis. Political scientist Morton Inger, for instance, argued that the school board, mayor, and civic elite permitted chaos to reign by removing themselves from politics. Historian Kim Lacy Rogers countered that the board's apolitical posturing was a calculated move intended to appease the white masses. Similarly, Edward Haas blamed New Orleans mayor DeLesseps "Chep" Morrison for his lack of leadership as the date for desegregation approached. Psychiatrist Robert Coles, by contrast, emphasized the humanity of both Ruby Bridges and the white segregationists who opposed her, exploring the latter's actions in relation to their personal frustrations, insecurities, and anxieties. To a greater extent than Coles, Steinbeck chalked up the white protestors' fury to "three hundred years of fear and anger and terror of change in a changing world." Historian Adam Fairclough in turn examined the crisis within the broader context of the civil rights movement. He argued that it set the stage for a new, more aggressive phase in the black freedom struggle by highlighting the depths of white elite commitment to segregation. In her narrative account of school desegregation in New Orleans, Liva Baker emphasized the power of the federal judiciary and the courage of individuals such as Bridges and Wright to persist in the face of violent hostility. More recently, Jason Sokol analyzed the School Crisis in the context of white southerners' reaction against and accommodation to Jim Crow's demise, while Donald DeVore stressed the strength of the black community in the face of adversity.[7]

Despite their merits, none of these interpretations fully acknowledges the links between the 1960 crisis and New Orleans's past. The desegregation crisis was the latest and most dramatic manifestation of a centuries-old struggle over schools, race, and the future of the city. Denied the services lavished upon racially homogenous middle-class suburbs such as Gentilly, the Ninth Ward's poor and working-class white residents confronted a situation familiar to previous generations of white New Orleanians. Like the whites who lived in the racially mixed neighborhoods near McDonogh No. 13 and the Bayou Road School earlier in the century, the Ninth Ward residents recognized their neighborhood's precarious position in the municipal pecking order. Also like these earlier New Orleanians, they clung to the racial status of their schools as the one thing that could save their neighborhoods from complete neglect. As historian Juliette Landphair writes, "The protestors' vitriol was a product of the neighborhoods around them. To whites the decision to initiate school desegregation in the Ninth Ward represented another example of the city's disregard for their community."[8]

The city's inattention to the Ninth Ward also drove the black civil rights activism that sparked the 1960 School Crisis. The plaintiffs in the NAACP's school equalization and desegregation suits both hailed from the Ninth Ward.[9] Yet here too there were parallels to the earlier struggles in other parts of the city. During the nineteenth century, the Catholic Institution became a bedrock of the city's free black community and a springboard for its campaign for racial equality. That campaign was rooted in the school's Faubourg Marigny neighborhood and the adjacent Tremé, where the Reconstruction-era effort to desegregate public schools began. Similarly, after the school board eliminated black public schooling beyond the fifth grade in 1900, black parents joined with civic leaders such as Walter L. Cohen to press for greater educational opportunity. Those campaigns focused on the situations that were the most dire and the black communities the most in need: the unsanitary school buildings on Bayou Road, the elementary school adjacent to "black Storyville" in the Third Ward, the double sessions that limited classroom instruction for black students in Central City, and the lack of opportunities for high school education.

Whenever black educational activism butted up against white needs, the reaction was swift and furious. During the antebellum era, New Orleans joined the rest of the nation in cracking down on black schooling in the face of an intensifying abolitionist movement and the advent of universal white male suffrage. This backlash was also as evident during the Reconstruction-era riots as during the twentieth century. The new school facilities that the board provided to the white residents in burgeoning neighborhoods such as Broadmoor and the Fellman tract during the 1920s and 1930s, for instance, only stoked the resentment of the whites who remained in the older, racially mixed sections of the city. With government officials and real estate professionals (who were often one and the same) stressing the link between racial homogeneity and property value, these white schools bolstered the growth of the newer neighborhoods and ensured that they received additional city services and zoning that safeguarded their residential status. Neighborhoods with black schools, however, did not simply fail to receive similar protections; the presence of black schools and students also marked the surrounding areas as declining ones, and wrecking balls often followed close on the heels of their introduction.

In this climate, it was not surprising that city, school, and federal officials opted to build New Orleans's educational Soweto—the Desire Housing Project and its accompanying "school village"—out of sight and mind from the rest of the city. Much like the acerbic former School Board president James Fortier, village founder Charles Colbert—the board's nationally renowned planner—embraced public schools as engines of the city's physical and demographic development. Residents attached similar importance to schools, which accounted for the backlash against black education during the antebellum era and Reconstruction and the equally vicious protests over McDonogh No. 13 in 1917, the Bayou Road School in 1923, and Frantz and McDonogh No. 19 in 1960.

The intensity of the 1960 crisis affirmed one of the primary assumptions behind the NAACP's decades-long campaign against segregated education: schools were central to the maintenance of Jim Crow. They acted as economic gatekeepers that provided—or inhibited—pathways to mainstream success. Schools were also symbolically important to both black and white people; as long as segregated schools persisted, many seemed to think, the color line would as well. As this book has shown, segregated schools also created the racially segregated and uneven landscapes that became so common in the nation's cities. This divided geography enabled whites to accrue wealth through property while sharply inhibiting African American efforts to do the same.

But if schools played a central role in making Jim Crow, deducing how they could unmake it was no easy task. In Raleigh and Nashville, historians have shown how the residential segregation that school policies fostered complicated the process of school desegregation by requiring extensive busing between predominantly white suburbs and the predominantly black inner city. In New Orleans, which never implemented busing, school desegregation was essentially a one-way process, particularly in the high schools: black students attended formerly white schools such as Fortier, but white students almost never attended black schools such as Cohen, Clark, McDonogh 35, or Carver. School desegregation was also short-lived in the Crescent City. After judicial leniency (following Skelly Wright's elevation to the Court of Appeals for the District of Columbia in 1962) permitted the school board to limit the amount of desegregation through the early sixties, the courts ordered it to pick up the pace later in the decade. At the time, blacks comprised two-thirds of the city's 108,000 public school students. By 1978, however, only 15,000 white students remained in what was then an 89,000-student system—hardly enough to achieve desegregation on any meaningful scale.[10]

More significantly, school desegregation alone offered insufficient compensation for the spatially grounded inequalities that segregated schooling and neighborhoods fostered. While desegregation could bring black and white students together in the same classrooms, it guaranteed neither equitable education nor equitable access to jobs, housing, basic services, or wealth. These limitations became particularly clear as white families fled the city and its desegregating public schools for those in outlying parishes during the 1970s. Tax dollars and consumer services followed whites to parishes such as Jefferson and St. Tammany. As in Oakland, Detroit, Boston, and other major cities, the containerization of the Port of New Orleans and declines in manufacturing eliminated many of the jobs that had supported a well-paid black working class. Public and private investment in a tourism-based economy simultaneously promoted the growth of a low-wage, largely nonunion, workforce in the service industry. These shifts coincided with the nationwide "criminalization of urban space" through stricter drug and sentencing laws, a process that unfolded with remarkable brutality in Louisiana. By 2012, Louisiana imprisoned more people per capita than any other state in the nation, giving it the highest incarceration rate in the world.[11]

These developments exacerbated the racial and spatial divisions that already existed within New Orleans, hitting the city's segregated black neighborhoods—especially Central City and the Desire area—the hardest. With roughly one in fourteen black men in jail in New Orleans and nationally, the criminal justice system ripped families and communities apart in a manner reminiscent of the domestic slave trade two centuries before. Violent crime also increased nationally *following* the introduction of lengthy mandatory minimum sentences, compounding these communities' dire straits. The Desire Housing Project alone was the scene of nineteen homicides in 1988, giving it a murder rate seven times the city average. As New Orleans recorded nearly two thousand murders between 1989 and 1994, Central City residents also became increasingly familiar with violence. By the close of the twentieth century, 41 percent of the city's children were living in poverty—a rate that has mostly held steady since then. New Orleans's public school system, which by then served a population that was almost exclusively poor and black, also gained a reputation as among the most organizationally dysfunctional in the country.[12]

Despite this grim picture, the historical role that public schools played in driving metropolitan inequality offers some lessons for the future. Most significantly, it underscores that the issues affecting urban schools cannot be separated from urban history, just as the issues affecting cities cannot be separated from the history of their schools. This reciprocal relationship between cities and schools is generally lost in present-day debates about school reform, which often focus narrowly on issues such as testing, standards, teachers' unions, and school choice. Divorcing public education from the history of metropolitan change also encourages people to both expect too much from, and to ask too little of, urban schools.

President Barack Obama was guilty of this line of thinking in a 2010 speech on education reform before the National Urban League Centennial Conference. In that speech, Obama discussed the educational gap between white and minority children, and he attributed the conditions facing students living in what he termed "the wrong neighborhood" to "a turn of fate" rather than to well-documented historical contingencies. Later in the speech, he touted a slate of reforms that had enjoyed remarkably broad support during the preceding decade, including initiatives to "turn around" low-performing schools. According to the president, a critical piece of the effort to overhaul struggling schools was the belief that doing so was possible in spite of the challenging circumstances they faced. To emphasize his point, Obama offered the example of the Mastery charter schools in Philadelphia, which are run by a private organization according to the terms of a contract—or charter— with the local education agency. "In just two years, three of the schools that Mastery has taken over have seen reading and math levels nearly double—in some cases, triple," Obama said. "Now, if a school like Mastery can do it," he continued, "every troubled school can do it."[13]

Following Hurricane Katrina in 2005, New Orleans became the vanguard of a national charter school movement through the overhaul of its school system. By 2017, 93 percent of its public school students attended a charter. Proponents for charter schools, which also figure prominently in cities such as Detroit, Washington, DC, and Philadelphia, emphasize the capacity of privately operated schools such as Mastery to revolutionize public education. Specifically, these advocates argue that "school choice" provides expanded educational opportunity to students from the "wrong neighborhood" by allowing them to select a school other than the one nearest their home. Since schools must compete for students—and the public funds that come with them—these reformers claim that "choice" creates an educational market that will propel systemic improvement. The successful schools will flourish and replicate, the thinking goes, while the unsuccessful ones will close due to insufficient enrollment or the revocation of their charter. (When a school loses its charter, another "operator" may reconstitute a new school at the same site as part of a "turnaround" effort, or the existing school building may close its doors for good.)[14]

In the transition from the Obama to the Trump administration, the drive for expanded school choice outside of public school systems has only accelerated. Trump has called for more charter schools, more publicly funded vouchers for students to attend private schools, and more opportunities for low-income students to leave their neighborhood public school for another one while taking the public money allocated for their education with them.[15]

Some readers may reach this point in this account of the inequalities that public schools historically promoted and conclude that the traditional system of public education is so broken that radical reforms such as "school choice" are sorely needed. That is not my intention. Rather, I seek to stress that the common school ideal—like American democracy itself—remains a viable and necessary objective even if its reality has fallen short of its ideals. By highlighting the ways in which schools aided the construction and institutionalization of white supremacy, I hope to provide policymakers and the general public with the context for developing approaches to redress past wrongs and to promote equitable futures. School choice does not meet either of these aims.

While there are certainly reasons to cheer when schools such as Mastery appear to succeed against all odds, overemphasizing these individual success stories distracts from the persistence of segregated schools and neighborhoods within metropolitan America and the impact of past and present discrimination upon opportunity, resource allocation, and wealth accumulation.[16] School choice essentially takes segregation and metropolitan inequality as a given, providing students with an opportunity to leave struggling neighborhoods rather than investing in those communities. The closure of a neighborhood public school, moreover, has the potential to affect the surrounding area in much the same way that slum clearance affected McDonogh 35's Third Ward neighborhood and Joseph Craig's Tremé environs. The instability inherent in school "turnaround" efforts, which overwhelmingly affect poor and minority neighborhoods, also rivals the upheaval that these areas experienced during previous periods of redevelopment. In considering how schools can direct a city's future, policymakers should remember the role they played in creating and managing racialized markets for opportunity in the past.[17]

While school choice advocates may be guilty of expecting too much from individual schools, recognizing public education's historical capacity to affect metropolitan development and the broader racial order also raises the prospect that people can ask much more of urban schools and school reform. Rather than focusing on strategies for succeeding in spite of the racially isolated, economically depressed neighborhoods that prior school policies helped to create, reformers should explore ways of harnessing the power of schools to rebuild those neighborhoods. This will involve reestablishing the links between schools, housing, community development, and urban planning that previous generations of policymakers cherished yet too often abused. It will also require prioritizing public interests over private ones and redistributing power and resources to those who have historically had limited access to both. Throughout much of New Orleans's history, public schools played a central role in segregating the city. In the future, one can only hope that they serve a more unifying and equitable purpose.[18]

NOTES

INTRODUCTION

1. Ruby Bridges, *Through My Eyes* (New York: Scholastic, 1999), 8, 15, 19.

2. Ibid., 6, 8; Social Explorer Tables (SE), Census 1960 Tracts Only Set, Social Explorer & U.S. Census Bureau—DUALabs, based upon data from *U.S. Censuses of Population and Housing: 1960, Census Tracts, Final Report PHC(1)-11* (Washington, DC: U.S. Government Printing Office, 1962). On the history of racial oppression and black community organizing in Bridges's native Walthall County and other southwestern Mississippi counties, see Charles M. Payne, *I've Got the Light of Freedom: The Organizing Tradition and the Mississippi Freedom Struggle* (Berkeley: University of California Press, 1995), 111–18; and Louis M. Kyriakoudes and Hayden Noel McDaniel, "Listening to Freedom's Voices: Forty-Four Years of Documenting the Mississippi Civil Rights Movement," *Southern Quarterly* 52, no. 1 (Fall 2014): 72–73. For another study highlighting the long history of racial oppression and African American community organizing and activism in the rural South, see Hasan Kwame Jeffries, *Bloody Lowndes: Civil Rights and Black Power in Alabama's Black Belt* (New York: New York University Press, 2009).

3. Bridges, *Through My Eyes*, 8; Liva Baker, *The Second Battle of New Orleans: The Hundred-Year Struggle to Integrate the Schools* (New York: Harper Collins, 1996), 397.

4. Bridges, *Through My Eyes*, 15; Baker, *Second Battle of New Orleans*, 399–401. On the NAACP's legal campaign, see Baker, *Second Battle of New Orleans*, passim; Mark V. Tushnet, *The NAACP's Legal Strategy Against Segregated Education, 1925–1950* (Chapel Hill: University of North Carolina Press, 1987); Richard Kluger, *Simple Justice: The History of* Brown v. Board of Education *and Black America's Struggle for Equality* (New York: Knopf, 1975); Michael J. Klarman, *From Jim Crow to Civil Rights: The Supreme Court and the Struggle for Racial Equality* (Oxford: Oxford University Press, 2004); James T. Patterson, *Brown v. Board of Education: A Civil Rights Milestone and its Troubled Legacy* (Oxford: Oxford University Press, 2001). I was able to develop a picture of the Bridges home and neighborhood through a remarkable series of photographs that Paul Slade took in 1960. These images are in the *Paris Match* archive and are available for viewing via Getty Images at http://www.gettyimages.com/photos/william-frantz?excludenudity=true&family=editorial&page=1&phrase=%22William%20Frantz%22&sort=mostpopular#license.

5. Bridges, *Through My Eyes*, 15–16; PBS NewsHour, "A Class of One: Ruby Bridges," 18 February 1997 (Arlington, VA: MacNeil-Lehrer Productions, 1997) (for quote).

6. Baker, *Second Battle of New Orleans*, 394–401; Henry Louis Gates Jr., *The African Americans: Many Rivers to Cross*, Episode 5 (Arlington, VA: PBS Distribution, 2013) (for quote).

7. Louisiana State Advisory Committee to the United States Commission on Civil Rights, *The New Orleans School Crisis* (Washington, DC: Government Printing Office, 1961), 12–17.

8. Ibid.; *Brown v. Board of Education* 347 U.S. 483 (1954); Baker, *Second Battle of New Orleans*, 403–6, 410–18; Adam Fairclough, *Race and Democracy: The Civil Rights Struggle in Louisiana*, 2nd edition (Athens: University of Georgia Press, 2008), 195–97, 207–11, 223–26, 234–44; Walter C. Stern, "Black, White, Silver, and Blue: Race and Desegregation at New Orleans' Fortier High, 1960–1975" (Master's thesis, Tulane University, 2010). While one New Orleans high school technically desegregated in 1964, large-scale desegregation did not occur in the city's high schools until the 1967–1968 school year. See Donald E. DeVore and Joseph Logsdon, *Crescent City Schools: Public Education in New Orleans, 1841-1991* (Lafayette: University of Southwestern Louisiana Press, 1991), 264–65.

9. See Klarman, *Jim Crow to Civil Rights*, chap. 7 (quote on p. 350).

10. The curriculum framework for the AP US History exam, which nearly 500,000 high school students take annually, provides one of the best (albeit rough) indicators of the prevalence of "backlash" as an explanation for key developments in postwar American history. While the AP curriculum framework includes "key concepts" rather than historical content, those concepts emphasize a 1960s backlash against a postwar liberal consensus. See The College Board, "AP Course and Exam Description: AP United States History, Including the Curriculum Framework" (New York: College Board, 2015), especially p. 81, available at https://secure-media.collegeboard.org/digital Services/pdf/ap/ap-us-history-course-and-exam-description.pdf. For the number of AP exams administered, see The College Board, "Program Summary Report," 2016, https://secure-media .collegeboard.org/digitalServices/pdf/research/2016/Program-Summary-Report-2016.pdf. Examples of textbooks that feature the "backlash" narrative include James West Davidson, *Experience History: Interpreting America's Past*, vol. 2, 8th edition (New York: McGraw Hill, 2014); and George Brown Tindall and David Emory Shi, *America: A Narrative History*, 8th edition (New York: W. W. Norton, 2010).

11. A generation of scholars have challenged the "backlash" narrative, looking instead to New Deal and postwar liberalism as the source of later social, political, and economic fissures. Urban historians in particular have emphasized the role that race and political economy played in unevenly distributing public and private benefits during the decades bracketing World War II. These scholars, however, generally pay little attention to schools. Key works in this area include Arnold R. Hirsch, *Making the Second Ghetto: Race and Housing in Chicago, 1940-1960* (Cambridge: Cambridge University Press, 1983); Kenneth Jackson, *Crabgrass Frontier: The Suburbanization of the United States* (New York: Oxford University Press, 1985); Thomas J. Sugrue, *The Origins of the Urban Crisis: Race and Inequality in Postwar Detroit* (Princeton, NJ: Princeton University Press, 1996); Robert O. Self, *American Babylon: Race and the Struggle for Postwar Oakland* (Princeton, NJ: Princeton University Press, 2003); David M. P. Freund, *Colored Property: State Policy & White Racial Politics in Suburban America* (Chicago: University of Chicago Press, 2007); Kevin Kruse, *White Flight: Atlanta and the Making of Modern Conservatism* (Princeton, NJ: Princeton University Press, 2005); Matthew D. Lassiter, *Silent Majority: Suburban Politics in the Sunbelt South* (Princeton, NJ: Princeton University Press, 2006); Amanda I. Seligman, *Block By Block: Neighborhoods and Public Policy on Chicago's West Side* (Chicago: University of Chicago Press,

2005); Donna Jean Murch, *Living for the City: Migration, Education, and the Rise of the Black Panther Party in Oakland, California* (Chapel Hill: University of North Carolina Press, 2010). For a work that traces the roots of white southern resistance to the two decades before *Brown*, see Jason Morgan Ward, *Defending White Democracy: The Making of a Segregationist Movement and the Remaking of Southern Politics* (Chapel Hill: University of North Carolina Press, 2011). For a helpful overview of the broader historiography, see Meg Jacobs, "The Uncertain Future of American Politics," in *American History Now*, ed. Eric Foner and Lisa McGirr (Philadelphia: Temple University Press, 2011).

12. In conceptualizing how my work challenges the "backlash" thesis, I benefited from insights that David Freund, Jefferson Cowie, Kevin Kruse, Donna Murch, Andrew K. Sandoval-Strausz, and Heather Ann Thompson provided during an Organization of American Historians session on "Revisiting 'White Flight' and the 'Backlash' Thesis: Racial Politics in the American Metropolis," OAH Annual Meeting, New Orleans, LA, 7 April 2017.

13. The question of continuity versus change that C. Vann Woodward attempted to answer more than sixty years ago in *The Strange Career of Jim Crow* still figures prominently in the literature on the origins of segregation. While historians such as Howard Rabinowitz sharply questioned Woodward's "forgotten alternatives" thesis—that the segregation that took root in the late nineteenth and early twentieth century reflected a break with the past—others such as Glenda Gilmore partially revived it. This study partially sides with Woodward by emphasizing that New Orleans's spatial reorganization into distinct black and white areas during the early twentieth century marked a profound change. At the same time, it emphasizes the remarkable continuity of white supremacy and white anxiety from the antebellum through the Jim Crow era. Key works on the origins of segregation include C. Vann Woodward, *The Strange Career of Jim Crow* (New York: Oxford University Press, 1955); Howard N. Rabinowitz, *Race Relations in the Urban South* (New York: Oxford University Press, 1978); Joel Williamson, *The Crucible of Race: Black-White Relations in the American South Since Emancipation* (New York: Oxford University Press, 1984); John W. Cell, *The Highest Stage of White Supremacy: The Origins of Segregation in South Africa and the American South* (Cambridge: Cambridge University Press, 1982); Glenda Gilmore, *Gender and Jim Crow: Women and the Politics of White Supremacy in North Carolina, 1896–1920* (Chapel Hill: University of North Carolina Press, 1996); Grace Elizabeth Hale, *Making Whiteness: The Culture of Whiteness in the South, 1890–1940* (New York: Pantheon Books, 1998); Leon Litwack, *Trouble in Mind: Black Southerners in the Age of Jim Crow* (New York: Knopf, 1998). On New Orleans, see Dale A. Somers, "Black and White in New Orleans: A Study in Urban Race Relations, 1865–1900," *Journal of Southern History* 40, no. 1 (February 1974): 19–42; Roger A. Fischer, "Racial Segregation in Ante Bellum New Orleans," *American Historical Review* 74, no. 3 (February 1969): 926–37; Roger A. Fischer, *The Segregation Struggle in Louisiana, 1862–1877* (Urbana: University of Illinois Press, 1974); John Blassingame, *Black New Orleans, 1860–1880* (Chicago: University of Chicago Press, 1973); Donald E. DeVore, *Defying Jim Crow: African American Community Development and the Struggle for Racial Equality in New Orleans, 1900–1960* (Baton Rouge: Louisiana State University Press, 2015); Michael A. Ross, *The Great New Orleans Kidnapping Case: Race, Law, and Justice in the Reconstruction Era* (Oxford: Oxford University Press, 2015); James B. Bennett, *Religion and the Rise of Jim Crow in New Orleans* (Princeton, NJ: Princeton University Press, 2005). For summaries of the historiographical debate, see James Beeby and Donald G. Nieman, "The Rise of Jim Crow, 1880–1920," in *A Companion to the Amer-*

ican South, ed. John B. Boles (Malden, MA: Blackwell Publishing, 2004); and Howard N. Rabinowitz, "More Than the Woodward Thesis: Assessing *The Strange Career of Jim Crow,*" *Journal of American History* 75, no. 3 (December 1988): 842-56.

14. On the Reconstruction-era desegregation of New Orleans public schools and their resegregation after 1877, see Louis R. Harlan, "Desegregation in New Orleans Public Schools During Reconstruction," *American Historical Review* 67, no. 3 (April 1962): 663-75.

15. DeVore and Logsdon, *Crescent City Schools,* 143. On New Orleans's lack of sewerage, drainage, and water facilities at the turn of the twentieth century and the inequities that marred the initial distribution of these and other amenities, see Craig E. Colton, *Unnatural Metropolis: Wresting New Orleans from Nature* (Baton Rouge: Louisiana State University Press, 2005), chap. 3. On the rise of mass schooling, see David Tyack, *The One Best System: A History of American Urban Education* (Cambridge, MA: Harvard University Press, 1974); David Nasaw, *Schooled to Order: A Social History of Public Schooling in the United States* (New York: Oxford University Press, 1981); Ira Katznelson and Margaret Weir, *Schooling for All: Class, Race, and the Decline of the Democratic Ideal* (New York: Basic Books, 1985).

16. The court initially struck down residential segregation ordinances in *Buchanan v. Warley,* 245 U.S. 60 (1917). It upheld this ruling in *Harmon v. Tyler,* 273 U.S. 668 (1927), which originated in New Orleans, and in *City of Richmond v. Deans,* 281 U.S. 704 (1930). See also Klarman, *Jim Crow to Civil Rights,* 143, 507 n. 107. The Louisiana Supreme Court also struck down New Orleans's "first residential segregation ordinance based primarily on racial criteria," which pertained to prostitutes, in 1917. See Alecia P. Long, *The Great Southern Babylon: Sex, Race, and Respectability in New Orleans, 1865-1920* (Baton Rouge: Louisiana State University Press, 2005), 214-24 (quote on 217). The New Orleans ordinances and cases are discussed in greater detail in chapters 3 and 5. While Carl Nightingale argues that the post-*Buchanan* power vacuum in the United States meant that "public authorities had to defer to real estate agents and land economists to develop a more camouflaged route for racial segregationism," I show that real estate professionals and public school officials cooperated quite openly to advance segregation. See Nightingale, *Segregation: A Global History of Divided Cities* (Chicago: University of Chicago Press, 2012), 361.

17. Total Community Action, Department of Program Development, *Profile of Poverty in New Orleans* (New Orleans: 1973), 3-5, 18, 20-21(first and third quote on 4; second quote on 5).

18. While African Americans figure prominently in this narrative, white actors receive what may strike some readers as an excessive share of attention. This reflects my focus on the joint creation of white supremacy and the urban built environment, or what Arnold Hirsch artfully refers to as "the construction of the ball park within which the urban game is played." Since whites held a disproportionate share of power in this construction project, they receive a disproportionate amount of the coverage here. Other historians have also provided excellent accounts of African American community development in New Orleans during much of the time period covered here. See, in particular, John Blassingame's *Black New Orleans* for the late nineteenth century and Donald DeVore's *Defying Jim Crow* for the first six decades of the twentieth. On young black women's experiences with Jim Crow in New Orleans, see LaKisha Michelle Simmons, *Crescent City Girls: The Lives of Young Black Women in Segregated New Orleans* (Chapel Hill: University of North Carolina Press, 2015). On African American life and community development in colonial New Orleans, see Lawrence N. Powell, *The Accidental City: Improvising New Orleans* (Cambridge,

MA: Harvard University Press, 2012); Jennifer M. Spear, *Race, Sex, and Social Order in Early New Orleans* (Baltimore: Johns Hopkins University Press, 2010); Gwendolyn Midlo Hall, *Africans in Colonial Louisiana: The Development of Afro-Creole Culture in the Eighteenth Century* (Baton Rouge: Louisiana State University Press, 1992); and Kimberly Hanger, *Bounded Lives, Bounded Places: Free Black Society in Colonial New Orleans, 1769–1803* (Durham, NC: Duke University Press, 1997). For antebellum New Orleans, see Caryn Cossé Bell, *Revolution, Romanticism, and the Afro-Creole Protest Tradition in Louisiana, 1718–1868* (Baton Rouge: Louisiana State University Press, 1997); and Elizabeth Clark Neidenbach, "The Life and Legacy of Marie Couvent: Social Networks, Property Ownership, and the Making of a Free People of Color Community in New Orleans." (PhD diss., College of William and Mary, 2015). For Hirsch quote, see *Making the Second Ghetto*, xvi.

19. Edmund S. Morgan, *American Slavery, American Freedom: The Ordeal of Colonial Virginia* (New York: W. W. Norton, 1975); Lynn Hunt, *Inventing Human Rights: A History* (New York: W. W. Norton, 2007); Barbara Jeanne Fields, "Slavery, Race, and Ideology in the United States of America," *New Left Review* 181 (May–June 1990): 95–118; Ibram X. Kendi, *Stamped from the Beginning: The Definitive History of Racist Ideas in America* (New York: Nation Books, 2016), 38–39, 84–85; Nightingale, *Segregation: A Global History*, 83–85. On the Haitian Revolution's impact on efforts to codify race, see Emily Clark, *The Strange History of the American Quadroon: Free Women of Color in the Revolutionary Atlantic World* (Chapel Hill: University of North Carolina Press, 2013), 1–10.

20. Heather Andrea Williams, *Self-Taught: African American Education in Slavery and Freedom* (Chapel Hill: University of North Carolina Press, 2007), 14–16, 204–5; Hilary J. Moss, *Schooling Citizens: The Struggle for African American Education in Antebellum America* (Chicago: University of Chicago Press, 2009), 18–20, 44–46, 56–57, 62; David R. Roediger, *The Wages of Whiteness: Race and the Making of the American Working Class*, rev. edition (London: Verso, 1999), chap. 7.

21. Frederick Douglass, *Narrative of the Life of Frederick Douglass, An American Slave* (Boston: The Anti-Slavery Office, 1845), 33 (for quote), available at http://docsouth.unc.edu/neh/douglass/douglass.html.

22. Carl H. Nightingale, "The Transnational Context of Early Twentieth-Century American Urban Segregation," *Journal of Social History* 39, no. 3 (Spring 2006): 673–74; Nightingale, *Segregation: A Global History*, 269–71, 273, 284, 289, 294, 303–4, 316–17; Hale, *Making Whiteness*, chap. 4; James R. Grossman, *Land of Hope: Chicago, Black Southerners, and the Great Migration* (Chicago: University of Chicago Press, 1989); St. Clair Drake and Horace Cayton, *Black Metropolis: A Study of Negro Life in a Northern City* (New York: Harcourt, Brace, 1945); DeVore, *Defying Jim Crow*, 24–25, 29; Klarman, *Jim Crow to Civil Rights*, 12; Williamson, *Crucible of Race*, chap. 4; Kendi, *Stamped from the Beginning*, 301–02, 310–11.

23. For a similar formulation of the United States' ever-changing racial structure, albeit one that emphasizes the more recent development of mass incarceration rather than spatial reorganization, see Michelle Alexander, *The New Jim Crow: Mass Incarceration in the Age of Colorblindness*, rev. edition (New York: The New Press, 2012). Mass incarceration of African Americans, of course, has had a particularly profound impact upon cities because of the residential concentration of African Americans within them. On the significance of mass incarceration to postwar urban

history, see Heather Ann Thompson, "Why Mass Incarceration Matters: Rethinking Crisis, Decline, and Transformation in Postwar American History," *Journal of American History* 97, no. 3 (December 2010): 703–34.

24. Works that discuss segregation in the United States in relationship to colonialism include N. D. B. Connolly, *A World More Concrete: Real Estate and the Remaking of Jim Crow South Florida* (Chicago: University of Chicago Press, 2014); Nightingale, *Segregation: A Global History;* and Cell, *The Highest Stage of White Supremacy.* For Nightingale, transnationalism and imperialism provide critical context for understanding the "ghetto." See also Nightingale, "A Tale of Three *Global* Ghettos: How Arnold Hirsch Helps Us Internationalize U.S. Urban History," *Journal of Urban History* 29, no. 3 (March 2003): 257–71. These works revive the colonial analogies that the Black Panthers and other black radicals used to describe American apartheid during the late 1960s and 1970s. See, for instance, Self, *American Babylon,* 14, 291. Important challenges and alternatives to the "ghetto formation" framework include Joe William Trotter, *Black Milwaukee: The Making of an Industrial Proletariat, 1915–1945* (Urbana: University of Illinois Press, 1985); Rhonda Y. Williams, *The Politics of Public Housing: Black Women's Struggles Against Urban Inequality* (Oxford: Oxford University Press, 2004); Murch, *Living for the City;* and Drake and Cayton, *Black Metropolis.* For further discussion of the "ghetto" and "ghetto formation" as well as evidence of their persistence, see the special section on "Urban History, Arnold Hirsch, and the Second Ghetto Thesis" in *Journal of Urban History* 29, no. 3 (March 2003). See also Mitchell Duneier, *Ghetto: The Invention of a Place, the History of an Idea* (New York: Farrar, Straus, and Giroux, 2016) and the essays accompanying the 2nd edition of Trotter's *Black Milwaukee* (Urbana: University of Illinois Press, 2007).

25. A work that employs a similar framework to discuss segregation is Dane Kennedy, *Islands of White: Settler Society and Culture in Kenya and Rhodesia, 1890–1939* (Durham, NC: Duke University Press, 1987), 3–6, 187–92. See also Cell, *The Highest Stage of White Supremacy.* My thinking about power relations within colonial contexts has also been shaped by scholars working under the wide banners of Atlantic and African diasporic history. Particularly influential works include Daniel H. Usner Jr., *Indians, Settlers, & Slaves in a Frontier Exchange Economy: The Lower Mississippi Valley Before 1783* (Chapel Hill: University of North Carolina Press, 1992); Jane G. Landers, *Atlantic Creoles in the Age of Revolutions* (Cambridge, MA: Harvard University Press, 2010); Laurent Dubois, *A Colony of Citizens: Revolution & Slave Emancipation in the French Caribbean, 1787–1804* (Chapel Hill: University of North Carolina Press, 2004); Rebecca J. Scott, *Degrees of Freedom: Louisiana and Cuba After Slavery* (Cambridge, MA: Belknap Press of Harvard University Press, 2005); John K. Thornton, *Africa and Africans in the Making of the Atlantic World, 1400–1800,* 2nd edition (New York: Cambridge University Press, 1998); Robin D. G. Kelley, "'But a Local Phase of a World Problem': Black History's Global Vision, 1883–1950," *Journal of American History* 86, no. 3 (December 1999): 1045–77.

26. Case studies of urban school systems have traditionally paid little attention to political economy, housing policy, and processes of urban transformation. This is largely true of the seminal study of public education in New Orleans, Donald E. DeVore and Joseph Logsdon's *Crescent City Schools* as it is of Jeffrey Mirel's landmark *The Rise and Fall of an Urban School System, Detroit: 1907–1981,* 2nd edition (Ann Arbor: University of Michigan Press, 1999). Key works on the political economy of urban education include Jean Anyon, *Ghetto Schooling: A Political Economy of Urban Educational Reform* (New York: Teachers College Press, 1997); Harvey Kantor

and Barbara Brenzel, "Urban Education and the 'Truly Disadvantaged': The Historical Roots of the Contemporary Crisis, 1945-1990," in *The 'Underclass' Debate: Views from History*, ed. Michael B. Katz (Princeton, NJ: Princeton University Press, 1993); and John L. Rury and Jeffrey E. Mirel, "The Political Economy of Urban Education," *Review of Research in Education* 22 (1997): 49–110. On the longstanding disconnect between the history of education and urban history, see Jack Dougherty, "Bridging the Gap Between Urban, Suburban, and Educational History," in *Rethinking the History of American Education*, ed. Wiliam J. Reese and John L. Rury (New York: Palgrave Macmillan, 2008). Dougherty's essay was particularly influential in the formulation of this study.

27. For recent challenges to the prevailing assumption that housing patterns shaped schooling in both the North and South, see Ansley T. Erickson, *Making the Unequal Metropolis: School Desegregation and Its Limits* (Chicago: University of Chicago Press, 2016); Andrew Highsmith, *Demolition Means Progress: Flint, Michigan, and the Fate of the American Metropolis* (Chicago: University of Chicago Press, 2015); and the special section on "Schools and Housing in Metropolitan History" in the *Journal of Urban History* 38, no. 2 (March 2012). See also Karen A. Benjamin, "Progressivism Meets Jim Crow: Segregation, School Reform, and Urban Development in the Interwar South" (PhD diss., University of Wisconsin–Madison, 2007); Ansley T. Erickson, "The Rhetoric of Choice: Segregation, Desegregation, and Charter Schools," *Dissent* (Fall 2010): 41–46; Kevin Fox Gotham, "Missed Opportunities, Enduring Legacies: School Segregation and Desegregation in Kansas City, Missouri," *American Studies* 43, no. 2 (Summer 2002): 5–41; Gotham, *Race, Real Estate, and Uneven Development: The Kansas City Experience, 1900-2000* (Albany: State University of New York Press, 2002), chap. 5; Seligman, *Block by Block*, chap. 5; Dougherty, "Bridging the Gap Between Urban, Suburban, and Educational History"; Michael Clapper, "School Design, Site Selection, and the Political Geography of Race in Postwar Philadelphia," *Journal of Planning History* 5, no. 3 (August 2006): 241–63. Gregory Jacobs touches on this theme briefly in *Getting Around Brown: Desegregation, Development, and the Columbus Public Schools* (Columbus: Ohio State University Press, 1998), which focuses largely on busing during the 1970s. A recent example of a work that integrates the history of education and the history of metropolitan transformation is Emily E. Straus, *Death of a Suburban Dream: Race and Schools in Compton, California* (Philadelphia: University of Pennsylvania Press, 2014).

28. For an overview of these developments, see John L. Rury, *Education and Social Change: Contours in the History of American Schooling*, 4th edition (New York: Routledge, 2013), chap. 2–3. A work that examines race and antebellum education in relation to urban change is Moss, *Schooling Citizens*.

29. Two exceptions to this are Karen A. Benjamin, "Suburbanizing Jim Crow: The Impact of School Policy on Residential Segregation in Raleigh," *Journal of Urban History* 38, no. 2 (March 2012): 225–46, and Highsmith, *Demolition Means Progress*, which examines Flint, Michigan, before and after World War II.

30. Davison M. Douglas, *Jim Crow Moves North: The Battle Over Northern School Segregation, 1865-1954* (New York: Cambridge University Press, 2005), 131–49 (the details on Chicago are on p. 147).

31. Arnold R. Hirsch, "With or Without Jim Crow: Black Residential Segregation in the United States," in *Urban Policy in Twentieth-Century America*, ed. Arnold R. Hirsch and Raymond A. Mohl (New Brunswick, NJ: Rutgers University Press, 1993),75–77.

32. Key works on *Brown* include, but are certainly not limited to, Tushnet, *NAACP's Legal Strategy;* Kluger, *Simple Justice;* Klarman, *Jim Crow to Civil Rights;* Patterson, *Brown v. Board of Education;* "Round Table: *Brown v. Board of Education,* Fifty Years After," *Journal of American History* 91, no. 1 (June 2004); *History of Education Quarterly* 44, no. 1: A Special Issue on the Fiftieth Anniversary of the *Brown v. Board of Education* Decision (Spring 2004). As these scholars acknowledge, African Americans never unanimously supported the NAACP's decision to place segregated education at the center of its struggle against racial inequality. W. E. B. Du Bois was perhaps the most famous critic of this strategy. See, for instance, "Does the Negro Need Separate Schools?" *Journal of Negro Education* 4, no. 3 (July 1935): 328–35. For more recent critiques of the campaign against segregated education, see especially Derrick A. Bell, *Silent Covenants: Brown v. Board of Education and the Unfulfilled Hopes for Racial Reform* (New York: Oxford University Press, 2004) and Risa L. Goluboff, *The Lost Promise of Civil Rights* (Cambridge, MA: Harvard University Press, 2007).

33. While Risa Goluboff casts the NAACP's prioritizing of education cases over labor and employment ones as a decision to attack the social and political rather than economic aspects and Jim Crow, my work suggests schools provided a means for attacking economic inequality as well. See Goluboff, *Lost Promise of Civil Rights.* On the wealth gap, see Melvin L. Oliver and Thomas M. Shapiro, *Black Wealth/White Wealth: A New Perspective on Racial Inequality,* 2nd edition (New York: Routledge, 2006); James Surowiecki, "The Widening Racial Wealth Divide," *The New Yorker,* 10 October 2016, http://www.newyorker.com/magazine/2016/10/10/the-widening -racial-wealth-divide.

34. On *Brown's* failure to address the structural nature of racial inequality, see Lani Guinier, "From Racial Liberalism to Racial Literacy: *Brown v. Board of Education* and the Interest–Divergence Dilemma," *Journal of American History* 91 (June 2004): 92–118. Guinier's description of Jim Crow as "the visible manifestation of a larger, constantly mutating racialized hierarchy" also supports the picture developed here. See "Racial Liberalism to Racial Literacy," 99.

35. Goluboff, *Lost Promise of Civil Rights,* chap. 7–9.

36. Klarman, *Jim Crow to Civil Rights,* 348. The relationship between school and housing segregation receives little to no attention in the major studies of *Brown* cited in note 32 above and is absent from many school desegregation case studies. Representative case studies include David S. Cecelski, *Along Freedom Road: Hyde County, North Carolina, and the Fate of Black Schools in the South* (Chapel Hill: University of North Carolina Press, 1994); Baker, *Second Battle of New Orleans;* Karen Anderson, *Little Rock: Race and Resistance at Central High* (Princeton, NJ: Princeton University Press, 2009); Robert A. Pratt, *The Color of Their Skin: Education and Race in Richmond, Virginia, 1954–1989* (Charlottesville: University Press of Virginia, 1992). For examinations of later desegregation cases that tackled the connections between segregated schools and housing, see Davison M. Douglas, *Reading, Writing, & Race: The Desegregation of the Charlotte Schools* (Chapel Hill: University of North Carolina Press, 1995); Lassiter, *Silent Majority;* and Erickson, *Making the Unequal Metropolis.*

37. I will leave it to future legal scholars and historians to travel the potentially treacherous counterfactual terrain necessary to assess 1) the extent to which the NAACP could have crafted alternate arguments in *Brown* (e.g., based on the due process clause of the Fourteenth and/or Fifth Amendments) that more effectively targeted the material consequences of school segregation, 2) the potential impact those alternate approaches might have had, and 3) the extent to which

opportunities existed for the NAACP to target the connections between school and housing seg-regation sooner. The Supreme Court did decide *Brown*'s Washington, DC-based companion case, *Bolling v. Sharpe* 347 U.S. 497, based upon the due process clause of the Fifth Amendment since the Fourteenth Amendment's prohibition against *states* denying equal protection did not apply to the nation's capital. But standing in the shadow of *Brown*, the *Bolling* decision applied the due process clause through the lens of equal protection. On *Bolling*, see Goluboff, *Lost Promise of Civil Rights*, 241.

38. See, for instance, Jackson, *Crabgrass Frontier*, 12–13, 135–37.

39. On the slippery nature of the term *Creole*, see Rien Fertel, *Imagining the Creole City: The Rise of Literary Culture in Nineteenth-Century New Orleans* (Baton Rouge: Louisiana State University Press, 2014), 9–10 and 127, n. 32. While historians of Louisiana frequently define *Creole* more expansively—as Louisiana natives of either European or European and African descent—they often use the term both more narrowly and more broadly than their own definitions. A prime example of this is Caryn Cossé Bell's *Revolution, Romanticism, and the Afro-Creole Protest Tradition in Louisiana, 1718–1868*. In that seminal work on Afro-Creoles, Cossé Bell defines that group as "native-born Louisianians of African and Latin European descent" but focuses almost exclusively on francophone people of color and rarely distinguishes between those actually born in Louisiana of "Latin European" descent and those who emigrated to Louisiana from elsewhere in the francophone Atlantic world. My definition is an attempt to recognize, as Cossé Bell does in practice if not in her definition of the word, that Afro-Creoles' shared connection to the franco-phone Atlantic world was generally of greater importance than their actual place of birth. See Cossé Bell, *Afro-Creole Protest Tradition*, p. 2, n. 2.

40. On this point, see Dougherty, "Bridging the Gap."

41. This dynamic was similar to early twentieth-century suburbanization in other southern cities such as Raleigh, where annexation incorporated post–World War I suburbs into the city. See Benjamin, "Suburbanizing Jim Crow." During the nineteenth century, New Orleans annexed several neighboring cities that had been part of Jefferson Parish. For a succinct history of the city's expansion, see Richard Campanella, "The Turbulent History Behind the Seven New Orleans Municipal Districts," *Times-Picayune/NOLA.com*, October 9, 2013, http://www.nola.com/home garden/index.ssf/2013/10/new_orleans_seven_municipal_di.html.

42. See, for instance, Emily Clark, *The Strange History of the American Quadroon: Free Women of Color in the Revolutionary Atlantic World* (Chapel Hill: University of North Carolina Press, 2013); David P. Geggus, ed., *The Impact of the Haitian Revolution in the Atlantic World* (Columbia: University of South Carolina Press, 2001); Clare A. Lyons, *Sex Among the Rabble: An Intimate History of Gender & Power in the Age of Revolution, Philadelphia, 1730–1830* (Chapel Hill: University of North Carolina Press, 2006); Spear, *Race, Sex, and Social Order*; Ashli White, *Encountering Revolution: Haiti and the Making of the Early Republic* (Baltimore: Johns Hopkins University Press, 2010).

43. Scott P. Marler effectively captures antebellum New Orleans's position as an essential part of, and yet apart from, the rest of the United States when he notes that the "processes of industrialization [elsewhere in the Atlantic world] were fueled largely by the millions of bales of slave-produced cotton shepherded through New Orleans. There, however, the relatively effortless profits from this trade lulled businessmen into complacent habits that suppressed the invest-ment patterns and class cohesion that undergirded economic modernization in free labor urban

environments in Europe and the North." See Marler, *The Merchants' Capital: New Orleans and the Political Economy of the Nineteenth-Century South* (Cambridge: Cambridge University Press, 2013), 27.

44. Mary Niall Mitchell, *Raising Freedom's Child: Black Children and Visions of the Future After Slavery* (New York: New York University Press, 2008), 9. On the nineteenth-century creation of the myth of New Orleans exceptionalism, see Fertel, *Imagining the Creole City.*

45. On this point, see Bennett, *Religion and the Rise of Jim Crow,* 7.

46. While Howard Rabinowitz concludes that residential segregation was the norm in the urban South by 1890, Arnold Hirsch notes that in the early twentieth-century North and South the black population "lived in scattered clusters" that were occasionally racially mixed and almost always intersected with predominantly white areas. Hirsch rightly adds that "the vast urban expanses of almost exclusively black settlement that propelled themselves into the national consciousness during the 1960s were twentieth-century" developments, but he overstates the extent to which they were strictly "northern creations." See Hirsch, "With or Without Jim Crow," 69; Rabinowitz, *Race Relations in the Urban South,* chap. 5. Hirsch's and Rabinowitz's contrasting characterizations of southern residential segregation underscore the importance of scale when assessing levels of urban segregation. While a city may appear segregated at the ward level, the picture may be very different when one looks at where people lived within a given ward. For more on late nineteenth- and early twentieth-century black residential patterns, see David Goldfield, *Cotton Fields and Skyscrapers: Southern City and Region* (Baltimore: Johns Hopkins University Press, 1992), 166–67; Gotham, *Race, Real Estate, and Uneven Development: The Kansas City Experience, 1900–2000* (Albany: State University of New York Press, 2002), chap. 1; Karl E. Taeuber and Alma F. Taeuber, *Negroes in Cities: Residential Segregation and Neighborhood Change* (Chicago: Aldine Publishing, 1965), 3; Gilbert Osofsky, "The Enduring Ghetto," *Journal of American History* 55, no. 2 (September 1968): 243–55; August Meier and Elliott Rudwick, *From Plantation to Ghetto,* 3rd edition (New York: Hill and Wang, 1976), 234–35; St. Clair Drake and Horace Cayton, *Black Metropolis: A Study of Negro Life in a Northern City* (New York: Harcourt, Brace, 1945).

47. Douglas S. Massey and Nancy A. Denton, *American Apartheid: Segregation and the Making of the Underclass* (Cambridge, MA: Harvard University Press, 1993), 23–24.

48. Citing the tendency of blacks in older southern cities to live in back alleys or smaller streets behind or adjacent to exclusively white avenues, Massey and Denton claim that black "ghettos" took shape more slowly in the South than in the North. While black and white residents may have been segregated by block, they write, those blocks were often within the same integrated neighborhood on the eve of World War II. Yet the New Orleans neighborhood now known as Central City was a clearly distinguished black zone by 1940. Blacks comprised more than 85 percent of the population in each of the area's eight census tracts and 90 percent of its overall population. The 36,000 black residents who lived in Central City in 1940 made up about one-quarter of New Orleans's black population. See Bureau of the Census, *16th Census of the United States, 1940, Population and Housing: Statistics for Census Tracts, New Orleans, La.,* (Washington: Government Printing Office, 1941); Massey and Denton, *American Apartheid,* 17–42 (41–42 for their claims about ghetto formation in the South).

49. Lassiter, *Silent Majority,* chap. 12.

50. See, for instance, "Negro Problems in Africa," *Times-Picayune,* 9 March 1920, 8.

51. See James Grossman, *Land of Hope: Chicago, Black Southerners, and the Great Migration* (Chicago: University of Chicago Press, 1989); Nightingale, *Segregation: A Global History*, 315–17.

52. "Northern Race Riots," *New Orleans Item*, 31 July 1919, 8.

CHAPTER ONE

1. J. D. B. De Bow, "The Moral Advance of New Orleans," *De Bow's Review* 2 (November 1846): 349.

2. Ibid. On De Bow, see John F. Kvach, "J. D. B. De Bow's South Carolina: The Antebellum Origins of the New South Creed," *The South Carolina Historical Magazine* 113, no. 1 (January 2012): 4–23; Ottis Clark Skipper, "J. D. B. De Bow, the Man," *Journal of Southern History* 10, no. 4 (November 1944): 404–23; "De Bow, James Dunwoody Brownson," *Louisiana Dictionary of Biography*, http://www.lahistory.org/site21.php. On the context in which De Bow was making his comment, see Scott P. Marler, *The Merchants' Capital: New Orleans and the Political Economy of the Nineteenth-Century South* (Cambridge: Cambridge University Press, 2013), 22–27.

3. Quoted in Donald E. DeVore and Joseph Logsdon, *Crescent City Schools: Public Education in New Orleans, 1841–1991* (Lafayette: University of Southwestern Louisiana Press, 1991), 18.

4. Kvach, "J. D. B. De Bow's South Carolina"; Carl F. Kaestle, *Pillars of the Republic: Common Schools and American Society, 1780–1860* (New York: Hill and Wang, 1983), ix–xii, 102; Michael B. Katz, *The Irony of School Reform: Educational Innovation in Mid-Nineteenth Century Massachusetts* (Boston: Beacon Press, 1968); William J. Reese, *America's Public Schools: From the Common School to "No Child Left Behind"* (Baltimore: Johns Hopkins University Press, 2005), chap. 1; David Nasaw, *Schooled to Order: A Social History of Public Schooling in the United States* (Oxford: Oxford University Press, 1979).

5. For a transcription of the 1841 legislation authorizing the creation of a public school system in New Orleans for the education of "all resident white children," see Board of Directors of Public Schools of the Second Municipality of New Orleans, Minutes, 13 May 1847, Orleans Parish School Board Collection (Mss 147), Louisiana and Special Collections Department, Earl K. Long Library, University of New Orleans (cited hereinafter as OPSB-147). On black exclusion from early public school systems, see Hilary J. Moss, *Schooling Citizens: The Struggle for African American Education in Antebellum America* (Chicago: University of Chicago Press, 2009); Kaestle, *Pillars of the Republic*, ix–xii, 171–77; Robert L. McCaul, *The Black Struggle for Public Schooling in Nineteenth-Century Illinois* (Carbondale and Edwardsville: Southern Illinois University Press, 1987), 4–5, 9–10, 29, 45, 54; John L. Rury, "The New York African Free School, 1827–1836: Conflict Over Community Control of Black Education," *Phylon* 44, no. 3 (3rd Qtr. 1983): 187–97; Gary Nash, *Forging Freedom: The Formation of Philadelphia's Black Community, 1720–1840* (Cambridge, MA: Harvard University Press, 1988), 208–9, 267–71; and Leon Litwack, *North of Slavery: The Negro in the Free States, 1790–1860* (Chicago: University of Chicago Press, 1961), chap. 4.

6. *History of the Catholic Indigent Orphan Institute, Dauphine and Touro Streets, Destroyed by the Hurricane, September 1915, Rebuilt in 1916, published by the Board of Directors*, 1916, Archives of the Archdiocese of New Orleans (cited hereinafter as AANO); Elizabeth Neidenbach, "Marie Bernard Couvent, the Couvent School, and African American Education in New Orleans" (Honors thesis, Tulane University, 2003), 104; Caryn Cossé Bell, *Revolution, Romanticism, and*

the Afro-Creole Protest Tradition in Louisiana, 1718–1868 (Baton Rouge: Louisiana State University Press, 1997), 123–27.

7. Elizabeth Clark Neidenbach, "The Life and Legacy of Marie Couvent: Social Networks, Property Ownership, and the Making of a Free People of Color Community in New Orleans" (PhD diss., College of William and Mary, 2015), 399–403 (Reverend Theodore Clapp quoted on 403).

8. Ibid., 295, 310, 312, 391–92, 400, 403 (testament of Marie Justine Cirnaire, Widow Bernard Couvent, November 12, 1832, quoted in Neidenbach, 312); Bureau de Santé, Séance de Mardi, 13 novembre, *L'Abeille*, 15 November 1832, p. 1, col. 2 (translation from French by the author).

9. DeVore and Logsdon, *Crescent City Schools*, 42 (for quote); Neidenbach, "Legacy of Marie Couvent," 391–93, 404. The Catholic Institution's history is also discussed in John W. Blassingame, *Black New Orleans, 1860–1880* (Chicago: University of Chicago Press, 1973), chap. 5; Cossé Bell, *Afro-Creole Protest Tradition;* Marcus Christian, "The Negro in Louisiana," 1942, chap. 20, Marcus Christian Collection, UNO; Rodolphe Lucien Desdunes, *Our People and Our History*, translated and edited by Sister Dorothea Olga McCants (Baton Rouge: Louisiana State University Press, 1973); Mary Niall Mitchell, *Raising Freedom's Child: Black Children and Visions of the Future After Slavery* (New York: New York University Press, 2008), chap. 1, p. 5, Conclusion; Alice Dunbar Nelson, "Free People of Color in Louisiana: Part II, *Journal of Negro History* 2, no. 1 (January 1917): 65; Charles Barthelemy Roussève, *The Negro in Louisiana: Aspects of His History and His Literature* (New Orleans: Xavier University Press, 1937), 43.

10. Mitchell, *Raising Freedom's Child*, 18–19; Cossé Bell, *Afro-Creole Protest Tradition*, 127; DeVore and Logsdon, *Crescent City Schools*, 42; Alma Hobbs Peterson, "The Administration of the Public Schools in New Orleans" (PhD diss., Louisiana State University, 1964), 65. The quote is from Directeurs de l'Institution Catholique des Orphelins Indigents, Séance du 26 Avril 1851, Séance Book I, AANO (unless otherwise noted, this and all other translations from this source are by the author).

11. Neidenbach, "Legacy of Marie Couvent," 25–27, 83, 86, 120–23.

12. Ibid., 125–26, 135, 160–61; Neidenbach, "'Mes dernières volontés': Testaments to the Life of Marie Couvent, a Former Slave in New Orleans," *Transatlantica* [online] 2 (2012), 3–4; Rebecca J. Scott and Jean M. Hébrard, *Freedom Papers: An Atlantic Odyssey in the Age of Emancipation* (Cambridge, MA: Harvard University Press, 2012), 27–30; Laurent Dubois, *Avengers of the New World: The Story of the Haitian Revolution* (Cambridge, MA: The Belknap Press of Harvard University Press, 2004), 157–58; Emily Clark, *The Strange History of the American Quadroon: Free Women of Color in the Revolutionary Atlantic World* (Chapel Hill: University of North Carolina Press, 2013), 39, 210 n. 6. On the broader impact of the Haitian Revolution on the United States, see Ashli White, *Encountering Revolution: Haiti and the Making of the Early Republic* (Baltimore: Johns Hopkins University Press, 2010).

13. Scott and Hébrard, *Freedom Papers,* 71; Neidenbach, "Legacy of Marie Couvent," 165, 172–76, 314–16, 370; Neidenbach, "'Mes dernières volontés,'" 3–5; Ashli White, *Encountering Revolution: Haiti and the Making of the Early Republic* (Baltimore: Johns Hopkins University Press, 2010), 203.

14. Neidenbach, "Legacy of Marie Couvent," 137, 145–46, 370; Neidenbach, "'Mes dernières volontés,'" 3–5; Greater New Orleans Community Data Center, "Marigny Neighborhood," http://www.datacenterresearch.org/pre-katrina/orleans/7/21/index.html; Richard Campanella, *Bienville's*

Dilemma: A Historical Geography of New Orleans (Lafayette: University of Louisiana at Lafayette Press, 2008), 27, 143; Amy R. Sumpter, "Segregation of the Free People of Color and the Construction of Race in Antebellum New Orleans," *Southeastern Geographer* 48, no. 1 (May 2008), 23; Rien Fertel, *Imagining the Creole City: The Rise of Literary Culture in Nineteenth-Century New Orleans* (Baton Rouge: Louisiana State University Press, 2014), 1; Juliette Lee Landphair, "'For the Good of the Community': Reform Activism and Public Schools in New Orleans, 1920–1960" (PhD diss., University of Virginia, 1999), 28–31; Lawrence N. Powell, *The Accidental City: Improvising New Orleans* (Cambridge, MA: Harvard University Press, 2012), 269–70.

15. School and property locations are based upon Elizabeth C. Neidenbach, "The Life and Legacy of Marie Couvent: Social Networks, Property Ownership, and the Making of a Free People of Color Community in New Orleans" (PhD diss., College of William and Mary, 2015), 497; E. Robinson and R. H. Pidgeon, *Robinson's Atlas of the City of New Orleans, Louisiana* (New York: E. Robinson, 1883), plate 18, available at http://www.orleanscivilclerk.com/robinson/index.htm.

16. Joseph G. Tregle Jr., "Creoles and Americans," in *Creole New Orleans: Race and Americanization*, ed. Arnold R. Hirsch and Joseph Logsdon (Baton Rouge: Louisiana State University Press, 1992), 143 (for quote); Joseph Logsdon and Caryn Cossé Bell, "The Americanization of Black New Orleans, 1850–1900," in *Creole New Orleans*, 206; Neidenbach, "Legacy of Marie Couvent," 312; Rashauna Johnson, *Slavery's Metropolis: Unfree Labor in New Orleans during the Age of Revolutions* (New York: Cambridge University Press, 2016), 93.

17. Logsdon and Cossé Bell, "Americanization of Black New Orleans," 205–6; Powell, *Accidental City*, 337. Many of the émigrés whom New Orleans officials listed as slaves were likely free people who were pressed back into slavery either upon their initial departure from Saint-Domingue or upon their arrival in New Orleans. See Scott and Hébrard, *Freedom Papers*, 67–71.

18. Walter Johnson, *Soul by Soul: Life Inside the Antebellum Slave Market* (Cambridge, MA: Harvard University Press, 2001); Steven Deyle, *Carry Me Back: The Domestic Slave Trade in American Life* (Oxford: Oxford University Press, 2005), 4–11; Sven Beckert, "History of American Capitalism," in *American History Now*, ed. Eric Foner and Lisa McGirr (Philadelphia: Temple University Press, 2011); Marler, *Merchants' Capital*, 4; Steven Deyle, "Review of *River of Dark Dreams: Slavery and Empire in the Cotton Kingdom*," *William and Mary Quarterly* 71, no. 4 (October 2014): 632–36; Eric Foner, "A Brutal Process," *New York Times Sunday Book Review*, 3 October 2014; Campbell Gibson, *Population of the 100 Largest Cities and Other Urban Places in the United States: 1790 to 1990*, Population Division Working Paper No. 27 (Washington, DC: U.S. Bureau of the Census, June 1998), Table 5, http://www.census.gov/population/www/documentation/twps0027/twps0027.html. My understanding of the domestic slave trade also benefited greatly from the Historic New Orleans Collection's exhibit, "Purchased Lives: New Orleans and the Domestic Slave Trade, 1808–1865," March 17–July 18, 2015, and the accompanying symposium it hosted on March 21, 2015.

19. Powell, *Accidental City*, 350; Tregle, "Creoles and Americans," 154–55.

20. Tregle, "Creoles and Americans," 155; Powell, *Accidental City*, 348–49; Neidenbach, "Legacy of Marie Couvent," 370–74.

21. Neidenbach, "Legacy of Marie Couvent," 315, 370–74.

22. Ibid., 314–15, 360–63 (quote on 363); Tregle, "Creoles and Americans," 143.

23. Powell, *Accidental City*, 73–77, 348–49 (for quote); Ira Berlin, *Many Thousands Gone: The First Two Centuries of Slavery in North America* (Cambridge, MA: Harvard University Press,

1998); Neidenbach, "Legacy of Marie Couvent," 369–70; 376; Samuel Wilson Jr., *New Orleans Architecture*, Vol. 4: *The Creole Faubourgs* (Gretna, LA: Pelican Publishing, 1996), 17; Nash, *Forging Freedom*, 167–71.

24. Neidenbach, "Legacy of Marie Couvent," 365–67, 374–75, 499; Claude Hémécourt, "Plan de la Ville et des faubourgs incorporés de la Nouvelle Orleans," c. 1875 after 1812 Tanesse plan, Historic New Orleans Collection, 1966.33.30, http://cdm16313.contentdm.oclc.org/cdm/ref/collection /p15140c01128/id/116. Bernard Marigny later developed the portion of his property on the northern, or lakeside, of Bons Enfans (St. Claude) and dubbed it the Nouveau Faubourg Marigny. The New Marigny name has been recently revived amidst that area's rapid gentrification. See Neidenbach, 373; Richard A. Webster, "'New Marigny' newcomers and poor squatters give St. Roch a split personality," NOLA.com/*Times-Picayune*, posted 9 June 2015, updated 16 June 2015, http://www .nola.com/neighborhoods/2015/06/st_roch_neighborhoods_2.html.

25. Neidenbach, "Legacy of Marie Couvent," 358, 375–76; Moss, *Schooling Citizens*, 60; Joe William Trotter Jr., "Shifting Perspectives on Segregation in the Emerging Postindustrial Age," paper presented at The Future of the African American Past Conference, May 19–21, 2016, Washington, DC, https://futureafampast.si.edu/sites/default/files/03_Trotter%20Joe.pdf.

26. Cossé Bell, *Afro-Creole Protest Tradition*, chap. 1 (quote on p. 19); Powell, *Accidental City*, chap. 10. See also Jennifer M. Spear, *Race, Sex, and Social Order in Early New Orleans* (Baltimore: Johns Hopkins University Press, 2010), chap. 4–5; Kimberly Hanger, *Bounded Lives, Bounded Places: Black Society in Colonial New Orleans, 1769–1803* (Durham, NC: Duke University Press, 1997).

27. Cossé Bell, *Afro-Creole Protest Tradition*, 29–37 (quote on p. 30); Carl Nightingale, *Segregation: A Global History of Divided Cities* (Chicago: University of Chicago Press, 2012), 83–85. On the Haitian Revolution's impact on efforts to codify race, see Clark, *History of the American Quadroon*, 1–10.

28. Clark, *History of the American Quadroon*, 31–40.

29. Neidenbach, "'Mes Dernières Volontés,'" 5, 7; Neidenbach, "Legacy of Marie Couvent," 222 (for quote; italics added), 263–76. On the complicated nature of free black slave ownership, see Scott and Hébrard, *Freedom Papers*, 76. Scott and Hébrard also provide a masterful account of the ways in which people of African descent used legal documentation to safeguard their freedom.

30. Neidenbach, "Legacy of Marie Couvent," 271, 357.

31. Emily Clark, *Masterless Mistresses: The New Orleans Ursulines and the Development of a New World Society, 1727–1834* (Chapel Hill: University of North Carolina Press, 2007).

32. Clark, *Masterless Mistresses*, 7, 35–41, chap. 1, p. 56 (for quote), "Appendix 1, Convent Population, 1727–1803," 271–73; Walter C. Stern, "Ursuline Nuns Establish School," *An Interactive Timeline of New Orleans Public Education, 1718–Present* (New Orleans: Cowen Institute, 2015), http://www.spen02015.com/timeline.html.

33. Clark, *Masterless Mistresses*, 57, chap. 3, p. 162 (for quote), 255; Albert J. Raboteau, *Slave Religion: The 'Invisible Institution' in the Antebellum South* (Oxford: Oxford University Press, 1978), 112–20.

34. Neidenbach, "Legacy of Marie Couvent," 357–58, 396.

35. On this point, see ibid., 390. Quote is from Nash, *Forging Freedom*, 259.

36. Neidenbach, "Legacy of Marie Couvent," 359–60, 381–82.

37. Ibid., 321–22, 380–89.

38. Heather Andrea Williams, *Self-Taught: African American Education in Slavery and Freedom* (Chapel Hill: University of North Carolina Press, 2007), 14–16; Moss, *Schooling Citizens*, 46, 56–57, 61–62; David R. Roediger, *The Wages of Whiteness: Race and the Making of the American Working Class*, rev. edition (London: Verso, 1999), chap. 7; David Walker, *Walker's Appeal, in Four Articles, Together with a Preamble, to the Coloured Citizens of the World, but in Particular, and Very Expressly, to Those of the United States of America*, DocSouth Books edition (Chapel Hill: University of North Carolina Press, 2011).

39. Roussève, *The Negro in Louisiana*, 47–48; Christian, "The Negro in Louisiana," chap. 20, pp. 9–12; Cossé Bell, *Afro-Creole Protest Tradition*, 91–94, 123; Williams, *Self-Taught*, Appendix: African Americans, Literacy, and the Law in the Antebellum South, 204–5 (for quote); Lawrence N. Powell, "Introduction: A Novelist Turns Historian," in *The New Orleans of George Washington Cable: The 1887 Census Office Report*, ed. Lawrence N. Powell (Baton Rouge: Louisiana University Press, 2008), 21; Moss, *Schooling Citizens*, 66, 96. As Cossé Bell notes, free blacks either passing as white or telling census enumerators that they were white, likely accounted for a portion of the decrease in the free black population during the 1840s. Baltimore and New Orleans each had the nation's largest free black population at various points during the first half of the nineteenth century. The two cities' free black populations were nearly identical in 1810 and 1830, while New Orleans had the larger population in 1840 and Baltimore in 1820 and 1850. For specific population figures, see "Table 19. Louisiana—Race and Hispanic Origin for Selected Large Cities and Other Places: Earliest Census to 1990" and "Table 21. Maryland—Race and Hispanic Origin for Selected Large Cities and Other Places: Earliest Census to 1990," in Gibson and Jung, *Historical Census Statistics On Population Totals By Race, 1790 to 1990, and By Hispanic Origin, 1970 to 1990, For Large Cities And Other Urban Places In The United States*, http://www.census.gov/population/www/documentation/twps0076/twps0076.html.

40. David S. Cecelski, *The Waterman's Song: Slavery and Freedom in Maritime North Carolina* (Chapel Hill: University of North Carolina Press, 2001), 30, 53; Williams, *Self-Taught*, chap. 1, pp. 203–9 (204 for first quote); Peter Wallenstein, "Antiliteracy Laws," in Junios P. Rodriguez, *Slavery in the United States: A Social, Political, and Historical Encyclopedia*, vol. 1 (Santa Barbara: ABC-CLIO, 2007), 172; Frederick Douglass, *Narrative of the Life of Frederick Douglass, An American Slave* (Boston: The Anti-Slavery Office, 1845), 33 (second quote; emphasis added), available at http://docsouth.unc.edu/neh/douglass/douglass.html; Leonard L. Richards, *The Slave Power: The Free North and Southern Domination, 1780–1860* (Baton Rouge: Louisiana State University Press, 2000), 127–33.

41. Moss, *Schooling Citizens*, 18–20, 44–45 (quote on 45); James Brewer Stewart, "The New Haven Negro College and the Meanings of Race in New England, 1776–1870," *New England Quarterly* 76, no. 3 (September 2003): 323–55; Moss, "New Haven's Ill-Fated Attempt to Establish the First Black College," *Journal of Blacks in Higher Education*, no. 58 (Winter 2007/2008): 78–79; Williams, *Self-Taught*, 17, 219 n. 34; *Special Report of the Commissioner of Education on the Condition and Improvement of Public Schools in the District of Columbia* (Washington, DC: Government Printing Office, 1871), 328–34.

42. Litwack, *North of Slavery*, 74–93; McCaul, *Black Struggle for Public Schooling*; Moss, *Schooling Citizens*, 9 (for quote), 10–12, 25–26. On the antebellum construction of "white" as a privileged racial category, see Roediger, *Wages of Whiteness*. See also Eric Arnesen, "Whiteness and the Historians' Imagination," *International Labor and Working-Class History*, no. 60 (Fall

2001): 3-32; Eric Foner, "Response to Eric Arnesen," *International Labor and Working-Class History,* no. 60 (Fall 2001): 57-60.

43. Cossé Bell, *Afro-Creole Protest Tradition,* 123–25; Neidenbach, "Legacy of Marie Couvent," 388–89; *Prospectus de l'Institution Catholique des Orphelins Indigent* (New Orleans: Maitre Desarzant, 1847), Louisiana Research Collection, Tulane University (cited hereinafter as LaRC); Desdunes, *Our People and Our History,* 68.

44. Neidenbach, "Legacy of Marie Couvent," 390 (for quote). Neidenbach revises an interpretation initially advanced by Rodolphe Lucien Desdunes and embraced by numerous other scholars. See Desdunes, *Our People and Our History.* Like Neidenbach, Marcus Christian blames white opposition to black schooling for the school's delayed opening, though his assessment of Fletcher is less complimentary than Neidenbach's. See Christian, "The Negro in Louisiana," chap. 20, pp. 14–15.

45. John L. Rury, *Education and Social Change: Contours in the History of American Schooling,* 4th edition (New York: Routledge, 2013), 76–82. See also Joseph W. Newman, "Antebellum School Reform in the Port Cities of the Deep South" and David L. Angus, "The Origins of Urban Schools in Comparative Perspective," both in *Southern Cities, Southern Schools: Public Education in the Urban South,* ed. David N. Plank and Rick Ginsberg (Westport, CT: Greenwood Press, 1990); Carl F. Kaestle, *Pillars of the Republic;* Reese, *America's Public Schools;* Litwack, *North of Slavery,* chap. 4. On the 1834 attack against the Ursuline convent, see Clark, *Masterless Mistresses,* 258–59.

46. New Orleans's divided governance structure, which enabled Americans to dominate the uptown Second Municipality, meant that common school reformers in the Crescent City may have been less concerned than those elsewhere about the role schools could play in unifying ethnically and religiously diverse populations. But reformers throughout the nineteenth-century urban United States faced the challenge of producing the stability amid extensive mobility. As Thomas Sugrue notes, "The population of industrial America was remarkably unstable, for many cities were mere way stations; the poor and jobless moved rapidly from place to place in search of employment. From year to year in Boston between 1830 and 1860, as much as 20 percent of the population turned over; data from throughout the United States show that on average about 40 percent of the urban population remained in cities between the decennial censuses from the 1830s through the early twentieth century." Sugrue makes this point in "The Structure of Urban Poverty: The Reorganization of Space and Work in Three Periods in American History," in *The "Underclass" Debate: Views from History,* ed. Michael Katz (Princeton, NJ: Princeton University Press, 1993), 91. On the transience of people—and capital—in antebellum New Orleans, see Marler, *Merchants' Capital,* 22–26, 65–67.

47. Robert C. Reinders, "New England Influences on the Formation of Public Schools in New Orleans," *Journal of Southern History* 30, no. 2 (May 1964): 181–95.

48. "Table 19. Louisiana—Race and Hispanic Origin for Selected Large Cities and Other Places: Earliest Census to 1990," in Gibson and Jung, *Historical Census Statistics On Population Totals By Race, 1790 to 1990, and By Hispanic Origin, 1970 to 1990, For Large Cities And Other Urban Places In The United States,* http://www.census.gov/population/www/documentation/twps0076/twps0076.html; Powell, "A Novelist Turns Historian," 9–11; Clark, *Masterless Mistresses,* 242–43; Richard Campanella, *Geographies of New Orleans: Urban Fabrics Before the Storm* (Lafayette: Center for Louisiana Studies, 2006), 372; Social Explorer Dataset (SE), Cen-

sus 1850, Digitally transcribed by Inter-university Consortium for Political and Social Research. Edited, verified by Michael Haines. Compiled, edited, and verified by Social Explorer.

49. DeVore and Logsdon, *Crescent City Schools,* 11.

50. Walter C. Stern, "Public School System Begins," *An Interactive Timeline of New Orleans Public Education,* http://spen02015.com/timeline.html; Reinders, "New England Influences on the Formation of Public Schools in New Orleans," 183 (quote); Marler, *Merchants' Capital,* 27, 42–43, 56.

51. DeVore and Logsdon, *Crescent City Schools,* 5, 11–17 (quote on 13); Moss, *Schooling Citizens,* 156–58.

52. This 1841 quote from the New Orleans school directors' first annual report appears in *Annual Report of the Directors of the Public Schools of the First District of New Orleans for the Year Ending December 31, 1860,* which is itself reprinted in *Annual Report of the Public Schools of New Orleans of the Parish of Orleans, 1919–1920,* Annual Reports, box 9, OPSB-147; Minutes, Board of Directors of Public Schools of the Second Municipality of New Orleans, 23 October 1843, OPSB-147 (second quote); Second Annual Report of the Board of Directors of Public Schools of the Second Municipality of New Orleans, 1844, quoted in "Schools in New Orleans (Second Municipality), *The Common School Journal,* 1 July 1844, p. 216 (third quote); DeVore and Logsdon, *Crescent City Schools,* 19.

53. David L. Angus, "The Origins of Urban Schools in Comparative Perspective," in *Southern Cities, Southern Schools: Public Education in the Urban South,* 70–71 (quote on 70).

54. Christian, "The Negro in Louisiana," chap. 20, p. 11 (for quote); DeVore and Logsdon, *Crescent City Schools,* 364, n. 20; Walter C. Stern, "First Public Schools Open," *An Interactive Timeline of Public Education in New Orleans, 1718–Present,* http://www.spen02015.com/timeline.html.

55. Moss, *Schooling Citizens,* 68–69, chap. 3–4; Social Explorer Dataset (SE), Census 1850, digitally transcribed by Inter-university Consortium for Political and Social Research. Edited, verified by Michael Haines. Compiled, edited, and verified by Social Explorer. The data reported here are for Baltimore County, which encompassed Baltimore City prior to the city's separation from the county in 1851. Eighty percent of Baltimore Country's population lived within the City of Baltimore in 1850. For the history of the county-city jurisdictional relationship in Baltimore, see Maryland State Archives, "Baltimore City, Maryland," *Maryland Manual On-Line: A Guide to Maryland and its Government,* http://msa.maryland.gov/msa/mdmanual/3610c/bcity/html/bcity.html. In an analysis of heads of households in Baltimore's Ward 17, Moss places the 1850 literacy rate for African Americans at 27 percent. Her analysis of school attendance in Ward 17 places the 1850 rate for African Americans at 17 percent overall. She also notes that 26.5 percent of black households had at least one child in school. Moss, *Schooling Citizens,* 89, 109.

56. Christian, "The Negro in Louisiana," chap. 20, pp. 11–13, Marcus Christian Collection; Cossé Bell, *Afro-Creole Protest Tradition,* 95–98, 105–6, 120–21.

57. Marcus Christian, "The Negro in Louisiana," Ch. 20, 11–13; Elizabeth C. Neidenbach, "The Life and Legacy of Marie Couvent: Social Networks, Property Ownership, and the Making of a Free People of Color Community in New Orleans" (PhD diss., College of William and Mary, 2015), 497; E. Robinson and R. H. Pidgeon, *Robinson's Atlas of the City of New Orleans, Louisiana* (New York: E. Robinson, 1883), plate 6, 18, 21, available at http://www.orleanscivilclerk.com/robinson/index.htm; *Norman's Plan of New Orleans & Environs,* 1845, Library of Congress, Geography and Map Division, available at http://hdl.loc.gov/loc.gmd/g4014n.ct000243; Emily Clark and

Virginia Meacham Gould, "The Feminine Face of Afro-Catholicism in New Orleans, 1727–1852," *William and Mary Quarterly* 59, no. 2 (April 2002): 409–48; Friends of the Cabildo, *New Orleans Architecture, vol. 6: Faubourg Tremé and the Bayou Road* (Gretna, LA: Pelican Publishing Company, 1980), 99–100; Michel & Co., *New Orleans Annual and Commercial Register for 1846* (New Orleans: E. A. Michel & Co., 1845), Appendix, 55–56; Alma Hobbs Peterson, "The Administration of the Public Schools in New Orleans" (PhD diss., Louisiana State University, 1964), 65, 99–104. Thanks to Richard Campanella for help translating antiquated addresses to their correct locations.

58. Walter C. Stern, "Church's Education Role Expands," *An Interactive Timeline of Public Education in New Orleans, 1718–Present*, http://www.spen02015.com/timeline.html; Clark, *Masterless Mistresses*, 256; DeVore and Logsdon, *Crescent City Schools*, 41.

59. Cossé Bell, *Afro-Creole Protest Tradition*, 127–33; Emily Clark and Virginia Meacham Gould, "The Feminine Face of Afro-Catholicism in New Orleans, 1727–1852," *William and Mary Quarterly* 59, no. 2 (April 2002): 409–48; Friends of the Cabildo, *New Orleans Architecture*, Vol. 6: *Faubourg Tremé and the Bayou Road* (Gretna, LA: Pelican Publishing, 1980), 99–100. While Clark and Gould refer to Sister Marthe Fontiere, Cossé Bell refers to Sister Marth Fortière.

60. *Prospectus de l'Institution Catholique des Orphelins Indigent*, LaRC; *History of the Catholic Indigent Orphan Institute, Dauphine and Touro Streets, Destroyed by the Hurricane, September 1915, Rebuilt in 1916, published by the Board of Directors*, 1916, AANO; Cossé Bell, *Afro-Creole Protest Tradition*, 125.

61. DeVore and Logsdon, *Crescent City Schools*, 42; "Free Colored Schools in Louisiana," *Common School Journal*, 15 January 1849, pp. 30–31, American Periodicals Database, http://search.proquest.com/docview/125578476?accountid=14437; Clarence L. Mohr, "Education in the South," in Clarence L. Mohr, ed., *The New Encyclopedia of Southern Culture*, Vol. 17: *Education* (Chapel Hill: University of North Carolina Press, 2011), 4–6 (5–6 for quote); Moss, *Schooling Citizens*, 97; "Table 1. Alabama—Race and Hispanic Origin for Selected Large Cities and Other Places: Earliest Census to 1990," and "Table 21. Maryland," in Gibson and Jung, *Historical Census Statistics On Population Totals By Race, 1790 to 1990, and By Hispanic Origin, 1970 to 1990, For Large Cities And Other Urban Places In The United States*, http://www.census.gov/population/www/documentation/twps0076/twps0076.html.

62. La Direction de l'Institution Catholique des Orphelins Indigents, Séance Extraordinaire, 3 Avril 1852 (for quote), 3 Mai 1852, 4 Septembre 1853; Séance, 1 Décembre 1851, 15 Avril 1852, 1 Juillet 1853, 1 Aout 1853, 2 Novembre 1853, all in Séance Book I, AANO; Mitchell, *Raising Freedom's Child*, 17; Neidenbach, "Legacy of Marie Couvent," 413.

63. *Prospectus de l'Institution Catholique des Orphelins Indigents*, LaRC (for quotes); Neidenbach, "Marie Bernard Couvent, the Couvent School, and African American Education in New Orleans," 44; Desdunes, *Our People and Our History*, 104; Nathan Wiley, "Education of the Colored Population of Louisiana," *Harper's New Monthly Magazine* 33, no. 1 (July 1866), 248; Neidenbach, "Legacy of Marie Couvent," 413.

64. Neidenbach, "Marie Bernard Couvent, the Couvent School, and African American Education in New Orleans," 44; Neidenbach, "Legacy of Marie Couvent," 412–13; Mitchell, *Raising Freedom's Child*, 16 (for quotes).

65. Séance Extraordinaire, 22 Juillet 1854, Séance Book I, AANO; Mitchell, *Raising Freedom's Child*, 237 n. 26.

66. Cossé Bell and Logsdon, "The Americanization of Black New Orleans," 208; Cossé Bell, *Afro-Creole Protest Tradition*, 126, 133; Christian, "The Negro in Louisiana," chap. 20, p. 18; Neidenbach, "Legacy of Marie Couvent," 417–19; Mitchell, *Raising Freedom's Child*, 36. Both Christian and Cossé Bell place the city ordinance calling on police to search free black schools in 1852. In fact, it was passed in 1853. See *Daily Picayune*, 29 June 1853, p. 2, col. 6.

67. Mitchell, *Raising Freedom's Child*, 36.

68. John W. Blassingame, "The Union Army as an Educational Institution for Negroes, 1862–1865," *Journal of Negro Education* 34, no. 2 (Spring 1965): 152–59; James B. Anderson, *The Education of Blacks in the South, 1860-1935* (Chapel Hill: University of North Carolina Press, 1988), 4–9; DeVore and Logsdon, *Crescent City Schools*, 47, 54–55; *The Anglo-African*, 13 June 1863, p. 1, col. 3–4. While Blassingame and subsequent scholars credit the Union Army with taking the lead in forming schools for former slaves, Heather Andrea Williams effectively highlights the role that African Americans played in the creation of these schools. See Williams, *Self-Taught*, 47, 228 n. 7.

69. DeVore and Logsdon, *Crescent City Schools*, 47; Nathan Wiley, "Education of the Colored Population of Louisiana," 248; Neidenbach, "Legacy of Marie Couvent," 423–24 (for quote); Mitchell, *Raising Freedom's Child*, 17; Walter C. Stern, "First Black Public Schools," *An Interactive Timeline of Public Education in New Orleans, 1718-Present*, http://www.spen02015.com/timeline .html. The $7,536 the school received through Butler's Bureau of Education likely exceeded its annual operational costs. In 1850–1851, for instance, the school's expenses totaled $2,587.73 for approximately 165 students. While its enrollment increased to about 250 by 1862, the Bureau of Education funds would have more than covered that increase, assuming per-pupil costs remained relatively stable. In Wiley's 1866 article referencing the $7,536 allocation, however, the author does not make clear whether the amount was an annual appropriation or a cumulative one since 1862. For the 1850–1851 budget, see Séance, 1 Mai 1851, Séance Book I, AANO.

70. Blassingame, "The Union Army as an Educational Institution for Negroes," 154; DeVore and Logsdon, *Crescent City Schools*, 47–57.

71. DeVore and Logsdon, *Crescent City Schools*, 55; Neidenbach, "Legacy of Marie Couvent," 420, 430–32 (quote on 432); Mitchell, *Raising Freedom's Child*, 9.

72. Lincoln quoted in Eric Foner, *Reconstruction: America's Unfinished Revolution, 1863-1875* (New York: Perennial Classics, 1988), 49. See also Neidenbach, "Legacy of Marie Couvent," 434.

73. Logsdon and Cossé Bell, "The Americanization of Black New Orleans," 227–28 (quote on 227); Neidenbach, "Legacy of Marie Couvent," 435–36; Cossé Bell, *Afro-Creole Protest Tradition*, 251–55.

74. Williams, *Self-Taught*, 94 (for quote); Hannah Rosen, *Terror in the Heart of Freedom: Citizenship, Sexual Violence, and the Meaning of Race in the Postemancipation South* (Chapel Hill: University of North Carolina Press, 2009), 61–68; Shelby County Historical Commission, "Schools for Freedmen," 1980 (photo of historical marker in author's possession).

75. Justin A. Nystrom, *New Orleans After the Civil War: Race, Politics, and a New Birth of Freedom* (Baltimore: Johns Hopkins University Press, 2010), 66–68; Foner, *Reconstruction: America's Unfinished Revolution*, 271–80; James K. Hogue, *Uncivil War: Five New Orleans Street Battles and the Rise and Fall of Radical Reconstruction* (Baton Rouge: Louisiana State University Press, 2006), 34–45.

76. The first quote is from Article 2 of the 1868 Constitution. See *Official Journal of the*

Proceedings of the Convention, for Framing a Constitution for the State of Louisiana (New Orleans: J. B. Roudanez & Co., 1867–1868), 293. Delegate list from *Constitution Adopted by the State Constitutional Convention of the State of Louisiana, March 7, 1868* (New Orleans: The New Orleans Republican, 1868), 21–22. On the Creoles' transatlantic conception of rights, see Rebecca J. Scott, "Public Rights and Private Commerce: A Nineteenth Century Atlantic Creole Itinerary," *Current Anthropology* 28, no. 2 (2007): 237–56. For the second quote, see David C. Rankin, "The Origins of Black Leadership in New Orleans During Reconstruction," *Journal of Southern History* 40, no. 3 (1974): 417–40 (quote on 420). To determine the number of Catholic School affiliates on Rankin's list of 201 black leaders, I compared Rankin's list with the teachers, board members, and school benefactors included in *History of the Catholic Indigent Orphan Institute, Dauphine and Touro Streets, Destroyed by the Hurricane, September 1915, Rebuilt in 1916, published by the Board of Directors,* 1916, AANO; with those listed in the minutes of the school's board meetings; and with the names of school affiliates identified in Neidenbach, "The Life and Legacy of Marie Couvent."

77. Roger A. Fischer, *The Segregation Struggle in Louisiana, 1862–1877* (Urbana: University of Illinois Press, 1974), 110–11; School Board Minutes, 21 May 1868; OPSB-147. Demographics largely explained the divergent outcomes between the 1868 municipal elections and the referendum on the new constitution. While black people comprised a majority of voters statewide, whites outnumbered blacks by a nearly three-to-one margin in New Orleans. See Fischer, 111.

78. For early references to the Bayou Road School, see *Daily Picayune,* 26 November 1858, and *Annual Report of the Superintendent of Public Schools to the Legislature of the State of Louisiana,* January, 1861 (Baton Rouge: J. M. Taylor, State Printer, 1861), 59. It is referred to as a girls' school in *Report of the State Superintendent of Public Education to the General Assembly of the State of Louisiana,* October, 1864 (New Orleans: W. R. Fish, State Printer, 1864), 26. Both state reports are available at http://www2.state.lib.la.us/doeafsr/.

79. This incident is related in School Board Minutes, 21 May 1868, which also include reprints of Rogers's May 7, 1868 letter to Bigot and her response to him. See also Fischer, *Segregation Struggle in Louisiana.*

80. All quotes are from School Board Minutes, 27 May 1868. See also Mitchell, *Raising Freedom's Child,* 215–16.

81. DeVore and Logsdon, *Crescent City Schools,* 55; Fischer, *Segregation Struggle in Louisiana,* 110. The Barracks School, where the 1862 desegregation fight occurred, was in the same district as the Bayou Road School. See *Report of the State Superintendent of Public Education to the General Assembly of the State of Louisiana,* October 1864 (New Orleans: W. R. Fish, State Printer), 26.

82. DeVore and Logsdon, *Crescent City Schools,* 66–67.

83. Ibid.; Board of Directors of Public Schools of New Orleans Minutes, 16 September 1867, OPSB-147. The teachers who directly stated their opposition to segregated schools included Edmonia G. Highgate of Syracuse, New York, and Edouard Tinchant, a French-born man of Haitian descent who served as a delegate to the 1867–1868 constitutional convention, where he vociferously supported the Afro-Creoles' civil rights platform. On Tinchant, see Scott and Hébrard, *Freedom Papers.* On Highgate, see Dorothy Sterling, ed., *We Are Your Sisters: Black Women in the Nineteenth Century* (New York, 1984), 294–305. In addition to her regular contributions in black newspapers, Highgate's wartime and Reconstruction-era correspondences are included in

American Missionary Association Archives, Amistad Research Center, Tulane University, and the Gerrit Smith Papers, Special Collections Research Center, Syracuse University.

84. Louis R. Harlan, "Desegregation in New Orleans Public Schools During Reconstruction," *American Historical Review* 67, no. 3 (April 1962): 663–75; DeVore and Logsdon, *Crescent City Schools*, 86. Harlan included Bayou Road in his list of desegregated schools. See p. 666, n. 14.

85. Harlan, "Desegregation During Reconstruction," 671–72; Marler, *Merchants' Capital*, 9; DeVore and Logsdon, *Crescent City Schools*, 76, 81; Fischer, *Segregation Struggle in Louisiana*, 123–25. For a reference to the Upper Girls' High School's location, see *Annual Report of the State Superintendent of Public Education, for the Year 1874* (New Orleans: Republican Office, 1875), 169; Steven Hahn, *A Nation Under Our Feet: Black Political Struggles in the Rural South from Slavery to the Great Migration* (Cambridge: The Belknap Press of Harvard University Press, 2003), chap. 6.

86. Harlan, "Desegregation During Reconstruction," 671–72. The references to the "committee" and "youthful regulators" are from *Times-Picayune*, 18 December 1874, p. 1.

87. *Annual Report of the State Superintendent of Public Education, for the Year 1875* (New Orleans: Republican Office, 1876), 151.

88. DeVore and Logsdon, *Crescent City Schools*, 76.

89. "War Sure Enough," *Times-Picayune*, 18 December 1874; Fischer, *Segregation Struggle in Louisiana*, 125–27.

90. "Color in the New Orleans Schools," *Harper's Weekly*, 13 February 1875, 147.

91. Harlan, "Desegregation During Reconstruction," 668.

92. Cable quoted in Powell, "A Novelist Turns Historian," 5–6.

93. School Board Minutes, 1 August 1877.

94. Joseph S. Schwertz, "The History of Warren Easton Boys' High School" (Master's thesis, Tulane University, 1941), 52; Ethel Walker, "History of the Sophie B. Wright High School" (Master's thesis, Tulane University, 1939), 52–56; David Tyack and Elisabeth Hansot, *Learning Together: A History of Coeducation in American Schools* (New Haven, CT: Yale University Press, 1990), 114; DeVore and Logsdon, *Crescent City Schools*, 33, 89–103 (quote on 103).

95. Desdunes, *Our People and Our History*, 107.

96. Mitchell, *Raising Freedom's Child*, 224–27 (quotes on 224).

97. Ibid. On the Fillmore School, see also Mishio Yamanaka, "The Fillmore Boys School in 1877: Racial Integration, Creoles of Color and the End of Reconstruction in New Orleans," http://fillmoreschool.web.unc.edu.

98. Desdunes, *Our People and Our History*, 68, 107; Mitchell, *Raising Freedom's Child*, 229; *History of the Catholic Indigent Orphan Institute, Dauphine and Touro Streets, Destroyed by the Hurricane, September 1915, Rebuilt in 1916, published by the Board of Directors*, 1916, AANO.

99. *History of the Catholic Indigent Orphan Institute*, AANO; David Levering Lewis, *W. E. B. Du Bois*; *Biography of a Race, 1868–1919* (New York: Henry Holt, 1993), 58–72.

100. C. Vann Woodward, *Origins of the New South, 1877–1913* (Baton Rouge: Louisiana State University Press, 1951), 211–12; Neidenbach, "Legacy of Marie Couvent," 443–45; Mitchell, *Raising Freedom's Child*, 228.

101. Cossé Bell, *Afro-Creole Protest Tradition*, 280–82; Neidenbach, "Marie Bernard Couvent, the Couvent School, and African American Education in New Orleans," 57.

CHAPTER TWO

1. "Ku Klux Brought Into Discussion by School Board," *Times-Picayune*, 13 January 1923, 1, 10; "Weather News," *Times-Picayune*, 13 January 1923, p. 5; Sanborn Map Company, *Insurance Maps of New Orleans, Louisiana*, vol. 3, 1908, sheets 238, 240, and vol. 1A, 1940, sheet 10A, available at http://sanborn.umi.com/la/3376/dateid-000009.htm?CCSI=3057n; Orleans Parish School Board Minutes, 12 January 1923, Orleans Parish School Board Collection (MSS 147), Louisiana and Special Collections Department, Earl K. Long Library, University of New Orleans (cited hereinafter as OPSB Minutes); John Smith Kendall, *History of New Orleans*, vol. 2 (Chicago and New York: Lewis Publishing, 1922), 679–81. Malcolm Rosenberg noted that the school district's offices were on the third floor of the Municipal Building (also known as the City Hall Annex) in "The Orleans Parish Schools Under the Superintendency of Nicholas Bauer" (PhD diss., Louisiana State University, 1963), 134. The quote is from OPSB Minutes, 12 January 1923, p. 184.

2. "A Grave Injustice," *Times-Picayune*, 2 February 1923, 8; OPSB Minutes, 25 August and 13 December 1922; Samuel Hoskins, "Citizens Have Been Pleading to Orleans School Board 22 Years for Better Schools," *Louisiana Weekly*, 24 January 1942, 1.

3. OPSB Minutes, 12 January 1923; James J. A. Fortier Passport Application, 16 June 1924, *Passport Applications, January 2, 1906–March 31, 1925*, National Archives and Records Administration (NARA), Microfilm Roll 2570, Certificates 442350–442849, 14 Jun 1924–16 Jun 1924, accessed via Ancestry.com; *Soards' New Orleans City Directory*, 1923 (New Orleans: Soards Directory Co., 1923), 635; "Pen Pictures: Men of Louisiana," *Times-Picayune*, 1 September 1917, 10; "Seven Candidates in the Field for School Board Vacancies," *Times-Picayune*, 5 November 1922, 19; "Semi-Annual Financial Statement of the Pyramid Homestead Association," *Times-Picayune*, 13 July 1919, 16-C; "Semi-Annual Financial Statement of the Pyramid Homestead Association," *Times-Picayune*, 15 January 1922, sec. 5, p. 9; "Career of Mr. James Fortier is Brilliant," *Silver and Blue*, 18 March 1932, Lusher Charter School Library (cited hereinafter as LCS).

4. *Buchanan v. Warley*, 245 U.S. 60 (1917). All quotes are from OPSB Minutes, 12 January 1923.

5. Carl H. Nightingale, "The Transnational Contexts of Early Twentieth-Century American Urban Segregation, *Journal of Social History* 39, no. 3 (Spring 2006): 667–702; Carl H. Nightingale, *Segregation: A Global History of Divided Cities* (Chicago: University of Chicago Press, 2012), chap. 10; Christopher Silver, "The Racial Origins of Zoning: Southern Cities from 1910–40," *Planning Perspectives* 6 (1991): 189–205; Roger L. Rice, "Residential Segregation by Law, 1910–1917," *The Journal of Southern History* 34, no. 2 (May 1968): 179–99; Arthur T. Martin, "Segregation of Residences of Negroes," *Michigan Law Review* 32, no. 6 (April 1934): 721–42; David M. P. Freund, *Colored Property: State Policy & White Racial Politics in Suburban America* (Chicago: University of Chicago Press, 2007), esp. chap. 2; *Tyler v. Harmon*, 158 La. 439 (1925); *Harmon v. Tyler*, 273 U.S. 668 (1927).

6. Arnold R. Hirsch, "With or Without Jim Crow: Black Residential Segregation in the United States," in *Urban Policy in Twentieth Century America*, ed. Arnold R. Hirsch and Raymond A. Mohl (New Brunswick, NJ: Rutgers University Press, 1993), 73–78; William Ivy Hair, *Carnival of Fury: Robert Charles and the New Orleans Race Riot of 1900* (Baton Rouge: Louisiana State University Press, 1976); Joel Williamson, *Crucible of Race: Black-White Relations in the American South Since Emancipation* (Oxford: Oxford University Press, 1985), 201–9; "Another Effort to Bomb Negro's Residence Fails," *Times-Picayune*, 15 November 1926, 2. The population schedules

for the 1920 U.S. Census attest to the alternating black and white stretches in the area surrounding the 2000 block of Louisiana Avenue, which was the scene of two of the 1926 bombings. See Manuscript Census Returns, Fourteenth Census of the United States, 1920, New Orleans, La., Population (hereinafter cited as 1920 U.S. Census, New Orleans, La., Population), National Archives Microfilm Series T-625, reel 623, available through Heritage Quest Online; hereinafter cited as NAMS T-625/Heritage Quest.

7. W. E. B. Du Bois, *The Souls of Black Folk: Essays and Sketches* (Chicago: A. C. McClurg, 1904), vii (first quote); interview with Herbert Melvin Cappie and Ruth Irene Cappie (btvct07063), interviewed by Michele Mitchell, New Orleans, LA, July 2, 1994, Behind the Veil: Documenting African-American Life in the Jim Crow South Digital Collection, John Hope Franklin Research Center, Duke University Libraries (second quote). Booker T. Washington expressed sentiments similar to Herbert Cappie's in his 1909 essay, "The Negro's Place in American Life": "[The Negro] often hears the opinion expressed that [he] should keep his place or that he is 'all right in his place,'" Washington wrote. "People who make use of these expressions seldom understand how difficult it is, considering the different customs in different parts of the country, to find out just what his place is." Booker T. Washington, "The Negro's Place in American Life," *Outlook*, 13 November 1909.

8. Scholarship on the origins of Jim Crow often revolves around the extent to which segregation reflected continuity versus change in terms of southern race relations. This study adds weight to the argument that Jim Crow marked a historical break while also stressing the continuity of white supremacy and the fluidity of Jim Crow's evolution. On the origins of Jim Crow, see C. Vann Woodward, *The Strange Career of Jim Crow* (New York: Oxford University Press, 1955); Howard N. Rabinowitz, *Race Relations in the Urban South* (New York: Oxford University Press, 1978); Glenda Gilmore, *Gender and Jim Crow: Women and the Politics of White Supremacy in North Carolina, 1896–1920* (Chapel Hill: University of North Carolina Press, 1996); Grace Elizabeth Hale, *Making Whiteness: The Culture of Whiteness in the South, 1890–1940* (New York: Pantheon Books, 1998); Williamson, *Crucible of Race*.

9. New Orleans was the sixteenth largest city in the country in 1930, with a population of 458,762. Houston was the next largest city in the former Confederacy with a population less than two-thirds that of New Orleans. Houston still had 110,000 fewer residents than New Orleans in 1940, and Atlanta trailed the Crescent City by nearly 200,000 residents. See Campbell Gibson, *Population of the 100 Largest Cities and Other Urban Places in the United States: 1790 to 1990*, Population Division Working Paper No. 27 (Washington: U.S. Bureau of the Census, June 1998), http://www.census.gov/population/www/documentation/twps0027/twps0027.html.

10. Campbell Gibson and Kay Jung, *Historical Census Statistics On Population Totals By Race, 1790 to 1990, and By Hispanic Origin, 1970 to 1990, For Large Cities And Other Urban Places In The United States*, Population Division Working Paper No. 76 (Washington: U.S. Bureau of the Census, February 2005), http://www.census.gov/population/www/documentation/twps0076/twps0076.html.

11. New Orleans had nearly 400,000 residents in 1920; Atlanta barely topped 200,000. See Blaine A. Brownell, "The Commercial-Civic Elite and City Planning in Atlanta, Memphis, and New Orleans in the 1920s," *Journal of Southern History* 41, no. 3 (August 1975): 342.

12. Davison Douglas, *Jim Crow Moves North: The Battle Over Northern School Segregation, 1865–1954* (New York: Cambridge University Press, 2005), chap. 4.

13. My definition of Jim Crow as a system of legal, political, social, and economic oppression is based upon Risa L. Goluboff, *The Lost Promise of Civil Rights* (Cambridge, MA: Harvard University Press, 2007), 6–8; Michael J. Klarman, *From Jim Crow to Civil Rights: The Supreme Court and the Struggle for Racial Equality* (Oxford: Oxford University Press, 2004), chap. 1; Manning Marable, *Race, Reform, and Rebellion: The Second Reconstruction and Beyond in Black America, 1945–2006*, 3rd edition (Oxford: University Press of Mississippi, 2007), 10; Fairclough, *Race and Democracy*, 5–11; DeVore, *Defying Jim Crow;* and the sources cited in note 8. On the economic nature of Jim Crow, see especially Goluboff and Marable. On Jim Crow in the North, see Douglas, *Jim Crow Moves North;* Matthew Lassiter and Joseph Crespino, "Introduction: The End of Southern History," and Lassiter, "De Jure/De Facto Segregation: The Long Shadow of a National Myth," in *The Myth of Southern Exceptionalism*, ed. Matthew Lassiter and Joseph Crespino (Oxford: Oxford University Press, 2009); Joe William Trotter, *Black Milwaukee: The Making of an Industrial Proletariat, 1915–1945* (Urbana: University of Illinois Press, 1985); and Andrew R. Highsmith, *Demolition Means Progress: Flint, Michigan, and the Fate of the American Metropolis* (Chicago: University of Chicago Press, 2015).

14. Williamson, *Crucible of Race*, 225–56; Woodward, *The Strange Career of Jim Crow*, chap. 3; Klarman, *Jim Crow to Civil Rights*, 10–11, 17–28; Fairclough, *Race and Democracy*, 9–10, 64, 483 n. 23; Robert Margo, *Race and Schooling in the South, 1880–1950: An Economic History* (Chicago: University of Chicago Press, 1990), 18–23; DeVore, *Defying Jim Crow*, 166–73; Michael A. Ross, *The Great New Orleans Kidnapping Case: Race, Law, and Justice in the Reconstruction Era* (Oxford: Oxford University Press, 2015), 214. In 1882, Tennessee became the first state to pass a law mandating segregation beyond schooling. See Williamson, *Crucible of Race*, 253.

15. Marable, *Race, Reform, and Rebellion*, 10–11; Barbara Bair, "Though Justice Sleeps, 1880–1900," in *To Make Our World Anew: A History of African Americans*, vol. 2, *From 1880*, ed. Robin D. G. Kelley and Earl Lewis (Oxford: Oxford University Press, 2000), 28; Joe William Trotter Jr., *The African American Experience*, vol. 2, *From Reconstruction* (Boston: Houghton Mifflin, 2001), 336–39, 404–6; Trotter, "Shifting Perspectives on Segregation in the Emerging Postindustrial Age," 12–13, paper presented at The Future of the African American Past Conference, May 19–21, 2016, Washington, DC, https://futureafampast.si.edu/sites/default/files/03_Trotter%20 Joe.pdf; Richard Kluger, *Simple Justice: The History of* Brown v. Board of Education *and Black America's Struggle for Equality* (New York: Knopf, 1976), 110–13.

16. Michael Honey, "Class, Race, and Power in the New South: Racial Violence and the Delusion of White Supremacy," in *Democracy Betrayed: The Wilmington Race Riot of 1898 and Its Legacy*, ed. David S. Cecelski and Timothy B. Tyson (Chapel Hill: University of North Carolina Press, 1998), 171–75; Gilmore, *Gender and Jim Crow*, chap. 4; Woodward, *The Strange Career of Jim Crow*, chap. 12; Edward L. Ayers, *Promise of the New South: Life After Reconstruction* (New York: Oxford University Press, 1992), chap. 10–11; Edward F. Haas, "John Fitzpatrick and Political Continuity in New Orleans, 1896–1899," *Louisiana History* 22, no. 1 (Winter 1981): 21–23; Haas, "Political Continuity in the Crescent City: Toward an Interpretation of New Orleans Politics, 1874–1986, *Louisiana History* 39, no. 1 (Winter 1998): 5–10; Barbara J. Fields, "*Origins of the New South* and the Negro Question," *Journal of Southern History* 67, no. 4 (November 2001): 811–26; Michael Perman, *Struggle for Mastery: Disfranchisement in the South, 1888–1908* (Chapel Hill: University of North Carolina Press, 2001), chap. 7–8; Glenda Gilmore, "Review of *Struggle for Mastery: Disfranchisement in the South, 1888–1908*," *American Historical Review* 107, no. 3 (June 2002): 885–86.

17. Klarman, *Jim Crow to Civil Rights*, 12–15; Goluboff, *Lost Promise of Civil Rights*, 18–20; Lawrence N. Powell, "Why Louisiana Mattered," *Louisiana History* 53, no. 4 (Fall 2012): 389–401; Kluger, *Simple Justice*, 56–83. As James Bennett notes, black Creole New Orleanians had resources at their disposal that the black petitioners in other court challenges to railroad segregation did not have. While resources help to explain the large number of civil rights cases from New Orleans that reached the Supreme Court, Afro-Creole New Orleanians' commitment to the ideals articulated in the 1868 state constitution also distinguished them from black activists elsewhere. Significantly, Louisiana's 1868 Constitution set a higher standard for equality than the Fourteenth Amendment by explicitly rejecting racial classification. See Bennett, *Religion and the Rise of Jim Crow*, 180; Klarman, *Jim Crow to Civil Rights*, 18; Powell, "Why Louisiana Mattered."

18. Nightingale, "Transnational Context," 673–74; Nightingale, *Segregation: A Global History*, 269–71, 273, 284, 289, 294, 303–4, 316–17; Hale, *Making Whiteness*, chap. 4; James R. Grossman, *Land of Hope: Chicago, Black Southerners, and the Great Migration* (Chicago: University of Chicago Press, 1989); St. Clair Drake and Horace Cayton, *Black Metropolis: A Study of Negro Life in a Northern City* (New York: Harcourt, Brace, 1945); DeVore, *Defying Jim Crow*, 24–25, 29; Klarman, *Jim Crow to Civil Rights*, 12; Williamson, *Crucible of Race*, chap. 4; Ibram X. Kendi, *Stamped from the Beginning: The Definitive History of Racist Ideas in America* (New York: Nation Books, 2016), 301–2, 310–11.

19. A vast literature exists on the role of race within American imperialism. For works that specifically discuss the evolution of Jim Crow within a transnational context, see Nightingale, *Segregation: A Global History*; Cell, *Highest Stage of White Supremacy*; Woodward, *The Strange Career of Jim Crow*, 72–74. For more detailed examinations of the role of race within American colonial administration, see for example Louis A. Pérez Jr., *The War of 1898: The United States & Cuba in History and Historiography* (Chapel Hill: University of North Carolina Press, 1998); Stuart Creighton Miller, *"Benevolent Assimilation": The American Conquest of the Philippines, 1899–1903* (New Haven, CT: Yale University Press, 1982); Mary A. Renda, *Taking Haiti: Military Occupation & the Culture of U.S. Imperialism, 1915–1949* (Chapel Hill: University of North Carolina Press, 2001); Julie Greene, *The Canal Builders: Making America's Empire at the Panama Canal* (New York: The Penguin Press, 2009); Paul Kramer, "Race-Making and Colonial Violence in the U.S. Empire: The Philippine-American War as Race War," *Diplomatic History* 30, no. 2 (April 2006): 169–210.

20. OBSP Minutes, 12 January 1923 (first quote); W. E. B. Du Bois, *Black Reconstruction in America, An Essay Toward a History of the Part Which Black Folk Played in the Attempt to Reconstruct Democracy in America, 1860–1880* (New York: Harcourt, Brace, 1935; reprint, Cleveland and New York: Meridian Books, 1969), 693–701 (quote on 701; page citations are to the reprint edition). See also Eric Arnesen, "Whiteness and the Historians' Imagination," *International Labor and Working-Class History*, no. 60 (Fall 2001), 9–13; Fairclough, *Race and Democracy*, 6; Fields, "Origins of the New South."

21. On the "racial theory of property value," see Nightingale, *Segregation: A Global History*. On the role of schools as economic gatekeepers, see David Labaree, *The Making of an American High School: The Credentials Market and the Central High School of Philadelphia, 1838–1939* (New Haven, CT: Yale University Press, 1988); Grossman, *Land of Hope*, chap. 9. On the links between segregated schooling and segregated job markets, see Ansley T. Erickson, *Making the Unequal Metropolis: School Desegregation and Its Limits* (Chicago: University of Chicago Press, 2016), 95–101.

22. Hirsch, "A Matter of Black and White"; Logsdon and Cossé Bell, "Americanization of Black New Orleans"; and Hirsch and Logsdon, "Introduction to Part III: Franco-Africans and African-Americans," in *Creole New Orleans: Race and Americanization*, ed. Arnold R. Hirsch and Joseph Logsdon (Baton Rouge: Louisiana State University Press, 1992); Juliette Lee Landphair, "'For the Good of the Community': Reform Activism and Public Schools in New Orleans, 1920–1960" (PhD diss., University of Virginia, 1999), 9, 69–72; Scott, "Public Rights and Private Commerce"; Foner, *Reconstruction: America's Unfinished Revolution*, 47–50; Donald DeVore, "The Rise from the Nadir: Black New Orleans Between the Wars, 1920–1940" (Master's thesis, University of New Orleans, 1983), 49; DeVore, *Defying Jim Crow*, 123.

23. Hirsch's characterization of racial settlement patterns in the urban South corrects Howard Rabinowitz's contention that residential segregation was the norm in the South by 1890. See Hirsch, "With or Without Jim Crow," 69; Rabinowitz, *Race Relations in the Urban South, 1865–1890* (New York: Oxford University Press, 1978), chap. 5. On southern residential patterns around the turn of the century, see also David Goldfield, *Cotton Fields and Skyscrapers: Southern City and Region* (Baltimore: Johns Hopkins University Press, 1892), 166–67. On black residential patterns in the late nineteenth- and early twentieth-century North, see Karl E. Taeuber and Alma F. Taeuber, *Negroes in Cities: Residential Segregation and Neighborhood Change* (Chicago: Aldine Publishing, 1965), 3; Gilbert Osofsky, "The Enduring Ghetto," *Journal of American History* 55, no. 2 (September 1968): 243–55; August Meier and Elliott Rudwick, *From Plantation to Ghetto*, 3rd edition (New York: Hill and Wang, 1976), 234–35; Drake and Cayton, *Black Metropolis*.

24. "Backyard pattern" is quoted in Daphne Spain, "Race Relations and Residential Segregation in New Orleans: Two Centuries of Paradox," *Annals of the American Academy of Political and Social Sciences* 441 (January 1979): 82–96. See also Peirce F. Lewis, *New Orleans: The Making of an Urban Landscape* (Pensacola, FL: Ballinger Publishing, 1976), 44–45; Mitchell Duneier, *Ghetto: The Invention of a Place, the History of an Idea* (New York: Farrar, Straus, and Giroux, 2016), 33.

25. Ari Kelman, *A River and Its City: The Nature of Landscape in New Orleans* (Berkeley: University of California Press, 2006), 4; Richard Campanella, *Geographies of New Orleans: Urban Fabrics Before the Storm* (Lafayette: Center for Louisiana Studies, 2006), 58–60; Spain, "Race Relations and Residential Segregation."

26. Lawrence N. Powell, *The Accidental City: Improvising New Orleans* (Cambridge, MA: Harvard University Press, 2012), 204 (first quote); Lewis, *Making of an Urban Landscape*, 45 (second quote). On the development of the Sixth Ward, see City of New Orleans Office of Policy and Planning, "Sixth Ward/Treme/Lafitte Neighborhood Profile (6A)," December 1978, pp. 3.02–3.03. On nineteenth-century immigration in New Orleans, see Hirsch and Logsdon, "Franco-Africans and African-Americans," 190; Logsdon and Cossé Bell, "Americanization of Black New Orleans," 207–8; and Tregle, "Creoles and Americans," 163–64.

27. Hair, *Carnival of Fury*, 69, 87–89 (the unnamed sanitation expert is quoted on p. 69).

28. One of the earliest examples of this dates to 1888, when the school board temporarily transferred the McDonogh No. 6 School, which was located in a predominantly white neighborhood, from black to white use. Examples from the early twentieth century are discussed at length in subsequent chapters. On McDonogh No. 6, see Donald E. DeVore and Joseph Logsdon, *Crescent City Schools: Public Education in New Orleans, 1841–1991* (Lafayette: University of Southwestern Louisiana Press, 1991), 116.

29. The term *facts on the ground* derives from the Israeli settler movement and in that context refers to settlers' attempts after 1967 to establish a sufficiently large presence in the West Bank to ensure permanent Israeli control of Palestinian lands. It is also the title of a book by anthropologist Nadia Abu El-Haj. See David Rosen, "Searching for 'Facts' on the Ground," *The Columbia Current*, Fall 2007, available at http://www.columbia.edu/cu/current/articles/fa112007/searching-for-facts-on-the-ground.html, and Karen W. Arenson, "Fracas Erupts Over Book on Mideast by a Barnard Professor Seeking Tenure," *New York Times*, 10 September 2007, B1.

30. DeVore, "Rise from the Nadir," 86; DeVore, *Defying Jim Crow*, esp. chap. 2 and 5. For examples of blacks donating land for the construction of schools in existing black neighborhoods, see "Site is Offered for Public School," *New Orleans Item*, 21 November 1910, and Newton E. Renfro, "'Open Space' Concept Takes Getting Used to at Rosenwald," *Times-Picayune*, 4 November 1973, section 3, p. 6. James Anderson has written about similar instances of "double taxation" in the context of the black rural school building boom of the early twentieth century. In addition to paying regular school taxes, black people regularly paid extra money out of their own pockets for school land, labor, and construction. See James Anderson, *The Education of Blacks in the South: 1860–1935* (Chapel Hill: University of North Carolina Press, 1988), chap. 5.

31. Erickson, *Making the Unequal Metropolis*, 29–32 (quote on 30); Carol McMichael Reese, "The Once and Future New Orleans of Planners Milton Medary and Harland Bartholomew, 1920–1960," in *New Orleans Under Reconstruction: The Crisis of Planning*, ed. Carol McMichael Reese, Michael Sorkin, and Anthony Fontenot (London: Verso, 2014), 99–105; "Education Week," *Association of Commerce News Bulletin*, November 28, 1922, p. 5. For sources documenting Fortier's wide-ranging business activities in law, real estate, and finance, see note 3 in this chapter.

32. Perry quoted in Erickson, *Making the Unequal Metropolis*, 32. See also Andrew R. Highsmith and Ansley T. Erickson, "Segregation as Splitting, Segregation as Joining: Schools, Housing, and the Many Modes of Jim Crow," *American Journal of Education* 121, no. 4 (August 2015), 568–73; Karen Benjamin, "Segregation Built to Last: Schools and the Construction of Segregated Housing Patterns in Early Twentieth-Century Atlanta," paper presented at the Annual Meeting of the History of Education Society, 4 November 2016; Highsmith, *Demolition Means Progress*, 65.

33. Freund, *Colored Property*, 65 (second quote), 76–87 (first quote on 80). See also Nightingale, *Segregation: A Global History*, 319–27.

34. Duneier, *Ghetto: The Invention of a Place*, 30 (for quote); Freund, *Colored Property*, 80; Nightingale, *Segregation: A Global History*, 322–27.

35. Laura Amsberryaugier and Marilyn Hankel, "Mining the Decennnial Census for Louisiana Data, 1940–2000," *Louisiana Libraries* (Winter 2004): 8–12.

36. Examples include Alecia P. Long, *The Great Southern Babylon: Sex, Race, and Respectability in New Orleans, 1865–1920* (Baton Rouge: Louisiana State University Press, 2005); Hair, *Carnival of Fury*; Juliette Landphair, "Sewerage, Sidewalks, and Schools: The New Orleans Ninth Ward and Public School Desegregation," *Louisiana History* 40, no. 1 (Winter 1999): 35–62, as well as the Friends of the Cabildo's eight-volume *New Orleans Architecture* series. See in particular vol. 6, *Faubourg Tremé and the Bayou Road*.

37. See for example H. W. Gilmore, "The Old New Orleans and the New: A Case for Ecology," *American Sociological Review* 9, no. 4 (August 1944): 385–94; Spain, "Race Relations and Residential Segregation"; and Lewis, *The Making of an Urban Landscape*.

38. For an explanation of enumeration districts, see "1940 Federal Population Census, Indexes

and Other Finding Aids," National Archives Web site, http://www.archives.gov/research/census /1940/finding-aids.html#maps, accessed 20 April 2013. See also U.S. Census Bureau, "Measuring America: The Decennial Censuses From 1790 to 2000," available at www.census.gov/prod/2002 pubs/p0102marv-pt2.pdf, accessed 20 April 2013. Campanella's data do not fully account for racially mixed households since he used the head of household's race as the indicator of household race. It does, however, account for homes that included boarders of different races—a fairly common phenomenon in early twentieth-century New Orleans—since the Heritage Quest index isolates each individual with a unique surname within and across households.

39. Richard Campanella, e-mail correspondence with author, 24 November 2012. Campanella previously published these 1910 data, though not the map that appears here, in *Delta Urbanism: New Orleans* (Chicago: American Planning Association, 2010). He also draws upon that data in "'Two Centuries of Paradox': The Geography of New Orleans' African-American Population, from Antebellum to Postdiluvian Times," in *Hurricane Katrina in Transatlantic Perspective,* ed. Randy Sparks and Romain Huret (Baton Rouge: Louisiana State University Press, 2014).

40. Estimates are based upon Heritage Quest's indexed derivation of the 1920 census population schedules at the precinct level. The percentages are inexact since the Heritage Quest database returns both heads of households and individuals with unique surnames for each address. See 1920 U.S. Census, New Orleans, La., Population, NAMS T-625, reel 620, via Heritage Quest Online, accessed 14 September 2012.

41. 1920 U.S. Census, New Orleans, La., Population, NAMS T-625, reel 621; Sanborn Map Company, *Insurance Maps of New Orleans, Louisiana,* vol. 2, 1908, sheet 139; Office of Policy and Planning, "Sixth Ward/Treme/Lafitte Neighborhood Profile (6A)."

42. Tregle, "Creoles and Americans"; Lawrence N. Powell, "Introduction: A Novelist Turns Historian," in *The New Orleans of George Washington Cable: The 1887 Census Office Report,* ed. Lawrence N. Powell (Baton Rouge: Louisiana University Press, 2008), 9–11.

43. Friends of the Cabildo, *New Orleans Architecture,* vol. 4, 41–46, 61–62, 71–75, vol. 6, 112–13, 132–37; City of New Orleans Historic District Landmark Commission, "Garden District Historic District," May 2011, available at http://www.nola.gov/nola/media/HDLC/Historic%20 Districts/Garden.pdf.

44. Campanella, *Geographies of New Orleans,* 276; 1900 U.S. Census, New Orleans, La., Population, NAMS T-623, reel 574, accessed through Heritage Quest Online; Sam Borden, "A Saint in His City: Archie Manning in New Orleans," *New York Times,* 26 January 2013.

45. Campanella, *Geographies of New Orleans,* 270–76. Campanella bases his argument about these streets' role as commercial interfaces upon racial composition maps that the Works Progress Administration compiled in the 1930s. As discussed in the next chapter, however, my analysis of the 1910, 1920, and 1930 censuses challenges the idea of a uniformly black back-of-town and white front-of town.

46. Eric Arnesen, *Waterfront Workers of New Orleans: Race, Class, and Politics, 1863–1923* (New York: Oxford University Press, 1991); Hair, *Carnival of Fury,* 10, 109–110; C. Vann Woodward, *Origins of the New South, 1877–1913* (Baton Rouge: Louisiana State University Press, 1951), 180–86; Julius Rosenwald Foundation, "Report of a Special Inquiry Undertaken in New Orleans into the Industrial Status of Negroes," 1930, Isaac Heller folder, General Files, OPSB-147; DeVore, *Defying Jim Crow,* chap. 6; Fairclough, *Race and Democracy,* 483 n. 23.

47. 1920 U.S. Census, New Orleans, La., Population, NAMS T-625, reel 621.

48. School Board Minutes, 29 June 1900; DeVore and Logsdon, *Crescent City Schools*, 117–19; Anderson, *Education of Blacks in the South*, 188, 192–93.

49. DeVore and Logsdon, *Crescent City Schools*, 112–14, 117–19, 189–93; *Official Journal of the Proceedings of the Constitutional Convention of the State of Louisiana* (New Orleans: R. J. Hearsey, 1898), 10 (for quote).

50. Haas, "John Fitzpatrick and Political Continuity in New Orleans, 1896–1899," 16.

51. While Louisiana's 1879 Constitution eliminated the 1868 Constitution's prohibition against school segregation, it did not require segregation. Since the public schools in New Orleans had been segregated via local fiat since 1877, the 1898 Constitution ratified existing practice. See *Official Journal of the Proceedings of the Convention, for Framing a Constitution for the State of Louisiana* (New Orleans: J. B. Roudanez & Co., 1867–1868); *Official Journal of the Proceedings of the Constitutional Convention of the State of Louisiana* (New Orleans: R. J. Hearsey, 1898); *Constitution of the State of Louisiana, Adopted in Convention at the City of New Orleans, the Twenty-Third Day of July, A. D. 1879* (New Orleans: J. H. Cosgrove, 1879).

52. DeVore and Logsdon, *Crescent City Schools*, 114–17, 125–26.

53. Arnesen, *Waterfront Workers*, ix, 211–17; George M. Reynolds, *Machine Politics in New Orleans, 1897–1926* (New York: Columbia University Press, 1936), 32–37, 93–107, 233. See also John R. Kemp, "Introduction," in *Martin Behrman of New Orleans*, ed. John R. Kemp (Baton Rouge: Louisiana State University Press, 1977).

54. Juliette Landphair, "Sewerage, Sidewalks, and Schools," 37–39; Lewis, *The Making of an Urban Landscape*, 64–66; "'Paradise' on Lakefront Without Cost to Citizens Pictured by Col. Garsaud," *Times-Picayune*, 14 August 1925, section 1, pp. 1, 9 (quote).

55. Reynolds, *Machine Politics*, 108–37; Juliette Landphair, "Sewerage, Sidewalks, and Schools," 37–39; Rick Ginsberg, "Boss Behrman Reforms the Schools: The 1912 New Orleans School Reform," in Rick Ginsberg and David Plank, ed., *Southern Cities, Southern Schools* (New York: Greenwood Press, 1990); DeVore and Logsdon, *Crescent City Schools*, 164–66.

56. DeVore and Logsdon, *Crescent City Schools*, 148, 361–62; Robert Meyer Jr., *Names Over New Orleans Public Schools* (New Orleans: Namesake Press, 1975), 33, 45, 81, 180; *Soards' New Orleans City Directory, 1916* (New Orleans: Soards Directory Co., 1916), 1138, 1501; "Mr. Soniat Long Leading Notary in New Orleans," *Times-Picayune*, 20 January 1918, 4; *Soards' New Orleans City Directory, 1921* (New Orleans: Soards Directory Co., 1921), 1109, 1520; *Soards' New Orleans City Directory, 1914* (New Orleans: Soards Directory Co., 1916), 204; "Perry-Buckley Company," *Times-Picayune*, 10 December 1905, 17; *Soards' New Orleans City Directory, 1912* (New Orleans: Soards Directory Co., 1912), 1924; "Valloft & Dreux," *Times-Picayune*, 16 August 1915; "Men Who Preside Over Homesteads," *Times-Picayune*, 4 May 1917, p. B-3; "Homestead Men Studying Bills for Legislature," *Times-Picayune*, 26 March 1922, sec. 5, p. 1; "Two May Stores Sold, Third in Big Demand," *Daily Picayune*, 3 December 1912, 5.

57. DeVore and Logsdon, *Crescent City Schools*, 360; *Soards' New Orleans City Directory, 1908* (New Orleans: Soards Directory Co., 1908), 595, 634; *Soards' New Orleans City Directory, 1910* (New Orleans: Soards Directory Co., 1910), 1092; *Soards' New Orleans City Directory, 1911* (New Orleans: Soards Directory Co., 1911), 268, 311, 369, 570, 660, 685, 738, 749, 795, 930, 1012, 1154, 1277, and the following pages whose numbers start anew with the section listing individuals by profession: 110, 128, 129, 136, 176; *Soards' New Orleans City Directory, 1916* (New Orleans: Soards Directory Co., 1916), 1501; "Kenner Electric Finally Framed," *Daily Picayune*, 15 October

1913, 5; "Homestead News from Near and Far," *Daily Picayune,* 21 September 1902; "A Splendid Investment," *Daily Picayune,* 28 May 1901, 6; "Homestead Men Studying Bills for Legislature," *Times-Picayune,* 26 March 1922, sec. 5, p. 1; Meyer, *Names Over New Orleans Schools,* 45, 81.

58. Robert W. Williams Jr., "Martin Behrman and New Orleans Civic Development, 1904–1920," *Louisiana History* 2, no. 4 (Autumn 1961): 374–75 (first quote on 374); Craig E. Colton, *Unnatural Metropolis: Wresting New Orleans from Nature* (Baton Rouge: Louisiana State University Press, 2005), 82 (second quote).

59. Williams Jr., "Martin Behrman and New Orleans Civic Development, 1904–1920," 374–375; Jeffrey Mirel, *The Rise and Fall of an Urban School System, Detroit: 1907–1981,* 2nd edition (Ann Arbor: University of Michigan Press, 1999), 17, 27; DeVore and Logsdon, *Crescent City Schools,* 182–183.

60. Samuel Hoskins, "Citizens Have Been Pleading to Orleans School Board 22 Years for Better Schools," *Louisiana Weekly,* 24 January 1942, 1, 3 (quote is on 1).

61. O. C. W. Taylor, "The Public School Your Child Attends," *Louisiana Weekly,* 9 April 1927.

62. Ibid.; OPSB Minutes, 27 October 1922; DeVore and Logsdon, *Crescent City Schools,* 187–89.

63. DeVore and Logsdon, *Crescent City Schools,* 189, 191, 205–6; DeVore, *Defying Jim Crow,* 165–66.

64. DeVore, *Defying Jim Crow;* Walter C. Stern, "Review of Donald E. DeVore, *Defying Jim Crow: African American Community Development and the Struggle for Racial Equality in New Orleans, 1900–1960,*" *Urban History* 43, no. 2 (May 2016): 351–52, doi: https://doi.org/10.1017/S0963926816000213; interview with Delores Mary Aaron (btvct07060), interviewed by Michele Mitchell, New Orleans (LA), June 30, 1994, and Interview with Emmett Emmanuel Cheri (btvct07064), interviewed by Kate Ellis, New Orleans (LA), June 23, 1994, both in Behind the Veil: Documenting African-American Life in the Jim Crow South Digital Collection, John Hope Franklin Research Center, Duke University Libraries (see Aaron interview for quote).

65. DeVore and Logsdon, *Crescent City Schools,* 141; Leonard P. Ayres, *Laggards in Our Schools: A Study of Retardation and Elimination in City School Systems* (New York: Russell Sage Foundation, 1909; New York: Survey Associates, 1913), 162. Citations refer to the Survey Associates edition.

66. *Annual Report of the New Orleans Public Schools, 1919–1920,* 23, Annual Reports, Box 9, OPSB-147.

67. *Report of the Commissioner of Education for the Year Ended June 30, 1914,* vol. 2 (Washington: Government Printing Office, 1915), 29, 34.

68. *Report of the Commissioner of Education for the Year Ended June 30, 1920,* vol. 1 (Washington: Government Printing Office, 1920), 17–18; *Annual Report of the New Orleans Public Schools of the Parish of Orleans, 1920–1921,* Annual Reports, Box 9, p. 16, OPSB-147; DeVore and Logsdon, *Crescent City Schools,* 162; Cowen Institute for Public Education Initiatives, "Creating a Governing Framework for Public Education in New Orleans: School District Political Leadership," November 2009, 6–7, http://www.coweninstitute.com/our-work/applied-research/creating-a-governing-framework-for-public-education-in-new-orleans/.

69. *A Brief Summary and Thirty-Eight Maps Showing the Public School Situation in Louisiana in a Few Essential Respects, Session of 1918–1919,* vol. 3 of Biennial Report, Sessions of 1917–18 and 1918–19 (Baton Rouge: Louisiana State Department of Education, 1920), 40, 46, 63;

Public School Situation in Louisiana, Session of 1919-1920, vol. 1 of Biennial Report, Sessions of 1919-20 and 1920-21 (Baton Rouge: Louisiana State Department of Education, 1921), 52, 58, 74, available at http://www2.state.lib.la.us/doeafsr/; DeVore and Logsdon, *Crescent City Schools*, 164, 166, 168. Adjustments for inflation based upon U.S. Department of Labor, Bureau of Labor Statistics, "CPI Inflation Calculator," http://www.bls.gov/data/inflation_calculator.htm. Expenses per student exclude capital outlays and debt payments.

70. *Report of the Chief Superintendent of the Public Schools of the City of New Orleans, LA, to the State Board of Education*, January 1886, 241, 266–67 (the report is included in *Biennial Report of the State Superintendent of Public Education of the State of Louisiana, 1884-1885*, available at http://www2.state.lib.la.us/doeafsr/); DeVore and Logsdon, *Crescent City Schools*, 70, 91, 102, 128. Father Adam J. Ryan is quoted in Louis R. Harlan, "Desegregation in New Orleans Public Schools During Reconstruction," *American Historical Review* 67, no. 3 (April 1962): 669.

71. Harlan judiciously estimates that private schools enrolled roughly 10,000 in 1869 based on his reading of numbers included in city and state reports and the Catholic press. See Harlan, "Desegregation During Reconstruction," 669 n. 33. The city's public schools likely enrolled about 24,000 students that year. See the slightly different numbers reported by the state (23,284) and city (23,284 and 25,000) in *Annual Report of the State Superintendent of Public Education for 1869, to the General Assembly* (New Orleans: A. L. Lee, 1870), 26, 76, 78, available at http://www2.state.lib.la.us/doeafsr/.

72. *Report of the Chief Superintendent of the Public Schools of the City of New Orleans, LA, to the State Board of Education*, January 1886, 241, 266–67 (the report is included in *Biennial Report of the State Superintendent of Public Education of the State of Louisiana, 1884-1885*, available http://www2.state.lib.la.us/doeafsr/); DeVore and Logsdon, *Crescent City Schools*, 70, 91, 102, 128; Harlan, "Desegregation During Reconstruction," 669, 669 n. 33 (quote is on 669); *Annual and Biennial Reports*, 1900, 1910, 1930, 1940, http://www2.state.lib.la.us/doeafsr/.

73. Bennett, *Religion and the Rise of Jim Crow*, chap. 5, esp. 153, 168; John B. Alberts, "Black Catholic Schools: The Josephite Parishes of New Orleans During the Jim Crow Era," *U.S. Catholic Historian* 12, no. 1 (Winter 1994), 81. Citing estimates ranging from 50,000 to 100,000, Alberts places the black Catholic population of New Orleans in the 1890s at roughly 60,000. Bennett, meanwhile, cites a contemporary estimate of 75,000 to 100,000 for the entire diocese, whose borders extended beyond the city limits. Since New Orleans was home to fewer than 65,000 African Americans in 1890, the city's black Catholic population was almost certainly well below 60,000. For 1890 population statistics by race, see Campbell Gibson and Kay Jung, *Historical Census Statistics On Population Totals By Race, 1790 to 1990, and By Hispanic Origin, 1970 to 1990, For Large Cities And Other Urban Places In The United States*, U.S. Census Bureau Population Division, Working Paper No. 76 (Washington, DC: U.S. Census Bureau, 2005).

74. Bennett, *Religion and the Rise of Jim Crow*, chap. 6, pp. 193–94, 206.

75. Ibid., 156–59, 171–73; Alberts, "Black Catholic Schools"; Justin D. Poché, "Crescent City Catholicism: Catholic Education in New Orleans," in *Urban Catholic Education: Tales of Twelve American Cities*, ed. Thomas C. Hunt and Timothy Walch (Notre Dame, IN: Alliance for Catholic Education Press, 2010), 232–34.

76. Bennett, *Religion and the Rise of Jim Crow*, 206–23.

77. Ibid., 193, 197–98, 204, 219–22 (quote on 222).

78. Ibid., 206, 214–15; Benedict Westrick, "The History of Catholic Negro Education in the

City of New Orleans, 1724–1950" (Master's thesis, St. Mary's University of San Antonio, Texas, 1950), 72–73; Campanella, *Geographies of New Orleans*, 299, 216–17; Orleans Parish School Board—Office of Planning and Construction, *A Planning and Building Program for New Orleans' Schools* (New Orleans: Orleans Parish School Board, 1952), second map following p. 10, report courtesy of Ken Ducote, also available at Amistad Research Center and Earl K. Long Library, University of New Orleans; Catalog Description for Postcard of St. Dominic's Church, c. 1923, Item No. 1981.350.260, Historic New Orleans Collection; Bureau of the Census, *Population and Housing: Statistics for Census Tracts, New Orleans, La.* (Washington, DC: Government Printing Office, 1941), iv, 5. On the ways in which "the permanence of Catholic parishes anchored Catholics to particular neighborhoods," see James T. McGreevy, *Parish Boundaries: The Catholic Encounter with Race in the Twentieth-Century Urban North* (Chicago: University of Chicago Press, 1996), 17–20 (quote on 20) and Gerald Gamm, *Urban Exodus: Why the Jews Left Boston and the Catholics Stayed* (Cambridge, MA: Harvard University Press, 1999). St. Dominic/Joan of Arc was located near Cambronne and Burthe Streets, and Mater Dolorosa was located a few blocks away on Carrollton Avenue.

79. Bennett, *Religion and the Rise of Jim Crow*, 218–19, 225–26 (quote on 226); Poché, "Crescent City Catholicism," 234–35, 240.

80. DeVore and Logsdon, *Crescent City Schools*, chap. 3.

81. "Occupation of Parents, Session 1901–1902," *Annual Report for the Board of Education and the Superintendent of Schools of the City of New Orleans, 1901–1902*, 138–139, Annual Reports Box 2, OPSB-147; *Twelfth Census of the United States*, Census Reports, vol. 2: Population, Part 2 (Washington: U.S. Census Office, 1902), 578. Since the Census did not disaggregate occupational data for cities by race in 1900, I have subtracted the numbers of black doctors, lawyers, and brokers in 1910 (47, 12, and 2, respectively) from the 1900 totals in order to estimate the number of white doctors, lawyers, and brokers in 1900. For the 1910 numbers, see *Thirteenth Census of the United States: 1910*, vol. 4, Occupation Statistics, Table VIII, p. 570. These census reports are available at https://www.census.gov/prod/www/decennial.html.

82. Reid Mitchell, *All on Mardi Gras Day: Episodes in the History of New Orleans Mardi Gras* (Cambridge, MA: Harvard University Press, 1995); Woodward, *Origins of the New South*, chap. 3.

83. Kenneth Jackson, *Crabgrass Frontier: The Suburbanization of the United States* (New York: Oxford University Press, 1985), 275.

84. See, for instance, Grossman, *Land of Hope*, especially ch. 7 and 8; Drake and Cayton, *Black Metropolis*; Douglas, *Jim Crow Moves North*.

CHAPTER THREE

1. Louis Armstrong, *Satchmo: My Life in New Orleans*, centennial edition reprint (New York: Da Capo Press, 1986), 33–37; Thomas Brothers, *Louis Armstrong's New Orleans* (New York: W. W. Norton, 2006), 2, 96–99.

2. Armstrong, *Satchmo*, 33; Sanborn Map Company, *Insurance Maps of New Orleans, Louisiana*, vol. 3, 1908, sheets 263 and 266; available at http://sanborn.umi.com/la/3376/dateid-000009 .htm?CCSI=3057; Alecia P. Long, "Poverty Is the New Prostitution: Race, Poverty, and Public

Housing in Post-Katrina New Orleans," *Journal of American History* 94 (December 2007): 798–800. See also Long, *The Great Southern Babylon: Sex, Race, and Respectability in New Orleans, 1865–1920* (Baton Rouge: Louisiana State University Press, 2005), 161.

3. From multiple accounts, it is clear that Armstrong began his evening at Perdido and South Liberty and fired the gun at Perdido and South Rampart. While Armstrong does not state which route he took from his home to South Rampart, I am assuming it was along Perdido since that would have been the most direct path between the two known points in that evening's sequence of events. See Louis Armstrong, *Satchmo*, 33–37, and Brothers, *Louis Armstrong's New Orleans*, 96.

4. Brothers, *Louis Armstrong's New Orleans*, 74, 150; DeVore and Logsdon, *Crescent City Schools*, 189, 191; Sanborn Map Company, *Insurance Maps of New Orleans, Louisiana*, vol. 3, 1908, sheets 261, 264, 268, available at http://sanborn.umi.com/la/3376/dateid-000009.htm ?CCSI=3057.

5. 1910 U.S. Census, New Orleans, La., Population, NAMS T-624, reel 520; Armstrong, *Satchmo*, 57.

6. Using the 1910 U.S. Census population schedules, I tallied the number of residents identified as white, black, and mulatto living in this area by square block. Of the 2,169 residents (adults and children) I identified, 1,142 were black or mulatto and 1,026 were white.

7. A recent redevelopment project aims to return the Rampart Street corridor to its mixed residential and commercial past, albeit for a wealthier demographic. Initial plans called for retail shops and more than two hundred luxury apartments on the block opposite the former McDonogh No. 13. See John Magill, "Then and Now: New Orleans' South Market District," *Louisiana Cultural Vistas* 23, no. 4 (Winter 2012–2013): 66–73. For additional details on the development, see http://www.southmarketdistrict.com/index.php.

8. The Federal Writers Project of the Works Progress Administration, *New Orleans City Guide* (Boston: Houghton Mifflin, 1938; Garrett County Press reprint edition, 2009), 364; interview with Herbert Melvin Cappie and Ruth Irene Cappie (btvct07063), interviewed by Michele Mitchell, New Orleans, LA, July 2, 1994, Behind the Veil: Documenting African-American Life in the Jim Crow South Digital Collection, John Hope Franklin Research Center, Duke University Libraries (emphasis added).

9. OPSB Minutes, 14 September 1917; Sanborn Map Company, *Insurance Maps of New Orleans, Louisiana*, vol. 3, 1908, sheets 258–59, 268.

10. Using the 1910 U.S. Census population schedules, I identified 1,793 residents (adults and children) in the area bounded by South Rampart, Carondelet, Julia, and Poydras Streets. Of these, 1,385 were white, 403 were black and mulatto, and five were other races. See 1910 U.S. Census, New Orleans, La., Population, NAMS T-624, reel 520.

11. OPSB Minutes, 14 September 1917; 1910 U.S. Census, New Orleans, La., Population, NAMS T-624, reel 520; 1920 U.S. Census, New Orleans, La., Population, NAMS T-625, reel 618; Sanborn Map Company, *Insurance Maps of New Orleans, Louisiana*, vol. 3, 1908, sheets 257–62; Campanella, *Geographies of New Orleans*, 270; Ralph Blumenthal, "Digging Up Satchmo's Roots in the City that Spawned Him," *New York Times*, 15 April 2000, section E, 1. While Armstrong's relationship with the Karnofsky family is widely recounted, writers often stumble over the precise facts of the relationship. Armstrong recalled late in life that his relationship with the Karnofsky family began when he was only seven. But Thomas Brothers convincingly argued that Armstrong

likely started working for the family after his stay at the Waif's Home. See Brothers, *Louis Armstrong's New Orleans*, 324. Campanella incorrectly stated that Armstrong worked at the family's music store, not as a junk collector and coal deliverer. Based on information presumably gleaned from the late jazz historian Tad Jones, Ralph Blumenthal also incorrectly identified Morris Karnofsky, who was roughly the same age as Armstrong, as the family patriarch. The population schedule from the 1920 Census, however, indicates that Morris's father Louie owned the family store at 427 South Rampart.

12. Brothers, *Louis Armstrong's New Orleans*, 32.

13. Brothers, *Louis Armstrong's New Orleans*, 166; Juliette Lee Landphair, "'For the Good of the Community': Reform Activism and Public Schools in New Orleans, 1920–1960" (PhD diss., University of Virginia, 1999), 41. On southern children's interactions across—and understandings of—the color line more broadly, see Jennifer Ritterhouse, *Growing Up Jim Crow: How Black and White Southern Children Learned Race* (Chapel Hill: University of North Carolina Press, 2006).

14. The intensity of anti-Italian discrimination in New Orleans likely made assimilation a less viable option for Italians than Jews, thereby limiting Italians' ability to differentiate themselves from their black neighbors. While anti-Jewish discrimination existed as well, the fact that many Jews had ascended into—or at least approached—the upper echelons of New Orleans society suggests that working-class Jews could aspire to follow a similar trajectory. See, for instance, Walda Katz Fishman and Richard L. Zweigenhaft, "Jews and the New Orleans Economic and Social Elites," *Jewish Social Studies* 44, no. 3/4 (Summer–Autumn 1982): 291–98; John V. Baiamonte Jr., "'Who Killa de Chief' Revisited: The Hennessey Assassination and Its Aftermath, 1890–1991," *Louisiana History* 33, no. 2 (Spring 1992): 117–46. On the different roles public education played in Jewish and Italian immigrants' social structure and mobility, see Joel Perlmann, *Ethnic Differences: Schooling and Social Structure Among the Irish, Italians, Jews, and Blacks in an American City, 1880–1935* (New York: Cambridge University Press, 1988) and Thomas Kessner, *The Golden Door: Italian and Jewish Immigrant Mobility in New York, 1880–1915* (New York: Oxford University Press, 1977).

15. See, for instance, OPSB Minutes, 2 July 1913, 8 August 1913, 27 August 1913, 15 June 1914, 26 January 1915, and 23 March 1917.

16. Charles B. Rousséve, *The Negro in Louisiana: Aspects of His History and His Literature* (New Orleans: Xavier University Press, 1937), 130–32 (quote is on 130); Arnold R. Hirsch, "Simply a Matter of Black and White: The Transformation of Race and Politics in Twentieth-Century New Orleans," in *Creole New Orleans: Race and Americanization*, ed. Arnold R. Hirsch and Joseph Logsdon (Baton Rouge: Louisiana State University Press, 1992), 264.

17. *Annual Report of the New Orleans Public Schools of the Parish of Orleans*, 1913–1914, box 6, Annual Reports, OPSB-147; OPSB Minutes, 9 July 1914 and 13 August 1914. Fisk served 685 students and its nearby annex, known as Fisk Branch, served another 262.

18. OPSB Minutes, 13 August 1914.

19. OPSB Minutes, 11 November 1915 and 19 July 1914 (the quote is from these minutes).

20. A. E. Perkins, ed., *Who's Who in Colored Louisiana* (Baton Rouge: Douglas Loan Co., 1930), 61, 137–38; DeVore and Logsdon, *Crescent City Schools*, 179, 182; DeVore, *Defying Jim Crow*, 72–76.

21. DeVore, *Defying Jim Crow*, 76, 153–55 (quote on 76).

22. "Walter L. Cohen, Negro Political Leader, Is Dead," *Times-Picayune,* 30 December 1930, 3; *Gardner's New Orleans Directory for 1861* (New Orleans: Charles Gardner, 1861), 107; U.S. Census, 1860, New Orleans, La., Population, National Archives Microfilm Series M653, Reel 417, accessed via Heritage Quest Online; Sanborn Map Company, *Insurance Maps of New Orleans, Louisiana,* vol. 2, 1885, sheets O-A, 38-B; Campanella, *Geographies of New Orleans,* 265.

23. *L'Abbeille,* 11 October 1884, 1, col. 5; *Gardner's New Orleans Directory for 1861* (New Orleans: Charles Gardner, 1861), 61; U.S. Census, 1860, Natchez, Ms., Population, NAMS M653, Reel 577; U.S. Census, 1910, New Orleans, La., Population, NAMS T-624, Reel 521, U.S. Census, 1920, New Orleans, La., Population, NAMS T-625, Reel 620, all accessed via Heritage Quest Online; *New Orleans Daily Creole,* 12 August 1856, 2; *Daily Picayune,* 1 April 1853, 1; *Daily Picayune,* 22 November 1852, 4, col. 4. The latter article was an ad Bingaman placed for a runaway slave named Stephen. Considering Bingaman's description of Stephen as "a very light mulatto, with blue eyes and brownish hair," it is quite possible that he was Amelia's brother. Henrietta Bingaman, a free woman of color who lived several houses down from Amelia in New Orleans in 1861, was likely a relative as well.

24. The 1861 City Directory listed Bernard Cohen's residence as 72 Marais Street and Amelia Bingaman's as 56 Gasquet. Bingaman Cohen's 1884 obituary, which was prepared by her family, noted that her "body was exposed for viewing at No. 72 ½ Marais Street, between Bienville and Conti." See *Gardner's New Orleans Directory for 1861,* 61, 107; *L'Abbeille,* 11 October 1884, 1, col. 5 (the translation from French is my own).

25. Joseph Logsdon and Caryn Cossé Bell, "The Americanization of Black New Orleans, 1850–1900," in *Creole New Orleans: Race and Americanization,* ed. Arnold R. Hirsch and Joseph Logsdon (Baton Rouge: Louisiana State University Press, 1992), 207–15.

26. Donald E. DeVore, "The Rise from the Nadir: Black New Orleans Between the Wars" (Master's thesis, University of New Orleans, 1983), 17–18; Rousséve, *The Negro in Louisiana,* 130–32; Logsdon and Cossé Bell, "Americanization of Black New Orleans," 201–2, 250–51; Caryn Cossé Bell, *Afro-Creole Protest Tradition* (Baton Rouge: Louisiana State University Press, 1997), 268–69, 272–74.

27. Logsdon and Cossé Bell, "Americanization of Black New Orleans," 251–61 (Pinchback is quoted on 252).

28. Ibid.

29. Robert Meyer Jr., *Names Over New Orleans Schools* (New Orleans: Namesake Press, 1975), 44; Perkins, *Who's Who in Colored Louisiana,* 113; Booker T. Washington to William Howard Taft [New York City], 23 April 1909, and Robert Elijah Jones to Booker T. Washington, New Orleans, 3 June 1909, in *The Booker T. Washington Papers,* ed. Louis R. Harlan and Raymond W. Smock, vol. 10, 1909–11 (Urbana: University of Illinois Press, 1981), 91, 129–30 (for quote); Rousséve, "The Negro in Louisiana," 131. For an example of white New Orleanians extending the honorific "Captain" to Cohen, see "New Orleans Sends Heartfelt Prayers," *Times-Picayune,* 8 September 1901, 3; *Soards' New Orleans City Directory for 1890* (New Orleans: L. Soards, 1890), 249.

30. DeVore, "Rise from the Nadir," 18; Theodore Roosevelt to Booker T. Washington, 8 June 1904, quoted in *The Booker T. Washington Papers,* ed. Harlan and Smock, vol. 7, 1903–4 (Urbana: University of Illinois Press, 1977), 531 n. 1; Emmett Jay Scott to Booker T. Washington, Washington, 1 April 1909, in *The Booker T. Washington Papers,* ed. Harlan and Smock, vol. 10, 1909–11

(Urbana: University of Illinois Press, 1981), 80–81. On Washington's involvement in protecting Cohen's appointment and combating the Lily White movement in Louisiana, see *The Booker T. Washington Papers*, vol. 7, 180–81, 455, 497–98, 531, and *The Booker T. Washington Papers*, ed. Harlan and Smock, vol. 8, 1904–6 (Urbana: University of Illinois Press, 1979), 10, 103.

31. DeVore, "Rise from the Nadir," 20; Perkins, *Who's Who in Colored Louisiana*, 113; Fairclough, *Race and Democracy*, 18–19. On the waning days of the Republican Party in nineteenth-century Louisiana, see Michael Perman, *Struggle for Mastery: Disfranchisement in the South, 1888–1908* (Chapel Hill: University of North Carolina Press, 2001), chap. 7.

32. Hirsch, "A Matter of Black and White," 264. On the complicity of elite members of oppressed groups in systems of apartheid, see N. D. B. Connolly, *A World More Concrete: Real Estate and the Remaking of Jim Crow South Florida* (Chicago: University of Chicago Press, 2014); John W. Cell, *The Highest Stage of White Supremacy: The Origins of Segregation in South Africa and the American South* (Cambridge: Cambridge University Press, 1982), 19.

33. OPSB Minutes, 13 August 1914; *Directory of the Public Schools of New Orleans, Session 1930–31*, box 4, School Directories, OPSB-147.

34. OPSB Minutes, 13 August 1914; James Anderson, *The Education of Blacks in the South, 1860–1935* (Chapel Hill: University of North Carolina Press, 1988), especially chap. 2 and pp. 213–21. Anderson's lengthy discussion of the failed effort to build an industrial high school for blacks in New Orleans during the 1930s notes black opposition to this plan but not the noticeable amount of black support it also received. This oversight was likely the result of both his strict reliance on sources produced by white philanthropists, journalists, and school officials and his failure to consider this episode in the context of local blacks' longer struggle for secondary education. Had he looked at the black-owned *Louisiana Weekly* or the numerous appearances of black New Orleanians before the school board recorded in the board minutes, he would have discovered a different narrative. For an alternate interpretation of the black movement for secondary education and the trade school debate, see DeVore and Logsdon, *Crescent City Schools*, 189–98, and DeVore, *Defying Jim Crow*, 145–50.

35. Gwendolyn P. Watts, "Against All Odds: McDonogh 35 High School, 1917–1937" (Master's thesis, University of New Orleans, 1998), 5–6; DeVore and Logsdon, *Crescent City Schools*, 189; Perkins, *Who's Who in Colored Louisiana*, 94 (for the Clark quote); John B. Alberts, "Black Catholic Schools: The Josephite Parishes of New Orleans During the Jim Crow Era," *U.S. Catholic Historian* 12, no. 1 (Winter 1994): 89.

36. OPSB Minutes, 2 July 1913.

37. OPSB Minutes, 8 August 1913.

38. Joseph S. Schwertz Jr., "The History of Warren Easton Boys' High School" (Master's thesis, Tulane University, 1941), 72–73; Ethel L. Walker, "History of the Sophie B. Wright High School" (Master's thesis, Tulane University, 1939), 85; "Public Works," *Daily Picayune*, 9 February 1912; "Schools Open with 1000 More Pupils Than at Start Last Year," *New Orleans Item*, 24 September 1913; DeVore and Logsdon, *Crescent City Schools*, 131–34, 191.

39. Charles Melden, "A Modern Exodus," *Southwestern Christian Advocate*, 18 October 1917, 6–7. Melden noted that the board spent $1,750,000 on white school buildings versus $35,000 on black ones in the five years preceding 1917.

40. OPSB Minutes, 26 January 1915; New Orleans Public Schools, *School Directory, 1910–1911*, box 1, School Directories, OPSB-147.

41. "New Institute for Negroes is Ready," *New Orleans States,* 24 September 1916, 16.

42. Janice Richard Johnson, "Leland University in New Orleans, 1870–1915" (PhD diss., University of New Orleans, 1996), 186–87; Robert J. Cangelosi Jr., "Residential Parks," in *New Orleans Architecture, Vol. 7: The University District,* ed. Robert J. Cangelosi Jr. and Dorothy G. Schlesinger (Gretna, LA: Pelican Publishing, 1997), 88–89.

43. "Negroes Emphasize Need of High School," *New Orleans Item,* 19 May 1916.

44. James Bennett, *Religion and the Rise of Jim Crow in New Orleans* (Princeton, NJ: Princeton University Press, 2005), 206, 221–22 (first quote on 221; second quote on 222).

45. Ibid., 222–25. Bureau of the Census, *Population and Housing: Statistics for Census Tracts, New Orleans, LA* (Washington, DC: Government Printing Office, 1941), iv, 5.

46. Watts, "Against All Odds," 7; "Negroes Ask Better School Facilities," *Times-Picayune,* 13 May 1917, A-10. The ministerial alliance quote is from "Negro High School," *Times-Picayune,* 1 August 1917, 13 (emphasis added). See also DeVore and Logsdon, *Crescent City Schools,* 191, on the persistence of black petitioners and the restoration of grades seven and eight. Coghill is listed as the Bayou Road principal in *School Directories,* 1910–1920, box 1, School Directories, OPSB-147.

47. "Budget Adopted for Local Schools Reaches $1,202,978," *Times-Picayune,* 28 July 1917, 11; "The School Board Budget," *Times-Picayune,* 30 July 1917, 6; DeVore and Logsdon, *Crescent City Schools,* 191; DeVore, *Defying Jim Crow,* 141.

48. Long, *Great Southern Babylon,* 217; Sanborn Map Company, *Insurance Maps of New Orleans, Louisiana,* vol. 3, 1908, sheets 263, 266, 268; Ordinance 4485 C.C.S., July 17, 1917; Ordinance 13,485 C.S., July 6, 1897, both available at City Archives, Louisiana Division, New Orleans Public Library (cited hereinafter as NOPL).

49. "Want M'Donogh 13 to Remain School for White Pupils," *Times-Picayune,* 7 September 1917.

50. OPSB Minutes, 24 August 1917.

51. For a comparison of the buildings, see OPSB Minutes, 9 July 1914.

52. "Parents Protest School No. 13 Change, Board Asked to Retain White Status," *New Orleans Item,* 27 August 1917; "Board Withholds Action in McDonogh School Case," *New Orleans Item,* 29 August 1917; "M'Donogh Fate to be Known Soon," *New Orleans Daily States,* 8 September 1917; Sanborn Map Company, *Insurance Maps of New Orleans, Louisiana,* vol. 3, 1908, sheets 259–60, available at http://sanborn.umi.com/la/3376/dateid-000009.htm?CCSI=3057.

53. *John Fitzpatrick et al. v. The Board of Directors of the Public Schools for the City of New Orleans,* Orleans Parish Civil District Court, Division D, Docket 5, Case No. 121508, City Archives, Louisiana Division, NOPL.

54. I was able to identify forty-two protestors by name, and at least thirty-two of these appeared to be Jewish, based upon their last name, nativity, and/or mother tongue as recorded by census enumerators. While the census did not record religious affiliation, nativity categories such as Russ-Yiddish, Aust-Yiddish, or Russia-Hebrew (which denoted both place of birth and mother tongue) served as proxy identifiers for Jews. Protestors' names come from "Board Asked to Retain White Status," *New Orleans Item,* 27 August 1917; "Board Withholds Action in McDonogh School Case," *New Orleans Item,* 29 August 1917; "Protest Against M'Donogh No. 13 as Negro School," *Times-Picayune,* 29 August 1917; "M'Donogh 13 Fate to Be Known Soon," *New Orleans Daily States,* 8 September 1917; OPSB Minutes, 14 September 1917; and *Fitzpatrick v. Board.* Nativity and mother tongue data are from U.S. Census, 1910, New Orleans, La., Population, and U.S.

Census, 1920, New Orleans, La., Population. On Census questionnaires and categories, see U.S. Census Bureau, "Measuring America: The Decennial Censuses from 1790 to 2000," April 2002, available at http://www.census.gov/prod/2002pubs/p0102-ma.pdf.

55. U.S. Census, 1910, New Orleans, La., Population; U.S. Census, 1920, New Orleans, La., Population; Ralph Blumenthal, "Digging Up Satchmo's Roots in the City that Spawned Him," *New York Times*, 15 April 2000, section E, 1; Brothers, *Louis Armstrong's New Orleans*, 225. For the sake of consistency, I rely upon census categories when identifying an individual's place of birth. These categories, however, are notoriously unreliable. For instance, while the 1910 Census identifies Rosa Rubenstein's place of birth as Austria, her great-grandson informed me that she came from Kiev, which was then part of Russia. Communication with David Willenzik, March 16, 2017.

56. *Fitzpatrick et al. v. The Board of Directors of the Public Schools for the City of New Orleans.* John McDonogh also made a similar bequest for the benefit of poor children in his native Baltimore. See DeVore and Logsdon, *Crescent City Schools*, 33 (for quote).

57. *Fitzpatrick et al. v. The Board of Directors of the Public Schools for the City of New Orleans.*

58. Emily Lieb, "How Segregated Schools Built Segregated Cities," *CityLab*, 2 February 2017, http://www.citylab.com/housing/2017/02/how-segregated-schools-built-segregated-cities/515373/ (first quote); Carl H. Nightingale, "The Transnational Context of Early Twentieth-Century American Urban Segregation," *Journal of Social History* 39, no. 3 (Spring 2006): 674; Mitchell Duneier, *Ghetto: The Invention of a Place, the History of an Idea* (New York: Farrar, Straus, and Giroux, 2016), 33; Hilary J. Moss, *Schooling Citizens: The Struggle for African American Education in Antebellum America* (Chicago: University of Chicago Press, 2009), 139–47 (quote on 139–40).

59. "Parents Protest School No. 13 Change; Board Asked to Retain White Status," *New Orleans Item*, 27 August 1917.

60. Mrs. P. [Sophia] Jacobson, Letter to the Editor, *Daily States*, 30 August 1917.

61. "Board Withholds Action in McDonogh School Case," *New Orleans Item*, 29 August 1917; "Protest Against M'Donogh No. 13 As Negro School," *Times Picayune*, 29 August 1917. The quote is from the *Picayune* article.

62. U.S. Census, 1910, New Orleans, La., Population; U.S. Census, 1920, New Orleans, La., Population; Sanborn Map Company, *Insurance Maps of New Orleans, Louisiana*, vol. 3, 1908, sheets 259–60.

63. *Fitzpatrick et al. v. The Board of Directors of the Public Schools for the City of New Orleans.*

64. My thinking here has been influenced by Ritterhouse, *Growing Up Jim Crow*, 15.

65. Arnold R. Hirsch, "With or Without Jim Crow: Black Residential Segregation in the United States," in *Urban Policy in Twentieth-Century America*, ed. Arnold R. Hirsch and Raymond A. Mohl (New Brunswick, NJ: Rutgers University Press), 71; David M. P. Freund, *Colored Property: State Policy & White Racial Politics in Suburban America* (Chicago: University of Chicago Press, 2007), 45–87.

66. "Zones of Quiet Will Curb Noise," *Times-Picayune*, 11 February 1917; *New Orleans Item*, 12 April 1917; "L. R. & N. Submits Map and Statements in Plea for New Depot Permit," *New Orleans Daily States*, 26 March 1917; "L. R. & N to Get Depot Permit, is Forecast," *New Orleans Daily States*, 17 April 1917; "Illinois Central's New Freight Terminals Inspected by Public," *Times-Picayune*, 1 June 1911; Sanborn Map Company, *Insurance Maps of New Orleans, Louisiana*, vol. 3, 1908, sheets 258–61, 268, available at http://sanborn.umi.com/la/3376/dateid-000009

.htm?CCSI=3057, accessed 16 December 2011. To gauge the scale of the railroad terminals and their impact on the neighborhood, I compared the 1908 Sanborn maps with the updates Sanborn pasted over the 1908 base maps in 1934. See Sanborn Map Company, *Insurance Maps of New Orleans, Louisiana,* vol. 3, 1908, corrected to 1934, sheets 258–61, 268, Southeastern Architectural Archive, Special Collections Division, Tulane University.

67. "L. R. & N. Road Seeks Franchise for New Station," *Times-Picayune,* 26 March 1917.

68. "L. R. & N. Submits Map and Statement in Plea for New Depot Permit," *New Orleans Daily States,* 26 March 1917.

69. L. R. & N. Public Statement, *New Orleans Item,* 12 April 1917.

70. Ibid.

71. "L. R. & N. to Get Depot Permit, is Forecast, *Daily States,* 17 April 1917 (emphasis added).

72. Ibid.

73. Ibid.

74. "The L. R. and N. Withdrawal," *Daily States,* 2 May 1917; "City Commissioner Will Not Consider Edenborn Letter," *Times-Picayune,* 13 May 1917.

75. Brian Gary Ettinger, "John Fitzpatrick and the Limits of Working-Class Politics in New Orleans, 1892–1896," *Louisiana History* 26, no. 4 (Autumn 1985): 341–67 (esp. 341, 347–48, 367); Edward F. Haas, "John Fitzpatrick and Political Continuity in New Orleans, 1896–1899," *Louisiana History* 22, no. 1 (Winter 1981): 7–29; "Administrations of the Mayors of New Orleans: John Fitzpatrick (1844–1919)," Louisiana Division, NOPL, http://www.neworleanspubliclibrary .org/~nopl/info/louinfo/admins/fitzpatrick.htm; *Fitzpatrick et al. v. The Board of Directors of the Public Schools for the City of New Orleans.*

76. "Board Withholds Action in McDonogh School Case," *New Orleans Item,* 29 August 1917; "Protest Against M'Donogh No. 13 as Negro School," 29 August 1917, *Times-Picayune.*

77. "M'Donogh 13 Fate to be Known Soon," *New Orleans Daily States,* 8 September 1917.

78. *Fitzpatrick et al. v. The Board of Directors of the Public Schools for the City of New Orleans.*

79. A Mother, Letter to the Editor, *Times-Picayune,* 28 August 1917.

80. "Parents Protest School No. 13 Change, Board Asked to Retain White Status," *New Orleans Item,* 27 August 1917.

81. "McDonogh 13 Will Be Colored School," *Daily States,* 15 September 1917. Showcasing the purple prose of early twentieth-century journalism, this article provides additional examples of the gendered dimensions of the men's and women's protest. Describing a school board where protestors challenged the conversion, the *Daily States* wrote, "The clamor of two hundred children, the pleas of *mothers* to 'give us back old No. 13'; arguments of *father*s that their property would be ruined and the threat of an impending civil suit failed to move the Orleans Parish School Board Friday night" (emphasis added).

82. The *States* reported that "no negroes attended the meeting" on September 7, and the minutes from the September 14th meeting do not mention any African Americans appearing before the board to discuss McDonogh No. 13. See "M'Donogh 13 Fate to Be Known Soon," *Daily States,* 8 September 1917, and OPSB Minutes, 14 September 1917.

83. F. P. Ricard, Letter to the Editor, *Item,* 10 September 1917. On Ricard, see E. A. Perkins, *Who's Who in Colored Louisiana,* 138.

84. Partly due to redevelopment projects that targeted the former "black Storyville" and Rampart Street area, Dryades Street between Phillip Street and Howard Avenue became the city's

premier black shopping district following World War II. Jews continued to operate many of these stores after the war, as they had for many years before it. In the spring of 1960, black civic leaders formed the Consumers' League to protest discriminatory hiring practices at retail stores. They first targeted Dryades Street since blacks accounted for up to 80 percent of sales yet held only about one-third of the jobs, primarily in positions no higher than janitor. The Consumers' League started its campaign with a two-thousand-person march followed by a boycott that crippled businesses during the normally bustling period before Easter. See Campanella, *Geographies of New Orleans*, 276–78; Liva Baker, *The Second Battle of New Orleans: The Hundred-Year Struggle to Integrate the Schools* (New York: Harper Collins, 1996), 326–27; Kim Lacy Rogers, *Righteous Lives: Narratives of the New Orleans Civil Rights Movement* (New York: New York University Press, 1993), 67–69; and Walter C. Stern, "Black, White, Silver, and Blue: Race and Desegregation at New Orleans' Fortier High, 1960–1975" (Master's thesis, Tulane University, 2010), 12.

85. OPSB Minutes, 14 September 1917; "M'Donogh No. 13 Made Negro School by Board," *New Orleans Item*, 15 September 1917; "M'Donogh 13 Will Be Colored School," *New Orleans Daily States*, 15 September 1917. The quote is from "Board Refuses to Change Stand on M'Donogh 13," *Times-Picayune*, 15 September 1917.

86. James K. Hogue, *Uncivil War: Five New Orleans Street Battles and the Rise and Fall of Radical Reconstruction* (Baton Rouge: Louisiana State University Press, 2006), 127–38.

87. OPSB Minutes, 14 September 1917 (source of quote); *Times-Picayune*, 15 September 1917. On Spearing's professional background, see *Soards' New Orleans City Directory, 1916* (New Orleans: Soards Directory Co., 1916), 1501. The listings of real estate sales in the *Times-Picayune* are littered with transactions in which Spearing was involved as an attorney or notary. He is also listed as an attorney for homestead associations in "Homestead Men Studying Bills for Legislature," *Times-Picayune*, 26 March 1922, sec. 5, p. 1.

88. OPSB Minutes, 14 September 1917.

89. Ibid.

90. DeVore and Logsdon, *Crescent City Schools*, 194.

91. Watts, "Against All Odds," 7–9; *The Roneagle* (McDonogh 35 Yearbook), 1928, 13, 19, McDonogh 35 High School Library; DeVore and Logsdon, *Crescent City Schools*, 212; "Scope and Contents, George Longe Papers, 1849–1971," Amistad Research Center, available http://www.amistadresearchcenter.org/archon/index.php?p=accessions/accession&id=547. For a list of some of McDonogh 35's most prominent graduates, see Watts, "Against All Odds," 40–45.

92. Interview with Herbert Melvin Cappie and Ruth Irene Cappie (btvct07063), interviewed by Michele Mitchell, New Orleans, LA, July 2, 1994, Behind the Veil Digital Collection. See also the Behind the Veil Interview with Delores Mary Aaron (btvct07060), interviewed by Michele Mitchell, New Orleans (La.), June 30, 1994. For a more critical take on black high school teachers in Jim Crow New Orleans, see the Behind the Veil Interview with Emmett Cheri (btvct07064), interviewed by Kate Ellis, New Orleans (La.), June 23, 1994. Cheri describes the discrimination he faced on account of his dark skin while in high school in the late 1930s through the early 1940s, though he does not specify whether he faced this discrimination at McDonogh 35 or at Albert Wicker, the school he attended through tenth grade. For a discussion of McDonogh No. 35's early academic success that corroborates Cappie's and Aaron's personal recollections, see DeVore, *Defying Jim Crow*, 141–43. For accounts of academic excellence at segregated African American high schools outside of New Orleans, see Vanessa Siddle Walker, *Their Highest Potential: An African*

American School Community in the Segregated South (Chapel Hill: University of North Carolina Press, 1996); Alison Stewart, *First Class; The Legacy of Dunbar, America's First Black High School* (Chicago: Lawrence Hill Books, 2013). On tracking and class-based inequities in black and white schools during the Jim Crow era, see Beverly Jacques Anderson, *Cherished Memories: Snapshots of Life and Lessons from a 1950s Creole Village* (Bloomington, IN: iUniverse, 2011), 143; DeVore and Logsdon, *Crescent City Schools*, 141–43, 172–78; Adam Fairclough, "The Costs of *Brown:* Black Teachers and School Integration," *Journal of American History* 91, no. 1 (June 2004): 46.

93. The Greater New Orleans Community Data Center writes that the Tremé neighborhood experienced "more destruction of property than in any other part of town." But unlike Louis Armstrong's childhood neighborhood, much of early twentieth-century Tremé remains standing today. See Greater New Orleans Community Data Center, "Tremé/Lafitte Neighborhood Snapshot," http://www.gnocdc.org/orleans/4/42/snapshot.html. Redevelopment and residential displacement within Tremé is taken up in chapter 4.

94. Sanborn Map Company, *Insurance Maps of New Orleans, Louisiana*, vol. 3, 1908, sheets 257–68; Sanborn Map Company, *Insurance Maps of New Orleans, Louisiana*, vol. 3, 1908, corrected to 1934, sheets 257–68, Southeastern Architectural Archive; New Orleans City Planning and Zoning Commission, "New Orleans, Louisiana, District Map & Key to Official District Maps," July 1930, box 126, Record Group 195, Records of the Federal Home Loan Bank Board, Home Owners' Loan Corporation, Records Relating to the City Survey File, 1935–40, National Archives II (cited hereinafter as RG 195, National Archives II); Long, "Poverty is the New Prostitution," 801. For more on the city's comprehensive zoning ordinance and neighborhood-specific zoning, see Carol McMichael Reese, "The Once and Future New Orleans of Planners Milton Medary and Harland Bartholomew, 1920–1960," in *New Orleans Under Reconstruction: The Crisis of Planning*, ed. Carol McMichael Reese, Michael Sorkin, and Anthony Fontenot (London: Verso, 2014); and "Finding Aid for City Planning and Zoning Commission, Records Relating to the Creation of the 1929 Comprehensive Zoning Ordinance," City Archive, NOPL, http://www.neworleanspublic library.org/~nopl/inv/zone1929.htm.

95. Sanborn Map Company, *Insurance Maps of New Orleans, Louisiana*, vol. 3, 1940, 206–8, 212, and *Insurance Maps of New Orleans, Louisiana*, vol. 1a, sheets 1a–4a, microfilm roll 9, Historic New Orleans Collection (HNOC), 96–37-L; Nirenstein's National Realty Map Company, "Business Section, City of New Orleans," 1947, HNOC, 1976.92.1; Michael E. Crutcher Jr., *Tremé: Race and Place in a New Orleans Neighborhood* (Athens: University of Georgia Press, 2010), 14; Edward F. Haas, *DeLesseps S. Morrison and the Image of Reform: New Orleans Politics, 1946–1961* (Baton Rouge: Louisiana State University Press, 1974), 58; Arnold R. Hirsch, "Race and Renewal in the Cold War South: New Orleans, 1947–1968," in *The American Planning Tradition: Culture and Policy*, ed. Robert Fishman (Washington, DC: Woodrow Wilson Center Press, 2000), 228, 238 n. 31 (228 for Rousseau quote).

96. Robert O. Self, *American Babylon: Race and the Struggle for Postwar Oakland* (Princeton, NJ: Princeton University Press, 2003), 138–40; Ansley T. Erickson, *Making the Unequal Metropolis: School Desegregation and Its Limits* (Chicago: University of Chicago Press, 2016), 39.

97. *Annual Report of the New Orleans Public Schools, 1920–21*, "Original Enrollment for the Session," folded chart following p. 16, p. 109, box 9, Annual Reports, OPSB-147.

98. OPSB Minutes, 25 February 1921 and 11 March 1921; *Annual Report of the New Orleans Public Schools, 1920–21*, p. 11.

99. OPSB Minutes, 24 June 1921.

100. OPSB Minutes, 22 August 1924.

101. OPSB Minutes, 22 September 1922 and 27 October 1922.

102. U.S. Census, New Orleans, La., Population, 1910–1930, NAMS T-624, Reel 520, NAMS T-625, reel 618, and NAMS 5163, Reel 21. Compilation and analysis by the author.

103. Amy E. Hillier, "Residential Security Maps and Neighborhood Appraisals: The Home Owners' Loan Corporation and the Case of Philadelphia," *Social Science History* 29, no. 2 (Summer 2005): 207–33; Hillier, "Redlining and the Home Owners' Loan Corporation," *Journal of Urban History* 29, no. 4 (May 2003): 394–420; "Real Estate Area Map, New Orleans, Louisiana" [1936], pp. 1, 9, box 126, RG 195, National Archives II; Residential Security Map, New Orleans, LA, 1936; Residential Security Map, New Orleans, LA, 1939, both in box 126, RG 195, National Archives II.

104. "Real Estate Area Map, New Orleans, Louisiana" [1936], pp. 1, 9, box 126, RG 195, National Archives II; Division of Research & Statistics, Federal Home Loan Bank Board, "Summary of Economic, Real Estate and Mortgage Survey and Security Area Descriptions of New Orleans, Louisiana," 28 April 1939, New Orleans, LA #2 folder, box 88, RG 195, National Archives II.

105. Division of Research & Statistics, Federal Home Loan Bank Board, "Summary of Economic, Real Estate and Mortgage Survey and Security Area Descriptions of New Orleans, Louisiana," 28 April 1939, New Orleans, LA #2 folder, box 88, RG 195, National Archives II; Andrew Highsmith, *Demolition Means Progress: Flint, Michigan, and the Fate of the American Metropolis* (Chicago: University of Chicago Press, 2015), 44–45.

106. Reynolds, *Machine Politics in New Orleans, 1897–1926* (New York: Columbia University Press, 1936), 230–31.

107. Reynolds, *Machine Politics*, 108–37; Landphair, "'For the Good of the Community,'" 37–39; Rick Ginsberg, "Boss Behrman Reforms the Schools: The 1912 New Orleans School Reform," in *Southern Cities, Southern Schools*, ed. Rick Ginsberg and David Plank (New York: Greenwood Press, 1990); DeVore and Logsdon, *Crescent City Schools*, 164–66; Jeffrey Mirel, *The Rise and Fall of an Urban School System, Detroit: 1907–1981*, 2nd edition (Ann Arbor: University of Michigan Press, 1999), 20–27; David Tyack, *The One Best System: A History of American Urban Education* (Cambridge, MA: Harvard University Press, 1974), 126–76.

108. Arnesen, *Waterfront Workers*, 238; Reynolds, *Machine Politics*, 208–16; DeVore and Logsdon, *Crescent City Schools*, 164–66; "New Regulars Take Helm of School Board," *New Orleans Item*, 9 December 1922, 3.

109. On the prominence of civic and commercial elites nationally among urban school reformers, see Tyack, *The One Best System*, 126–98.

110. *Soards' New Orleans City Directory*, 1923 (New Orleans: Soards Directory Co., 1923), 635; *Soards' New Orleans City Directory*, 1921 (New Orleans: Soards Directory Co., 1921), 1579; "Pen Pictures: Men of Louisiana," *Times-Picayune*, 1 September 1917, 10; "Seven Candidates in the Field for School Board Vacancies," *Times-Picayune*, 5 November 1922, 19; "Semi-Annual Financial Statement of the Pyramid Homestead Association," *Times-Picayune*, 13 July 1919, 16-C; "Semi-Annual Financial Statement of the Pyramid Homestead Association," *Times-Picayune*, 15 January 1922, sec. 5, p. 9; 1921 *City Directory*, 1579; "Homestead Men Studying Bills for Legislature," *Times-Picayune*, 26 March 1922, sec. 5, p. 1.

111. *Soards' New Orleans Directory, 1921*, 278, 1082; *Simmons Spice Mill*, January 1916,

22; U.S. Census, New Orleans, La., Population, 1920, NAMS T-625, roll 623, accessed via Heritage Quest.

112. DeVore and Logsdon, *Crescent City Schools*, 361–62; *Soards' New Orleans Directory, 1921*, 1109, 1244; "Sixth Semiannual Statement of the Orleans Homestead Association," *Daily Picayune*, 14 July 1912, 8; "Twenty-Fourth Financial Statement of the Orleans Homestead Association," *Times-Picayune*, 10 July 1921, sec. 7, p. 8.

113. DeVore and Logsdon, *Crescent City Schools*, 360; *Soards' New Orleans City Directory, 1908* (New Orleans: Soards Directory Co., 1908), 595, 634; *Soards' New Orleans City Directory, 1910* (New Orleans: Soards Directory Co., 1910), 1092; *Soards' New Orleans City Directory, 1911* (New Orleans: Soards Directory Co., 1911), 268, 311, 369, 570, 660, 685, 738, 749, 795, 930, 1012, 1154, 1277, and the following pages whose numbers start anew with the section listing individuals by profession: 110, 128, 129, 136, 176; *Soards' New Orleans City Directory, 1916* (New Orleans: Soards Directory Co., 1916), 1501; "Kenner Electric Finally Framed," *Daily Picayune*, 15 October 1913, 5; "Homestead News from Near and Far," *Daily Picayune*, 21 September 1902; "A Splendid Investment," *Daily Picayune*, 28 May 1901, 6; "Homestead Men Studying Bills for Legislature," *Times-Picayune*, 26 March 1922, sec. 5, p. 1; Meyer, *Names Over New Orleans Schools*, 45, 81. For a detailed description of the composition of the ward-based board, see chap. 2.

114. For a list of board members, see DeVore and Logsdon, *Crescent City Schools*, 361–62. Data on occupation compiled from Robert Meyer Jr., *Names Over New Orleans Public Schools* (New Orleans: Namesake Press, 1975), 33, 45, 81, 180; *Soards' New Orleans City Directory, 1912*, 1924; *Soards' New Orleans City Directory, 1914*, 204; *Soards' New Orleans City Directory, 1916*, 1138, 1501, 1502; *Soards' New Orleans City Directory, 1919*, 1109; *Soards' New Orleans City Directory, 1921*, 278, 1082, 1109, 1244, 1520, 1579, 1706; *Soards' New Orleans City Directory, 1922*, 704; *Soards' New Orleans City Directory, 1927*, 687, 1299; *Soards' New Orleans City Directory, 1930*, 664; *Soards' New Orleans City Directory, 1932*, 1099, 1350; *Soards' New Orleans City Directory, 1933*, 680; U.S. Census, New Orleans, La., Population, 1930, NAMS T-626, roll 813, accessed via Heritage Quest; "Mr. Soniat Long Leading Notary in New Orleans," *Times-Picayune*, 20 January 1918, 4; "Perry-Buckley Company," *Times-Picayune*, 10 December 1905, 17; "Valloft & Dreux," *Times-Picayune*, 16 August 1915; "Men Who Preside Over Homesteads," *Times-Picayune*, 4 May 1917, B-3; "Homestead Men Studying Bills for Legislature," *Times-Picayune*, 26 March 1922, sec. 5, p. 1; "Two May Stores Sold, Third in Big Demand," *Daily Picayune*, 3 December 1912, 5; "Pen Pictures: Men of Louisiana," *Times-Picayune*, 1 September 1917, 10; "Seven Candidates in the Field for School Board Vacancies," *Times-Picayune*, 5 November 1922, 19; "Semi-Annual Financial Statement of the Pyramid Homestead Association," *Times-Picayune*, 13 July 1919, 16-C; "Semi-Annual Financial Statement of the Pyramid Homestead Association," *Times-Picayune*, 15 January 1922, sec. 5, p. 9; "Dixie Homestead Association," *Daily Picayune*, 14 February 1912, sec. 2, p. 7.

CHAPTER FOUR

1. McShane reduced the basis for assessing property taxes from 90 to 85 percent of the property value. Donald E. DeVore and Joseph Logsdon, *Crescent City Schools: Public Education in New Orleans, 1841–1991* (Lafayette: University of Southwestern Louisiana Press, 1991), 168; Leslie Gale Parr, *A Will of Her Own: Sarah Towles Reed and the Pursuit of Democracy in Southern Public*

Education (Athens: University of Georgia Press, 1998); *Annual Report of the New Orleans Public Schools of the Parish of Orleans, 1919-1920,* Annual Reports Box 9 and OPSB Minutes, 29 November 1922, both in OPSB-147. On the board's fiscal crisis, see also OPSB Minutes, 8 December, and 13 December 1922.

2. DeVore and Logsdon, *Crescent City Schools,* 200; DeVore, "Race Relations and Community Development," 98.

3. On the dynamics between reform and machine politics in late nineteenth and early twentieth-century New Orleans, see Eric Arnesen, *Waterfront Workers of New Orleans: Race, Class, and Politics, 1863-1923* (New York: Oxford University Press, 1991); George M. Reynolds, *Machine Politics in New Orleans, 1897-1926* (New York: Columbia University Press, 1936); and Edward F. Haas, "Political Continuity in the Crescent City: Toward an Interpretation of New Orleans Politics, 1874-1986," *Louisiana History* 39, no. 1 (Winter 1998): 5-18. On efforts to enforce racial, class, and gender hierarchies through residential segregation ordinances restricting where prostitutes could live, see Alecia P. Long, *The Great Southern Babylon: Sex, Race, and Respectability in New Orleans, 1865-1920* (Baton Rouge: Louisiana State University Press, 2005). Two additional, excellent studies of female political activity in New Orleans during the Progressive Era are Pamela Tyler, *Silk Stockings and Ballot Boxes: Women and Politics in New Orleans, 1920-1960* (Athens: University of Georgia Press, 1996) and Parr, *A Will of Her Own.* While Sarah T. Reed and other female progressives challenged the status quo to a greater extent than male reformers, both Tyler and Parr note that these women operated—and must be understood—within the context of southern norms of respectability. Reed and other female teachers' embrace of unionism and their willingness to challenge male authority, however, distinguished them from Tyler's "silk stocking" activists.

4. On the prominence of civic and commercial elites among Progressive Era school reformers, see David B. Tyack, *The One Best System: A History of American Urban Education* (Cambridge, MA: Harvard University Press, 1974), 126-98. For an examination of white reformers who, like those in New Orleans, viewed segregation as a tool to promote social cohesion, see Andrew R. Highsmith and Ansley T. Erickson, "Segregation as Splitting, Segregation as Joining: Schools, Housing, and the Many Modes of Jim Crow," *American Journal of Education* 121, no. 4 (August 2015): 563-95.

5. Jeanne E. Crombie, "Professor Alcée Fortier, 1856-1914," *Louisiana Historical Quarterly* 55, no. 1 (Winter-Spring 1972): 1-62; Lawrence N. Powell, *The Accidental City: Improvising New Orleans* (Cambridge, MA: Harvard University Press, 2012), 57, 68-69, 73. For an account that downplays the impact of exiled prostitutes upon New Orleans's early development but does not question its early instability, see Erin M. Greenwald, *Marc-Antoine Caillot and the Company of the Indies in Louisiana: Trade in the French Atlantic World* (Baton Rouge: Louisiana State University Press, 2016), 80-86.

6. Crombie, "Professor Alcée Fortier," 2-3; Alcée Fortier, *A History of Louisiana,* vol. 2: *The Spanish Domination and the Cession to the United States, 1769-1803* (New York: Manzi, Joyant & Co., 1904), 246; "Fortier, Miguel (Michel) II," *Dictionary of Louisiana Biography,* http://www.lahistory.org/site23.php; "Jean Michel Fortier," *KnowLA: Encyclopedia of Louisiana,* http://www.knowla.org/image.php?rec=85; Caryn Cossé Bell, *Revolution, Romanticism, and the Afro-Creole Protest Tradition in Louisiana, 1718-1868* (Baton Rouge: Louisiana State University Press, 1997), 32.

7. Crombie, "Professor Alcée Fortier," 4–7; Eliza Ripley, *Social Life in Old New Orleans: Being Recollections of My Girlhood* (New York and London: D. Appleton, 1912), 186, 188–89 (the first quote is on 188 and the second on 186).

8. Crombie, "Professor Alcée Fortier"; "Fortier, Alcée," *Dictionary of Louisiana Biography*, http://www.lahistory.org/site23.php; "Dedicatory Address of George H. Terriberry, Alcée Fortier High School, April 28, 1931," in *Memorial Program, Dedicatory Exercises, Alcée Fortier Boys' High School*, p. 7, Louisiana Reference Collection, NOPL. The quote is from Alcée Fortier, *Louisiana Studies: Literature, Customs and Dialects, History and Education* (New Orleans: F. F. Hansell & Bro., 1894), 4–5; "History Instructor Points out Real Meaning of 'Creole,'" *Times-Picayune*, 23 April 1922, in James J. A. Fortier Scrapbook, folder RG 65 1983.65.57a, box 5, Alcée Fortier Collection (RG 65), Louisiana State Museum. On Alcée Fortier, see also Rien Fertel, *Imagining the Creole City: The Rise of Literary Culture in Nineteenth-Century New Orleans* (Baton Rouge: Louisiana State University Press, 2014).

9. Joseph G. Tregle Jr., "Creoles and Americans," and Joseph Logsdon and Caryn Cossé Bell, "The Americanization of Black New Orleans, 1850–1900," in *Creole New Orleans: Race and Americanization*, ed. Arnold R. Hirsch and Joseph Logsdon (Baton Rouge: Louisiana State University Press, 1992); Berndt Ostendorf, "Creole Cultures and the Process of Creolization: With Special Attention to Louisiana," in *Louisiana Culture from the Colonial Era to Katrina*, ed. John Lowe (Baton Rouge: Louisiana State University Press, 2008), 112–13; Lawrence N. Powell, "Introduction: A Novelist Turns Historian," in *The New Orleans of George Washington Cable: The 1887 Census Office Report*, ed. Lawrence N. Powell (Baton Rouge: Louisiana State University Press, 2008), 9–13; Fertel, *Imagining the Creole City*, chap. 4.

10. "Creole Association," *Times-Democrat*, 18 October 1886, 2, col. 6 (first quote); Alcée Fortier, Letter to the Editor, *Times-Democrat*, 20 October 1886, 8, col. 3 (second quote); Fortier, *Louisiana Studies*, 134; Crombie, "Professor Alcée Fortier," 19–20, 34; Hale, *Making Whiteness: The Culture of Whiteness in the South, 1890–1940* (New York: Pantheon Books, 1998), 45. Fortier's letter was in response to a review of his MLA paper that ran in the *Times-Democrat* earlier that week. See "A Sketch of the Creole Patois," *Times-Democrat*, 17 October 1886, 4, col. 4. Ironically, subsequent historians contradicted Fortier's efforts to dissociate white and black Creole French. Summarizing the work of Gwendolyn Midlo Hall, historian Adam Fairclough wrote that "the type of French that came to be spoken in Louisiana was not simply a modified version of the metropolitan tongue that the French colonists imparted to their slaves, but rather a simplified form of the language fashioned by the slaves themselves and subsequently adopted as a lingua franca. Louisiana Creole, notable for the pleasing musicality of its speech patterns, came to be spoken by many whites as well as by newly imported African slaves." See Adam Fairclough, *Race and Democracy: The Civil Rights Struggle in Louisiana, 1915–1972*, 2nd edition (Athens: University of Georgia Press, 2008), 2.

11. Crombie, "Professor Alcée Fortier," 15; Joe Gray Taylor, *Louisiana Reconstructed, 1863–1877* (Baton Rouge: Louisiana State University Press, 1974), 291–96; James K. Hogue, *Uncivil War: Five New Orleans Street Battles and the Rise and Fall of Radical Reconstruction* (Baton Rouge: Louisiana State University Press, 2006), 127–38; Lawrence N. Powell, "Reinventing Tradition: Liberty Place, Historical Memory, and Silk-Stocking Vigilantism in New Orleans," *Slavery and Abolition: A Journal of Slave and Post-Slave Studies* 20, no. 1 (1999): 129–31, 135, 138, and *passim* (the quote is from p. 138). For the persistence of the Liberty Place myth, see Crombie's 1972

statement that the White League's street battles during Reconstruction "were not the only times Fortier was to carry a gun *in the cause of honesty and justice*" (italics are mine; quote is from p. 15).

12. Crombie, "Professor Alcée Fortier," 17, 26; Powell, "Reinventing Tradition," 136–38 (the *Times-Democrat* is quoted on p. 138).

13. Crombie, "Professor Alcée Fortier," 31–32 (first quote is on 32); James J. A. Fortier, "I Remember When I Was a Boy," undated news clipping, James J. A. Fortier Scrapbook, folder RG 65 1983.65.57a, box 5, Alcée Fortier Collection (RG 65), Louisiana State Museum.

14. Reynolds, *Machine Politics*, 214; "Outline of the Organization and Work of the Public School Alliance of New Orleans, 1905–1909," 1–6, 15–16, Education. Public School Alliance folder, Ephemera Collection, LaRC; Delwyn Bonds, "Career of Mr. James Fortier is Brilliant," *Silver and Blue*, 18 March 1932, Lusher Charter School Library (cited hereinafter as LCS). For additional evidence of James Fortier's private school attendance, see "Activity Among the Southern Colleges," *Times-Picayune*, 8 February 1902; "News from Southern Colleges," *Times-Picayune*, 5 December 1903; "Elocution Contest," *Times-Picayune*, 6 May 1905. These articles indicate that James Fortier was a senior at Jesuit in 1905. Fortier's graduation from Tulane University four years later makes it unlikely that the James Fortier mentioned as attending Jesuit was different from the James J. A. Fortier who became school board president. Fortier received a liberal arts degree from Tulane in 1909 and an LLB in Law in 1912. Lori Shexnayder, Assistant University Archivist at Tulane, confirmed Fortier's graduation dates in an e-mail to the author, 6 June 2013.

15. OPSB Minutes, 12 January 1923 (italics are my own); James Fortier, ed., *Carpet-Bag Misrule in Louisiana: The Tragedy of The Reconstruction Era Following the War Between the States* (New Orleans: Louisiana State Museum, 1938). The pamphlet's second subtitle also deserves mention: "Louisiana's Part in Maintaining White Supremacy in the South." For an example of James and Alcée Fortier's shared vision of the Battle of Liberty Place, see the father's description of it in his *History of Louisiana*. His tribute to the White League dead in particular captured the white commemoration of the fight that would persist into and beyond his son's generation. "The victory was dearly bought," the elder Fortier wrote, "by the death of heroic citizens, whose names have been engraved on the monument erected to them in 1891 at Liberty Place, on the spot made sacred by the blood of martyrs who fell in defense of the freedom and honor of Louisiana." See Fortier, *A History of Louisiana*, vol. 4: *The American Domination*, part 2: *1861–1908* (New York: Manzi, Joyant, 1904), 153–54. In 2017, the city removed a monument commemorating the White League and the Battle of Liberty Place from public property following a protracted battle. During the 1990s, a lawsuit blocked a previous attempt to remove the monument from public view. See Jeff Adelson, "New Orleans' Battle of Liberty Place Monument Can Come Down, Judge Says," *New Orleans Advocate*, 8 March 2017, http://www.theadvocate.com/new_orleans/news/politics/article_db2818ac-045e-11e7-b65d-1311ddf0e635.html; Richard Fausset, "Confederate Monuments Fall, and Tempers Flare," *New York Times*, 8 May 2017, A1.

16. Hale, *Making Whiteness*, 79–81 (quotes on 80 and 81); W. E. B. Du Bois, *Black Reconstruction in America, An Essay Toward a History of the Part Which Black Folk Played in the Attempt to Reconstruct Democracy in America, 1860–1880* (New York: Harcourt, Brace, 1935; reprint, Cleveland and New York: Meridian Books, 1969), 711–29 (page citations are to the reprint edition).

17. David W. Blight, *Race and Reunion: The Civil War in American Memory* (Cambridge, MA: The Belknap Press of Harvard University Press, 2001), 3–5, 60–63, 338–97; Du Bois, *Black Reconstruction*, 723 (for quote).

18. *Directory of the Public Schools of New Orleans, La., Session 1910–1911*, Box 1, School Directories Series, OPSB-147; DeVore, "Race Relations and Community Development: The Education of Blacks in New Orleans, 1862–1960" (PhD diss., Louisiana State University, 1989), 95–96; Campbell Gibson and Kay Jung, *Historical Census Statistics On Population Totals By Race, 1790 to 1990, and By Hispanic Origin, 1970 to 1990, For Large Cities And Other Urban Places In The United States*, U.S. Census Bureau Population Division, Working Paper No. 76 (Washington, DC: U.S. Census Bureau, 2005), Table 19.

19. DeVore, "Race Relations and Community Development," 95–96 (the 1910 school board minutes are quoted on 95); School Board Minutes, 12 January 1914 (Wegmann quote); School Board Minutes, 16 February 1914; *Soards' New Orleans Directory for 1912* (New Orleans: Soards Directory Co., 1912), 1159.

20. U.S. Census, 1910, New Orleans, La., Population, NAMS T-624, Reel 521, U.S. Census, 1920, New Orleans, La., Population, NAMS T-625, Reel 620, both accessed via Heritage Quest Online.

21. "Hughes Site for Colored School," *Times-Picayune*, 6 February 1914 (both quotes); School Board Minutes, 12 January 1914.

22. "Hughes Site for Colored School," *Times-Picayune*, 6 February 1914 (Wexler quote); *Soards' New Orleans Directory for 1912* (New Orleans: Soards Directory Co., 1912), 1244; DeVore and Logsdon, *Crescent City Schools*, 200; DeVore, "Race Relations and Community Development," 95–98; OPSB Minutes, 24 June 1921, 25 November 1921, and 14 July 1922.

23. OPSB Minutes, 28 July 1922.

24. Ibid; *Soards' New Orleans Directory, 1921* (New Orleans: Soards Directory Co., 1921), 1109, 1082; *Annual Report of the New Orleans Board of Trade, 1917*, 144.

25. OPSB Minutes, 24 November 1922; School Board. Minutes, 22 June 1877. See also DeVore and Logsdon, *Crescent City Schools*, 84–87.

26. OPSB Minutes, 22 December 1922.

27. OPSB Minutes, 12 Januuary 1923.

28. OPSB Minutes, 12 January 1923; *Soards' New Orleans Directory, 1921*, 1579; *Soards' New Orleans Directory, 1925* (New Orleans: Soards Directory Co., 1925), 1509, 1681.

29. "Protest Against Negro School Plan," *Daily Picayune*, 12 June 1913.

30. See, for instance, OPSB Minutes, 11 February 1921, 27 January 1922, 27 October 1922, and 22 December 1922.

31. Fortier actually stated later in 1923 that "the amount spent above the sixth grade was not for the purpose of supplying the type of education best adapted for negroes of this community." He favored industrial education for blacks beyond grade six, but since that was prohibitively expensive he recommended "that since it would be admitted that the present type of education is not the right kind that we could eliminate that part of the system [i.e., black education beyond grade six] at a saving to the Board until the Board is in funds to provide the necessary industrial education without serious loss to the negroes." See OPSB Committee of the Whole Minutes, 20 November 1923.

32. OPSB Minutes, 12 January 1923.

33. For a discussion of the school board's later involvement with the Rosenwald Fund regarding a black trade school, see James D. Anderson, *The Education of Blacks in the South, 1860–1935* (Chapel Hill: University of North Carolina Press, 1988), 211–21.

34. OPSB Minutes, 12 January 1923.

35. Ibid.

36. OPSB Minutes, 26 January 1923.

37. OPSB Minutes 28 September 1917.

38. OPSB Minute 26 January 1923 (for quote). Recognizing that blacks' commitment to secondary education subverted any attempt to use high schools as a means of racial containment, the board voted to remove Chemistry, Spanish, and Physics from McDonogh 35's curriculum several months later. But it reinstated those subjects the next year following protests from African Americans. See OPSB Minutes, 14 September 1923; OPSB Committee of the Whole Minutes, 14 March 1924; DeVore and Logsdon, *Crescent City Schools*, 194. For context on the creation of black high schools in the urban South during the early twentieth century, see Anderson, *Education of Blacks in the South*, 211–21.

39. OPSB Minutes, 26 January 1923.

40. OPSB Minutes 23 December 1921. On the founding of McDonogh No. 6, see "The Public Schools," *Daily-Picayune*, 20 June 1876, and *Annual Report of the State Superintendent of Public Education for the Year 1875*, p. 193, http://www2.state.lib.la.us/doeafsr/ (the quotation is from this document).

41. OPSB Minutes 26 January 1923.

42. OPSB Minutes, 25 July 1924; "Residents Object to Negro School," *Times-Picayune*, 26 July 1924, 9; Orleans Parish School Board Committee of the Whole, Minutes, 19 August 1924; "Commerce High School Planned; First in South," *Times-Picayune*, 19 July 1924, 1, 5; "School Mothers' Club Disperses Equipment Fund," *Times-Picayune*, 9 August 1924, 4.

43. OPSB Minutes, 26 January 1923.

44. Ibid.; OPSB Minutes, 9 February 1923.

45. OPSB Minutes, 26 January 1923; "Board Decides Negroes Cannot Use New School," *Times-Picayune*, 27 January 1923, 2.

46. "Negroes Lodge Protest," *Times-Picayune*, 30 January 1923; "Negro Bodies Protest," *Times-Picayune*, 1 February 1923.

47. Ibid. "Patrons of Schools Voice Appreciation," *Times-Picayune*, 11 February 1923; OPSB Minutes, 9 February 1923; "Joseph A. Craig School to Reopen for Negro Pupils," *Times-Picayune*, 10 February 1923, 1; DeVore and Logsdon, *Crescent City Schools*, 202; DeVore, "Race Relations and Community Development," 103; A. E. Perkins, *Who's Who in Colored Louisiana* (Baton Rouge: Douglas Loan Co., 1930), 137.

48. Hirsch, "Simply A Matter of Black and White." See also DeVore, *Defying Jim Crow*.

49. Chas. D. Levy, Letter to the Editor, *Times-Picayune*, 31 January 1923.

50. Henry E. Braden, Letter to the Editor, *Times-Picayune*, 7 February 1923; Frances Joseph Gaudet, Letter to the Editor, *Times-Picayune*, 6 February 1923; Chas. D. Levy, Letter to the Editor, *Times-Picayune*, 31 January 1923; Mrs. C. E. Gates Phillips, Letter to the Editor, *Times-Picayune*, 8 February 1923.

51. OPSB Minutes, 26 August 1921.

52. "A Grave Injustice," *Times-Picayune*, 2 February 1923, 8.

53. "Negroes Lodge Protest," *Times-Picayune*, 30 January 1923, 11; "The Craig School," *Times-Picayune*, 9 February 1923, 8; OPSB Minutes, 9 February 1923; "Joseph A. Craig School to Reopen for Negro Pupils," *Times-Picayune*, 10 February 1923, 1; DeVore and Logsdon, *Crescent City Schools*, 124. Evidence of the prominent role wealthy uptown men—and particularly women—

played in the Public School Alliance can be found in the organization's membership lists, which are in box 13, Ida Weis Friend Papers, LaRC. See also *Outline of the Organization and Work of the Public School Alliance of New Orleans, 1905-1909,* Education. Public School Alliance Folder, LaRC Vertical Files.

54. "School Closing Protested," *Times-Picayune,* 4 February 1923.

55. OPSB Minutes, 9 February 1923; DeVore and Logsdon, *Crescent City Schools,* 202.

56. OPSB Minutes, 9 February 1923.

57. "Joseph A. Craig School to Reopen for Negro Pupils," *Times-Picayune,* 23 January 1923, p. 1.

58. OPSB Minutes, 9 February 1923.

59. Ibid.

60. OPSB Minutes, 9 February 1923 (emphasis added).

61. Carl H. Nightingale, "The Transnational Contexts of Early Twentieth-Century American Urban Segregation," *Journal of Social History* 39, no. 3 (Spring 2006): 667-702; Roger Rice, "Residential Segregation by Law, 1910-1917," *The Journal of Southern History* 34, no. 2 (May 1968): 179-99; Christopher Silver, "The Racial Origins of Zoning: Southern Cities from 1910-40," *Planning Perspectives* 6 (1991): 189-205; Nightingale, *Segregation: A Global History.*

62. OPSB Minutes, 9 February 1923.

63. Ibid.

64. The city officially renamed Beauregard Square Congo Square in 2011. Shane Lief, "Staging New Orleans: The Contested Space of Congo Square" (Master's thesis, Tulane University, 2011); Lawrence N. Powell, *The Accidental City: Improvising New Orleans* (Cambridge, MA: Harvard University Press, 2012), 98-99.

65. U.S. Census, 1920, New Orleans, La., Population, NAMS T-625, reel 620.

66. OPSB Minutes, 9 February 1923.

67. John A. Beeler, *Report to the Commissioner of Public Utilities, City of New Orleans, on the Street Railway Situation* (New York, 1923), p. 48, LaRC. Beeler submitted his report to the city's commissioner of public utilities on March 26, 1923.

68. H. W. Gilmore, "The Old New Orleans and the New: A Case for Ecology," *American Sociological Review* 9, no. 4 (August 1944): 385-94 (quote on 393).

69. OPSB Minutes, 9 February 1923.

70. Ibid. (for quote). On Thompson's involvement in the McDonogh No. 13 debate, see "Protest Against M'Donogh No. 13 as Negro School," *Times-Picayune,* 29 August 1917.

71. Andrew R. Highsmith, *Demolition Means Progress: Flint, Michigan, and the Fate of the American Metropolis* (Chicago: University of Chicago Press, 2015), 56-69 (quote on 66). For an elaboration on the role segregation played in advancing community cohesion in Flint, see Andrew R. Highsmith and Ansley T. Erickson, "Segregation as Splitting, Segregation as Joining: Schools, Housing, and the Many Modes of Jim Crow," *American Journal of Education* 121, no. 4 (August 2015): 563-95.

72. OPSB Minutes, 26 January 1923.

73. Karen Benjamin notes a similar dynamic in Raleigh, North Carolina, in "Progressivism Meets Jim Crow: Segregation, School Reform, and Urban Development in the Interwar South" (PhD diss., University of Wisconsin, 2007).

74. OPSB Minutes, 24 June 1921 (emphasis in original); *Cardinal Principles of Secondary*

Education: A Report of the Commission on the Reorganization of Secondary Education, Appointed by the National Education Association (Washington, DC: Government Printing Office, 1918).

75. OBSB Minutes, 24 June 1921.

76. U.S. Census, 1920, New Orleans, La. Population, via Heritage Quest. The Heritage Quest database catalogued individuals from the 1920 Census population schedules according to New Orleans's voting precincts, which permitted me to isolate people by voting precinct and then by race. The percentages are inexact since Heritage Quest counts both heads of households and individuals with unique surnames for each address.

77. LaBranche's comment is quoted above and in OPSB Minutes, 9 February 1923.

78. Broughton quoted in Karen Benjamin, "Suburbanizing Jim Crow: The Impact of School Policy on Residential Segregation in Raleigh," *Journal of Urban History* 38, no. 2 (2012): 236.

79. U.S. Census, 1920, New Orleans, La. Population, via Heritage Quest; *New Orleans Item*, 28 October 1920, 18; Sanborn Map Company, *Insurance Maps of New Orleans*, vol. 4, 1909, sheets 413–14, 419–20.

80. U.S. Census, 1920, New Orleans, La. Population, via Heritage Quest.

81. Sam R. Carter/Works Progress Administration, *A Report on Survey of Metropolitan New Orleans, Land Use, Real Property, and Low Income Housing Area* (Louisiana State Department of Public Works and Housing Authority of New Orleans, 1941), Map 19, Block Data Map, HNOC 68-19-L.7. Carter's map enabled me to examine block-level population data. According to Carter's tabulation, African Americans comprised more than 90 percent of Washington Avenue and South Robertson and South Galvez Streets. For the HOLC's assessment of the area, see "Summary of Economic, Real Estate and Mortgage Survey and Security Area Descriptions of New Orleans, Louisiana," 28 April 1939, Area Description D-34, in New Orleans, LA. #2 folder, box 88, RG 195, National Archives II (for quote).

82. Orleans Parish School Board—Office of Planning and Construction. *A Planning and Building Program for New Orleans' Schools* (New Orleans: Orleans Parish School Board, 1952), 40, document in author's possession.

83. The recommendations from Gwinn that the board implemented included: the construction of a black elementary school near Spruce and Monroe on the city's western edge, the erection of a second black school near Bienville and Claiborne north of the old Storyville neighborhood, the relocation of McCarthy to the Lower Ninth Ward, the creation of a school on the "lower coast" of Algiers on the west bank of the Mississippi River, and the construction of an annex and then a new structure for the Valena C. Jones School at Annette and North Miro. See New Orleans Public Schools, *Directory of the Public Schools of New Orleans, La, 1930–1931*, box 4, School Directories, OPSB-147.

84. Ibid.

85. OPSB Minutes, 12 January and 9 February 1923 (Moise's quote is from the February 9th minutes).

86. OPSB Minutes, 12 and 15 June 1923.

87. Of the 168 residents in the 1300–1500 block of St. Philip, more than 70 percent were identified as either black or mulatto. U.S. Census, 1920, New Orleans, La., Population, NAMS T-625, reel 620.

88. John B. Alberts, "Black Catholic Schools: The Josephite Parishes of New Orleans During the Jim Crow Era," *U.S. Catholic Historian* 12, no. 1 (Winter 1994): 93. See also Chapter 2.

89. OPSB Minutes, 13 August 1914.

90. "Site is Offered for Public School," *New Orleans Item*, 21 November 1910; "Seventh Ward League," *Daily Picayune*, 15 August 1909, 16, col. 3; "Real Estate Once More a Headliner," *Daily Picayune*, 27 November 1910, 11, col. 6; Newton Renfro, "'Open Space' Concept Takes Getting Used to at Rosenwald," *Times-Picayune*, 4 November 1973; Beverly Jacques Anderson, *Cherished Memories: Snapshots of Life and Lessons from a 1950s Creole Village* (Bloomington, IN: iUniverse, 2011), 55, 214–17; "Raise Money for School," *Cleveland Gazette*, 21 October 1911.

91. James Anderson discusses "double taxation" in the context of the post–World War I black school building boom in the rural South in *Education of Blacks in the South*, chap. 5.

92. DeVore and Logsdon, *Crescent City Schools*, 183; Anderson, *Cherished Memories*, 55; DeVore, *Defying Jim Crow*, 55; OPSB Minutes, 9 February 1923 (for quote). While Anderson quotes a 1954 Valena C. Jones School newsletter that dates the opening of the Miro School in a rented building to 1908, the school system's 1910 directory does not list the Miro School. By 1912, the school was open. See DeVore, *Defying Jim Crow*, 55; New Orleans Public School Directory, 1910, box 1, School Directories, OPSB-147.

93. DeVore, *Defying Jim Crow*, 104–5; "Hardin Playground Committee Testimonial to Dr. Joseph A. Hardin," 22 February 1951, box 2, Joseph A. Hardin Papers, Amistad Research Center at Tulane University, New Orleans, LA (for quote). For additional biographical information on Hardin, see also the biographical note accompanying the online finding aid for his papers at the Amistad Research Center, http://amistadresearchcenter.tulane.edu/archon/index.php?p=collections /findingaid&id=17&rootcontentid=6337&q=%22hardin+playground+committee%22#id6337.

94. DeVore, *Defying Jim Crow*, 55–56; Lucille Hutton, "Biography of Miss Fannie C. Williams," reproduced in Anderson, *Cherished Memories*, 218–19; Adam Fairclough, *A Class of Their Own: Black Teachers in the Segregated South* (Cambridge, MA: Harvard University Press, 2007), 279–80 (see 279 for quote); Fairclough, *Teaching Equality: Black Schools in the Age of Jim Crow* (Athens: University of Georgia Press, 2001), 43 (for quote). Valena C. Jones closed following Hurricane Katrina in 2005 and did not reopen. For examples of its continued prominence within African American historical memory, see Anderson, *Cherished Memories*, and Brenda Billips Square, "The Hijacking of an Education System," *New Orleans Tribune*, February/March 2012, 17.

95. For real estate assessments of the surrounding area, see "Summary of Economic, Real Estate and Mortgage Survey and Security Area Descriptions of New Orleans, Louisiana," 28 April 1939, Area Description D-18, in New Orleans, LA #2 folder, box 88, RG 195, National Archives II. This HOLC report placed the area's black population at 70 percent, which corresponds to the census's 1940 tract data and is about ten percentage points higher than the 1920 percentage of black households in the voting precinct that included Valena C. Jones. See U.S. Census, 1920, New Orleans, La., Population, Microfilm Series T-625, reel 625, via Heritage Quest, and Bureau of the Census, *Population and Housing: Statistics for Census Tracts, New Orleans, La.* (Washington, DC: Government Printing Office, 1941), 4.

96. OPSB Minutes, 9 January 1925; DeVore and Logsdon, *Crescent City Schools*, 204; "New School to Replace Old is Opened," *Louisiana Weekly*, 1 January 1927 (for quote)

97. "New School to Replace Old is Opened," *Louisiana Weekly*, 1 January 1927.

98. "Pick Beauregard Square as Site for Auditorium," *Times-Picayune*, 12 April 1928, 1, 3; Greater New Orleans Community Data Center, "Tremé/Lafitte Neighborhood Snapshot," http:// www.gnocdc.org/orleans/4/42/snapshot.html; Long, "Poverty is the New Prostitution," 800–1;

City of New Orleans, Office of Policy Planning, *Iberville Project Profile* (New Orleans: December 1978), p. 3.03; Sanborn Map Company, *Insurance Maps of New Orleans, Louisiana,* vol. 2, 1908, sheets 132, 137.

99. Martha Mahoney, "The Changing Nature of Public Housing in New Orleans, 1930–1974" (Master's thesis, Tulane University, 1985), 36–37; Long, "Poverty is the New Prostitution," 800–1; City of New Orleans, Office of Policy Planning, "Iberville Project Profile (6C)" (New Orleans: December 1978), p. 3.04.

100. Greater New Orleans Community Data Center, "Tremé /Lafitte Neighborhood Snapshot"; Trushna Parekh, "Inhabiting Tremé: Gentrification Memory and Racialized Space in a New Orleans Neighborhood" (PhD diss., University of Texas, 2008), 15–17; Michael E. Crutcher Jr., *Tremé: Race and Place in a New Orleans Neighborhood* (Athens: University of Georgia Press, 2010), chap. 1.

101. Lawrence J. Vale, "When Walmart Landed on Public Housing: Development Displacement and Historic Preservation in New Orleans," paper presented at the Eighth Biennial Urban History Association Conference, Chicago, IL, 15 October 2016, 8–9 (Mohl quoted on p. 8; unpublished manuscript in author's possession); Juliette Lee Landphair, "'For the Good of the Community': Reform Activism and Public Schools in New Orleans, 1920–1960" (PhD diss., University of Virginia, 1999), 73; City of New Orleans Office of Policy and Planning, "Sixth Ward/Tremé/Lafitte Neighborhood Profile (6A)," (New Orleans: December 1978), p. 3.07 (second quote); "Summary of Economic, Real Estate and Mortgage Survey and Security Area Descriptions of New Orleans, Louisiana," 28 April 1939, New Orleans, LA #2 folder, box 88, RG 195, National Archives II; Sanborn Map Company, *Insurance Maps of New Orleans, Louisiana,* vol. 2, 1908, sheet 132; New Orleans Public Schools, *School Directory,* 1940–41, box 4, School Directories, OPSB-147; Bureau of the Census, *16th Census of the United States, 1940, Population and Housing: Statistics for Census Tracts, New Orleans, La.,* (Washington: Government Printing Office, 1941), iv, 4.

102. Nicholas Bauer to John Klorer, New Orleans, La., 6 July 1927, Orleans Parish School Board Folder, box 3, New Orleans Department of Public Property Records, City Archive, NOPL; OPSB Minutes, 10 September 1926 and 10 August 1928; Joseph S. Schwertz, "The History of Warren Easton Boys' High School" (Master's thesis, Tulane University, 1941), 79.

CHAPTER FIVE

1. "Section of Fine Homes Where Land Was Waste Quarter Century Ago," *Times-Picayune,* 10 June 1923.

2. Ibid.; "Succession of Bernard Fellman, No. 36658, Orleans Parish Civil District Court, Division A," 4 November 1892, Conveyance Office Book 145, folios 490–496 (cited hereinafter as COB 145/490–496), Conveyance Division, Orleans Parish Civil District Court, New Orleans, La. (cited hereinafter as Conveyance Division, OPCDC); "Sheriff's Sale, Samuel Ricker, Jr. to John H. Pearson," 22 March 1853, recorded in Book 1, Jefferson Parish, Conveyance Division, OPCDC; Dorothy G. Schlesinger, Robert J. Cangelosi Jr., and Sally Kittredge Reeves, *New Orleans Architecture, vol 7: Jefferson City* (Gretna, LA: Pelican Publishing, 1989), 5, 24; Henry W. W. Reynolds, "Perspective View of New Orleans and Environs from the South," 1884, Historic New Orleans Collection, 1974.25.18.125, available through the LOUISiana Digital Library, http://cdm16313.content

dm.oclc.org/cdm/ref/collection/p15140c01128/id/87; Craig E. Colton, *Unnatural Metropolis: Wresting New Orleans from Nature* (Baton Rouge: Louisiana State University Press, 2005), 83. Distance estimate based upon property descriptions included in conveyance records and Google Maps.

3. Nicole Romagossa, "Albert Baldwin Wood, the Screw Pump, and the Modernization of New Orleans" (Master's thesis, University of New Orleans, 2010), 12; Ordinance No. 7194, Commission Council Series, 28 December 1922, City Archives, NOPL; Daney and Waddill, Plan No. 2382, 17 July 1915, and "Act of Sale for Site No. 3 on Octavia Street in Block No. 651 (formerly 83) in Sixth District, Bernard Co., Inc. to Louis V. Burka, 9 March 1923" (first quote), both in *Notarial Acts, 1–79, 1923, Arthur B. Leopold, Notary Public,* New Orleans Notarial Archives Research Center (hereafter referred to as NONARC); "Section of Fine Homes Where Land Was Waste Quarter Century Ago," *Times-Picayune,* 10 June 1923 (second quote); Colton, *Unnatural Metropolis,* 78, 84–7.

4. OPSB Minutes, 13 August 1923.

5. "A Leading Dry Goods Merchant of This City," *Daily Picayune,* 3 September 1892, 6, col. 3; Schlesinger, Cangelosi, and Reeves, *New Orleans Architecture, vol. 7: Jefferson City,* 3–4, 24–29.

6. Schlesinger, Cangelosi, and Reeves, *New Orleans Architecture, vol. 7: Jefferson City,* 24, 28.

7. Ibid., 44–45; "Act Passed by James G. Fanning, Sheriff of the Parish of Jefferson," 22 March 1853, Conveyance Book 1, Jefferson, pages 662–64, OPCDC.

8. Schlesinger, Cangelosi, and Reeves, *New Orleans Architecture, vol. 7: Jefferson City,* 48–49; Eric Foner, *Reconstruction: America's Unfinished Revolution, 1863–1877* (New York: Harper Collins, 1988), 529–30.

9. "A Leading Dry Goods Merchant of This City," *Daily Picayune,* 3 September 1892, 6, col. 3; *Daily Picayune,* 20 February 1873, p. 4, 2 November 1873, p. 3, and 31 March 1874, 8, col. 4 (for quote).

10. Schlesinger, Cangelosi, and Reeves, *New Orleans Architecture, vol. 7: Jefferson City,* 41–46; Sale of Property Abby W. Pearson et al. to Bernard Fellman, 17 September 1885, COB 123/496, OPCDC; Benjamin F. Butler, *Butler's Book: A Review of His Legal, Political, and Military Career* (Boston: A. M. Thayer, 1892), 968–69, 981.

11. "Fellman Tract to Fill Gap Left in Fair City's Heart," *Times-Picayune,* 15 March 1931. See also COB 121/782, 17 September 1885, COB 121/816–820, 5 October 1885, COB 124/716, 2 May 1887, and COB 145/490–496, 4 November 1892, OPCDC.

12. "Benjamin Cohn Dead from Heart Disease," *New Orleans Item,* 7 November 1918; "Felix Dreyfous Taken By Death," *Times-Picayune,* 16 November 1946; 1860 U.S. Census, New Orleans, La., Population-Free Inhabitants, Heritage Quest Online, Series M-593, Reel 419, available through Heritage Quest; "Leo Fellman, 59, Dies After Long Illness at Home," *Times-Picayune,* 22 November 1934, 1, 8. Felix Dreyfous also served as Bernard Fellman's attorney when he purchased his Rickerville properties. See COB 121/816–820 and COB 123/496, OPCDC.

13. On the lawsuit stemming from the fire, see "Sues for $16,000 Insurance," *New Orleans Item,* 17 January 1902; "Value Placed by Mrs. Dreyfous on Her Burned Property," *New Orleans Item,* 13 December 1902; "To Be Tried Next Term," *Daily Picayune,* 16 June 1906; "New Trial Asked," *Times-Picayune,* 7 January 1908; *Fellman v. Royal Insurance Co.,* 184 F. 577 (5th Cir. 1911); *Fellman v. Royal Insurance Co.,* 185 F. 689 (5th Cir. 1911). Details about the Rickerville lawsuit are included in "George B. Taylor Found Guilty by Jury," *Daily Picayune,* 20 March 1908.

14. "Leo Fellman, 59, Dies After Long Illness at Home," *Times-Picayune,* 22 November 1934, 1, 8. For Bernard Fellman's succession, see COB 145/490, OPCDC.

15. "Suburban Growth Raises Questions," *Daily Picayune*, 5 September 1909, 16.

16. "Section of Fine Homes Where Land Was Waste Quarter Century Ago," *Times-Picayune*, 10 June 1923, section 2, p. 1 (quote); Daney and Waddill, Plan No. 2382, 17 July 1915, attached to "Act of Sale for Site No. 3 on Octavia Street in Block No. 651 (formerly 83) in Sixth District, Bernard Co., Inc. to Louis V. Burka," 9 March 1923, in *Notarial Acts, 1–79, 1923, Arthur B. Leopold, Notary Public*, NONARC.

17. Ordinance No. 7194, Commission Council Series, 28 December 1922, City Archives, NOPL; "Act of Sale for Site No. 3 on Octavia Street in Block No. 651 (formerly 83) in Sixth District, Bernard Co., Inc. to Louis V. Burka," 9 March 1923, in *Notarial Acts, 1–79, 1923, Arthur B. Leopold, Notary Public*, NONARC; "Succession of Mrs. Anna Fellman," Civil District Court of the Parish of Orleans, No. 128,206, 8 August 1919, COB 308/365–368; "Act of Sale, Rose Fellman Lownes to Leo Fellman," 18 March 1922, COB 347/450–454; "Act of Sale, Leo Fellman, Celina Elias, Emanuel Fellman, Lily Fellman, Morris Fellman, and Laurel Fellman unto Bernard Company, Inc.," 15 May 1922, COB 353/89–96, all in OPCDC. Conversion from 1922 to 2017 dollars made via CPI Inflation Calculator, https://data.bls.gov/cgi-bin/cpicalc.pl.

18. Joseph S. Schwertz Jr., "The History of Warren Easton Boys' High School" (Master's thesis, Tulane University, 1941), 73, 76.

19. OPSB Committee of the Whole Minutes, 31 May 1923; OPSB Minutes, 28 July 1922, 12 June, and 13 August 1923; "Pay of Teachers Unchanged Until Revenues Known," *Times-Picayune*, 14 August 1923, 3; "Harris Appeals for More Money to Run Schools," *Times-Picayune*, 15 September 1923, 20; Sanborn Map Company, *Insurance Maps of New Orleans, Louisiana*, vol. 5, 1909, sheet 527, available at http://sanborn.umi.com/la/3376/dateid-000009.htm?CCSI=3057.

20. OPSB Minutes, 13 August 1923.

21. The *Times-Picayune*'s Sunday Real Estate section provided ample, though oftentimes overblown, evidence of this area's growth. The quote is from "Volume of Realty Business Approaches Two Million," *Times-Picayune*, 21 January 1923, sec. 5, p. 1, col. 2. For construction activity, see Beeler, *Report to the Commissioner of Public Utilities, City of New Orleans, on the Street Railway Situation*, "Map of New Orleans Showing Buildings Erected in 1920"; "Map of New Orleans Showing Buildings Erected in 1921"; "Map of New Orleans Showing Buildings Erected in 1922," LaRC. On the board's plan to build the school in 1928, see OPSB Committee of the Whole Minutes, 23 November 1926.

22. Beeler, *Report to the Commissioner of Public Utilities, City of New Orleans, on the Street Railway Situation*, "Population Map and Proposed Track Layout," Exhibit 2-B, LaRC.

23. See, for instance, Sanborn Map Company, *Insurance Maps of New Orleans, Louisiana*, vol. 5, new sheet, Sept. 1922, sheets 524–25; vol. 6, new sheet, Nov. 1922, sheets 575–76, 666; vol. 6A, 1940, sheets 627, 645–46, 648.

24. "Subdivisions in City and Suburbs," *Times-Picayune*, 28 October 1923, section 2, p. 1; "Section of Fine Homes Where Land Was Waste Quarter Century Ago," *Times-Picayune*, 10 June 1923, section 2, p. 1.

25. "Catholic Education Victories Vital," *Daily Picayune*, 1 September 1911, p. 3; K. K. Blackmar, "The Ursulines and Their New Home," *Daily Picayune*, 18 August 1912, third section, 1, 13. On the Ursuline nuns, see Emily Clark, *Masterless Mistresses: The New Orleans Ursulines and the Development of a New World Society, 1727–1834* (Chapel Hill: University of North Carolina Press, 2007).

26. Sanborn Map Company, *Insurance Maps of New Orleans, Louisiana*, vol. 6, additional sheets 665 and 666, November 1922; James B. Bennett, *Religion and the Rise of Jim Crow in New Orleans* (Princeton, NJ: Princeton University Press, 2005), 156.

27. OPSB Committee of the Whole Minutes, 9 September 1924.

28. OPSB Minutes, 13 April 1925.

29. "Subdivisions in City and Suburbs," *Times-Picayune*, 28 October 1923, section 2, p. 1. On the development of semiprivate residential parks in New Orleans, see Robert J. Cangelosi Jr., "Residential Parks," in *New Orleans Architecture, Vol. 7: The University District*, ed. Robert J. Cangelosi Jr. and Dorothy G. Schlesinger (Gretna, LA: Pelican Publishing, 1997), 66–91.

30. "Many Large Sales Made During Week," *Times-Picayune*, 20 January 1924, section 2, p. 1 (quote).

31. While the *Picayune* claimed that Fellman sold the first portion of his lakeside tract early in 1924, conveyance records and later news coverage suggest he did not open the area in any significant fashion until the 1930s. For early reports of activity in this area, see "Many Large Sales Made During Week," *Times-Picayune*, 20 January 1924, section 2, p. 1. For coverage showing that full development came later, see, for instance, "Act of Partition by and Between Bernard Co Inc and Leo Fellman," 27 February 1932, COB 464/521; "Act of Sale," Widow of Leo Fellman et al. unto M. E. Pick, September 24, 1941, COB 517/413; "Exchange of Property," Estate of Leo Fellman and Bernard Company, 18 August 1939, COB 505/413; and Bernard Company unto Elias Cohen, 7 January 1941, COB 515/335, all at OPCDC; "Fellman Tract to Fill Gap Left in Fair City's Heart," *Times-Picayune*, 15 March 1931, section 3, pp. 10, 12.

32. Greater New Orleans Community Data Center, "Broadmoor Neighborhood Snapshot," http://www.gnocdc.org/orleans/3/63/snapshot.html; Romagossa, "Albert Baldwin Wood," 14–16, 23–25. The Broadmoor boundaries are based upon a 2002 map produced by the Greater New Orleans Community Data Center, available at http://www.gnocdc.org/orleans/3/63/index.html; Gary Krist, *Empire of Sin: A Story of Sex, Jazz, Murder, and the Battle for Modern New Orleans* (New York: Crown, 2014), 2; Colton, *Unnatural Metropolis*, 93. During the 1920s, the Broadmoor Civic Improvement Association had a much more expansive yet less clearly defined sense of Broadmoor's boundaries because much of the area on the lakeside of Claiborne was in the process of being developed. For the sake of clarity, I therefore use the neighborhood's present-day boundaries. On the neighborhood association, see the Broadmoor Civic Improvement Association, 1927–1928 folder, box 2, New Orleans Department of Public Property Records, City Archives, NOPL.

33. Romagossa, "Albert Baldwin Wood," 27; George B. Tindall, *The Emergence of the New South, 1913–1945* (Baton Rouge: Louisiana State University Press, 1967), 95, 104–7.

34. *Annual Report of the New Orleans Public Schools, 1919–1920*, 23, Annual Reports, Box 9, OPSB-147.

35. See, for instance, 1920 U.S. Census, New Orleans, La., Population, Series T-625, Roll 623.

36. Interview with John Harold Boucree (btvct07061), interviewed by Kate Ellis, New Orleans (La.), July 5, 1994, Behind the Veil: Documenting African-American Life in the Jim Crow South Digital Collection, John Hope Franklin Research Center, Duke University Libraries. The transcription of Boucree's interview identifies Boucree as saying that he grew up in the 8700 block of South Galvez. However, the 1920 Census places Boucree's parents and older siblings in a house they owned at 3529 South Galvez. The 1940 Census, meanwhile, places the sixteen-year-old Boucree and his family one block further uptown at 3723 South Galvez, also in a house they

owned. Most likely, Boucree's father built the smaller houses at 3723, and his grandfather built the larger house at 3529 South Galvez. These locations are consistent with Boucree's statement that he lived about ten blocks from the St. Monica Catholic school, located on First Street between South Galvez and South Miro. Boucree and his three living siblings sold the house at 3723 South Galvez in 2016 for $95,000. See 1920 U.S. Census, New Orleans, La., Population, Series T-625, Roll 623; 1940 U.S. Census, New Orleans, La., Population, NAMS T627–1431, both accessed via Heritage Quest; "New Orleans Property Transfers for Feb. 22–27, 2016," *The Advocate*, 8 March 2016, http://www.theadvocate.com/new_orleans/entertainment_life/home_garden/article_d32f2a6e -a0af-5195- 894f-3ff1b3f63e86.html.

37. Sanborn Map Company, *Insurance Maps of New Orleans, Louisiana*, vol. 5, additional sheet 531, September 1920, and additional sheets 532–34, September 1922, all available at http:// sanborn.umi.com/la/3376/dateid-000036.htm?CCSI=3057n; John A. Beeler, *Report to the Commissioner of Public Utilities, City of New Orleans, on the Street Railway Situation* (New York, 1923), "Map of New Orleans Showing Buildings Erected in 1920"; "Map of New Orleans Showing Buildings Erected in 1921"; "Map of New Orleans Showing Buildings Erected in 1922," LaRC.

38. *Annual Report of the New Orleans Public Schools, 1920–21*, 10–11, OPSB-147.

39. OPSB Minutes, 23 September 1921 and 28 July 1922.

40. Robert Meyer Jr., *Names Over New Orleans Public Schools* (New Orleans: Namesake Press, 1975), 238.

41. OPSB Minutes, 12 August 1921; Juliette Lee Landphair, "'For the Good of the Community': Reform Activism and Public Schools in New Orleans, 1920–1960" (PhD diss., University of Virginia, 1999), 76; Arnold R. Hirsch, "Simply a Matter of Black and White: The Transformation of Race and Politics in Twentieth-Century New Orleans," in *Creole New Orleans: Race and Americanization*, ed. Arnold R. Hirsch and Joseph Logsdon (Baton Rouge: Louisiana State University Press, 1992), 266; A. E. Perkins, *Who's Who in Colored Louisiana* (Baton Rouge: Douglas Loan Co., 1930), 101; 1920 U.S. Census, New Orleans, La., Population, Heritage Quest Online, Series T-625, Roll 623, available through Heritage Quest. I located Broadmoor's 1920 black residents by searching "12-WD; 8-PCT; New Orleans" (12th Ward-8th Precinct) in Heritage Quest.

42. James E. Allison & Co., *Report on the Street Railway Service of the City of New Orleans, Made to the Committee on Transportation Facilities of New Orleans* (St. Louis, 1917), "Map of New Orleans Showing Street Car Lines and Density of Population," Louisiana and Special Collections, Earl K. Long Library, University of New Orleans; Beeler, *Report to the Commissioner of Public Utilities, City of New Orleans, on the Street Railway Situation*, "Population Map and Proposed Track Layout," Exhibit 2-B; "Map of New Orleans Showing Buildings Erected in 1920"; "Map of New Orleans Showing Buildings Erected in 1921"; "Map of New Orleans Showing Buildings Erected in 1922," LaRC.

43. Sanborn Map Company, *Insurance Maps of New Orleans, Louisiana*, vol. 5, additional sheet 532, September 1922.

44. Search of *Times-Picayune* via America's Historical Newspapers, http://infow *eb.newsbank .com/*.

45. "Auction Sales," *Times-Picayune*, 4 April 1935, 28, column 3; Greater New Orleans Community Data Center, "Broadmoor Neighborhood Snapshot," http://www.gnocdc.org/orleans/3/63 /snapshot.html; OPSB Minutes, 22 December 1922 and 11 December 1925.

46. OPSB Committee of the Whole (COW) Minutes, 24 July 1923 and 7 August 1923; OPSB

Minutes, 13 August 1923; Sanborn Map Company, *Insurance Maps of New Orleans, Louisiana,* vol. 7, 1937, sheet 725; http://sanborn.umi.com/la/3376/dateid-000016.htm?CCSI=3057n; "$200 in Cash Prizes for Winning Essay of 'Build in Algiers,'" *Times-Picayune,* 3 June 1923, section 2, p. 13; Herman J. Seiferth, "Algiers Takes Vigorous Steps to Become Great N.O. Residential Suburb," *Times-Picayune,* 20 May 1923, section 2, p. 1.

47. OPSB COW Minutes, 21 October 1925, 13 November 1925.

48. Crestmont Park advertisement, *Times-Picayune,* 15 July 1923; Jefferson Heights advertisements, *Times-Picayune,* 5 August 1923, 26 August 1923, and 9 September 1923.

49. Karen Benjamin, "Suburbanizing Jim Crow: The Impact of School Policy on Residential Segregation in Raleigh," *Journal of Urban History* 38, no. 2 (2012): 225–46, DOI 10.1177/0096144211427114.

50. Lewis, *The Making of an Urban Landscape,* 65.

51. OPSB Minutes, 11 December 1925 (quote); U.S. Census, 1920, New Orleans, La., Population; Meyer, *Names Over New Orleans Schools,* 243. On Kruttschnitt's death, see *Daily Picayune,* 17 April 1906, 1, col. 2.

52. OPSB Minutes, 11 December 1925.

53. U.S. Census, 1920, New Orleans, La., Population, National Archives Microfilm Series T-625, reel 622, via Heritage Quest; Sanborn Map Company, *Insurance Maps of New Orleans,* vol. 1, 1908, sheets 32–33, 37–38, http://sanborn.umi.com/splash.html.

54. OPSB Committee of the Whole Minutes, 5 October 1926.

55. Donald E. DeVore, "The Rise from the Nadir: Black New Orleans Between the Wars" (Master's thesis, University of New Orleans, 1983), 70; "Blast in Front of Negro Home Heard for Mile," *Times-Picayune,* 2 November 1926, 1; Henry E. Braden Letter to the Editor, *Times-Picayune,* 7 February 1923; 1920 U.S. Census, New Orleans, La., Population, Heritage Quest, NAMS T625, Reel 623. The 1920 Census placed Braden and Ricard respectively at 1917 and 1919 Delachaise Street, which was in the next block from the Krutschnitt School and one and one-half blocks from the 2000 block of Louisiana, where the *Picayune* placed Braden in 1926. DeVore, meanwhile, placed Braden's bombed house in the 2200 block of Louisiana. By 1930, Ricard lived at 2902 Louisiana Avenue, which was roughly ten blocks from his 1920 address. See Perkins, *Who's Who in Colored Louisiana,* 138.

56. DeVore, "Rise from the Nadir," 70–71; "Another Effort to Bomb Negro's Residence Fails," *Times-Picayune,* 15 November 1926, 2.

57. James Weldon Johnson and Herbert J. Seligmann, "Legal Aspects of the Negro Problem," *Annals of the American Academy of Political and Social Science* 140 (November 1928): 94; Thomas Sugrue, *The Origins of the Urban Crisis: Race and Inequality in Postwar Detroit* (Princeton, NJ: Princeton University Press, 1996), 24; Joe William Trotter Jr., *The African American Experience,* vol. 2, *From Reconstruction* (Boston: Houghton Mifflin, 2001), 336–39, 404–6; Trotter, "Shifting Perspectives on Segregation in the Emerging Postindustrial Age," 12–13, paper presented at The Future of the African American Past Conference, May 19–21, 2016, Washington, DC, https://futureafampast.si.edu/sites/default/files/03_Trotter%20Joe.pdf.

58. DeVore, "Rise from the Nadir," 61–62; "White Residents Prepare to Test Segregation Act," *Times-Picayune,* 19 September 1924, 9 (quoting the ordinance).

59. DeVore, "Rise from the Nadir," 61–62; "Negroes Barred from Building Too Near Whites," *Times-Picayune,* 17 September 1924, 14 (quote); Sanborn Map Company, *Insurance Maps of New*

Orleans, Louisiana, vol. 5, September 1922, additional sheet 532; Sanborn Map Company, *Insurance Maps of New Orleans, Louisiana,* vol. 6a, 1940, sheets 613a and 614a.

60. "White Residents Prepare to Test Segregation Act," *Times-Picayune,* 19 September 1924, 1, 9 (quote is on p. 9).

61. Ibid., *Louisiana Weekly* quoted in DeVore, "Rise from the Nadir," 70.

62. DeVore, "Rise from the Nadir," 63–64; "Woman Will Fight Conviction Under Segregation Law," *Times-Picayune,* 29 May 1925, 28; "Segregation Law Violation Brings Fine for Woman," *Times-Picayune,* 6 June 1925, 7; Sanborn Map Company, *Insurance Maps of New Orleans, Louisiana,* vol. 5, additional sheet 532, September 1922.

63. Interview with John Harold Boucree, Behind the Veil Collection. For additional examples of New Orleans police officers' stopping black male teenagers as they walked by white homes or schools, see Jennifer Ritterhouse, *Growing Up Jim Crow: How Black and White Southern Children Learned Race* (Chapel Hill: University of North Carolina Press, 2006), 191–92.

64. Interview with John Harold Boucree, Behind the Veil Collection.

65. "Segregation Law Conference Set," *Times-Picayune,* 16 October 1925, 3; DeVore, "Rise from the Nadir," 64–65 (first quote); "Seeks to Delay Bill for Decision," *Times-Picayune,* 8 November 1925, 22 (second quote).

66. DeVore, "Rise from the Nadir," 65–66.

67. Ibid., 66–67; Roger L. Rice, "Residential Segregation by Law, 1910–1917," *Journal of Southern History* 34, no. 2 (May 1968): 179–99; Arthur T. Martin, "Segregation of Residences of Negroes," *Michigan Law Review* 32, no. 6 (April 1934): 727–31; *Buchanan v. Warley,* 245 U.S. 60 (1917).

68. DeVore, "Rise from the Nadir," 68–69; *Tyler v. Harmon,* 158 La. 439 (1925) (quote); *Harmon v. Tyler,* 273 U.S. 668 (1927); Rice, "Residential Segregation by Law," 193.

69. Quoted in DeVore, "Rise from the Nadir," 73.

70. U.S. Bureau of the Census, *16th Census of the United States, 1940: Population and Housing, Statistics for Census Tracts, New Orleans, La.* (Washington: Government Printing Office, 1941), 5; 1940 U.S. Census, New Orleans, La., Population, NAMS T627–1431, via Heritage Quest.

71. Mayor [Martin Behrman] to Nicholas Bauer, New Orleans, 6 August 1925, Correspondence-Public Schools folder, carton 3, series II, Mayor Martin Behrman Papers, City Archives, NOPL.

72. Sanborn Map Company, *Insurance Maps of New Orleans,* vol. 5, 1909, sheets 507, 509, 510, http://sanborn.umi.com/la/3376/dateid-000009.htm?CCSI=3057n; OPSB Minutes, 12 October 1928.

73. Sanborn Map Company, *Insurance Maps of New Orleans,* vol. 5, 1909, sheets 509, http://sanborn.umi.com/la/3376/dateid-000009.htm?CCSI=3057n; Robert J. Cangelosi Jr. and Dorothy G. Schlesinger, eds., *New Orleans Architecture,* vol. 7: *The University District* (Gretna, LA: Pelican Publishing, 1997), 8; "The Newest School," *Daily Picayune,* 17 March 1904, 4 (for quote).

74. Cangelosi and Schlesinger, eds., *New Orleans Architecture,* vol. 7, pp. 43, 46–50, 65–66, 77–81; Nightingale, *Segregation: A Global History,* 319–20; Nels Abrams, "The Making of Audubon Park: Competing Ideologies of Public Space" (Master's Thesis, University of New Orleans, 2010). See also Robert M. Fogelson, *Bourgeois Nightmares: Suburbia, 1870–1930* (New Haven, CT: Yale University Press, 2005).

75. Janice Richard Johnson, "Leland University in New Orleans, 1870–1915" (PhD diss., University of New Orleans, 1996), 93, 186–87, 231; Cangelosi and Schlesinger, eds., *New Orleans Architecture*, vol. 7, pp. 57–62, 88–89.

76. Cangelosi and Schlesinger, eds., *New Orleans Architecture*, vols. 7, 18; 1920 U.S. Census, New Orleans, La., Population, Heritage Quest, NAMS T-625, Roll 624; Sanborn Map Company, *Insurance Maps of New Orleans*, vol. 5, 1909, sheet 507, http://sanborn.umi.com/splash.html.

77. The author's father, Maurice M. Stern, was born in 1916 and lived at 3 Richmond Place, opposite the Alms House grounds, into the 1930s. He recalled that Fabacher's cows grazed on the land between Nashville, Joseph, South Liberty, and Freret prior to the construction of a school on that site. This recollection is consistent with contemporary reports of cows roaming the nearby Fellman tract during the 1920s. See "Section of Fine Homes Where Land Was Waste Quarter Century Ago," *Times-Picayune*, 10 June 1923; 1920 U.S. Census, New Orleans, La., Population, Series T-625, Roll 624.

78. OPSB Committee of Whole Minutes, 6 April 1926.

79. "Mrs. Baumgartner for New Schools," *Times-Picayune*, 30 October 1920, 20. On Friend's complaints about Allen, see OPSB Minutes, 14 October 1921 and 9 January 1925. See also Pamela Tyler, *Silk Stockings and Ballot Boxes: Women and Politics in New Orleans, 1920–1960* (Athens: University of Georgia Press, 1996), 46. On Weis Friend, see "Biographical Note," Ida Weis Friend Papers, LaRC, available at http://specialcollections.tulane.edu/archon/index.php?p=collections/findingaid&id=78&q=Ida+Weiss+Friend&rootcontentid=.

80. OPSB Minutes, 28 November 1924.

81. "Joseph Street Will be Closed in Four Blocks," *Times-Picayune*, 12 February 1929, 1. On the public battle over the creation of a new road through the Fellman Tract, see Fellman Tract folder, Box 1, New Orleans Department of Public Property Records, City Archives, NOPL. See also "Citizens Protest Mission Proposal at Council Meet," *Times-Picayune*, 19 June 1928, 9; "Planning Board Forming Policy on Subdivision Streets," *Times-Picayune*, 23 September 1927; "Council Pledges Lakeview Sewer Project Priority," *Times-Picayune*, 6 February 1929; "Park Commission Approves Plans to Beautify City," *Times-Picayune*, 23 August 1928, 4.

82. OPSB Minutes, 12 October 1928; "A. B. Nicholas Made President of Realty Board," *Times-Picayune*, 24 March 1928 (quote); "Schools Will Stress Importance of Health Through Coming Year," *Times-Picayune*, 1 January 1930.

83. OPSB Minutes, 12 February 1930; "$2,250,000 for Eight New School Buildings Is Approved by Board," *Times-Picayune*, 13 February 1930, 1.

84. Gwen Bristow, "Great Educational Center Rising in Small Uptown Area," *Times-Picayune*, 16 March 1930, 20.

85. OPSB Minutes, 9 January 1925; G. A. Mahe to John C. Klorer, New Orleans, 18 June 1927, New Orleans Real Estate Board folder, box 2, New Orleans Department of Public Property Records, City Archives, NOPL. Quote is from G. F. Cocker to John C. Klorer, New Orleans, 18 June 1929, Fourteenth Ward Civic League folder, box 2, New Orleans Department of Public Property Records, City Archives, NOPL.

86. City Planning & Zoning Commission, "New Orleans Louisiana District Map & Key to Official District Maps," July 1930, box 126, RG 195, National Archives II; Cangelosi and Schlesinger, eds., *New Orleans Architecture*, vol. 7, 69; "Act of Sale for Site No. 3 on Octavia Street in Block No. 651 (formerly 83) in Sixth District," Bernard Co., Inc. to Louis V. Burka, 9 March 1923, *No-*

tarial Acts, 1–79, 1923, Arthur B. Leopold, Notary Public, New Orleans Notarial Archives Research Center; David M. P. Freund, *Colored Property: State Policy & White Racial Politics in Suburban America* (Chicago: University of Chicago Press, 2007), 46–66; Blaine A. Brownell, "The Commercial-Civic Elite and City Planning in Atlanta, Memphis, and New Orleans in the 1920s," *Journal of Southern History* 41, no. 3 (August 1975): 339–68.

87. Notable exceptions include Ansley T. Erickson, *Making the Unequal Metropolis: School Desegregaion and Its Limits* (Chicago: University of Chciago Press, 2016); Andrew R. Highsmith, *Demolition Means Progress: Flint, Michigan, and the Fate of the American Metropolis* (Chicago: University of Chicago Press, 2015); Karen Benjamin, "Segregation Built to Last: Schools and the Construction of Segregated Housing Patterns in Early Twentieth-Century Atlanta," paper presented at the History of Education Society Annual Conference, 5 November 2016.

88. "Superb Fortier High School Will Receive Students Monday, *Times-Picayune,* 1 February 1931, 20; OPSB Minutes, 9 January 1931, 15 May 1931; "School Congestion Opposed," *Times-Picayune,* 15 May 1931, 14; "Fellman Tract to Fill Gap Left in Fair City's Heart," *Times-Picayune,* 15 March 1931; "Leo Fellman, 59, Dies After Long Illness at Home," *Times-Picayune,* 22 November 1934, 1, 8.

89. "Leo Fellman, 59, Dies After Long Illness at Home," *Times-Picayune,* 22 November 1934, 8; "Sale of Property, Alice Lemann, widow of Leo Fellman, Mary Anna Fellman, wife of Julian B. Feibelman, and John Henry Fellman to Milton E. Pick," 23 September 1941, in *Acts, August 29, 1940 to October 16, 1941,* vol. 53, *J. D. Dresne*r, NONARC; "Sale of Property by Bernard Company, Inc. to Elias Cohen," 7 January 1940, in vol. 2, *Notarial Acts, 1939–1941 inclusive, 1–202, Manuel I. Fisher, Notary Public,* Notarial Archives; "Area Description, Security Map of Metropolitan New Orleans, La.," Area A-9, 1939, New Orleans, LA #2 folder, box 88, RG 195, National Archives II. N.B. While also part of Orleans Parish Civil District Court, the Notarial Archives is distinct from the Notarial Archives Research Center.

90. Division of Research and Statistics, Federal Home Loan Bank Board, *Summary, Survey of Economic, Real Estate and Mortgage Finance Conditions in New Orleans, Louisiana* (Washington, DC: 1939), 6, 8–9, "New Orleans Re-Survey Report # 2" folder, box 67; interview with Stanley M. LeMarie, Partner in Leo Fellman & Co., Real Estate Brokers, p. 194-A, in "Appendix: Report of Re-Survey, New Orleans, Louisiana for the Division of Research and Statistics, Home Owners' Loan Corporation" [1939], folder #1, box 127, all in RG 195, National Archives II; Sanborn Map Company, *Insurance Maps of New Orleans, Louisiana,* vol. 6A, 1940, sheets 627A, 646A, 650A.

91. Sanborn Map Company, *Insurance Maps of New Orleans, Louisiana,* vol. 5, 1933, sheet 527, Southeastern Architectural Archive, Tulane University; Sanborn Map Company, *Insurance Maps of New Orleans, Louisiana,* vol. 5, 1951, sheet 527.

92. Interview with F. Poché Waguespack, pp. 196-A and 197-A, in "Appendix: Report of Re-Survey, New Orleans, Louisiana for the Division of Research and Statistics, Home Owners' Loan Corporation" [1939], folder #1, box 127, RG 195, National Archives II; Sanborn Map Company, *Insurance Maps of New Orleans, Louisiana,* vol. 5, 1933, sheet 510, Southeastern Architectural Archive, Tulane University; Sanborn Map Company, *Insurance Maps of New Orleans, Louisiana,* vol. 5, 1951, sheet 510.

93. Interview with Stanley M. LeMarie, Partner in Leo Fellman & Co., Real Estate Brokers, in 194-A, in "Appendix: Report of Re-Survey, New Orleans, Louisiana for the Division of Research and Statistics, Home Owners' Loan Corporation" [1939], folder #1, box 127, RG 195, National

Archives II. Several other interviews in this appendix corroborate LeMarie's assessment of the University Section.

94. Division of Research and Statistics, Federal Home Loan Bank Board, "Summary of Economic, Real Estate and Mortgage Survey and Security Area Descriptions of New Orleans, Louisiana," 28 April 1939, pp. 2-A, 3-A, New Orleans, LA #2 folder, box 88, RG 195, National Archives II.

95. Division of Research and Statistics, Federal Home Loan Bank Board, "Summary of Economic, Real Estate and Mortgage Survey and Security Area Descriptions of New Orleans, Louisiana," 28 April 1939, pp. 2-A, 3-A, and Area Descriptions for Areas A-9, B-18, and B-19, New Orleans, LA #2 folder, box 88 (quote is from description of Area A-9); "Residential Security Map," New Orleans, LA, 1939, box 126, RG 195, National Archives II.

96. The quote is from the Area Description for Area B-6, Madison, WI, accessed via Robert K. Nelson, LaDale Winling, Richard Marciano, Nathan Connolly, et al., "Mapping Inequality," *American Panorama*, ed. Robert K. Nelson and Edward L. Ayers, accessed April 21, 2017, https://dsl.richmond.edu/panorama/redlining/#loc=14/43.0712/-89.4058&opacity=0.8&city=madison-wi&area=B6. The Area Descriptions for Atlanta areas A-8, B-13, B-14, B-15, which are also accessible via the "Mapping Inequality" web site, provide glimpses of the importance surveyors placed upon proximity to schools. Additionally, Area A-9 in Philadelphia is an example of a highly rated neighborhood for which surveyors took note of access to schools. The Philadelphia area descriptions are available via Amy Hillier's "Redlining in Philadelphia" web site, http://www.nis.cml.upenn.edu/redlining/.

97. The quote is from a report simply titled "Federal Housing Administration," located in the New Orleans, Louisiana, Confidential Reports folder, box 127, RG 195, National Archives II. The summaries of interviews with real estate brokers and officials which accompany the report are dated May 3 and 4, 1939. The most comprehensive source on the Federal Housing Administration is Freund, *Colored Property*, esp. chap. 3 and 4.

98. Leo Fellman & Co., "New Orleans' New Home Section: A Real Place to Live," n.d., "Real Estate Agents. Leo Fellman" folder, Ephemera Collection, LaRC.

99. "Grads Took Final Bow Last Night," *Silver and Blue,* 29 January 1932, p. 3, Lusher Library; 1940 U.S. Census, New Orleans, La., Population, Heritage Quest Online, Series T-627, Roll 1433, available through Heritage Quest; Sanborn Map Company, *Insurance Maps of New Orleans, Louisiana*, vol. 6, 1909, corrected to 1934, sheet 571, Southeastern Architectural Archive, Special Collections Division, Tulane University; Cangelosi and Schlesinger, eds., *New Orleans Architecture*, vol. 7, 185.

100. U.S. Bureau of the Census, *16th Census of the United States, 1940, Population and Housing, Statistics for Census Tracts, New Orleans, La.* (Washington: Government Printing Office, 1941), iv, 55, 62; Cangelosi and Schlesinger, eds., *New Orleans Architecture*, vol. 7, 185; 1940 U.S. Census, New Orleans, La., Population, Heritage Quest Online, Series T-627, Roll 1433; 1930 U.S. Census, New Orleans, La., Population, Heritage Quest Online, Series T-626, both available through Heritage Quest.

101. U.S. Bureau of the Census, *16th Census of the United States, 1940, Population and Housing, Statistics for Census Tracts, New Orleans, La.* (Washington: Government Printing Office, 1941), iv, 58; Nirenstein's National Realty Map Company, "Business Section, City of New Orleans," 1947, HNOC, 1976.92.1.

102. DeVore and Logsdon, *Crescent City Schools*, 184; OPSB Minutes, 11 December 1925 and 14 September 1928.

103. OPSB Committee of the Whole Minutes, 7 October 1924.

104. Ibid.

105. Colored Civic League of New Orleans to John Klorer, New Orleans, 26 March 1927, Colored Civic League of New Orleans/Colored Civic and Business League folder, box 1, New Orleans Department of Public Property Records, City Archives, NOPL.

106. A. E. Perkins to John Klorer, New Orleans, 21 July 1927, Colored Civic League of New Orleans/Colored Civic and Business League folder, box 1, New Orleans Department of Public Property Records, City Archives, NOPL.

107. Sanborn Map Company, *Insurance Maps of New Orleans, Louisiana*, vol. 6a, 1940, sheet 665a.

108. State Department of Education of Louisiana, *Ninety-second Annual Report for the Session 1940–41*, 181–82; New Orleans Public Schools, *School Directory*, 1940–41, box 4, School Directories, OPSB-147.

109. Legal filing quoted in Charles L. deLay, "Schools Target in 2 Law Suits Filed," *Louisiana Weekly*, 12 June 1948, 1, 7.

CHAPTER SIX

1. OPSB Minutes, 18 March 1948, 12 April 1948, 7 June 1948 (for quote), and 30 November 1948.

2. OPSB Minutes, 30 November 1948; Mary Lee Muller, "The Orleans Parish School Board and Negro Education, 1940–1960" (Master's thesis, University of New Orleans, 1975), 14–20; Donald E. DeVore and Joseph Logsdon, *Crescent City Schools: Public Education in New Orleans, 1841–1991* (Lafayette: University of Southwestern Louisiana Press, 1991), 224–25.

3. "Understanding, Sympathy Seen as World War Result," *Times-Picayune*, 28 November 1947, 39; "Three Shifts Set for High School," *Times-Picayune*, 8 July 1948, 13; "Rules at Negro Schools Listed," *Times-Picayune*, 26 August 1948, 24; Lionel J. Bourgeois to A. P. Tureaud, 30 September 1947, folder 3, box 43, Subseries 4, Subseries 27, Series VII/microfilm reel 32, frames 1081–2, A. P. Tureaud Papers, Amistad Research Center at Tulane University, New Orleans, Louisiana (cited hereinafter as APT Papers).

4. H. S. Baham, Mrs. B. Brown, Mrs. M. B. Johnson, and Mrs. L. Blacke to the Honorable Members of the School Board, 13 October 1950, folder 6, box 43/microfilm reel 32/frame 1148, APT Papers (for quote). The Educational Committee of the New Orleans Branch NAACP also submitted a petition regarding Clark's platoon system on 18 August 1950. See New Orleans Branch NAACP to Orleans Parish School Board, 18 August 1950, "Petition in re: Platoon System in Clark High School," Joseph S. Clark Senior High School, August 18, 1950–February 17, 1970 folder, School Board General Files, OPSB-147.

5. Lakeview's population, which was already almost entirely white, more than doubled from 4,670 in 1940 to 9,508 between 1940 and 1950. Population growth in Gentilly was so dramatic that the Census Bureau divided the two tracts that covered the area in 1940 into six by 1950. The total population in this part of the city increased from 8,422 in 1940 to 30,636 in 1950. With the

exception of the area in and around the black St. Bernard Housing Project in the southwestern corner of Gentilly, nearly everyone living in this section was white. U.S. Bureau of the Census, *16th Census of the United States, 1940, Population and Housing, Statistics for Census Tracts, New Orleans, La.* (Washington: Government Printing Office, 1941), iv, 4; "Original Variables(ORG), Census 1950 (All Geographies—Compatible Variables Only)," digitally transcribed by Inter-university Consortium for Political and Social Research. Edited and verified by Michael Haines. Compiled, edited, and verified by Social Explorer.

6. H. S. Baham, Mrs. B. Brown, Mrs. M. B. Johnson, and Mrs. L. Blacke to the Honorable Members of the School Board, 13 October 1950, folder 6, box 43/microfilm reel 32/frame 1148, APT Papers.

7. Thurgood Marshall to A. P. Tureaud, 11 October 1950, folder 5, box 43/microfilm reel 32, frame 1137, APT Papers (quote); Tureaud to Marshall, 12 October 1950, folder 6, box 43/microfilm reel 32, APT Papers; Richard Kluger, *Simple Justice: The History of* Brown v. Board of Education *and Black America's Struggle for Equality* (New York: Knopf, 1975), 281–94; Risa L. Goluboff, *Lost Promise of Civil Rights* (Cambridge, MA: Harvard University Press, 2007), 227–28.

8. Ira Berlin, *The Making of African America: Four Great Migrations* (New York: Viking, 2010), chap. 4; Original Variables(ORG), Census 1950 (All Geographies—Compatible Variables Only)," digitally transcribed by Inter-university Consortium for Political and Social Research. Edited and verified by Michael Haines. Compiled, edited, and verified by Social Explorer; Gibson and Jung, *Historical Census Statistics On Population Totals By Race, 1790 to 1990, and By Hispanic Origin, 1970 to 1990, For Large Cities And Other Urban Places In The United States,* "Table 19. Louisiana—Race and Hispanic Origin for Selected Large Cities and Other Places: Earliest Census to 1990," available at http://www.census.gov/population/www/documentation/twps0076/twps0076.html.

9. Martha Mahoney, "The Changing Nature of Public Housing in New Orleans, 1930–1974" (Master's thesis, Tulane University, 1985), 38–39, 59, 62–63; Donald E. DeVore, "The Rise from the Nadir: Black New Orleans Between the Wars, 1920–1940" (Master's thesis, University of New Orleans, 1983), 116–17; DeVore and Logsdon, *Crescent City Schools,* 219–20; Muller, "Orleans Parish School Board and Negro Education," 18–19; Orleans Parish School Board–Office of Planning and Construction, *A Planning and Building Program for New Orleans' Schools* (New Orleans: Orleans Parish School Board, 1952), 2, report courtesy of Ken Ducote, also available at Amistad Research Center and Earl K. Long Library, University of New Orleans; Louisiana Department of Education, *Annual Financial and Statistical Reports,* 1950–1952, available at http://www2.state.lib.la.us/doeafsr/; "Junk the Neighborhood School," *Architectural Forum,* April 1953, 130; New Orleans Public Schools, *Facts and Finances,* 1957–58, box 7, Financial Records, OPSB-147.

10. *A Planning and Building Program for New Orleans' Schools,* 4 (quote).

11. While Arnold Hirsch draws a bright line between the "first ghetto" and "second ghetto," my work highlights greater continuity between the earlier and later phases in an extended, government-sponsored process of restricting black residency in American cities. Specifically, this and previous chapters challenge the temporal and qualitative distinctions that Hirsch makes between the first and second ghetto. Hirsch famously distinguishes the second ghetto from the first on the basis of its larger size, its post–World War II development, and the government's outsized role in creating it. He writes that "direct government support for segregation, before the New Deal, consisted primarily of the judicial enforcement of privately drawn restrictive covenants."

While Hirsch rightly emphasizes the post–World War II impact of federal support for residential segregation, public schools enabled government officials (acting with state authorization at the local level) to promote residential segregation far earlier and more effectively than Hirsch and subsequent scholars acknowledge. See Hirsch, *Making the Second Ghetto: Race and Housing in Chicago, 1940–1960* (Chicago: University of Chicago Press, 1998; originally published 1983), 9–10 (for quote). In a reexamination of his influential book twenty years after its initial publication, Hirsch encouraged and partially anticipated revisions such as the one offered here with his suggestion that "a series of city-by-city case studies of school construction and renewal programs might well place educational issues and institutions . . . alongside highways as an unexplored facet of the second ghetto." See Hirsch, "Second Thoughts on the Second Ghetto," *Journal of Urban History* 29, no. 3 (March 2003): 305.

12. On Soweto's development in South Africa, which overlapped chronologically with the development of the "school village" and housing project in New Orleans's Ninth Ward, see Carl Nightingale, *Segregation: A Global History of Divided Cities* (Chicago: University of Chicago Press, 2012), 358–80.

13. Richard Campanella, e-mail correspondence with author, 22 January 2014. On St. Monica, see Arnold R. Hirsch, "Race and Renewal in the Cold War South: New Orleans, 1947–1968," in *The American Planning Tradition: Culture and Policy*, ed. Robert Fishman (Washington, DC: Woodrow Wilson Center Press, 2000), 219–39. The location of the St. Monica Catholic school is noted in *A Planning and Building Program for New Orleans' Schools,* "Existing Catholic Schools 1950–51," map following p. 10.

14. William Ivy Hair, *Carnival of Fury: Robert Charles and the New Orleans Race Riot of 1900* (Baton Rouge: Louisiana State University Press, 1976); "Thomy Lafon School Burned to the Ground," *Daily Picayune,* 28 July 1900, 8; "War Sure Enough," *Times-Picayune,* 18 December 1874; Fischer, *Segregation Struggle in Louisiana,* 125–27; Richard Campanella, *Geographies of New Orleans: Urban Fabrics Before the Storm* (Lafayette: Center for Louisiana Studies, 2006), 270–76.

15. "Social Explorer Tables (SE), Census 1950 Tracts Only Set," digitally transcribed by Interuniversity Consortium for Political and Social Research. Edited and verified by Michael Haines. Compiled, edited, and verified and additional data entered by Social Explorer. While the City of New Orleans currently distinguishes the Central City neighborhood from the adjacent B. W. Cooper, or Calliope, Housing Project, I group Calliope with Central City for two reasons. First, the two areas are contiguous and demographically indistinct during the time period under examination. Second, as discussed below, this broader area became racially homogenous through the same process of public and private support for residential segregation. For present-day neighborhood boundaries, see map 6.4.

16. U.S. Census, 1940, New Orleans, La., Population, National Archives Microfilm Series T-627, Reel 1431, accessed via Heritage Quest; Mahoney, "Changing Nature of Public Housing," 56–57. In 1940, Braden's home was worth $350,792 in 2017 dollars. Conversion made via U.S. Bureau of Labor Statistics, "CPI Calculator."

17. *A Planning and Building Program for New Orleans' Schools,* 35 (first quote); Mahoney, "Changing Nature of Public Housing," 49–50 (second quote); Muller, "The Orleans Parish School Board and Negro Education, 1940–1960," 23.

18. O. C. W. Taylor, "The Public School Your Child Attends," *Louisiana Weekly,* 9 April 1927; *A Planning and Building Program for New Orleans' Schools.*

19. On Kruttschnitt School, see chapter 5.

20. "$2,250,000 for Eight New School Buildings Is Approved by Board," *Times-Picayune*, 13 February 1930, 1 (quote); *Harmon v. Tyler*, 273 U.S. 668 (1927); *Buchanan v. Warley*, 245 U.S. 60 (1917); *City of Richmond v. Deans*, 281 U.S. 704 (1930); Mahoney, "Changing Nature of Public Housing," 24; Mahoney, "Law and Racial Geography: Public Housing and the Economy in New Orleans," *Stanford Law Review* 42, no. 5 (May 1990): 1269. For brief histories of specific housing projects, see, for instance, City of New Orleans, Office of Policy Planning, "Iberville Project Profile (6C)" (New Orleans: December 1978); City of New Orleans Office of Policy and Planning, "Sixth Ward/Tremé/Lafitte Neighborhood Profile (6A)" (New Orleans: December 1978); City of New Orleans Office of Policy and Planning, "Calliope Project Neighborhood Profile" (New Orleans: December 1978). As 1938 ended, the federal government had committed $30 million toward the construction of the St. Thomas and Iberville housing projects for whites and the Magnolia, Lafitte, Calliope, and St. Bernard projects for blacks. That amount nearly equaled Louisiana's *statewide* education spending for 1938–1939 and was roughly six times the expenditures for the public schools in New Orleans, which exceeded $5 million in 1938–1939 before increasing to more than $8 million by 1940–1941. See Mahoney, "Changing Nature of Public Housing," 24; State Department of Education of Louisiana, *Ninetieth Annual Report for the Session 1938–39*, 102, 137; State Department of Education of Louisiana, *Ninety-Second Annual Report for the Session 1940–41*, 165.

21. Mahoney, "Changing Nature of Public Housing," 20–27; A. Scott Henderson, "Housing Act of 1937," in *Encyclopedia of American Urban History*, ed. David Goldfield (Thousand Oaks, CA: Sage Publishing, 2007); Arnold R. Hirsch, "With or Without Jim Crow: Black Residential Segregation in the United States," in *Urban Policy in Twentieth-Century America*, ed. Arnold R. Hirsch and Raymond A. Mohl (New Brunswick, NJ: Rutgers University Press, 1993), 86 (quote).

22. Mahoney, "Changing Nature of Public Housing," 21; City of New Orleans Office of Policy and Planning, *Calliope Project Neighborhood Profile* (New Orleans: December 1978). "It shone like silver" is from the *Item-Tribune* newspaper, quoted in *Calliope Neighborhood Profile*, p. 3.03.

23. Mahoney, "Changing Nature of Public Housing," 22–23, 25–28; Michael E. Crutcher Jr., *Tremé; Race and Place in a New Orleans Neighborhood* (Athens: University of Georgia Press, 2010), 14. See also "Housing Authority of New Orleans," in New Orleans, Louisiana Confidential Reports folder, box 127, RG 195, National Archives II.

24. Secretary, Orleans Parish School Board, to Alvin M. Fromherz, 30 June 1948; Moise H. Goldstein & Associates, "Project No. LA 1–2, Housing Authority of New Orleans, Slum Clearance and Housing Project for Negroes, Site Plan, Scheme-'G,'" both in Housing Authority of New Orleans, June 18, 1938–July 27, 1953 folder, School Board General Files, OPSB-147; "Big New Orleans Slum-Clearance Works Approved in Roosevelt Act," *Times-Picayune*, 18 March 1938, 1; "Negro Advance in Science and Education Is Outlined," *Times-Picayune*, 23 November 1939, 29 (for Lafon enrollment); Carol McMichael Reese, "The Once and Future New Orleans of Planners Milton Medary and Harland Bartholomew, 1920–1960," in *New Orleans Under Reconstruction: The Crisis of Planning*, ed. Carol McMichael Reese, Michael Sorkin, and Anthony Fontenot (London: Verso, 2014), 108.

25. Alvin M. Fromherz to E. A. Christy, 30 October 1939, in Housing Authority of New Orleans, June 18, 1938–July 27, 1953 folder, School Board General Files, OPSB-147 (quote; emphasis added); OPSB Minutes, 13 August 1914; DeVore and Logsdon, *Crescent City Schools*, 197–98.

26. A. J. Tete to Housing Authority of New Orleans, 22 June 1941; A. J. Tete to Housing Authority of New Orleans, 16 April 1941; Secretary to J. Gilbert Scheib, 10 April 1947, all in Housing Authority of New Orleans, June 18, 1938–July 27, 1953 folder, School Board General Files, OPSB-147; Mahoney, "Changing Nature of Public Housing," 37–38, 46–47; *A Planning and Building Program for New Orleans' Schools*, 20–21; Ansley T. Erickson, *Making the Unequal Metropolis: School Desegregation and Its Limits* (Chicago: University of Chicago Press, 2016), 47–48, 122, 134–36.

27. Citizens Committee on Equal Education to Orleans Parish School Board, 5 May 1946, folder 3, box 43/Reel 32, frame 1061–66, APT Papers.

28. Muller, "Orleans Parish School Board and Negro Education," 19–23.

29. The black population in the eight census tracts that covered Central City and the Calliope Housing Project increased from 36,418 to 43,163 between 1940 and 1950. "Social Explorer Tables (SE), Census 1950 Tracts Only Set," digitally transcribed by Inter-university Consortium for Political and Social Research. Edited and verified by Michael Haines. Compiled, edited, and verified and additional data entered by Social Explorer; U.S. Bureau of the Census, *16th Census of the United States, 1940, Population and Housing, Statistics for Census Tracts, New Orleans, La.* (Washington: Government Printing Office, 1941), iv, 4–5.

30. *A Planning and Building Program for New Orleans' Schools*, 40–42 (for quotes).

31. Samson Paul Bordelon, "The New Orleans Public Schools Under the Superintendency of Lionel John Bourgeois" (PhD diss., University of Southern Mississippi, 1966), 51–54, 78–79 (quote on 78). On the American occupation of Haiti, see Mary Renda, *Taking Haiti: Military Occupation and the Culture of U.S. Imperialism, 1915–1940* (Chapel Hill: University of North Carolina Press, 2000).

32. Orleans Parish School Board, Office of the Superintendent, *Proposed Program for the Improvement of the Public Schools of New Orleans* (New Orleans: Orleans Parish School Board, 7 January 1948), 33 (for quote), available at Louisiana Division, Earl K. Long Library, University of New Orleans.

33. Ibid.

34. U.S. Const. amend. XIV, §1 (first quote); Mark V. Tushnet, *The NAACP's Legal Strategy Against Segregated Education, 1925–1950* (Chapel Hill: University of North Carolina Press, 1987), chap. 1–3, 171 n. 33 (see 13–14 for the second quote, which comes from a 1930 report from the NAACP to the Garland Fund); Goluboff, *Lost Promise of Civil Rights*, 178; Kluger, *Simple Justice*, 132–37; 186–88.

35. Adam Fairclough, *A Class of Their Own: Black Teachers in the Segregated South* (Cambridge, MA: Belknap Press of Harvard University Press, 2007), chap. 8–9; W. E. B. Du Bois, "Does the Negro Need Separate Schools?" *Journal of Negro Education* 4, no. 3 (July 1935): 328–35 (335 for quote); Michael Fultz, "The Displacement of Black Educators Post-*Brown*: An Overview and Analysis," *History of Education Quarterly* 44, no. 1 (Spring 2004): 11–45; DeVore, *Defying Jim Crow*, 195–205.

36. Adam Fairclough, *Race and Democracy: The Civil Rights Struggle in Louisiana*, 2nd edition (Athens: University of Georgia Press, 2008), 63, 99–100, 108; Kluger, *Simple Justice*, 215–17, 333–35.

37. Fairclough, *Race and Democracy*, 108.

38. Bordelon, "The New Orleans Public Schools Under the Superintendency of Lionel John Bourgeois," 78–79; "Interview with Mr. Paul B. Habans, State Manager H.O.L.C.," 4 May 1939, New Orleans, Louisiana Confidential Reports folder, box 127, RG 195; Division of Research & Statistics, Federal Home Loan Bank Board, "Summary of Economic, Real Estate and Mortgage Survey and Security Area Descriptions of New Orleans, Louisiana," 28 April 1939, p. 2-A, New Orleans, LA #2 folder, box 88, RG 195, National Archives II; Brooke H. Duncan to Lionel J. Bourgeois, 17 November 1949 (for quote); Ernest O. Becker to Brooke H. Duncan, 21 November 1949; Duncan to Bourgeois, 27 December 1949, Duncan to Bourgeois, 14 March 1950, all in folder 187, box 14, New Orleans City Planning Commission Subject Files, City Archives, NOPL.

39. Orleans Parish School Board, Office of the Superintendent, *Proposed Program for the Improvement of the Public Schools of New Orleans*, 55–60; DeVore and Logsdon, *Crescent City Schools*, 221, 361; *Soards' New Orleans City Directory*, 1930 (New Orleans: Soards Directory Co., 1930), 664; *Soards' New Orleans City Directory*, 1932 (New Orleans: Soards Directory Co., 1932), 1099; *Polk's New Orleans City Directory*, 1945–1946 (New Orleans: R. L. Polk & Co., 1946), 416, 739, 980.

40. Dorothy Shipps, *School Reform, Corporate Style: Chicago, 1880–2000* (Lawrence: University Press of Kansas, 2006), 67–69; Tracy L. Steffes, "Managing School Integration and White Flight: The Debate Over Chicago's Future in the 1960s," *Journal of Urban History* 42, no. 4 (July 2016): 711–13; John L. Rury, "Race, Space, and the Politics of Chicago's Public Schools: Benjamin Willis and the Tragedy of Urban Education," *History of Education Quarterly* 39, no. 2 (Summer 1999): 117–42.

41. Jeffrey Mirel, *The Rise and Fall of an Urban School System, Detroit: 1907–1981*, 2nd edition (Ann Arbor: University of Michigan Press, 1999), 192–94; Ruth Batson, *The Black Educational Movement in Boston: A Sequence of Historical Events: A Chronology* (Boston: Northeastern University School of Education, 2001), 168a, 176–79, 185, 187–88. Thanks to Jeanne Theoharis and Tess Bundy for alerting me to this Boston example and to Batson's remarkable chronicle of black educational activism in Boston. Batson's manuscript is available through multiple libraries in the Boston area.

42. Orleans Parish School Board, Office of the Superintendent, *Biennial Report of Progress* (New Orleans: Orleans Parish School Board, 1 March 1950), 40–41 (quotes on 41), available at Louisiana Division, Earl K. Long Library, University of New Orleans.

43. DeVore and Logsdon, *Crescent City Schools*, 219–21; Muller, "Orleans Parish School Board and Negro Education," 18. On black voter registration in New Orleans in 1948, see Fairclough, *Race and Democracy*, 123–24.

44. *A Planning and Building Program for New Orleans' Schools*, 35, 40–43; Lionel J. Bourgeois to Mrs. Erna Landix, Citizens Committee on Equal Education, NAACP, folder 5, box 43/Roll 32, frames 1124–1125, APT Papers.

45. *A Planning and Building Program for New Orleans' Schools*, 40–43; "Junk the Neighborhood School," 135. For additional discussion of the profitability of black housing for landlords, see Sugrue, *Origins of the Urban Crisis*, chap. 2, and Nightingale, *Segregation: A Global History*, 308–9.

46. *A Planning and Building Program for New Orleans' Schools*, 40–43 (quote on p. 40).

47. Ibid., 45–49 (quote on p. 49); "Junk the Neighborhood School," 134; Sanborn Map Com-

pany, *Insurance Maps of New Orleans*, vol. 9, 1937, corrected to 1951, sheets 0b, 1210, 1501; Sanborn Map Company, *Insurance Maps of New Orleans*, vol. 10, 1937, corrected to 1951, sheets 0a, 1012, 1022, available http://sanborn.umi.com. Colbert's "school village" bears a striking similarity to the "education parks" that educators later embraced as a means of advancing school desegregation. While Ansley T. Erickson has highlighted the popularity of the education park concept in northeastern and midwestern cities during the 1960s and 1970s, Colbert's proposal suggests that the idea may have originated a decade earlier in the South as a tool for preserving segregation. See Erickson, "Desegregation's Architects: Education Parks and the Spatial Ideology of Schooling," *History of Education Quarterly* 56, no. 4 (November 2016): 560–89.

48. "Junk the Neighborhood School," 129 (for quote), 178, 184; *A Planning and Building Program for New Orleans' Schools*, 6 (first quote), 45–49; Kluger, *Simple Justice*, 529–40; OPSB Minutes, 12 November 1951; Muller, "Orleans Parish School Board and Negro Education," 27–35; Nightingale, *Segregation: A Global History*, 357, 371.

49. *A Planning and Building Program for New Orleans' Schools*, 6 (first quote); "Junk the Neighborhood School," 129 (second quote).

50. "Contemporary School Architecture," *Architectural Forum*, February 1951, 104–6; Jacqueline T. Leonhard, "Statement re: new post of 'Supervising Architect for Planning and Construction' for the Orleans Parish School Board," 27 February 1951, Charles Colbert, February 27–December 15, 1951 folder, School Board General Files, OPSB-147; John C. Ferguson, "The Architecture of Education: The Public School Buildings of New Orleans," in DeVore and Logsdon, *Crescent City Schools*, 338–46; "New Orleans Said Building 'Monuments Not Schools,'" *Times-Picayune*, 3 April 1949, 1; "Charles R. Colbert, Architect and Educator," *Times-Picayune*, 16 February 2007, Metro section, p. 3. On Curtis and Davis, see Elizabeth G. Heavrin, *Recordation of Certain Buildings at the George Washington Carver School Campus, New Orleans, Louisiana* (New Orleans and Lexington, KY: Triagon Associates and Cultural Resource Analysts, 2010), FEMA-George Washington Carver School Collection (Mss 363), Louisiana and Special Collections Department, Earl K. Long Library, University of New Orleans; "Finding Aid to Nathaniel C. Curtis, Jr. Drawings, Southeastern Architectural Archive Collection 24," Tulane University, http://seaa.tulane.edu/sites/all/themes/Howard_Tilton/docs/finding_aids/Nathaniel%20C.%20Curtis,%20Jr.%20Drawings.pdf.

51. "Candidate Urges More Efficiency," *Times-Picayune*, 2 November 1948, 12; "AIA Will Advise Board on School," *Times-Picayune*, 9 April 1949, 1; "Club Asks Delay on School Plans," *Times-Picayune*, 5 April 1949, 31; "New Orleans Said Building 'Monuments Not Schools,'" *Times-Picayune*, 3 April 1949, 1; "Contemporary School Architecture," *Architectural Forum*, February 1951, 104–6; "Junk the Neighborhood School," 135; "Statement re: new post of 'Supervising Architect for Planning and Construction' for the Orleans Parish School Board," 27 February 1951.

52. "Statement re: new post of 'Supervising Architect for Planning and Construction' for the Orleans Parish School Board"; Sanborn Map Company, *Insurance Maps of New Orleans*, vol. 10, 1937, corrected to 1951, sheets 0a, 1020, 1034–1037, available http://sanborn.umi.com; *A Planning and Building Program for New Orleans' Schools*, 4–5 and population density maps following p. 16. I generated the distance estimates using Apple Maps.

53. U.S. Bureau of the Census, *16th Census of the United States, 1940, Population and Housing, Statistics for Census Tracts, New Orleans, La.* (Washington: Government Printing Office, 1941), iv, 4; "Original Variables (ORG), Census 1950 (All Geographies—Compatible Variables

Only)," digitally transcribed by Inter-university Consortium for Political and Social Research. Edited and verified by Michael Haines. Compiled, edited, and verified by Social Explorer.

54. David M. P. Freund, *Colored Property: State Policy & White Racial Politics in Suburban America* (Chicago: University of Chicago Press, 2007), 118–33; Kenneth Jackson, *Crabgrass Frontier: The Suburbanization of the United States* (New York: Oxford University Press, 1985), 203–9. The role the FHA and other federal agencies played in the development of Parkchester and other Gentilly subdivisions was well documented in the *Times-Picayune*. See "Many Gaps in City Fill as Suburbs Spread Out," *Times-Picayune*, 25 January 1953, section 9, pp. 11, 18; "Construction to Begin on Homes," *Times-Picayune*, 23 January 1944, section 4, p. 11; "Mirabeau Manor Property is Sold," *Times-Picayune*, 9 September 1949, 19; "FHA Order Dims Housing Picture in New Orleans," *Times-Picayune*, 18 November 1947, 1; "Development to Make 350 Homes Available to Vets," *Times-Picayune*, 5 May 1946, section 4, p. 13; "Results of FHA Inquiry Awaited," *Times-Picayune*, 21 September 1954, 4; "Housing Project Funds Arranged," *Times-Picayune*, 9 January 1948, 11. See also Mahoney, "Law and Racial Geography," 1275.

55. Abrams quoted in Hirsch, "With or Without Jim Crow," 85.

56. Exceptions include Andrew R. Highsmith, *Demolition Means Progress: Flint, Michigan, and the Fate of the American Metropolis* (Chicago: University of Chicago Press, 2015); Andrew R. Highsmith and Ansley T. Erickson, "Segregation as Splitting, Segregation as Joining: Schools, Housing, and the Many Modes of Jim Crow," *American Journal of Education* 121, no. 4 (August 2015): 563–95; Shaun McGann and Jack Dougherty, "Federal Lending and Redlining," in Dougherty and contributors, *On the Line: How Schooling, Housing, and Civil Rights Shaped Hartford and Its Suburbs.* Book-in-progress, 2016, http://ontheline.trincoll.edu/book/chapter/federal-lending-and-redlining/.

57. Freund, *Colored Property*, 130; Federal Housing Administration, *Underwriting Manual: Underwriting Analysis Under Title II, Section 203 of the National Housing Act* (Washington, DC: National Housing Agency/Federal Housing Administration, 1938), paragraphs 950–52 (first quote at 951); Federal Housing Administration, *Underwriting Manual: Underwriting Analysis Under Title II, Section 203 of the National Housing Act* (Washington, DC: National Housing Agency/Federal Housing Administration, 1947), paragraphs 1320–23, 1344–46 (second quote at 1345(1)), paragraphs 1364–65, 1367–68, 1370–71.

58. NAACP attorneys stressed this point in *Swann v. Charlotte-Mecklenburg*. See Lassiter, *Silent Majority*, 131–37.

59. Freund, *Colored Property*, 131–32.

60. Division of Research & Statistics, Federal Home Loan Bank Board, "Summary of Economic, Real Estate and Mortgage Survey and Security Area Descriptions of New Orleans, Louisiana," 28 April 1939, Area Description D-12, New Orleans, LA #2 folder, box 88, RG 195, National Archives II; "Beat Scouts to Boulevards and Bought Bargains," *Times-Picayune*, 10 October 1926, section 2, pp. 1, 12; "Contractor Buys Tract on Bayou," *Times-Picayune*, 21 August 1948, 5; Ordinance No. 17,530, Commission Council Series, 17 December 1948, Oak Park School folder, School Board General Files, OPSB-147.

61. "Contractor Buys Tract on Bayou," *Times-Picayune*, 21 August 1948, 5; "420 Rental Units Being Considered," *Times-Picayune*, 5 June 1948, 12; "Bayou Residents to Protest Dam," *Times-Picayune*, 21 January 1949, 10; Ordinance No. 17,530, Commission Council Series, 17 December 1948, Oak Park School folder, School Board General Files, OPSB-147.

62. Gervais F. Favrot to Mayor and Commission Council, 19 October 1948, folder 187 (Schools, Orleans Parish School Board), box 14, New Orleans City Planning Commission Subject Files, NOPL (for quote); Ordinance No. 17,530, Commission Council Series, 17 December 1948, Oak Park School folder, School Board General Files, OPSB-147; "Real Estate for Sale, Lots," *Times-Picayune*, 30 August 1949, p. 30, col. 7; "Bids on School Projects Opened," *Times-Picayune*, 24 April 1952. For additional evidence of city-school collaboration and the tensions that sometimes accompanied it, see Bourgeois to Mayor Morrison, 7 November 1949 and 6 April 1950, and the exchanges between City Planning and Zoning Commission chairman Gervais Favrot and School Board president Clarence Scheps from May and June 1954, all in folder 187 (Schools, Orleans Parish School Board), box 14, New Orleans City Planning Commission Subject Files, NOPL; and "Memo for Mr. Colbert, 3 Feb 1953, for meeting of 27 January 1953," Colbert 1952–53 folder, School Board General Files, OPSB-147.

63. *A Planning and Building Program for New Orleans' Schools,* student population maps following pp. 16, 25. The fact that the Sanborn Map Company had not charted this section of Gentilly by March 1951 suggests that little construction activity had taken place as of that date. See Sanborn Map Company, *Insurance Maps of New Orleans,* vol. 10, 1937, corrected to 1951, sheet 0a, available at http://sanborn.umi.com.

64. *Swann v. Charlotte-Mecklenburg,* 402 U.S. 1 (1971).

65. Ansley T. Erickson, "Building Inequality: The Spatial Organization of Schooling in Nashville, Tennessee, after Brown," *Journal of Urban History* 38, no. 2 (2012), 248, 249–51, 265 n. 6; Highsmith and Erickson, "Segregation as Splitting, Segregation as Joining," 579; Becky M. Nicolaides, *My Blue Heaven: Life and Politics in the Working-Class Suburbs of Los Angeles, 1920–1965* (Chicago: University of Chicago Press, 2002), 288; Gregory S. Jacobs, *Getting Around Brown: Desegregation, Development, and the Columbus Public Schools* (Columbus: Ohio State University Press, 1998), 15; Kevin Fox Gotham, "Missed Opportunities, Enduring Legacies: School Segregation and Desegregation in Kansas City," *American Studies* 43, no. 2 (Summer 2002): 5–41.

66. Mahoney, "Law and Racial Geography," 1276; Mahoney, "Changing Nature of Public Housing," 54–58; *Report of the Housing Authority of New Orleans, for the Year Ending September 30, 1950,* p. 5, Louisiana Division, NOPL; Hirsch, *Making the Second Ghetto,* 224–29.

67. Mahoney, "Law and Racial Geography," 1284; Mahoney, "Changing Nature of Public Housing," 50 (quote), 56–57.

68. Carol McMichael Reese, "The New Orleans that Edgar (and Edith) Built," in *Longue Vue House and Gardens,* ed. Charles Davey and Carol McMichael Reese (New York: Skira Rizzoli, 2015), 186–90; Jane Wolff and Carol McMichael Reese, "Pontchartrain Park + Gentilly Woods Landscape Manual," in *New Orleans Under Reconstruction: The Crisis of Planning,* ed. Carol McMichael Reese, Michael Sorkin, and Anthony Fontenot (London: Verso, 2014), 381–85; *A Planning and Building Program for New Orleans' Schools,* 38; Arnold Hirsch, "Race and Renewal in the Cold War South: New Orleans, 1947–1968," in *The American Planning Tradition: Culture and Policy,* ed. Robert Fishman (Washington, DC: Woodrow Wilson Center Press, 2000), 219–39. The expansion of Magnolia and the construction of Pontchartrain Park aided a process of class-based spatial segmentation within New Orleans's black population that accelerated after 1960. On the relative persistence of socioeconomically diverse black residential areas in 1960 New Orleans, see Anthony Victor Margavio, "Residential Segregation in New Orleans: A Statistical Analysis of Census Data" (PhD diss., Louisiana State University, 1968), 34–50.

69. *Report of the Housing Authority of New Orleans, for the Year Ending September 30, 1951*, 17, 68. For details and numbers on families and businesses displaced by the housing project, see *Report of the Housing Authority of New Orleans, for the Year Ending September 30, 1954*, 26–27; Tennessee Williams, *A Streetcar Named Desire* (1947); *A Streetcar Named Desire*, directed by Elia Kazan (Burbank: Warner Brothers, 1951). For a description of the streetcar and bus route, see "Calling All Volunteers," *Times-Picayune*, 27 May 1951, section 4, p. 5.

70. Unfortunately, Hurricane Katrina damaged the HANO records that were most likely to provide greater detail about the chronology and nature of school and housing officials' joint consideration of the area that came to house the Desire Project. See Kevin Oufnac to Walter Stern, Response to Public Records Request, 18 September 2013, in author's possession.

71. OPSB Minutes, 28 June 1951 (the quotes are from the recorded discussion of the report, not the report itself); "Contracts Given For School Jobs," *Times-Picayune*, 29 June 1951, 14; "Memorandum for Mr. Colbert," 9 May 1951, Charles Colbert 1951 folder, School Board General Files, OPSB-147.

72. OPSB Minutes, 23 July 1951 (quotes); *Times-Picayune*, 24 July 1951.

73. OPSB Minutes, 23 July 1951.

74. DeVore and Logsdon, *Crescent City Schools*, 228–31.

75. OPSB Minutes, 23 July 1951.

76. Ibid.

77. Andrew Wiese, *Places of Their Own: African American Suburbanization in the Twentieth Century* (Chicago: University of Chicago Press, 2004), chap. 3; The Nine Times Social and Pleasure Club, *Coming Out the Door for the Ninth Ward* (New Orleans: Neighborhood Story Project, 2006), 21 (quotes).

78. OPSB Minutes, 23 July 1951 (quote); Jonathan Eig, "Desire Pays Price for Shortcuts," *Times-Picayune*, 19 June 1989, 1, 8.

79. Freda dePolitte to Gervais F. Favrot, 11 June 1952; Louis C. Bisso to Gervais F. Favrot, 16 June 1952, folder 187 (Schools, Orleans Parish School Board), box 14, New Orleans City Planning Commission Subject Files, City Archives, NOPL (for quote); "New School Idea Seen in Purchase," *Times-Picayune*, 18 July 1952, 17.

80. *Report of the Housing Authority of New Orleans, for the Year Ending September 30, 1953*, p. 9 (for quote); "Desire Project Schools Mapped," *Times-Picayune*, 12 November 1952, 47; Kluger, *Simple Justice*, 540.

81. "Memorandum for Mr. Colbert," 8 September 1952, Charles Colbert 1952–53 folder, School Board General Files, OPSB-147; OPSB Minutes, 19 June 1953, 8 March 1954, 21 June 1954; *Brown v. Board of Education of Topeka, Ka.*, 347 U.S. 483 (1954).

82. Ferguson, "The Architecture of Education," 347–49; Heavrin, *Recordation of Certain Buildings at the George Washington Carver School Campus, New Orleans, Louisiana;* Curtis & Davis, *The Architectural Report to the Orleans Parish School Board: George Washington Carver Junior-Senior High School, Basic Design Drawings, Analysis and Solution* (New Orleans: Curtis & Davis, 1955), folder 10, box 3, Charles B. Rousseve Collection, Amistad Research Center; Harold T. Porter to Members of the Carver School Committee, 13 December 1954, folder 10a, box 3, Rousseve Collection; OPSB Minutes, 29 January 1973.

83. OPSB Minutes, 26 November 1956 (for quote), 8 April 1957; Heavrin, *Recordation of Certain Buildings at the George Washington Carver School Campus, New Orleans, Louisiana;*

"Platooned Schools," *Times-Picayune*, 4 December 1954, "Costs Halved in Building of Newest School," 9 August 1954, all in folder 187 (Schools, Orleans Parish School Board), box 14, New Orleans City Planning Commission Subject Files, City Archives, NOPL.

84. Chris Adams, "Classroom Notes: Learning the Hard Way," *Times-Picayune*, 4 August 1992, A7; Chris Adams, "Drowning in Debt," *Times-Picayune*, 4 August 1992, A1.

85. OPSB Minutes, 30 March 1954, 10 May 1954, 19 February 1955, 23 January 1956, 13 February 1956; "Shorter School Year Discussed," *Times-Picayune*, 11 May 1954, 26 (quote).

86. Eig, "Desire Pays Price for Shortcuts" (all quotes); Mahoney, "Changing Nature of Public Housing," 61.

87. Eig, "Desire Pays Price for Shortcuts" (all quotes); Mahoney, "Changing Nature of Public Housing," 61–62, 66–67; City Planning and Zoning Commission, *Report and Recommendation for Selection of Low-Rent Housing Project Sites for Negro Occupancy* (New Orleans: City Planning & Zoning Commission, September 1952), 2, NOPL.

88. "Colbert Leaving Columbia to Resume as Architect," *New York Times*, 4 April 1963, 73 (quote); "Charles R. Colbert, Architect and Educator," *Times-Picayune*, 16 February 2007; "School Village Study Delayed," *Times-Picayune*, 30 July 1953.

89. The Nine Times Social and Pleasure Club, *Coming Out the Door for the Ninth Ward*, 62.

EPILOGUE

1. Liva Baker, *The Second Battle of New Orleans: The Hundred-Year Struggle to Integrate the Schools* (New York: Harper Collins, 1996), 394, 398; U.S. Weather Bureau, "The Weather," *Times-Picayune*, 15 November 1960, 10.

2. Baker, *Second Battle of New Orleans*, 403–6; Adam Fairclough, *Race and Democracy: The Civil Rights Struggle in Louisiana*, 2nd edition (Athens: University of Georgia Press, 2008), 234–44.

3. Baker, *Second Battle of New Orleans*, 398; Fairclough, *Race and Democracy*, 239.

4. Baker, *Second Battle of New Orleans*, 394–401.

5. Ibid., 410–15 (quotes on 411 and 415).

6. Ibid., 415–18; Louisiana State Advisory Committee to the United States Commission on Civil Rights, *The New Orleans School Crisis* (Washington, DC: Government Printing Office, 1961), 12–17; John Steinbeck, *Travels With Charley: In Search of America* (New York: Viking Press, 1962; New York: Bantam Books, 1963), 247. Citations refer to the Bantam edition.

7. Morton Inger, *Politics and Reality in an American City: The New Orleans School Crisis of 1960* (New York: Center for Urban Education, 1969); Kim Lacy Rogers, *Righteous Lives: Narratives of the New Orleans Civil Rights Movement* (New York: New York University Press, 1993); Edward F. Haas, *DeLesseps S. Morrison and the Image of Reform: New Orleans Politics, 1946–1961* (Baton Rouge: Louisiana State University Press, 1974); Robert Coles, *Children of Crisis: A Study of Courage and Fear*, vol. 1 (Boston: Little, Brown, 1967), see especially 82–6, 298–314; Steinbeck, *Travels With Charley*, 246 (for quote); Fairclough, *Race and Democracy*; Baker, *Second Battle of New Orleans*; Jason Sokol, *There Goes My Everything: White Southerners in the Age of Civil Rights, 1945–1975* (New York: Knopf, 2006); Donald E. DeVore, *Defying Jim Crow: African Amer-*

ican Community Development and the Struggle for Racial Equality in New Orleans, 1900–1960 (Baton Rouge: Louisiana State University Press, 2015).

8. Juliette Landphair, "'The Forgotten People of New Orleans': Community, Vulnerability, and the Lower Ninth Ward," *Journal of American History* 94 (December 2007), 840.

9. Ibid.

10. Karen Benjamin, "Suburbanizing Jim Crow: The Impact of School Policy on Residential Segregation in Raleigh," *Journal of Urban History* 38, no. 2 (March 2012): 225–46; Ansley T. Erickson, "Building Inequality: The Spatial Organization of Schooling in Nashville, Tennessee, after *Brown*," *Journal of Urban History* 38, no. 2 (March 2012): 247–70; Donald E. DeVore and Joseph Logsdon, *Crescent City Schools: Public Education in New Orleans, 1841–1991* (Lafayette: University of Southwestern Louisiana Press, 1991), 252–66; Mark Cortez, "The Faculty Integration of New Orleans Public Schools, 1972," *Louisiana History* 37, no. 4 (Autumn 1996): 405–34; New Orleans Public Schools, *Facts and Finances*, 1957–1981, boxes 7–9, Financial Records, OPSB-147.

11. On the changes in New Orleans's political economy during the late 1960s and 1970s, see Kent B. Germany, *New Orleans After the Promises: Poverty, Citizenship, and the Search for the Great Society* (Athens: University of Georgia Press, 2007), especially chap. 1, 2, Introduction, and Conclusion; Arnold R. Hirsch, "Simply a Matter of Black and White: The Transformation of Race and Politics in Twentieth-Century New Orleans," in *Creole New Orleans: Race and Americanization*, ed. Arnold R. Hirsch and Joseph Logsdon (Baton Rouge: Louisiana State University Press, 1992): 262–319; Michael Mizel-Nelson, "Batista-era Havana on the Bayou," *Reviews in American History* 36, no. 2 (June 2008): 231–42; J. Mark Souther, *New Orleans on Parade: Tourism and the Transformation of the Crescent City* (Baton Rouge: Louisiana State University Press, 2006); Landphair, "The Forgotten People," 842. On mass incarceration in New Orleans and nationally, see Cindy Chang, "Louisiana Is the World's Prison Capital," *Times-Picayune,* 13 May 2012, http://www.nola.com/crime/index.ssf/2012/05/louisiana_is_the_worlds_prison.html; Heather Ann Thompson, "Why Mass Incarceration Matters: Rethinking Crisis, Decline, and Transformation in Postwar American History," *Journal of American History* 97, no. 3 (December 2010): 703–34 (706 for quote). On Oakland, see Robert O. Self, *American Babylon: Race and the Struggle for Postwar Oakland* (Princeton, NJ: Princeton University Press, 2004), 157.

12. Jonathan Eig, "Decaying Homes; Blighted Hopes," *Times-Picayune,* 18 June 1989, A1; "N.O. Murder: Back to the Abyss," *Times-Picayune,* 29 November 1994, B4; Thompson, "Why Mass Incarceration Matters," 703, 728; Michelle Alexander, *The New Jim Crow: Mass Incarceration in the Age of Colorblindness,* rev. edition (New York: The New Press, 2012), 100; John Simmerman, "Prison Rips Up Families, Tears Apart Entire Communities," *Times-Picayune,* 18 May 2012, http://www.nola.com/crime/index.ssf/2012/05/prison_rips_up_families_tears.html; Lisa Frazier, "Violence Scars Family Once Again," *Times-Picayune,* 4 December 1994, A1; Adam Nossiter, "New Orleans' school system is a 'train wreck,'" Associated Press, 18 April 2005; Vicki Mack, "New Orleans Kids, Working Parents, and Poverty," The Data Center, 26 February 2015, 1. https://s3.amazonaws.com/gnocdc/reports/NewOrleansKidsWorkingParentsandPoverty.pdf; Andre Perry, "The New Orleans Youth Index," December 2016, The Data Center, p. 1, https://s3.amazonaws.com/gnocdc/reports/TheDataCenter_TheYouthIndex2016.pdf; Warren Simmons and Alethea Frazier Raynor, "K-12 Public Education Reform in New Orleans" (Providence, RI: The Annenberg Institute for School Reform, 2006).

13. On the necessity of viewing issues confronting urban schools within the broader context of urban history, see John L. Rury and Jeffrey E. Mirel, "The Political Economy of Urban Education," *Review of Research in Education* 22 (1997): 49–110. For Obama remarks, see The White House, Office of the Press Secretary, "Remarks by the President on Education Reform at the National Urban League Centennial Conference," 29 July 2010, available at http://www.whitehouse.gov/the-press-office/remarks-president-education-reform-national-urban-league-centennial-conference.

14. Sarah Carr, *Hope Against Hope: Three Schools, One City, and the Struggle to Educate America's Children* (New York: Bloomsbury Press, 2013); Diane Ravitch, *The Death and Life of the Great American School System: How Testing and Choice Are Undermining Education,* 3rd edition (New York: Basic Books, 2016); Kate Babineau, Dave Hand, and Vincent Rossmeier, "The State of Public Education in New Orleans, 2016–2017," Cowen Institute, February 2017, p. 14, http://www.coweninstitute.com/wp-content/uploads/2017/02/SPENO-2017-Final-Web.pdf; National Alliance for Public Charter Schools, "A Growing Movement: America's Largest Charter School Communities," November 2015, p. 3, http://www.publiccharters.org/wp-content/uploads/2015/11/enrollmentshare_web.pdf.

15. Anya Kamenetz, "President Trump's Budget Proposal Calls for Deep Cuts to Education," nprED, 22 May 2017, http://www.npr.org/sections/ed/2017/05/22/529534031/president-trumps-budget-proposal-calls-for-deep-cuts-to-education.

16. For a similar critique, see Jonathan Kozol, *The Shame of the Nation: The Restoration of Apartheid Schooling in America* (New York: Three Rivers Press, 2005), 200.

17. Ansley T. Erickson, "The Rhetoric of Choice: Segregation, Desegregation, and Charter Schools," *Dissent,* Fall 2011: 41–46; Lindsay Bell Weixler, Nathan Barrett, Douglas N. Harris, and Jennifer Jennings, "Did the New Orleans School Reforms Increase Segregation?" Education Research Alliance for New Orleans, 4 April 2017, http://educationresearchalliancenola.org/files/publications/040417-Bell-Weixler-Barrett-Harris-Jennings-Did-the-New-Orleans-School-Reforms-Increase-Segregation.pdf; Whitney Bross, Douglas N. Harris, and Lihan Liu, "Extreme Measures: When and How School Closures and Charter Takeovers Benefit Students," Education Research Alliance for New Orleans, 17 October 2016, http://educationresearchalliancenola.org/files/publications/Education-Research-Alliance-New-Orleans-Policy-Brief-Closure-Takeover.pdf; Valerie Strauss, "Education Department Investigating Three School Civil Rights Complaints," *Washington Post,* 15 October 2016, https://www.washingtonpost.com/news/answer-sheet/wp/2014/10/15/education-department-investigating-three-school-civil-rights-complaints/?utm_term=.b4d26391c049; Corey Mitchell, "Feds, Newark, N.J., Schools Reach Agreement Over Civil Rights Complaints," *Education Week's District Dossier Blog,* 14 December 2016, http://blogs.edweek.org/edweek/District_Dossier/2015/12/feds_newark_schools_reach_agre.html; Janelle Scott and Jennifer Jellison Holme, "The Political Economy of Market-Based Educational Policies: Race and Reform in Urban School Districts, 1915 to 2016," *Review of Research in Education* 40, no. 1 (March 2016): 250–97.

18. On the promise and perils of efforts to link school and housing reform, see Benjamin, "Suburbanizing Jim Crow," 241; Lawrence J. Vale, *Purging the Poorest: Public Housing and the Design Politics of Twice-Cleared Communities* (Chicago: University of Chicago Press, 2013), chap. 3, esp. 137–42.

BIBLIOGRAPHY

MANUSCRIPTS AND ARCHIVES

Amistad Research Center at Tulane University, New Orleans.
    Joseph A. Hardin Papers.
    A. P. Tureaud Papers.
    Charles B. Roussève Collection.

Archives of the Archdiocese of New Orleans.
    Records of l'Institution Catholique des Orphelins Indigents.

City Archives, New Orleans Public Library, New Orleans.
    Court Cases
    John Fitzpatrick et al. v. The Board of Directors of the Public Schools for the City of New Orleans, Orleans Parish Civil District Court, Division D, Docket 5, Case No. 121508.

    Ordinances
    Ordinance No. 13,485, Council Series, 6 July 1897.
    Ordinance No. 3,835, Commission Council Series, 10 October 1916.
    Ordinance No. 3,941, Commission Council Series, 29 November 1916.
    Ordinance No. 4,485, Commission Council Series, 17 July 1917.
    Ordinance No. 7,194, Commission Council Series, 28 December 1922.

    Records of the New Orleans Municipal Government.
    New Orleans City Planning Commission Subject Files.
    New Orleans Department of Public Property Records.
    Mayor Martin Behrman Papers.

Conveyance Division, Orleans Parish Civil District Court, New Orleans.
    Orleans Parish Conveyance Office Books.

Books 121, 123, 124, 145, 229, 308, 347, 353, 363, 368, 380, 403, 464, 505, 511, 515, 517, 562.

Jefferson Parish Conveyance Office Books.
Book 1.

Historic New Orleans Collection, New Orleans, La.
Manuscript Collections
Guy Seghers Survey Files.

Maps
Map 6. Economic Areas, New Orleans, Louisiana. Real Property Inventory, Sept. 15, 1939, Works Project Administration Project No 65–164–2215, HNOC Identification Number 68–19-L.7.

Map 10. Race of Household Map, New Orleans, Louisiana, Real Property Inventory, Sept. 15, 1939, Works Project Administration Project No 65–164–2215, HNOC Identification Number 68–19-L.7.

Map 19. Block Data Map, New Orleans, Louisiana, Real Property Inventory, Sept. 15, 1939, WPA Project No. 665–64–3-11, HNOC Identification Number 68–19-L.7.

Hémécourt, Claude. "Plan de la Ville et des faubourgs incorporés de la Nouvelle Orleans," c. 1875, after 1812 Tanesse plan, HNOC, 1966.33.30.

Nirenstein's National Realty Map Company, "Business Section, City of New Orleans," 1947, HNOC 1976.92.1.

Sanborn Map Company, *Insurance Maps of New Orleans,* volumes 1a and 3, 1908, corr. 1940.

Louisiana and Special Collections Department, Earl K. Long Library, University of New Orleans, New Orleans, La.
FEMA-George Washington Carver School Collection (MSS 363).
Marcus Christian Collection (MSS 011).
Orleans Parish School Board Collection (MSS 147).

Louisiana Research Collection, Tulane University, New Orleans, La.
Ephemera
Education. Public Schools Alliance folder.
Real Estate Agents. Leo Fellman folder.
Schools. Fortier High School folder.

Manuscript Collections
Ida Weis Friend Papers (Manuscripts Collection 287).

Louisiana State Museum, New Orleans.
 Alcée Fortier Collection (Record Group 65).
 Fortier Family Papers (Record Group 194).

Lusher Charter School Library, Fortier Campus, New Orleans.
 Silver and Blue (Fortier High School student newspaper).
 The Tarpon (Fortier High School yearbook).

McDonogh 35 High School Library, New Orleans.
 The Roneagle (McDonogh 35 High School yearbook).

National Archives and Records Administration, College Park, MD.
RG 31, Records of the Federal Housing Administration, 1930–1974, Real Property City
 Survey Maps, compiled 1934–1942.
RG 195, Records of the Federal Home Loan Bank Board, Entry 39, Home Owners'
 Loan Corporation, Records Relating to the City Survey File, 1935–1940.

New Orleans Notarial Archives, New Orleans.
 Manuel I. Fisher, *Notarial Acts, inclusive, 1–202, 1939–1941*, vol. 2.

New Orleans Notarial Archives Research Center, New Orleans.
 J. D. Dresner, *Acts, August 29, 1940 to October 16, 1941*, vol. 53.
 Arthur B. Leopold, *Notarial Acts, 1–79, 1923*.

Southeastern Architectural Archive, Tulane University, New Orleans.
 Sanborn Fire Insurance Company, *Insurance Maps of New Orleans*.

INTERVIEWS

From the Behind the Veil: Documenting African-American Life in the Jim Crow South
 Digital Collection, John Hope Franklin Research Center, Duke University Libraries.

Aaron, Delores Mary. Interviewed by Michele Mitchell, New Orleans, June 30, 1994
 (btvct07060).
Boucree, John Harold. Interviewed by Kate Ellis, New Orleans, July 5, 1994
 (btvct07061).
Cappie, Herbert Melvin, and Ruth Irene Cappie. Interviewed by Michele Mitchell, New
 Orleans, July 2, 1994 (btvct07063).
Cheri, Emmett Emmanuel. Interviewed by Kate Ellis, New Orleans, June 23, 1994
 (btvct07064).

NEWSPAPERS AND PERIODICALS

L'Abbeille (New Orleans, LA).

Anglo-African (New York).

Architectural Forum (New York).

Cleveland Gazette.

Common School Journal (Boston).

Daily Creole (New Orleans).

Harper's New Monthly Magazine (New York).

Harper's Weekly (New York).

Item (New Orleans).

Louisiana Cultural Vistas (Louisiana Endowment for the Humanities, New Orleans).

Louisiana Weekly (New Orleans).

New Orleans Advocate.

New Yorker (New York).

New York Times.

Outlook (New York).

Picayune; Daily Picayune (New Orleans).

Southwestern Christian Advocate (Methodist Book Concern, *New Orleans*).

States (New Orleans).

Times-Democrat (New Orleans).

Times-Picayune (New Orleans)

PUBLISHED PRIMARY SOURCES

Anderson, Beverly Jacques. *Cherished Memories: Snapshots of Life and Lessons from a 1950s Creole Village.* Bloomington, IN: iUniverse, 2011.

Armstrong, Louis. *Satchmo: My Life in New Orleans.* Centennial edition reprint. New York: Da Capo Press, 1986.

Ayres, Leonard P. *Laggards in Our Schools: A Study of Retardation and Elimination in City School Systems.* New York: Survey Associates, 1913. First published 1909 by the Russell Sage Foundation.

Batson, Ruth. *The Black Educational Movement in Boston: A Sequence of Historical Events: A Chronology.* Boston: Northeastern University School of Education, 2001.

Beeler, John A. *Report to the Commissioner of Public Utilities, City of New Orleans, on the Street Railway Situation.* New York, 1923.

Bridges, Ruby. *Through My Eyes.* New York: Scholastic, 1999.

Butler, Benjamin F. *Butler's Book: A Review of His Legal, Political, and Military Career.* Boston: A. M. Thayer, 1892.

Carter, Sam R., and Works Progress Administration. *A Report on Survey of Metro-*

politan New Orleans, Land Use, Real Property, and Low Income Housing Area. Louisiana State Department of Public Works and Housing Authority of New Orleans, 1941.

Desdunes, Rodolphe Lucien. *Our People and Our History,* translated and edited by Sister Dorothea Olga McCants. Baton Rouge: Louisiana State University Press, 1973.

Douglass, Frederick. *Narrative of the Life of Frederick Douglass, An American Slave.* Boston: The Anti-Slavery Office, 1845.

Du Bois, W. E. B. *The Souls of Black Folk: Essays and Sketches.* Chicago: A. C. McClurg, 1904.

The Federal Writers Project of the Works Progress Administration. *New Orleans City Guide.* New Orleans: Garrett County Press reprint edition, 2009. First published 1938 by Houghton Mifflin.

Fortier, James, ed. *Carpet-Bag Misrule in Louisiana: The Tragedy of the Reconstruction Era Following the War Between the States.* New Orleans: Louisiana State Museum, 1938.

Gardner's New Orleans Directory for 1861. New Orleans: Charles Gardner, 1861.

Harlan, Louis R., and Raymond W. Smock, eds. *The Booker T. Washington Papers,* 14 vols. Urbana: University of Illinois Press, 1972–1989.

James E. Allison & Co. *Report on the Street Railway Service of the City of New Orleans, Made to the Committee on Transportation Facilities of New Orleans.* St. Louis, 1917.

The Nine Times Social and Pleasure Club. *Coming Out the Door for the Ninth Ward.* New Orleans: Neighborhood Story Project, 2006.

Perkins, A. E., ed. *Who's Who in Colored Louisiana.* Baton Rouge: Douglas Loan Co., 1930.

Polk's New Orleans City Directory. New Orleans: R. L. Polk & Co., 1945.

Prospectus de l'Institution Catholique des Orphelins Indigent. New Orleans: Maitre Desarzant, 1847.

Ripley, Eliza. *Social Life in Old New Orleans: Being Recollections of My Girlhood.* New York and London: D. Appleton, 1912.

Sanborn Map Company. *Insurance Maps of New Orleans, Louisiana,* 1885–1951. Accessed via *Digital Sanborn Maps, 1867–1970.* http://sanborn.umi.com.

Soards' New Orleans City Directory, 1890–1932. New Orleans: Soards, 1890–1932.

Steinbeck, John. *Travels With Charley: In Search of America.* New York: Viking Press, 1962; New York: Bantam Books, 1963.

Total Community Action, Department of Program Development. *Profile of Poverty in New Orleans.* New Orleans, 1973.

GOVERNMENT DOCUMENTS

Annual Report of the New Orleans Public Schools. 1901–1902, 1910–1911, 1913–14, 1919–1920, 1920–21.

Bureau of the Census. *Twelfth Census of the United States, 1900. Census Reports,* vol. 2. *Population,* part 2. Washington, DC: US Census Office, 1902.

———. *Thirteenth Census of the United States, 1910. Occupation Statistics,* vol. 4. Washington, DC: US Census Office, 1914.

———. *Sixteenth Census of the United States, 1940. Population and Housing: Statistics for Census Tracts, New Orleans, La.* Washington, DC: Government Printing Office, 1941.

———. Manuscript Census Returns. *Thirteenth Census of the United States, 1910.* New Orleans, Louisiana, Population. National Archives Microfilm Series T-624, Reels 520, 521, 574. Also accessed through HeritageQuest Online, www.heritagequestonline.com.

———. Manuscript Census Returns. *Fourteenth Census of the United States, 1920.* New Orleans, La., Population. National Archives Microfilm Series T-625, Reels 618, 620–623. Also accessed through HeritageQuest Online, www.heritagequestonline.com.

———. Manuscript Census Returns. *Fifteenth Census of the United States, 1930.* New Orleans, La., Population. National Archives Microfilm Series 5163, Reel 21. Also accessed through HeritageQuest Online, www.heritagequestonline.com.

———. Manuscript Census Returns. *Sixteenth Census of the United States, 1940.* New Orleans, La., Population. National Archives Microfilm Series T-627. Also accessed through HeritageQuest Online, www.heritagequestonline.com.

City of New Orleans, Office of Policy and Planning. *Neighborhood Profiles.* Vols. 6A, 6C, 12D. New Orleans: Office of Policy and Planning, 1978.

City Planning and Zoning Commission. *Report and Recommendation for Selection of Low-Rent Housing Project Sites for Negro Occupancy.* New Orleans: City Planning & Zoning Commission, September 1952.

Constitution Adopted by the State Constitutional Convention of the State of Louisiana, March 7, 1868. New Orleans: The New Orleans Republican, 1868.

Constitution of the State of Louisiana, Adopted in Convention at the City of New Orleans, the Twenty-Third Day of July, A. D. 1879. New Orleans: J. H. Cosgrove, 1879.

Federal Housing Administration. *Underwriting Manual: Underwriting Analysis Under Title II, Section 203 of the National Housing Act.* Washington, DC: National Housing Agency/Federal Housing Administration, 1938.

———. *Underwriting Manual: Underwriting Analysis Under Title II, Section 203 of the National Housing Act.* Washington, DC: National Housing Agency/Federal Housing Administration, 1947.

Gibson, Campbell. *Population of the 100 Largest Cities and Other Urban Places in the United States: 1790 to 1990.* Population Division Working Paper No. 27. Washington, DC: U.S. Bureau of the Census, June 1998. *http://www.census.gov/population/www/documentation/twps0027/twps0027.html.*

Gibson, Campbell, and Kay Jung. *Historical Census Statistics On Population Totals*

By Race, 1790 to 1990, and By Hispanic Origin, 1970 to 1990, For Large Cities And Other Urban Places In The United States. Population Division Working Paper No. 76. Washington, DC: U.S. Bureau of the Census, February 2005. *http://www .census.gov/population/www/documentation/twps0076/twps0076.html.*

Housing Authority of New Orleans. *Report of the Housing Authority of New Orleans,*1948–1958.

Louisiana Department of Education. *Annual and Biennial Reports,* 1861–1960. *http:// www2.state.lib.la.us/doeafsr/.*

Louisiana State Advisory Committee to the United States Commission on Civil Rights. *The New Orleans School Crisis.* Washington, DC: Government Printing Office, 1961.

New Orleans Public School Directories. 1900, 1910, 1920, 1930, 1940.

Official Journal of the Proceedings of the Constitutional Convention of the State of Louisiana. New Orleans: R. J. Hearsey, 1898.

Official Journal of the Proceedings of the Convention, for Framing a Constitution for the State of Louisiana. New Orleans: J. B. Roudanez & Co., 1867–1868.

Orleans Parish School Board—Office of Planning and Construction. *A Planning and Building Program for New Orleans' Schools.* New Orleans: Orleans Parish School Board, 1952.

Orleans Parish School Board—Office of the Superintendent. *Biennial Report of Progress.* New Orleans: Orleans Parish School Board, 1 March 1950.

———. *Proposed Program for the Improvement of the Public Schools of New Orleans.* New Orleans: Orleans Parish School Board, 7 January 1948.

Report of the Commissioner of Education for the Year Ended June 30, 1914, vol. 2. Washington, DC: Government Printing Office, 1915.

Report of the Commissioner of Education for the Year Ended June 30, 1920, vol. 1. Washington, DC: Government Printing Office, 1920.

Statistical Report of the New Orleans Public Schools of the Parish of Orleans, 1930–31 and 1939–40.

SECONDARY SOURCES

Books and Movies

Alexander, Michelle. *The New Jim Crow: Mass Incarceration in the Age of Colorblindness.* Revised edition. New York: The New Press, 2012.

Allen, Danielle S. *Talking to Strangers: Anxieties of Citizenship Since* Brown v. Board of Education. Chicago: University of Chicago Press, 2004.

Anderson, James B. *The Education of Blacks in the South: 1860–1935.* Chapel Hill: University of North Carolina Press, 1988.

Anderson, Karen. *Little Rock: Race and Resistance at Central High.* Princeton, NJ: Princeton University Press, 2009.

Anyon, Jean. *Ghetto Schooling: A Political Economy of Urban Educational Reform.* New York: Teachers College Press, 1997.

Arnesen, Eric. *Waterfront Workers of New Orleans: Race, Class, and Politics, 1863–1923.* New York: Oxford University Press, 1991.

Ayers, Edward L. *Promise of the New South: Life After Reconstruction.* New York: Oxford University Press, 1992.

Baker, Liva. *The Second Battle of New Orleans: The Hundred-Year Struggle to Integrate the Schools.* New York: Harper Collins, 1996.

Bankston, Carl L., and Stephen J. Caldas. *A Troubled Dream: The Promise and Failure of School Desegregation in Louisiana.* Nashville, TN: Vanderbilt University Press, 2002.

Bell, Caryn Cossé. *Revolution, Romanticism, and the Afro-Creole Protest Tradition in Louisiana, 1718–1868.* Baton Rouge: Louisiana State University Press, 1997.

Bell, Derrick A. *Silent Covenants:* Brown v. Board of Education *and the Unfulfilled Hopes for Racial Reform.* New York: Oxford University Press, 2004.

Bennett, James B. *Religion and the Rise of Jim Crow in New Orleans.* Princeton, NJ: Princeton University Press, 2005.

Berlin, Ira. *The Making of African America: Four Great Migrations.* New York: Viking, 2010.

———. *Many Thousands Gone: The First Two Centuries of Slavery in North America.* Cambridge, MA: Harvard University Press, 1998.

Blassingame, John W. *Black New Orleans, 1860–1880.* Chicago: University of Chicago Press, 1976.

Blight, David W. *Race and Reunion: The Civil War in American Memory.* Cambridge, MA: The Belknap Press of Harvard University Press, 2001.

Brothers, Thomas. *Louis Armstrong's New Orleans.* New York: W. W. Norton, 2006.

Buras, Kristen L., Jim Randels, Kalamu ya Salaam, and Students at the Center. *Pedagogy, Policy, and the Privatized City: Stories of Dispossession and Defiance from New Orleans.* New York: Teachers College Press, 2010.

Cabildo, Friends of the. *New Orleans Architecture,* 8 vols. Gretna, LA: Pelican Publishing, 1971–1997.

Campanella, Richard. *Bienville's Dilemma: A Historical Geography of New Orleans.* Lafayette: University of Louisiana at Lafayette Press, 2008.

———. *Delta Urbanism: New Orleans.* Chicago: American Planning Association, 2010.

———. *Geographies of New Orleans: Urban Fabrics Before the Storm.* Lafayette: Center for Louisiana Studies, 2006.

Carr, Sarah. *Hope Against Hope: Three Schools, One City, and the Struggle to Educate America's Children.* New York: Bloomsbury Press, 2013.

Cecelski, David S. *Along Freedom Road: Hyde County, North Carolina, and the Fate of Black Schools in the South.* Chapel Hill: University of North Carolina Press, 1994.

———. *The Waterman's Song: Slavery and Freedom in Maritime North Carolina.* Chapel Hill: University of North Carolina Press, 2001.

Cell, John W. *The Highest Stage of White Supremacy: The Origins of Segregation in South Africa and the American South.* Cambridge: Cambridge University Press, 1982.

Clark, Emily. *Masterless Mistresses: The New Orleans Ursulines and the Development of a New World Society, 1727–1834.* Chapel Hill: University of North Carolina Press, 2007.

———. *The Strange History of the American Quadroon: Free Women of Color in the Revolutionary Atlantic World.* Chapel Hill: University of North Carolina Press, 2013.

Coles, Robert. *Children of Crisis: A Study of Courage and Fear,* vol. 1. Boston: Little, Brown, 1967.

College Board. "AP Course and Exam Description: AP United States History, Including the Curriculum Framework." New York: College Board, 2015. https://secure-media.collegeboard.org/digitalServices/pdf/ap/ap-us-history-course-and-exam-description.pdf.

———. "Program Summary Report." New York: College Board, 2016. https://secure-media.collegeboard.org/digitalServices/pdf/research/2016/Program-Summary-Report-2016.pdf.

Colton, Craig E. *Unnatural Metropolis: Wresting New Orleans from Nature.* Baton Rouge: Louisiana State University Press, 2005.

Connolly, N. D. B. *A World More Concrete: Real Estate and the Remaking of Jim Crow South Florida.* Chicago: University of Chicago Press, 2014.

Cossé Bell, Caryn. *Revolution, Romanticism, and the Afro-Creole Protest Tradition in Louisiana, 1718–1868.* Baton Rouge: Louisiana State University Press, 1997.

Cox, LaWanda. *Lincoln and Black Freedom: A Study in Presidential Leadership.* Columbia: University of South Carolina Press, 1981.

Crutcher, Michael E. Jr. *Tremé: Race and Place in a New Orleans Neighborhood.* Athens: University of Georgia Press, 2010.

Davidson, James West. *Experience History: Interpreting America's Past,* vol. 2. 8th edition. New York: McGraw Hill, 2014.

DeVore, Donald E. *Defying Jim Crow: African American Community Development and the Struggle for Racial Equality in New Orleans, 1900–1960.* Baton Rouge: Louisiana State University Press, 2015.

DeVore, Donald E., and Joseph Logsdon. *Crescent City Schools: Public Education in New Orleans, 1841–1991.* Lafayette: University of Southwestern Louisiana Press, 1991.

Deyle, Steven. *Carry Me Back: The Domestic Slave Trade in American Life*. Oxford: Oxford University Press, 2005.

Dictionary of Louisiana Biography. http://www.lahistory.org/site23.php.

Dougherty, Jack, and contributors. *On the Line: How Schooling, Housing, and Civil Rights Shaped Hartford and Its Suburbs*. In progress, 2016. http://ontheline.trincoll .edu/book.

Douglas, Davison M. *Jim Crow Moves North: The Battle Over Northern School Segregation, 1865–1954*. New York: Cambridge University Press, 2005.

———. *Reading, Writing, & Race: The Desegregation of the Charlotte Schools*. Chapel Hill: University of North Carolina Press, 1995.

Drake, St. Clair, and Horace Cayton. *Black Metropolis: A Study of Negro Life in a Northern City*. New York: Harcourt, Brace, 1945.

Dubois, Laurent. *Avengers of the New World: The Story of the Haitian Revolution*. Cambridge, MA: The Belknap Press of Harvard University Press, 2004.

———. *A Colony of Citizens: Revolution & Slave Emancipation in the French Caribbean, 1787–1804*. Chapel Hill: University of North Carolina Press, 2004.

Du Bois, W. E. B. *Black Reconstruction in America, An Essay Toward a History of the Part Which Black Folk Played in the Attempt to Reconstruct Democracy in America, 1860–1880*. New York: Harcourt, Brace, 1935; reprint, Cleveland and New York: Meridian Books, 1969.

Duneier, Mitchell. *Ghetto: The Invention of a Place, the History of an Idea*. New York: Farrar, Straus, and Giroux, 2016.

Erickson, Ansley T. *Making the Unequal Metropolis: School Desegregation and Its Limits*. Chicago: University of Chicago Press, 2016.

Fairclough, Adam. *Class of Their Own: Black Teachers in the Segregated South*. 2nd edition. Athens: University of Georgia Press, 2007.

———. *Race and Democracy: The Civil Rights Struggle in Louisiana, 1915–1972*. Athens: University of Georgia Press, 1995; 2nd edition, 2008.

———. *Teaching Equality: Black Schools in the Age of Jim Crow*. Athens: University of Georgia Press, 2001.

Fertel, Rien. *Imagining the Creole City: The Rise of Literary Culture in Nineteenth-Century New Orleans*. Baton Rouge: Louisiana State University Press, 2014.

Fischer, Roger A. *The Segregation Struggle in Louisiana, 1862–77*. Urbana: University of Illinois Press, 1974.

Foner, Eric. *Reconstruction: America's Unfinished Revolution, 1863–1877*. New York: Harper & Row, 1988.

Fortier, Alcée. *A History of Louisiana*, vol. 2. *The Spanish Domination and the Cession to the United States, 1769–1803*. New York: Manzi, Joyant, 1904.

———. *A History of Louisiana*, vol. 4. *The American Domination*, part 2: *1861–1908*. New York: Manzi, Joyant, 1904.

———. *Louisiana Studies: Literature, Customs and Dialects, History and Education.* New Orleans: F. F. Hansell & Bro., 1894.

Freund, David M. P. *Colored Property: State Policy & White Racial Politics in Suburban America.* Chicago: University of Chicago Press, 2007.

Gamm, Gerald. *Urban Exodus: Why the Jews Left Boston and the Catholics Stayed.* Cambridge, MA: Harvard University Press, 1999.

Gates, Henry Louis Jr. *The African Americans: Many Rivers to Cross,* Episode 5. Arlington, VA: PBS Distribution, 2013.

Geggus, David P., ed. *The Impact of the Haitian Revolution in the Atlantic World.* Columbia: University of South Carolina Press, 2001.

Germany, Kent. *New Orleans After the Promises: Poverty, Citizenship, and the Search for the Great Society.* Athens: University of Georgia Press, 2007.

Gilmore, Glenda. *Gender and Jim Crow: Women and the Politics of White Supremacy in North Carolina, 1896–1920.* Chapel Hill: University of North Carolina Press, 1996.

Goldfield, David. *Cotton Fields and Skyscrapers: Southern City and Region.* Baltimore: Johns Hopkins University Press, 1992.

Goluboff, Risa L. *The Lost Promise of Civil Rights.* Cambridge, MA: Harvard University Press, 2007.

Gotham, Kevin Fox. *Race, Real Estate, and Uneven Development: The Kansas City Experience, 1900–2000.* Albany: State University of New York Press, 2002.

Greater New Orleans Community Data Center. *Pre-Katrina Data Center Web Site.* New Orleans: Greater New Orleans Nonprofit Knowledge Works, 2000–2007. http://www.gnocdc.org/prekatrinasite.html.

Greene, Julie. *The Canal Builders: Making America's Empire at the Panama Canal.* New York: The Penguin Press, 2009.

Greenwald, Erin M. *Marc-Antoine Caillot and the Company of the Indies in Louisiana: Trade in the French Atlantic World.* Baton Rouge: Louisiana State University Press, 2016.

Grossman, James. *Land of Hope: Chicago, Black Southerners, and the Great Migration.* Chicago: University of Chicago Press, 1989.

Haas, Edward F. *Delesseps S. Morrison and the Image of Reform: New Orleans Politics 1946–1961.* Baton Rouge: Louisiana State University Press, 1974.

Hahn, Steven. *A Nation Under Our Feet: Black Political Struggles in the Rural South from Slavery to the Great Migration.* Cambridge, MA: The Belknap Press of Harvard University Press, 2003.

Hair, William Ivy. *Carnival of Fury: Robert Charles and the New Orleans Race Riot of 1900.* Baton Rouge: Louisiana State University Press, 1976.

Hale, Grace Elizabeth. *Making Whiteness: The Culture of Whiteness in the South, 1890–1940.* New York: Pantheon Books, 1998.

Hall, Gwendolyn Midlo. *Africans in Colonial Louisiana: The Development of Afro-Creole Culture in the Eighteenth Century.* Baton Rouge: Louisiana State University Press, 1992.

Hanger, Kimberly. *Bounded Lives, Bounded Places: Free Black Society in Colonial New Orleans, 1769–1803.* Durham, NC: Duke University Press, 1997.

Highsmith, Andrew. *Demolition Means Progress: Flint, Michigan, and the Fate of the American Metropolis.* Chicago: University of Chicago Press, 2015.

Hirsch, Arnold R. *Making the Second Ghetto: Race and Housing in Chicago, 1940–1960.* Cambridge: Cambridge University Press, 1983.

Hirsch, Arnold R., and Joseph Logsdon, eds. *Creole New Orleans: Race and Americanization.* Baton Rouge: Louisiana State University Press, 1992.

Hogue, James K. *Uncivil War: Five New Orleans Street Battles and the Rise and Fall of Radical Reconstruction.* Baton Rouge: Louisiana State University Press, 2006.

Hunt, Lynn. *Inventing Human Rights: A History.* New York: W. W. Norton, 2007.

Inger, Morton. *Politics and Reality in an American City: The New Orleans School Crisis of 1960.* New York: Center for Urban Education, 1969.

Jackson, Kenneth. *Crabgrass Frontier: The Suburbanization of the United States.* New York: Oxford University Press, 1985.

Jacobs, Gregory. *Getting Around Brown: Desegregation, Development, and the Columbus Public Schools.* Columbus: Ohio State University Press, 1998.

Jeffries, Hasan Kwame. *Bloody Lowndes: Civil Rights and Black Power in Alabama's Black Belt.* New York: New York University Press, 2009.

Johnson, Rashauna. *Slavery's Metropolis: Unfree Labor in New Orleans during the Age of Revolutions.* New York: Cambridge University Press, 2016.

Johnson, Walter. *Soul by Soul: Life Inside the Antebellum Slave Market.* Cambridge, MA: Harvard University Press, 2001.

Kaestle, Carl F. *Pillars of the Republic: Common Schools and American Society, 1780–1860.* New York: Hill and Wang, 1983.

Katz, Michael B. *The Irony of School Reform: Educational Innovation in Mid-Nineteenth Century Massachusetts.* Boston: Beacon Press, 1968.

Katznelson, Ira, and Margaret Weir. *Schooling for All: Class, Race, and the Decline of the Democratic Ideal.* New York: Basic Books, 1985.

Kelman, Ari. *A River and Its City: The Nature of Landscape in New Orleans.* 2nd edition. Berkeley: University of California Press, 2006.

Kemp, John R., ed. *Martin Behrman of New Orleans.* Baton Rouge: Louisiana State University Press, 1977.

Kendall, John Smith. *History of New Orleans,* vol. 2. Chicago and New York: The Lewis Publishing Company, 1922.

Kendi, Ibram X. *Stamped from the Beginning: The Definitive History of Racist Ideas in America.* New York: Nation Books, 2016.

Kennedy, Dane. *Islands of White: Settler Society and Culture in Kenya and Rhodesia, 1890–1939*. Durham, NC: Duke University Press, 1987.

Kessner, Thomas. *The Golden Door: Italian and Jewish Immigrant Mobility in New York, 1880–1915*. New York: Oxford University Press, 1977.

Klarman, Michael J. *From Jim Crow to Civil Rights: The Supreme Court and the Struggle for Racial Equality*. Oxford: Oxford University Press, 2004.

Kluger, Richard. *Simple Justice: The History of* Brown v. Board of Education *and Black America's Struggle for Equality*. New York: Alfred A. Knopf, 1975.

Kozol, Jonathan. *The Shame of the Nation: The Restoration of Apartheid Schooling in America*. New York: Three Rivers Press, 2005.

KnowLA: Encyclopedia of Louisiana. http://www.knowla.org.

Krist, Gary. *Empire of Sin: A Story of Sex, Jazz, Murder, and the Battle for Modern New Orleans*. New York: Crown, 2014.

Kruse, Kevin. *White Flight: Atlanta and the Making of Modern Conservatism*. Princeton, NJ: Princeton University Press, 2005.

Labaree, David. *The Making of an American High School: The Credentials Market and the Central High School of Philadelphia, 1838–1939*. New Haven, CT: Yale University Press, 1988.

Landers, Jane G. *Atlantic Creoles in the Age of Revolutions*. Cambridge, MA: Harvard University Press, 2010.

Lassiter, Matthew D. *Silent Majority: Suburban Politics in the Sunbelt South*. Princeton, NJ: Princeton University Press, 2006.

Lewis, David Levering. *W. E. B. Du Bois: Biography of a Race, 1868–1919*. New York: Henry Holt, 1993.

Lewis, Peirce F. *New Orleans: The Making of an Urban Landscape*. Pensacola, FL: Ballinger Publishing, 1976.

Litwack, Leon. *North of Slavery: The Negro in the Free States, 1790–1860*. Chicago: University of Chicago Press, 1961.

———. *Trouble in Mind: Black Southerners in the Age of Jim Crow*. New York: Knopf, 1998.

Long, Alecia P. *The Great Southern Babylon: Sex, Race, and Respectability in New Orleans, 1865–1920*. Baton Rouge: Louisiana State University Press, 2004.

Lyons, Clare A. *Sex Among the Rabble: An Intimate History of Gender & Power in the Age of Revolution, Philadelphia, 1730–1830*. Chapel Hill: University of North Carolina Press, 2006.

Marable, Manning. *Race, Reform, and Rebellion: The Second Reconstruction and Beyond in Black America, 1945–2006*. 3rd edition. Oxford: University Press of Mississippi, 2007.

Margo, Robert. *Race and Schooling in the South, 1880–1950: An Economic History*. Chicago: University of Chicago Press, 1990.

Marler, Scott P. *Merchants' Capital: New Orleans and the Political Economy of the Nineteenth-Century South.* Cambridge: Cambridge University Press, 2013.

Massey, Douglas S., and Nancy A. Denton. *American Apartheid: Segregation and the Making of the Underclass.* Cambridge, MA: Harvard University Press, 1993.

McCaul, Robert L. *The Black Struggle for Public Schooling in Nineteenth-Century Illinois.* Carbondale and Edwardsville: Southern Illinois University Press, 1987.

McGreevy, James T. *Parish Boundaries: The Catholic Encounter with Race in the Twentieth-Century Urban North.* Chicago: University of Chicago Press, 1996.

McNeil, Genna Rae. *Groundwork: Charles Hamilton Houston and the Struggle for Civil Rights.* Philadelphia: University of Pennsylvania Press, 1983.

Meier, August, and Elliott Rudwick. *From Plantation to Ghetto.* 3rd edition. New York: Hill and Wang, 1976.

Meyer, Robert Jr. *Names Over New Orleans Public Schools.* New Orleans: Namesake Press, 1975.

Miller, Stuart Creighton. *"Benevolent Assimilation": The American Conquest of the Philippines, 1899–1903.* New Haven, CT: Yale University Press, 1982.

Mirel, Jeffrey. *The Rise and Fall of an Urban School System, Detroit: 1907–1981.* 2nd edition. Ann Arbor: University of Michigan Press, 1999.

Mitchell, Mary Niall. *Raising Freedom's Child: Black Children and Visions of the Future After Slavery.* New York: New York University Press, 2008.

Mitchell, Reid. *All on Mardi Gras Day: Episodes in the History of New Orleans Mardi Gras.* Cambridge, MA: Harvard University Press, 1995.

Mohr, Clarence L., ed. *The New Encyclopedia of Southern Culture,* vol. 17. *Education.* Chapel Hill: University of North Carolina Press, 2011.

Moore, Leonard. *Black Rage in New Orleans: Police Brutality and African American Activism from World War II to Hurricane Katrina.* Baton Rouge: Louisiana State University Press, 2010.

Morgan, Edmund S. *American Slavery, American Freedom: The Ordeal of Colonial Virginia.* New York: W. W. Norton, 1975.

Moss, Hilary J. *Schooling Citizens: The Struggle for African American Education in Antebellum America.* Chicago: University of Chicago Press, 2009.

Murch, Donna Jean. *Living for the City: Migration, Education, and the Rise of the Black Panther Party in Oakland, California.* Chapel Hill: University of North Carolina Press, 2010.

Nasaw, David. *Schooled to Order: A Social History of Public Schooling in the United States.* New York: Oxford University Press, 1981.

Nash, Gary. *Forging Freedom: The Formation of Philadelphia's Black Community, 1720–1840.* Cambridge, MA: Harvard University Press, 1988.

Nicolaides, Becky M. *My Blue Heaven: Life and Politics in the Working-Class Suburbs of Los Angeles, 1920–1965.* Chicago: University of Chicago Press, 2002.

Nightingale, Carl. *Segregation: A Global History of Divided Cities.* Chicago: University of Chicago Press, 2012.

Nystrom, Justin A. *New Orleans After the Civil War: Race, Politics, and a New Birth of Freedom.* Baltimore: Johns Hopkins University Press, 2010.

Oliver, Melvin L., and Thomas M. Shapiro. *Black Wealth/White Wealth: A New Perspective on Racial Inequality.* 2nd edition. New York: Routledge, 2006.

Parr, Leslie Gale. *A Will of Her Own: Sara Towles Reed and the Pursuit of Democracy in Southern Public Education.* Athens: University of Georgia Press, 1998.

Patterson, James T. *Brown v. Board of Education: A Civil Rights Milestone and Its Troubled Legacy.* New York: Oxford University Press, 2001.

Payne, Charles. *I've Got the Light of Freedom: The Organizing Tradition and the Mississippi Freedom Struggle.* Berkeley: University of California Press, 1995.

Perez, Louis A. Jr. *The War of 1898: The United States & Cuba in History and Historiography.* Chapel Hill: University of North Carolina Press, 1998.

Perlmann, Joel. *Ethnic Differences: Schooling and Social Structure Among the Irish, Italians, Jews, and Blacks in an American City, 1880–1935.* New York: Cambridge University Press, 1988.

Perman, Michael. *Struggle for Mastery: Disfranchisement in the South, 1888–1908.* Chapel Hill: University of North Carolina Press, 2001.

Plank, David, and Rick Ginsberg, eds. *Southern Cities, Southern Schools: Public Education in the Urban South.* New York: Greenwood Press, 1990.

Powell, Lawrence N. *The Accidental City: Improvising New Orleans.* Cambridge, MA: Harvard University Press, 2012.

Powell, Lawrence N., ed. *The New Orleans of George Washington Cable: The 1887 Census Office Report.* Baton Rouge: Louisiana University Press, 2008.

Pratt, Robert A. *The Color of Their Skin: Education and Race in Richmond, Virginia, 1954–1989.* Charlottesville: University Press of Virginia, 1992.

Rabinowitz, Howard N. *Race Relations in the Urban South.* New York: Oxford University Press, 1978.

Raboteau, Albert J. *Slave Religion: The 'Invisible Institution' in the Antebellum South.* Oxford: Oxford University Press, 1978.

Ravitch, Diane. *The Death and Life of the Great American School System: How Testing and Choice are Undermining Education.* 3rd edition. New York: Basic Books, 2016.

Reese, William J. *America's Public Schools: From the Common School to "No Child Left Behind."* Baltimore: Johns Hopkins University Press, 2005.

Renda, Mary. *Taking Haiti: Military Occupation and the Culture of U.S. Imperialism, 1915–1940.* Chapel Hill: University of North Carolina Press, 2000.

Reynolds, George M. *Machine Politics in New Orleans, 1897–1926.* New York: Columbia University Press, 1936.

Richards, Leonard L. *The Slave Power: The Free North and Southern Domination, 1780–1860.* Baton Rouge: Louisiana State University Press, 2000.

Ritterhouse, Jennifer. *Growing Up Jim Crow: How Black and White Southern Children Learned Race.* Chapel Hill: University of North Carolina Press, 2006.

Roediger, David R. *The Wages of Whiteness: Race and the Making of the American Working Class.* Revised edition. London: Verso, 1999.

Rogers, Kim Lacy. *Righteous Lives: Narratives of the New Orleans Civil Rights Movement.* New York: New York University Press, 1993.

Rosen, Hannah. *Terror in the Heart of Freedom: Citizenship, Sexual Violence, and the Meaning of Race in the Postemancipation South.* Chapel Hill: University of North Carolina Press, 2009.

Ross, Michael A. *The Great New Orleans Kidnapping Case: Race, Law, and Justice in the Reconstruction Era.* Oxford: Oxford University Press, 2015.

Roussève, Charles B. *The Negro in Louisiana: Aspects of His History and His Literature.* New Orleans: Xavier University Press, 1937.

Rury, John L. *Education and Social Change: Contours in the History of American Schooling.* 4th edition. New York: Routledge, 2013.

Scott, Rebecca J. *Degrees of Freedom: Louisiana and Cuba After Slavery.* Cambridge, MA: Belknap Press of Harvard University Press, 2005.

Scott, Rebecca J., and Jean M. Hébrard. *Freedom Papers: An Atlantic Odyssey in the Age of Emancipation.* Cambridge, MA: Harvard University Press, 2012.

Self, Robert O. *American Babylon: Race and the Struggle for Postwar Oakland.* Princeton, NJ: Princeton University Press, 2003.

Seligman, Amanda I. *Block by Block: Neighborhoods and Public Policy on Chicago's West Side.* Chicago: University of Chicago Press, 2005.

Shipps, Dorothy. *School Reform, Corporate Style: Chicago, 1880–2000.* Lawrence: University Press of Kansas, 2006.

Simmons, LaKisha Michelle. *Crescent City Girls: The Lives of Young Black Women in Segregated New Orleans.* Chapel Hill: University of North Carolina Press, 2015.

Sitkoff, Harvard. *The Struggle for Black Equality.* Revised edition. New York: Hill and Wang, 1993.

Sokol, Jason. *There Goes My Everything: White Southerners in the Age of Civil Rights, 1945–1975.* New York: Knopf, 2006.

Souther, J. Mark. *New Orleans on Parade: Tourism and the Transformation of the Crescent City.* Baton Rouge: Louisiana State University Press, 2006.

Spear, Jennifer. *Race, Sex, and Social Order in Early New Orleans.* Baltimore: Johns Hopkins University Press, 2010.

Stanonis, Anthony. *Creating the Big Easy: New Orleans and the Emergence of Modern Tourism, 1918–1945.* Athens: University of Georgia Press, 2006.

Sterling, Dorothy, ed. *We Are Your Sisters: Black Women in the Nineteenth Century.* New York: W. W. Norton, 1984.

Stewart, Alison. *First Class: The Legacy of Dunbar, America's First Black High School.* Chicago: Lawrence Hill Books, 2013.

Straus, Emily E. *Death of a Suburban Dream: Race and Schools in Compton, California.* Philadelphia: University of Pennsylvania Press, 2014.

Sugrue, Thomas J. *The Origins of the Urban Crisis: Race and Inequality in Postwar Detroit.* Princeton, NJ: Princeton University Press, 1996.

Taeuber, Karl E., and Alma F. Taeuber. *Negroes in Cities: Residential Segregation and Neighborhood Change.* Chicago: Aldine Publishing, 1965.

Taylor, Joe Gray. *Louisiana Reconstructed, 1863–1877.* Baton Rouge: Louisiana State University Press, 1974.

Thornton, John K. *Africa and Africans in the Making of the Atlantic World, 1400–1800.* 2nd edition. New York: Cambridge University Press, 1998.

Tindall, George B. *The Emergence of the New South, 1913–1945.* Baton Rouge: Louisiana State University Press, 1967.

Tindall, George Brown, and David Emory Shi. *America: A Narrative History.* 8th edition New York: W. W. Norton, 2010.

Trotter, Joe William. *Black Milwaukee: The Making of an Industrial Proletariat, 1915–1945.* Urbana: University of Illinois Press, 1985. 2nd edition, Urbana: University of Illinois Press, 2007.

———. *The African American Experience*, vol. 2. *From Reconstruction.* Boston: Houghton Mifflin, 2001.

Tushnet, Mark V. *The NAACP's Legal Strategy Against Segregated Education, 1925–1950.* Chapel Hill: University of North Carolina Press, 1987.

Tyack, David. *The One Best System: A History of American Urban Education.* Cambridge, MA: Harvard University Press, 1974.

Tyack, David, and Elisabeth Hansot. *Learning Together: A History of Coeducation in American Schools.* New Haven, CT: Yale University Press, 1990.

Tyler, Pamela. *Silk Stockings and Ballot Boxes: Women and Politics in New Orleans, 1920–1960.* Athens: University of Georgia Press, 1996.

Usner, Daniel H. *Indians, Settlers, & Slaves in a Frontier Exchange Economy: The Lower Mississippi Valley Before 1783.* Chapel Hill: University of North Carolina Press, 1992.

Vale, Lawrence J. *Purging the Poorest: Public Housing and the Design Politics of Twice-Cleared Communities.* Chicago: University of Chicago Press, 2013.

Walker, David. *Walker's Appeal, in Four Articles, Together with a Preamble, to the Coloured Citizens of the World, but in Particular, and Very Expressly, to Those of the United States of America.* DocSouth Books edition. Chapel Hill: University of North Carolina Press, 2011.

Walker, Vanessa Siddle. *Their Highest Potential: An African American School Community in the Segregated South.* Chapel Hill: University of North Carolina Press, 1996.

Ward, Jason Morgan. *Defending White Democracy: The Making of a Segregationist Movement and the Remaking of Southern Politics*. Chapel Hill: University of North Carolina Press, 2011.

White, Ashli. *Encountering Revolution: Haiti and the Making of the Early Republic*. Baltimore: Johns Hopkins University Press, 2010.

Wiese, Andrew. *Places of Their Own: African American Suburbanization in the Twentieth Century*. Chicago: University of Chicago Press, 2004.

Williams, Heather Andrea. *Self-Taught: African American Education in Slavery and Freedom*. Chapel Hill: University of North Carolina Press, 2007.

Williams, Rhonda Y. *The Politics of Public Housing: Black Women's Struggles Against Urban Inequality*. Oxford: Oxford University Press, 2004.

Williamson, Joel. *The Crucible of Race: Black-White Relations in the American South Since Emancipation*. New York: Oxford University Press, 1984.

Woodward, C. Vann. *Origins of the New South, 1877–1913*. Baton Rouge: Louisiana State University Press, 1951.

———. *The Strange Career of Jim Crow*. New York: Oxford University Press, 1955.

Articles, Chapters in Edited Collections, Published Reports, and Web Sites

Alberts, John B. "Black Catholic Schools: The Josephite Parishes of New Orleans During the Jim Crow Era." *U.S. Catholic Historian* 12, no. 1 (Winter 1994): 77–98.

Amsberryaugier, Lora, and Marilyn Hankel. "Mining the Decennial Census for Louisiana Data, 1940–2000." *Louisiana Libraries* (Winter 2004): 8–12.

Angus, David L. "The Origins of Urban Schools in Comparative Perspective." In *Southern Cities, Southern Schools*, edited by Rick Ginsberg and David Plank, 59–78. Westport, CT: Greenwood Press, 1990.

Arnesen, Eric. "Whiteness and the Historians' Imagination." *International Labor and Working-Class History* no. 60 (Fall 2001): 3–32.

Baiamonte, John V. Jr. "'Who Killa de Chief' Revisited: The Hennessey Assassination and Its Aftermath, 1890–1991." *Louisiana History* 33, no. 2 (Spring 1992): 117–46.

Bair, Barbara. "Though Justice Sleeps, 1880–1900." In *To Make Our World Anew: A History of African Americans*, vol. 2. *From 1880*, edited by Robin D. G. Kelley and Earl Lewis, 28. Oxford: Oxford University Press, 2000.

Baker, David P. "Schooling All the Masses: Reconsidering the Origins of American Schooling in the Postbellum Era." *Sociology of Education* 72, no. 4 (October 1999): 197–215.

Beckert, Sven. "History of American Capitalism." In *American History Now*, edited by Eric Foner and Lisa McGirr, 314–35. Philadelphia: Temple University Press, 2011.

Beeby, James, and Donald G. Nieman. "The Rise of Jim Crow, 1880–1920." In *A Com-*

panion to the American South, edited by John B. Boles, 336–47. Malden, MA: Blackwell Publishing, 2004.

Benjamin, Karen. "Suburbanizing Jim Crow: The Impact of School Policy on Residential Segregation in Raleigh." *Journal of Urban History* 38, no. 2 (March 2012): 225–46.

Blassingame, John. "The Union Army as an Educational Institution for Negroes, 1862–1865." *Journal of Negro Education* 34, no. 2 (Spring 1965): 152–59.

Brownell, Blaine A. "The Commercial-Civic Elite and City Planning in Atlanta, Memphis, and New Orleans in the 1920s." *Journal of Southern History* 41, no. 3 (August 1975): 339–68.

Buras, Kristen L. "Race, Charter Schools, and Conscious Capitalism: On the Spatial Politics of Whiteness as Property (and the Unconscionable Assault on Black New Orleans)." *Harvard Educational Review* 81, no. 2 (Summer 2011): 296–30.

Campanella, Richard. "Two Centuries of Paradox: The Geography of New Orleans' African-American Population, from Antebellum to Postdiluvian Times." In *Hurricane Katrina in Transatlantic Perspective,* edited by Randy Sparks and Romain Huret. Baton Rouge: Louisiana State University Press, 2014.

Clapper, Michael. "School Design, Site Selection, and the Political Geography of Race in Postwar Philadelphia." *Journal of Planning History* 5, no. 3 (August 2006): 241–63.

Clark, Emily, and Virginia Meacham Gould. "The Feminine Face of Afro-Catholicism in New Orleans, 1727–1852." *William and Mary Quarterly* 59, no. 2 (April 2002): 409–48.

Conway, Thomas G. "John A. Kennicott: A Teacher in New Orleans." *Louisiana History* 26, no. 4 (Autumn 1985): 399–415.

Cortez, Mark. "The Faculty Integration of New Orleans Public Schools, 1972." *Louisiana History* 37, no. 4 (Autumn 1996): 405–34.

Cowen Institute for Public Education Initiatives. "Creating a Governing Framework for Public Education in New Orleans: School District Political Leadership." New Orleans: Cowen Institute, November 2009.

Crombie, Jeanne E. "Professor Alcée Fortier, 1856–1914." *Louisiana Historical Quarterly* 55, no. 1 (Winter–Spring, 1972): 1–62.

Dart, Henry P. "Public Education in New Orleans in 1800." *Louisiana Historical Quarterly* 11 (1928): 241–43.

De Bow, J. D. B. "The Moral Advance of New Orleans." *De Bow's Review* 2 (November 1846).

Deyle, Steven. "Review of *River of Dark Dreams: Slavery and Empire in the Cotton Kingdom.*" *William and Mary Quarterly* 71, no. 4 (October 2014): 632–36.

Dougherty, Jack. "Bridging the Gap Between Urban, Suburban, and Educational History." In *Rethinking the History of American Education,* edited by Wiliam J. Reese and John L. Rury, 245–59. New York: Palgrave Macmillan, 2008.

———. "Shopping for Schools: How Public Education and Private Housing Shaped Suburban Connecticut." *Journal of Urban History* 38, no. 2 (March 2012): 205–24.

Du Bois, W. E. B. "Does the Negro Need Separate Schools?" *Journal of Negro Education* 4, no. 3 (July 1935): 328–35.

Erickson, Ansley T. "Building Inequality: The Spatial Organization of Schooling in Nashville, Tennessee, after *Brown.*" *Journal of Urban History* 38, no. 2 (March 2012): 247–70.

———. "Desegregation's Architects: Education Parks and the Spatial Ideology of Schooling." *History of Education Quarterly* 56, no. 4 (November 2016): 560–89.

———. "The Rhetoric of Choice: Segregation, Desegregation, and Charter Schools." *Dissent* (Fall 2010): 41–46.

Ettinger, Brian Gary. "John Fitzpatrick and the Limits of Working-Class Politics in New Orleans, 1892–1896." *Louisiana History* 26, no. 4 (Autumn 1985): 341–67.

Fairclough, Adam. "The Costs of *Brown:* Black Teachers and School Integration." *Journal of American History* 91, no. 1 (June 2004).

Fields, Barbara Jeanne. "*Origins of the New South* and the Negro Question." *Journal of Southern History* 67, no. 4 (November 2001): 811–26.

———. "Slavery, Race, and Ideology in the United States of America." *New Left Review* 181 (May–June 1990): 95–118.

Fischer, Roger A. "Racial Segregation in Ante Bellum New Orleans." *American Historical Review* 74, no. 3 (February 1969): 926–37.

Fishman, Walda Katz, and Richard L. Zweigenhaft. "Jews and the New Orleans Economic and Social Elites." *Jewish Social Studies* 44, no. 3/4 (Summer–Autumn, 1982): 291–98.

Foner, Eric. "Response to Eric Arnesen." *International Labor and Working-Class History*, no. 60 (Fall 2001): 57–60.

Fultz, Michael. "The Displacement of Black Educators Post-*Brown:* An Overview and Analysis." *History of Education Quarterly* 44, no. 1 (Spring 2004): 11–45.

Gilmore, H. W. "The Old New Orleans and the New: A Case for Ecology." *American Sociological Review* 9, no. 4 (August 1944): 385–94.

Ginsberg, Rick. "Boss Behrman Reforms the Schools: The 1912 New Orleans School Reform." In *Southern Cities, Southern Schools*, edited by Rick Ginsberg and David Plank. Westport, CT: Greenwood Press, 1990.

Gonzalez-Perez, Margaret C. "A House Divided: Public Housing Policy in New Orleans." *Louisiana History* 44, no. 4 (Autumn 2003): 443–61.

Gotham, Kevin Fox. "Missed Opportunities, Enduring Legacies: School Segregation and Desegregation in Kansas City, Missouri." *American Studies* 43, no. 2 (Summer 2002): 5–41.

Guinier, Lani. "From Racial Liberalism to Racial Literacy: *Brown v. Board of Education* and the Interest-Divergence Dilemma." *Journal of American History* 91 (June 2004): 92–118.

Haas, Edward F. "John Fitzpatrick and Political Continuity in New Orleans, 1896–1899." *Louisiana History* 22, no. 1 (Winter 1981): 7–29.

———. "Political Continuity in the Crescent City: Toward an Interpretation of New Orleans Politics, 1874–1986." *Louisiana History* 39, no. 1 (Winter 1998): 5–18.

Harlan, Louis R. "Desegregation in New Orleans Public Schools During Reconstruction." *American Historical Review* 67, no. 3 (April 1962): 663–75.

Henderson, A. Scott. "Housing Act of 1937." In *Encyclopedia of American Urban History*, edited by David Goldfield, 356–57. Thousand Oaks, CA: Sage Publishing, 2007. http://dx.doi.org/10.4135/9781412952620.n201.

Highsmith, Andrew, and Ansley T. Erickson. "Segregation as Splitting, Segregation as Joining: Schools, Housing, and the Many Modes of Jim Crow." *American Journal of Education* 121, no. 4 (August 2015): 563–95.

Hillier, Amy E. "Redlining and the Home Owners' Loan Corporation." *Journal of Urban History* 29, no. 4 (May 2003): 394–420.

———. "Residential Security Maps and Neighborhood Appraisals: The Home Owners' Loan Corporation and the Case of Philadelphia." *Social Science History* 29, no. 2 (Summer 2005): 207–33.

Hirsch, Arnold R. "Race and Renewal in the Cold War South: New Orleans, 1947–1968." In *The American Planning Tradition: Culture and Policy*, edited by Robert Fishman, 219–39. Washington, DC: Woodrow Wilson Center Press, 2000.

———. "Second Thoughts on the Second Ghetto." *Journal of Urban History* 29, no. 3 (March 2003): 298–309.

———. "Simply a Matter of Black and White: The Transformation of Race and Politics in Twentieth-Century New Orleans." In *Creole New Orleans: Race and Americanization*, edited by Arnold R. Hirsch and Joseph Logsdon, 262–319. Baton Rouge: Louisiana State University Press, 1992.

———. "With or Without Jim Crow: Black Residential Segregation in the United States." In *Urban Policy in Twentieth-Century America*, edited by Arnold R. Hirsch and Raymond A. Mohl, 65–99. New Brunswick, NJ: Rutgers University Press, 1993.

Honey, Michael. "Class, Race, and Power in the New South: Racial Violence and the Delusion of White Supremacy." In *Democracy Betrayed: The Wilmington Race Riot of 1898 and Its Legacy*, edited by David S. Cecelski and Timothy B. Tyson. Chapel Hill: University of North Carolina Press, 1998.

Jacobs, Meg. "The Uncertain Future of American Politics." In *American History Now*, edited by Eric Foner and Lisa McGirr, 151–74. Philadelphia: Temple University Press, 2011.

Kantor, Harvey, and Barbara Brenzel. "Urban Education and the 'Truly Disadvantaged': The Historical Roots of the Contemporary Crisis, 1945–1990." In *The 'Underclass' Debate: Views from History*, edited by Michael B. Katz, 366–402. Princeton, NJ: Princeton University Press, 1993.

Kelley, Robin D. G. "'But a Local Phase of a World Problem': Black History's Global Vision, 1883–1950." *Journal of American History* 86, no. 3 (December 1999): 1045–77.

Kramer, Paul. "Race-Making and Colonial Violence in the U.S. Empire: The Philippine-American War as Race War." *Diplomatic History* 30, no. 2 (April 2006): 169–210.

Kvach, John F. "J. D. B. De Bow's South Carolina: The Antebellum Origins of the New South Creed." *The South Carolina Historical Magazine* 113, no. 1 (January 2012): 4–23.

Kyriakoudes, Louis M., and Hayden Noel McDaniel. "Listening to Freedom's Voices: Forty-Four Years of Documenting the Mississippi Civil Rights Movement." *Southern Quarterly* 52, no. 1 (Fall 2014): 64–78.

Landphair, Juliette. "'The Forgotten People of New Orleans': Community, Vulnerability, and the Lower Ninth Ward." *Journal of American History* 94 (December 2007): 714–55.

———. "Sewerage, Sidewalks, and Schools: The New Orleans Ninth Ward and Public School Desegregation." *Louisiana History* 40, no. 1 (Winter 1999): 35–62.

Lassiter, Matthew D. "De Jure/De Facto Segregation: The Long Shadow of a National Myth." In *The Myth of Southern Exceptionalism,* edited by Matthew D. Lassiter and Joseph Crespino, 25–48. Oxford: Oxford University Press, 2009.

———. "Schools and Housing in Metropolitan History: An Introduction." *Journal of Urban History* 38, no. 2 (2012): 195–204.

Lassiter, Matthew D., and Joseph Crespino. "Introduction: The End of Southern History." In *The Myth of Southern Exceptionalism,* edited by Matthew D. Lassiter and Joseph Crespino, 3–22. Oxford: Oxford University Press, 2009.

Lieb, Emily. "How Segregated Schools Built Segregated Cities." *CityLab,* 2 February 2017. http://www.citylab.com/housing/2017/02/how-segregated-schools-built-segregated-cities/515373/.

Logsdon, Joseph, and Caryn Cossé Bell. "The Americanization of Black New Orleans, 1850–1900." In *Creole New Orleans: Race and Americanization,* edited by Arnold R. Hirsch and Joseph Logsdon, 201–61. Baton Rouge: Louisiana State University Press, 1992.

Long, Alecia P. "Poverty Is the New Prostitution: Race, Poverty, and Public Housing in Post-Katrina New Orleans." *Journal of American History* 94 (December 2007): 795–803.

Magill, John. "Then and Now: New Orleans' South Market District." *Louisiana Cultural Vistas* 23, no. 4 (Winter 2012–2013): 66–73.

Mahoney, Martha. "Law and Racial Geography: Public Housing and the Economy in New Orleans." *Stanford Law Review* 42, no. 5 (May 1990): 1251–90.

Manning, Diane T., and Perry Rogers. "Desegregation of the New Orleans Parochial Schools." *The Journal of Negro Education* 71, no. 1/2 (Winter–Spring 2002): 31–42.

Martin, Arthur T. "Segregation of Residences of Negroes." *Michigan Law Review* 32, no. 6 (April 1934): 721–42.

Michna, Catherine. "Stories at the Center: Story Circles, Educational Organizing, and Fate of Neighborhood Public Schools in New Orleans." *American Quarterly* 61, no. 3 (September 2009): 529–55.

Mirel, Jeffrey E. "Progressive School Reform in Comparative Perspective." In *Southern Cities, Southern Schools: Public Education in the Urban South,* edited by David N. Plank and Rick Ginsberg, 151–74. Westport, CT: Greenwood Press, 1990.

Mizel-Nelson, Michael. "Batista-era Havana on the Bayou." *Reviews in American History* 36, no. 2 (June 2008): 231–242.

Mohr, Clarence L. "Education in the South." In *The New Encyclopedia of Southern Culture,* vol. 17. *Education,* edited by Clarence L. Mohr, 1–30. Chapel Hill: University of North Carolina Press, 2011.

Muller, Mary Lee. "New Orleans Public School Desegregation." *Louisiana History* 17, no. 1 (Winter 1976): 69–88.

Neidenbach, Elizabeth C. "'Mes dernières volontés': Testaments to the Life of Marie Couvent, a Former Slave in New Orleans." *Transatlantica* [online] 2 (2012): 2–11.

Nelson, Alice Dunbar. "Free People of Color in Louisiana: Part II." *Journal of Negro History* 2, no. 1 (Jan. 1917): 51–78.

Newman, Joseph W. "Antebellum School Reform in the Port Cities of the Deep South." In *Southern Cities, Southern Schools: Public Education in the Urban South,* edited by David N. Plank and Rick Ginsberg, 17–35. Westport, CT: Greenwood Press, 1990.

Nightingale, Carl H. "A Tale of Three *Global* Ghettos: How Arnold Hirsch Helps Us Internationalize U.S. Urban History." *Journal of Urban History* 29, no. 3 (March 2003): 257–71.

———. "The Transnational Contexts of Early Twentieth-Century American Urban Segregation." *Journal of Social History* 39, no. 3 (Spring 2006): 667–702.

Noble, Stuart G. "Governor Claiborne and the Public School System of the Territorial Government of Louisiana." *The Louisiana Historical Quarterly* 11, no. 4 (October 1928): 535–52.

Noble, Stuart G., and Arthur G. Nuhrah. "Education in Colonial Louisiana." *Louisiana Historical Quarterly* 32, no. 4 (October 1949): 759–76.

Osofsky, Gilbert. "The Enduring Ghetto." *Journal of American History* 55, no. 2 (September 1968): 243–55.

Ostendorf, Berndt. "Creole Cultures and the Process of Creolization: With Special Attention to Louisiana." In *Louisiana Culture from the Colonial Era to Katrina,* edited by John Lowe, 103–35. Baton Rouge: Louisiana State University Press, 2008.

Poché, Justin D. "Crescent City Catholicism: Catholic Education in New Orleans." In *Urban Catholic Education: Tales of Twelve American Cities,* edited by Thomas C.

Hunt and Timothy Walch. Notre Dame, IN: Alliance for Catholic Education Press, 2010.

Powell, Lawrence N. "Reinventing Tradition: Liberty Place, Historical Memory, and Silk-Stocking Vigilantism in New Orleans." *Slavery and Abolition: A Journal of Slave and Post-Slave Studies* 20, no. 1 (1999): 127–49.

———. "Why Louisiana Mattered." *Louisiana History* 53, no. 4 (Fall 2012): 389–401.

Powell, Lawrence N., and Clarence L. Mohr, eds. "Through the Eye of Katrina: The Past as Prologue?" Special issue, *Journal of American History* 94, no. 3 (December 2007).

Rabinowitz, Howard N. "More than the Woodward Thesis: Assessing *The Strange Career of Jim Crow*." *Journal of American History* 75, no. 3 (December 1988): 842–56.

Rankin, David C. "The Origins of Black Leadership in New Orleans During Reconstruction." *The Journal of Southern History* 40, no. 3 (1974): 417–40.

Reese, Carol McMichael. "The New Orleans that Edgar (and Edith) Built." In *Longue Vue House and Gardens,* edited by Charles Davey and Carol McMichael Reese, 172–91. New York: Skira Rizzoli, 2015.

———. "The Once and Future New Orleans of Planners Milton Medary and Harland Bartholomew, 1920–1960." In *New Orleans Under Reconstruction: The Crisis of Planning,* edited by Carol McMichael Reese, Michael Sorkin, and Anthony Fontenot, 97–120. London: Verso, 2014.

Reinders, Robert C. "New England Influences on the Formation of Public Schools in New Orleans." *Journal of Southern History* 30, no. 2 (May 1964): 181–95.

Rice, Roger L. "Residential Segregation by Law, 1910–1917." *The Journal of Southern History* 34, no. 2 (May 1968): 179–99.

Rosen, David. "Searching for 'Facts' on the Ground." *The Columbia Current* (Fall 2007).

Rury, John L. "The New York African Free School, 1827–1836: Conflict Over Community Control of Black Education." *Phylon* 44, no. 3 (3rd Qtr. 1983): 187–97.

———. "Race, Space, and the Politics of Chicago's Public Schools: Benjamin Willis and the Tragedy of Urban Education." *History of Education Quarterly* 39, no. 2 (Summer 1999): 117–42.

Rury, John L., and Jeffrey E. Mirel. "The Political Economy of Urban Education." *Review of Research in Education* 22 (1997): 49–110.

Scott, Janelle, and Jennifer Jellison Holme. "The Political Economy of Market-Based Educational Policies: Race and Reform in Urban School Districts, 1915 to 2016." *Review of Research in Education* 40, no. 1 (March 2016): 250–97.

Scott, Rebecca J. "Public Rights and Private Commerce: A Nineteenth-Century Atlantic Creole Itinerary." *Current Anthropology* 28, no. 2 (2007), 237–56.

Shapiro, Thomas, and Hannah Thomas. "Prologue for Special Issue on Race and Wealth." *Race and Social Problems* 8, no. 1 (March 2016): 1–3.

Silver, Christopher. "The Racial Origins of Zoning: Southern Cities from 1910–40." *Planning Perspectives* 6 (1991): 189–205.

Simmons, Warren, and Alethea Frazier Raynor. "K–12 Public Education Reform in New Orleans." Providence, RI: The Annenberg Institute for School Reform, 2006.

Skipper, Ottis Clark. "J. D. B. De Bow, the Man." *Journal of Southern History* 10, no. 4 (November 1944): 404–23.

Somers, Dale A. "Black and White in New Orleans: A Study in Urban Race Relations, 1865–1900." *Journal of Southern History* 40, no. 1 (February 1974): 19–42.

Spain, Daphne. "Race Relations and Residential Segregation in New Orleans: Two Centuries of Paradox." *Annals of the American Academy of Political and Social Science* 441 (January 1979): 82–96.

Steffes, Tracy L. "Managing School Integration and White Flight: The Debate Over Chicago's Future in the 1960s." *Journal of Urban History* 42, no. 4 (July 2016): 711–13.

Stern, Walter C. *An Interactive Timeline of New Orleans Public Education, 1718–Present.* New Orleans: Cowen Institute, 2015. http://www.spen02015.com/timeline.html.

Stewart, James Brewer. "The New Haven Negro College and the Meanings of Race in New England, 1776–1870." *New England Quarterly* 76, no. 3 (September 2003): 323–55.

Sugrue, Thomas. "The Structure of Urban Poverty: The Reorganization of Space and Work in Three Periods in American History." In *The "Underclass" Debate: Views from History*, edited by Michael Katz, 91. Princeton, NJ: Princeton University Press, 1993.

Sumpter, Amy R. "Segregation of the Free People of Color and the Construction of Race in Antebellum New Orleans." *Southeastern Geographer* 48, no. 1 (May 2008): 19–37.

Thompson, Heather Ann. "Why Mass Incarceration Matters: Rethinking Crisis, Decline, and Transformation in Postwar American History." *Journal of American History* 97, no. 3 (December 2010): 703–34.

Tregle, Joseph. "Creoles and Americans." In *Creole New Orleans: Race and Americanization*, edited by Arnold R. Hirsch and Joseph Logsdon, 131–85. Baton Rouge: Louisiana State University Press, 1992.

Trotter, Joe William Jr. "Shifting Perspectives on Segregation in the Emerging Postindustrial Age." Paper presented at The Future of the African American Past Conference, May 19–21, 2016, Washington, DC. https://futureafampast.si.edu/sites/default/files/03_Trotter%20Joe.pdf.

Wallenstein, Peter. "Antiliteracy Laws." In *Slavery in the United States: A Social, Political, and Historical Encyclopedia*, vol. 1. Junios P. Rodriguez, 172. Santa Barbara: ABC-CLIO, 2007.

White, Monica A. "Paradise Lost? Teachers' Perspectives on the Use of Cultural Capital in the Segregated Schools of New Orleans, Louisiana." *Journal of African American History* 87 (Spring 2002): 269–81.

Wiley, Nathan. "Education of the Colored Population of Louisiana." *Harper's New Monthly Magazine* 33, no. 1 (July 1866): 248.

Williams, Robert W. Jr. "Martin Behrman and New Orleans Civic Development, 1904–1920." *Louisiana History* 2, no. 4 (Autumn 1961): 373–400.

Wolff, Jane, and Carol McMichael Reese. "Pontchartrain Park + Gentilly Woods Landscape Manual." In *New Orleans Under Reconstruction: The Crisis of Planning,* edited by Carol McMichael Reese, Michael Sorkin, and Anthony Fontenot, 381–92. London: Verso, 2014.

Yamanaka, Mishio. "The Fillmore Boys School in 1877: Racial Integration, Creoles of Color and the End of Reconstruction in New Orleans." http://fillmoreschool.web.unc.edu.

DISSERTATIONS, THESES, AND UNPUBLISHED MATERIAL

Abrams, Nels. "The Making of Audubon Park: Competing Ideologies of Public Space." Master's thesis, University of New Orleans, 2010.

Benjamin, Karen A. "Progressivism Meets Jim Crow: Segregation, School Reform, and Urban Development in the Interwar South." PhD diss., University of Wisconsin–Madison, 2007.

Bordelon, Samson Paul. "The New Orleans Public Schools Under the Superintendency of Lionel John Bourgeois." PhD diss., University of Southern Mississippi, 1966.

Buss, Andrew. "Doomed By Circumstance: Changing Perceptions of the Iberville Housing Development." Master's thesis, Temple University, 1998.

DeVore, Donald E. "Race Relations and Community Development: The Education of Blacks in New Orleans, 1862–1960." PhD diss., Louisiana State University, 1989. ProQuest (9025300).

———. "The Rise from the Nadir: Black New Orleans Between the Wars, 1920–1940." Master's thesis, University of New Orleans, 1983.

Devron, Gustave Pierre. "Warren Easton: The Educator." Master's thesis, 1937.

Erickson, Ansley T. "Schooling the Metropolis: Educational Inequality Made and Remade, Nashville, Tennessee, 1945–1985." PhD diss., Columbia University, 2010.

Fertel, Rien. "Imagining the Creole City: White Creole Print Culture, Community, and Identity Formation in Nineteenth-Century New Orleans." PhD diss., Tulane University, 2013.

Highsmith, Andrew. "Demolition Means Progress: Race, Class, and the Deconstruction of the American Dream in Flint, Michigan." PhD diss., University of Michigan, 2009.

Johnson, Janice Richard. "Leland University in New Orleans, 1870–1915." PhD diss., University of New Orleans, 1996.

Landphair, Juliette Lee. "'For the Good of the Community': Reform Activism and Public Schools in New Orleans, 1920–1960." PhD diss., University of Virginia, 1999. ProQuest (9935071).

Lief, Shane. "Staging New Orleans: The Contested Space of Congo Square." Master's thesis, Tulane University, 2011.

Mahoney, Martha. "The Changing Nature of Public Housing in New Orleans, 1930–1974." Master's thesis, Tulane University, 1985.

Margavio, Anthony Victor. "Residential Segregation in New Orleans: A Statistical Analysis of Census Data." PhD diss., Louisiana State University, 1968.

Muller, Mary Lee. "The Orleans Parish School Board and Negro Education, 1940–1960." Master's thesis, University of New Orleans, 1975.

Neidenbach, Elizabeth Clark. "The Life and Legacy of Marie Couvent: Social Networks, Property Ownership, and the Making of a Free People of Color Community in New Orleans." PhD diss, College of William and Mary, 2015.

——. "Marie Bernard Couvent, the Couvent School, and African American Education in New Orleans." Undergraduate honors thesis, Tulane University, 2003.

Ozenovich, Steve J. "The Development of Public Secondary Education in New Orleans, 1877–1914." Master's thesis, Tulane University, 1940.

Parekh, Trushna. "Inhabiting Tremé: Gentrification Memory and Racialized Space in a New Orleans Neighborhood." PhD diss., University of Texas, 2008.

Peterson, Alma Hobbs. "The Administration of the Public Schools in New Orleans." PhD diss., Louisiana State University, 1964.

Romagossa, Nicole. "Albert Baldwin Wood, the Screw Pump, and the Modernization of New Orleans." Master's thesis, University of New Orleans, 2010.

Rosenberg, Malcolm. "The Orleans Parish Schools Under the Superintendency of Nicholas Bauer." PhD diss., Louisiana State University, 1963.

Schwertz, Joseph S. "The History of Warren Easton Boys' High School." Master's thesis, Tulane University, 1941.

Slates, Stephanie Lyn. "To Clear a Rock-Bottom, Low-Density Slum: Using Public Housing Means to Meet Urban Renewal Ends in New Orleans, 1954–1959." Master's thesis, University of New Orleans, 2008.

Stern, Walter C. "Black, White, Silver, and Blue: Race and Desegregation at New Orleans' Fortier High, 1960–1975." Master's thesis, Tulane University, 2010.

——. "The Negro's Place: Schools, Race, and the Making of Modern New Orleans, 1900–1960." PhD diss., Tulane University, 2014.

Todd, Lewis. "The Development of Public Secondary Education in New Orleans, 1914–1941." Master's thesis, Tulane University, 1942.

Walker, Ethel. "History of the Sophie B. Wright High School." Master's thesis, Tulane University, 1939.

Watts, Gwendolyn P. "Against All Odds: McDonogh 35 High School, 1917–1937." Master's thesis, University of New Orleans, 1998.

Westrick, Benedict. "The History of Catholic Negro Education in the City of New Orleans, 1724–1950." Master's thesis, St. Mary's University of San Antonio, Texas, 1950.

INDEX

Abrams, Charles, 217

Advisory Committee on Zoning, 61

African Americans: activism of, 12, 195, 230, 242–43n18; African American teachers, 208; debate concerning the "place" of during the Jim Crow era, 12, 53, 84; "double taxation" of, 60, 136, 155, 265n30; and the labor market, 68–69; national debate concerning the future status of, 40–41; and the right to vote, 55; in the urban North in the nineteenth century, 12. *See also* free blacks; Jim Crow

African Methodist Episcopal (AME) Church, 102

Aimé, Valcour, 131, 133

Alcée Fortier High School, 169, 183

Algiers, 288n83

Allen Elementary School, 183, 189; overcrowding of, 185–86; proposed annex to, 186, 188

Alms House. *See* Touro-Shakespeare Alms House

American Civil War, 4, 5, 15, 59, 166; occupation of New Orleans by the Union army, 39–40; reimagining of, 134–35

American Institute of Architects (AIA), 216

Anderson, James D., 105, 274n34

Andrew Wilson School, 174, 175

AP US History curriculum framework, 240n10

A. P. Williams School, 122

Appeal to the Coloured Citizens of the World (Walker), 27–28

Armstrong, Louis, 5, 205; education of, 96; friendship of with the Karnofsky family, 98, 271–72n11; interaction of with whites as a young boy, 98–99; neighborhood of while a young boy, 96–98; trouble of with police as a young boy, 93, 94, 271n3

Armstrong, May Ann, 95

Association of Commerce, 61, 142, 159, 180

Astoria Hotel, 98, 142, 177

Atlanta, Georgia, 52, 54, 190, 261n9, 261n11, 299n96

Audubon Park, 66, 181, 183, 185

Autocrat Club, 104

Back of Town, 60, 200

Baker, Liva, 232

Baldwin, Joshua, 32, 33

Ball, Lena, 192

Ball, Samuel, 192

Baltimore, Maryland, 18, 44, 255n55; black schools in, 34; Roland Park subdivision of, 185

Barnard, Henry, 14–15, 32

Baton Rouge, Louisiana, 105, 195

Baton Rouge College, 106

Battle of Liberty Place, 118, 132–33, 134, 146, 284n15

Battle of New Orleans, 27, 130

Bauer, Nicholas, 170, 176, 177, 178, 183, 185

Baumgartner, Fannie, 126, 140, 141, 143, 155, 185
Bayou Road School, 58–59, 62–63, 232, 234; authorization for the construction of a new building for, 136; changes in the racial designation of, 5; controversy concerning blacks in, 43–44; debate concerning a new building for, 50–52, 128–29, 135–36, 141, 153–154, 159–60, 164; desegregation of, 44; poor physical conditions of, 74, 135; renaming of after Joseph A. Craig, 136; as a school for white girls, 43; student diversity of, 63–64; as the temporary home of the district's commercial high school for white boys, 158–59. *See also* Joseph A. Craig School
Bayou Road Parents' Club, 135
Bazanac, Joseph, 34, 36
Beauregard, P. G. T., 147
Beauregard Square, 147, 157, 158, 287n64
Beck, Anna, 179
Becker, Ernest O., 222, 224
Behrman, Martin, 71–72, 73, 125, 134, 183; opposition to the political machine of, 126, 127; political machine of (*see also* Choctaw Club of Louisiana), 129; support of for residential segregation, 129
Bell, Caryn Cossé, 102, 247n39, 253n39
Benjamin, Judah P., 68, 166
Bernard Company, 168
Bertonneau, Arnold, 41–42, 47
Bienville School, 106
Big Nose Sidney, 93
Bight of Benin, 17; Gbe-speaking region of, 17
Bigot, S., 43
Bingaman, A. L., 101, 273n23
Bingaman, Amelia, 101–2, 273nn23–24
Bingaman, Henrietta, 273n23
Birth of a Nation (1915), 56, 134
Bisso, Louis, 225
Blessed Sacrament Church, 107
Blumenthal, Esther, 116–17
Boguille, Ludger, 34, 36, 44
Boothby, C. W., 45
Bordeaux, 130

Boscoville, 218
Boston, Massachusetts, 18, 110–11; black educational activism in, 305n41
Boston School Committee, 210–11
Boucree, John, 173, 178, 182, 293–94n36; police harassment of, 180
Bourbon Democrats, 46
Bourgeois, Lionel J., 207–8, 216; building program of, 211; efforts of to concentrate black schools in the Central City area, 209–10; plan of for school construction, 208
Boys' High School, 45
Boys' House of Refuge, 183
Braden, Henry E., 142, 295n55; bombing of his home, 177
Braquet, Louis, 98
Bridges, Abon, 1, 2
Bridges, Lucille, 1, 2, 230
Bridges, Ruby, 1–2, 4, 13, 230, 232
Briggs v. Elliott (1952), 209
Broadmoor, 6, 170, 182, 210; black residents in, 174; drainage and initial development of, 171, 173–74; opening of an all-white school in, 174; residential segregation in, 179–80
Brouard, Françoise Palmyre, 30
Broughton, J. M., 152–53
Brown, Coleman, 111
Brown, Elizabeth, 111
Brown, Louisa, 111
Brown, Myrtle, 111
Brown v. Board of Education (1954), 2, 3, 10, 209, 228, 246–47n37
Buchanan v. Warley (1917), 52, 141, 181, 182, 242n16
Burger, Warren, 220
Butler, Benjamin F., 40–41, 166, 257n69
Byrnes, James, 209
Bywater, 151

Cable, George Washington, 46, 132
Calliope Housing Project, 121, 204, 205, 221, 278, 302n15, 303n20; black population of (1940-1950), 304n29
Camp Parapet, 39

Young, Andrew, 156
Young Men's Democratic Association
  (YMDA), 133

Zengel, Fred, 51, 126, 138, 141, 143, 169

j